WHEN WE GATHER

WHEN WE GATHER

A Book of Prayers for Worship

Revised Edition

For Years A, B, and C

James G. Kirk

Geneva Press
Louisville, Kentucky

Book design by Sharon Adams
Cover design by Grand Design

Published by Geneva Press
Louisville, Kentucky

This book is printed on acid-free paper that meets the American National Stan-dards Institute Z39.48 standard. ∞

PRINTED IN THE UNITED STATES OF AMERICA

01 02 03 04 05 06 07 08 09 10 — 10 9 8 7 6 5 4 3 2 1

Library of Congress Cataloging-in-Publication Data

A catalog record for this book is available from the Library of Congress.

ISBN 0-664-50114-1

Introduction

Prayer is the heartbeat of the soul. It is through prayer that the pulsating and life-bringing energy of the Holy Spirit flows into every sinew and tissue of our lives, aligns our thoughts with God's thoughts, focuses our capacities on the grace and mercy of the risen Christ, and moves us in the direction that, hopefully, will make us more faithful to God's will for our lives.

The prayers that follow were written with a conviction: a conviction that pastors don't have much time in the week to devote to the liturgical components of Sunday worship. They spend much time on the pastoral duties that beckon them daily. They have the administrative chores to look after. The demands of the parish can never be predicted and often consume more time than is allotted. Sermon preparation often seems as though Sunday comes every other day. And yet, there is cohesion to good Reformed worship that begs for time to be spent on the liturgical components as well.

The prayers that follow have been field tested for almost twenty years and have worn well the test of time. They were written to follow a pattern. The Call to Worship most often concentrates on the psalm for the day. The Prayer of Praise and Adoration puts in narrative form some of the thoughts contained in the psalm. The Litany of Confession or Affirmation draws its inspiration from the Epistle, while the Prayer of Dedication looks to the thoughts contained in the Gospel lesson. Often the Prayer of Thanksgiving and Supplication will seek out what thoughts are in the Old Testament lesson and, thus, throughout the service of worship one hears the scriptural themes played in various ways, which enhances the hearing of God's Word. With the revisions contained in this new volume, all of the prayers are now in accordance with the current Sunday lections.

Having been in the parish for the past fifteen years, I have had the occasion weekly to use the prayers in worship. The congregations have gotten used to them and have commented from time to time on what a particular prayer has meant to them. They appreciate the meter of the prayers in that they can be spoken in unison much as a hymn is sung. Also, using the prayers throughout the service provides a continuing opportunity for the congregation to participate in the liturgy.

Throughout my ministry I have taken exception to the common saying, "pray as though everything depended on God and work as though everything depended on you." In my opinion, that is backward. We should pray as though everything depended on us and work as though everything depended on God. The prayers of thanksgiving and supplication have been written with that thought in mind.

That is to say, the prayer begins, not ends, with the "Amen." All prayer begs the question, What are we going to do about what we've just prayed for? To go back to the thought that begins this Introduction, it is through prayer that the life-bringing energy of the Holy Spirit flows into every tissue and sinew of our lives. We pray to be energized, to become focused on what God would have us do. A woman was faced with two rather serious surgeries. She had suffered a mild heart attack in the midst of facing surgery for colon cancer. Which surgery should she have first, or should she have either? Both could be as life threatening as her heart and colon disease. She called me into her hospital room to pray with her, which I did. At the end of the prayer she asked me what I thought she should do. As we wrestled through what options lay before her it was as though the prayer of a short moment before was continuing. We were at the same time praying as though everything depended on us and working as though everything depended on God. The next time I saw her she had made up her mind to have the heart surgery, let herself heal, and then deal with the cancer. She said, "After all, if I had the colon surgery first and suffered a heart attack during the surgery, of what use would that be?" She had invited me to work with her after the "Amen" to take the next steps for which we had just prayed.

"Prayer aligns our thoughts with God's thoughts." Often prior to worship I pray with the choir and the associate pastor: "As we come before the throne of God's grace, may our thoughts be God's thoughts and our wills transformed into the mind of the living Christ as the Holy Spirit draws us into the realm of God's reign on earth." There is no doubt that the sanctuary is sacred space. It is there for whatever reasons people feel in touch with their God. It may be the olfactory, that strongest of all our senses, that provides the link. I have had people return to the sanctuary after having been gone for fifteen or twenty years and the first thing out of their mouths is, "it smells just the same as when I left it." It may also be the sight of some stained glass window. I can still recall the stained glass windows in the sanctuary in Alameda, California, where I grew up, almost in their proper order. It may be the sounds of the organ or musical instruments as the congregation prepares itself for worship. It may be the touch of a pew mate with whom we have come to pray and learn together what it means to be the faithful people of God. It may be the hearing of the liturgist's voice calling us to worship. Whatever the reasons, our thoughts are aligned with God's thoughts and we, indeed, find ourselves before the throne of God's grace.

Prayer also "focuses our capacities on the grace and mercy of the risen Christ." Mary never missed a Sunday in worship. She was there faithfully with her husband, and, after he died, continued to find the strength to occupy the same pew alone. Lately, Alzheimer's claimed her mind, and we had to find space for her in one of our local extended care facilities. Since she was no longer able to attend worship, we took the service to her. Our visits were tedious at times, because while Mary knew what it was she wanted to say, she was unable to find the words in the proper order to express herself. However, as we went through the liturgy with her we invited her to say the Lord's Prayer with us. What a transforming moment! She never missed a word. It was as though she was back in Sunday school, and the teacher had just called her to the front of the class. Whatever the Alzheimer's had done to her short-term memory it could not touch how the Lord's Prayer had focused for Mary the grace and mercy of the risen Christ.

Prayer then moves us in the direction that "will make us more faithful to God's will for our lives." My prayer time each day begins around 5:30 A.M. with a three-mile trek through the neighborhood. It has become such a routine that I jokingly have mentioned to people in the congregation that I knew it was time to pray for them when I got to a particular corner. One woman makes it a point during the receiving line after worship to make sure I am getting up early enough to deal with her family's needs. It is a comfort to them to know that their pastor faithfully keeps them in prayer each day. It is also a worthwhile discipline to begin each day focused on what God may have in store in the hours to come. Whatever may be your time and venue, I hope the prayers contained in this volume will help you to discern God's will for you on a regular basis.

It goes without saying that no work in print is the product of only one hand, especially a book of prayers. Countless people through the years have been kind enough to offer words of wisdom and guidance. I have been blessed with caring congregations and colleagues who have taught me what it means to "stand before the throne of God's grace." I want to thank four people in particular. My wife, Elizabeth, took the challenge upon herself to see to it that I would spend a portion of each day working on the manuscript. Otherwise, it would not have gotten done in a timely fashion. Chris and Jim Wolfe brought me into the dawn of the twenty-first century and patiently spent time with me introducing me to the intricacies of the computer, all the while assuring me that it would save me countless hours of time. Chris, in particular, massaged the manuscript and made sure it was worthy to send to the editor. The fourth person has been a good friend for a number of years and made it possible for the revision to occur. Tom Long, as director of Geneva Press, expressed an interest and then became my editor throughout this venture. To them and to all of you who come upon the following words of praise to the living God, "Gott sei Dank!"

JGK
Pentecost 2000

Note: In this book, prayers are provided for All Saints' Day in all three years. Prayers for Thanksgiving are provided only for year A but may be used in years B and C as well.

Year A

1ST SUNDAY OF ADVENT (A)

Isaiah 2:1–5; Psalm 122
Romans 13:11–14; Matthew 24:36–44

The people of God are to watch for the coming of the Lord. They are to be ready for the unexpected, and readiness takes preparation. Think of the unexpected ways the Lord appears in our lives. To watch means to live in expectation. How does such anticipation affect the routine course of the day? In Noah's day a flood overtook the people and swept them away. Watch and be ready!

Call to Worship   Psalm 122

Leader: I was glad when they said to me, "Let us go to the house of the Lord!"
People: For the sake of my relatives and friends I will say, "Peace be within you."
Leader: For the sake of the house of the Lord our God, I will seek your good.
People: Our feet are standing with your gates, O Jerusalem. Peace be within your walls.
Leader: Let us worship God!

Prayer of Praise and Adoration

The day is coming, O Lord, when people will say, "Come, let us go up to the mountain of the Lord, that you may teach us your ways and we may walk in your paths. As swords are beaten into plowshares and spears into pruning hooks, nation shall not lift up sword against nation, neither shall they learn war any more." In anticipation of the shalom Christ brings to all people we come now before your throne of grace to give your our praise and thanksgiving.

Prayer of Confession

Unison: God of forgiveness and mercy, hear our prayer as we confess our sin. With moments so critical we let time go by. With deliverance so near we linger in the darkness. With Christ as our armor, we yet fear the unknown foe. With the night having passed, we still hesitate to greet the new day. O God, lead us forth, that we may meet the moment you graciously give us. Dispel the shadows, so that your will may be clear. Clothed with light and new life in Christ, let us go forth as those awake to your will.

Assurance of Pardon

Leader: Jesus said that anyone who hears what he says and trusts in God has eternal life. The time is coming, indeed it is already here. All who heed God's voice shall have life and that, indeed, eternal. Rest in the assurance of God's grace made known to us in Jesus the Christ.

Prayer of Dedication

O God, your will is revealed in hidden places. We are told to be ready, for your Son comes at times we do not expect. We are told to clothe the naked, feed the hungry, and visit those in prison. Quiet our fears, so that we may venture confidently into the unknown and minister to strangers in our midst.

Prayer of Praise and Petition

Our eyes behold your grandeur, O God. Our feet stand within the gates of your house. Prophets have sung of your mountain, where nations shall come to learn of your ways. From out of Zion your law has gone forth; out of Jerusalem has proceeded your word. Confessing you to be our judge and redeemer, we gather to give you honor and praise.

Lift us to the heights of your abode, that we may learn how to make peace here on earth. We hear of swords beaten into plowshares, yet all around lands and peoples are battered by destructive weapons. We know that our spears are not being turned into pruning hooks but are poised to lash out at others. Turn our national obsession for security into deep concern for the safety and well-being of neighbors around the world. And grant that we may not only claim you as redeemer, but also serve you as agents of peace.

As Advent dawns, lead us from this courtyard of praise into paths filled with promise. Brighten our way, and help us to step out boldly in your love. When we venture into places that are hostile or strange, steady our nerves by your Spirit of truth and power. Go with us as we share with others the Advent hope.

Fill us with eagerness that waits for the dawn, curiosity that is willing to explore all truth, and impatience with injustice that refuses to leave till tomorrow the tasks of liberation. Come, Prince of Peace, in whose name we pray.

2ND SUNDAY OF ADVENT (A)

Isaiah 11:1–10; Psalm 72:1–7, 18–19
Romans 15:4–13; Matthew 3:1–12

Images abound! John wears strange garments and eats uncommon food. From stones God raises children to Abraham. An ax is laid to the roots of trees that fail to bear good fruit. People will be baptized with the Holy Spirit. The wheat is gathered, and the chaff is burned with unquenchable fire. All creation serves God's mercy and judgment.

Call to Worship   Psalm 72

Leader: Blessed be the Lord, the God of Israel, who alone does won-
            drous things.
People: Blessed be your glorious name forever, O God, may your
            glory fill the whole earth.
Leader: Let us worship God!

Prayer of Praise and Adoration

Most glorious God, you judge your people with righteousness and your poor with justice. The mountains yield prosperity for all your people and the hills are clothed with your splendor. You defend the cause of the poor and deliver the needy. You are like rain that falls on the mown grass, like showers that water the earth. Filled with the joy and peace of believing, we will sing you our praises and serve you with our whole being, to the end that the nations may affirm your glory.

Prayer of Confession

Unison: O God, you judge your people with righteousness; we judge our neighbors either right or wrong. Your Servant defended the cause of the poor; it is because of our greed that many still want. You bring deliverance to the needy, but we stand in the way of its being received. You send us a Savior who will crush the oppressor, but we raise up idols in his stead. Make us mindful of your dominion, how you rule while sun and moon endure. May we bow down before you and pay you the tribute that you are due.

Assurance of Pardon

Leader: Know this: if you are willing you will be taught. If you pause to listen you will gain knowledge. Reflect on God's statutes and meditate on the commandments. It is God who will give insight to your mind, and your desire for wisdom will be granted. Through Christ's intercession on our behalf we receive the assurance that through him we are forgiven.

Prayer of Dedication

The voice of one crying in the wilderness calls us to prepare your way, O Lord. Among the sounds of society you choose to reveal your will. Amid its clamor we yearn to hear voices seeking your mercy. Send us forth with clear minds so that your way is proclaimed with foresight. And grant us your benediction so that our acts are sanctified by your grace.

Prayer of Thanksgiving, Intercession, and Supplication

God of steadfastness and encouragement, you are a source of new life. When your creation moans in labor and your people cry out for compassion, you cause a sprig of hope to spring forth from a stump. You bring deliverance to the needy and justice to the oppressed. You cause your Spirit to rest on the faithful, bestowing wisdom, knowledge, and might. As a branch from the root of Jesse stands as a symbol of hope for your people, may nations respond by seeking to do your will, so that all our dwellings may reflect your glory.

Made wise by your prophets, help us to abide by your judgment. Cleansed with the water of baptism, may we not fear to confess you as our God. Not even a sparrow falls without your knowledge; may we also be mindful of your creation. You have planted in us the vision of shalom, when the wolf shall dwell with the lamb and none shall hurt or destroy. May we act on that dream to make peace here on earth. You send us the Christ who calls others to follow in his way; may we proclaim him the way of our lives. You assure us that you will not leave us alone; with that confidence may we become bold in our faith.

When we are confronted with poverty, give us the courage to act to free those who want. When we are aware of the lonely, let us be quick to provide comfort and companionship. When others face death, may our presence bring courage and help to fill the void. Where pain hinders movement, give us compassion to console those afflicted. As the shoot springs forth from the stump, let our actions cause it to break out into blossom, that all who hear of your love may come to rejoice with new life.

3RD SUNDAY OF ADVENT (A)

Isaiah 35:1–10; Psalm 146:5–10 or Luke 1:47–55
James 5:7–10; Matthew 11:2–11

John sends his disciples to find out if Jesus is the awaited Messiah. They are told by Jesus to report what they have seen and heard: the blind see, the deaf hear, lepers are cleansed, the poor hear good news, the dead are raised up. When John's disciples leave, Jesus tells the crowd John's identity: he is "more than a prophet," and one divinely sent to prepare the way for God's reign. The signs of that reign are already present in the midst of God's people.

Call to Worship   Psalm 146

> *Leader:* Happy are those whose help is the God of Jacob, whose hope is in the Lord their God.
>
> *People:* Who made heaven and earth, the sea, and all that is in them; who keeps faith forever.
>
> *Leader:* The Lord sets the prisoners free, opens the eyes of the blind, and lifts up those who are bowed down.
>
> *People:* The Lord will reign forever, your God, O Zion, for all generations. Praise the Lord!
>
> *Leader:* Let us worship God!

Prayer of Praise and Adoration

You are a God of bounteous gifts, O Lord, and we bless your name. You bestow mercies without end. Your people stand upright; you give sight to the blind. You have no patience with injustice, and the meek you do not turn away. We open our hearts to your presence, and our doors to the stranger. We gather as your people, brought together by your grace and made one by your love.

Prayer of Confession

Unison: You have taught us to be patient and promised to supply our needs, O God. Yet we grow weary of waiting and restless with our wants. We blame our troubles on brothers and sisters, withholding from them the tolerance and care you have shown to us. O God, forgive our indulgence and help us to stand firm. In Christ you showed patience with the world in spite of the cross. Teach us to be patient, that in Christ we may have endurance in spite of our need.

Assurance of Pardon

Leader: Know this: that we are assured of God's forgiveness, for we have a high priest set over the household of God, Jesus Christ, the new and living way. Let us therefore make our approach in sincerity and confidence, our guilty hearts sprinkled clean, our bodies washed with pure water. The Giver of the promise is to be trusted.

Prayer of Dedication

We offer ourselves, O God, as messengers of peace and goodwill. Where war threatens and strife is real, we seek by grace to demonstrate your reconciling love. When hostilities persist and your people are alienated, our gift is Christ's promise of intercession and accord. May our words be combined with commitment to act, and our actions conform to your abiding desire.

Prayer of Thanksgiving and Commitment

You cause new life to spring forth in the desert, O God, and that which was barren to yield. By your will waters cascade in dry places and rushing torrents subside to a flow. By your design, the crocus blooms as a sign that the winter shall end. As you have promised, weak hands are made strong, and feeble knees become firm. Those who are fearful gain boldness; the lost acquire sight of your haven. Your gifts are not exhausted by time, or depleted through use. You are a God of surprises. You are above us and beyond us, yet dwell among us. For all that you are and shall be we give you thanks, and praise your name.

Go before us and show us your will for our lives. As in the days of Israel, give us signs of your way, a cloud by day, and a fire by night. And stay behind to prod when we grow sluggish and lax. Let the prophets be heard, calling us to be faithful. Keep your commandments before us, encompassing your will. When we stumble and fall, we shall trust in Christ, our advocate, to intercede for us. He walked the path that we must walk and was obedient. He was tempted, yet did not submit. He taught us how you temper your judgment with mercy. We pray for a measure of patience as you wait at the doors of your kingdom.

You are a generous God who gives in abundance. As you spared not yourself but came even to dwell here on earth, may we respond by giving ourselves to your service. We commit ourselves anew to the journey of faith. Make straight the highway before us as we lead your people in Christ's name.

4TH SUNDAY OF ADVENT (A)

Isaiah 7:10–16; Psalm 80:1–7, 17–19
Romans 1:1–7; Matthew 1:18–25

"Emmanuel," God with us. What a glorious gift! The words of the prophet are fulfilled in the birth of a child. What is conceived of the Holy Spirit and carried in Mary's womb is the promise of eternal life to all that believe. Jesus will save God's people from their sins; God will dwell in their midst. The Spirit makes God's presence known now and forevermore.

Call to Worship   Psalm 80

Leader: Give ear, O Shepherd of Israel, you who lead Joseph like a flock!

People: Restore us, O God; let your face shine, that we may be saved.

Leader: Then we will never turn back from you; give us life, and we will call on your name.

People: Restore us, O Lord God of hosts; let your face shine, that we may be saved.

Leader: Let us worship God!

Prayer of Praise and Adoration

Your face has shone upon us, O God, in the young woman who is with child. She will bear a son and name him Emmanuel, "God with us." Your presence shall hereafter be a source of comfort and guidance to all that call on your name. Your footsteps shall accompany us, your breath shall give us new life, your arms will console us, and your hands will be there to welcome us home. You are a God for all seasons and give us all reason to worship your name.

Prayer of Confession

Unison: You shower gifts on your people, O God, and forgive their faults. We keep accounts and settle old scores. You make peace, sending Christ as a sign of reconciliation and hope. We make war and call it peacekeeping. You give us a source of confidence as your Spirit is sent into our midst. We cause others to be restless, in our anxiety and self-concern. Have mercy upon us, forgive, and free us, that we may be renewed to serve your people with goodwill.

Assurance of Pardon

Leader: The Most High is called *merciful,* because God has mercy on those who have not yet come into the world; and *gracious,* because God is rich in grace to those who repent and turn to the law; and *compassionate,* because God makes compassion abound more and more within all of creation. Live in this knowledge, and be confident that your sins are forgiven.

Prayer of Dedication

The stage is set for the presentation of your gift of life, O Christ, and we are part of the company of players. As the curtain is about to rise, we prepare ourselves for our roles. We commit what we have to the drama that changes lives. Help us to step onto the stage with anticipation and boldness. May we know the script so well that we shall not falter as we share your gift, and ours.

Prayer of Affirmation and Supplication

O God, by your prophet you promised a sign of your presence, a son called Emmanuel. And in Jesus Christ you chose to live in our midst, taste our suffering, and feel our needs. He made known your will, taught your way, and called us to follow in it. He entered the world as a tiny child, showing what dependence and promise would mean. Shepherds heard the angels' song and spread the news of the holy Child. The Magi traveled far to worship the newborn king and offer gifts. What you promised came to pass. What the prophet foretold we know now to be true.

As your story is retold and carols are sung, we hail the time appointed, and declare that your reign on earth has begun. As Jesus comes to break oppression, let us too set captives free. As he takes away transgression, let us strive for equity. We kneel in awe and wonder with shepherds and kings. As the Light of Lights descends, let us sweep away the darkness and receive the message he brings. "Watchman, tell us of the night, what its signs of promise are." Tell us of his sacrifice that banishes our terror and dread. "Come, thou long-expected Jesus, . . . born to reign in us forever." As you release us from our sins and fears, may we act to deliver your people everywhere.

O Strength and Consolation, you are the dayspring that we cheer. Yours is the time appointed; we hail the advent of your anointed One. As a woman conceived and bore for you a Son, we welcome Emmanuel, for by his birth our new life has begun.

CHRISTMAS EVE/DAY
Proper I (Year A B C)

Isaiah 9:2–7; Psalm 96
Titus 2:11–14; Luke 2:1–14 (15–20)

A decree. A census. A man and a woman arrive in Bethlehem to obey an emperor's wish. Shepherds on the night shift tend their sheep. In the midst of these ordinary events a baby's birth is announced with extraterrestrial fanfare. Glory is given to God in the highest; peace is promised on earth. Henceforth, the world shall be enlightened by God's Word made flesh.

Call to Worship
Psalm 96

Leader: O sing to the Lord a new song; tell of God's salvation from day to day.

People: For great is the Lord, and greatly to be praised; God is to be feared above all gods.

Leader: Worship the Lord in holy array; tremble before God, all the earth!

People: Honor and majesty are before God; strength and beauty are in God's sanctuary.

Prayer of Praise and Adoration

We praise your name, O God. You are glorified among the nations and in all creation. You cause the flowers to bloom; the honeycomb drips with sweetness according to your design. You dwell in teeming cities and in the quiet of the countryside. The whole earth is your habitation. You invite us into your sanctuary, where we worship and bow down before you. Fill us now with your Spirit, and let your presence be our blessing.

Prayer of Confession

Unison: Your grace, O God, has appeared for the salvation of all, calling us to renounce false gods and irresponsible love. In the midst of our sin, Christ has appeared as a sign of our hope, redeeming us and calling us to be a people eager to do your will. Make us zealous for good deeds in response to your wonderful deed in Jesus Christ. We confess the vain worship of ourselves and our neglect of your children. Forgive us and empower us to live upright and godly lives in this world.

Assurance of Pardon

Leader: Know this that the assurance of our forgiveness has come. "For a child has been born for us, a son given to us. . . . His authority shall grow continually, and there shall be endless peace for the throne of David and his kingdom. He will establish and uphold it with justice and with righteousness from this time onward and forevermore."

Prayer of Dedication

Your Word is made flesh and dwells among us, O God, full of grace and truth. For that gift and all you bestow, we say Alleluia and Amen! As we behold your glory, we commit ourselves to Christ's work. Make of us the body of Christ and dwell in us by your Spirit for the sake of the world that you love.

Prayer of Praise and Petition

The heavens tell of your glory, O God. All the trees of the wood sing for joy. For unto us a child is born, and into our midst has come a great light. You have come to deal justly with nations; with righteousness you rule your people. We hear of a Wonderful Counselor and know that your Spirit is near. The prophet proclaims you Mighty God, while the sea roars and fields exult. Your mercy is everlasting as you care for all your creation. We herald the Prince of Peace and await the time when his rule is complete. You are our God and are greatly to be praised. We sing unto you, honoring your name, and tell of your salvation from day to day.

Gifts have been opened and love has been exchanged. Keep us mindful that you are the source of all abundance and worth. Families have gathered and loved ones have returned home. May we always remember that Christ calls us to the Table with himself as the host. The tree has been trimmed and stockings have been hung. Let their garlands and tributes awaken assurance of your grace. Now that anticipation has given way to celebration, may we not lose sight of your continuing call to obedience and devotion.

To those who still seek a sign of your love, may we become that sign as we do justly and love mercy. To those who lack the warmth of home and friends, may we extend hospitality and good cheer. Where the sounds of war drown out Christ's call to peace, may we fulfill the tasks of reconciliation and love. You have established the world and sent the Prince of Peace. We go forth as his servants in praise of your reign!

CHRISTMAS EVE/DAY
Proper II (Year A B C)

Isaiah 62:6–12; Psalm 97
Titus 3:4–7; Luke 2:(1–7) 8–20

As shepherds watch over their flocks, an angel appears, bringing glad tidings of great joy. A child is born who will bring peace to the nations. A multitude gathers to witness the event; they are filled with wonder and awe at God's merciful deed. From this time forth and forevermore, justice and righteousness shall flow like streams of living water.

Call to Worship
Psalm 97

Leader: Rejoice in the Lord you righteous, and give thanks to God's holy name.

People: The heavens proclaim your righteousness, O God, and all the people behold your glory.

Leader: For you, O Lord, are most high over all the earth and are exalted above all gods.

People: Rejoice in the Lord you righteous, and give thanks to God's holy name.

Leader: Let us worship God!

Prayer of Praise and Adoration

O God of peace, to you we ascribe all honor and majesty, beauty and strength. You bring forth a child whom we call blessed, upon whose shoulders rests the destiny of nations. You give us the gift of life everlasting, a wonderful counselor who shall guide all your people. With shepherds and angels, we lift our voices rejoicing: All glory to you in the highest, and on earth peace among those with whom you dwell.

Litany of Affirmation

Leader: Be not afraid, for behold, I bring you good news of great joy for all the people.

People: God's grace has appeared for the salvation of all.

Leader: For to us is born a savior, who is Christ the Lord.

People: God's grace has appeared for the salvation of all.

Leader: When the goodness and loving-kindness of God our savior appeared, he saved us.

People: God's grace has appeared for the salvation of all.

Leader:	This Spirit he poured out on us richly through Jesus Christ our Savior.
People:	God's grace has appeared for the salvation of all.
Leader:	So that, having been justified by his grace, we might become heirs according to the hope of eternal life.
People:	God's grace has appeared for the salvation of all.

Prayer of Dedication

Our lives abound with signs of your matchless love, O God. Our days are full because of your mercy. As those long ago journeyed to Bethlehem and felt great joy at what had occurred, so also we come before you, praising your name for what you have made known to us. Accept our tributes to the Christ-child; use them that he may grow in stature among all people.

Prayer of Thanksgiving

O Giver of every good and perfect gift, we come rejoicing at the birth of your Son, our Savior Jesus Christ. We give you thanks that your light shines forth in the world. You illuminate our darkness, drive away the clouds of gloom and despair; you send forth rays of hope to cheer us and warm us with the radiance of your redeeming love.

The carols we sing tell of your glory, how angels sang and shepherds watched as glory shone round the place where Jesus lay. We give thanks for the amazement and wonder of your revelation, the many ways you surprise us, and visit us, and cause us to feel your presence. You can be found in the laughter and gaiety of noisy gatherings. On solemn occasions your majesty and strength evoke awe and praise.

The gifts we exchange are signs of your benevolence to us, how you came to earth and dwelt among us as Emmanuel, "God with us." The heavens are glad because of your presence, the earth rejoices with the peace you promise. The sea roars since you reign over it, and fields exult in praise of you. You have declared that you will not forsake your creation, and sealed your promise with the gift of a child. For that assurance we thank you and offer you our gratitude forevermore.

The joy we feel reflects our blessed hope: the appearance in glory of our Savior Jesus Christ. We give thanks that Christ calls us to follow him and gives us the ministry of reconciliation to fulfill in his name. At this glorious time of his birth, help us to reach out to those who feel no joy, for whom thanksgiving is difficult, because darkness enfolds them. Let us give to them a beacon of light that will lead them to your gift of new life.

CHRISTMAS EVE/DAY
Proper III (Year A B C)

Isaiah 52:7–10; Psalm 98
Hebrews 1:1–4 (5–12); John 1:1–14

"In the beginning was the Word, and the Word was with God, and the Word was God." John, sent from God, testifies to the light of the world, "so that all might believe through him." To all who believe in the name of the Lord the Word gives power to become children of God. They shall receive new life and be born not of blood or of the will of the flesh but by the will of God. The Word became flesh and lived among us, and we have seen his glory. Bathe in that radiance this day!

Call to Worship   Psalm 98

Leader: Make a joyful noise to the Lord, all the earth; break forth into joyous song and sing praises.
People: We will sing praises to the Lord with the lyre and the sound of the horn.
Leader: Let the sea roar, and all that fills it; the world and those who live in it.
People: We will sing you a new song, O God, for the marvelous things you have done.
Leader: Let us worship God!

Prayer of Praise and Adoration

O God, before whom mountains melt like wax, the earth trembles, and idols are humbled, we proclaim your righteousness as we behold your glory. You have sought out a people and proclaimed them holy. You have sent your chosen one, Jesus, to prepare your way. We have passed through the gates of salvation, which he opened for us, and now gather to worship you with our praise and thanksgiving.

Litany of Affirmation

Leader: Long ago God spoke to our ancestors in many and various ways, but in these last days God has spoken to us by a Son.
People: In the beginning, Lord, you founded the earth, and the heavens are the work of your hands.
Leader: He is the reflection of God's glory and the exact imprint of God's very being.

People:	In the beginning, Lord, you founded the earth, and the heavens are the work of your hands.
Leader:	When he had made purification for sins, he sat down at the right hand of the Majesty on high.
People:	In the beginning, Lord, you founded the earth, and the heavens are the work of your hands.
Leader:	Having become as much superior to angels as the name he has inherited is more excellent than theirs.
People:	In the beginning, Lord, you founded the earth, and the heavens are the work of your hands.

Prayer of Dedication

God of goodness and kindness, whose mercy is from everlasting to everlasting, all that we have are gifts of your grace. As the heavenly host sang of your glory, accept what we bring you as our offerings of praise. With the shepherds we have witnessed the birth of our Savior; our response is in gratitude for the hope of new life we receive in Christ Jesus.

Prayer of Thanksgiving

With "hosannas" we herald the birth of our Savior; we sing of glad tidings, O God our Redeemer. Through a child you have come to bring peace among us; we are reborn with the hope of new life. We hear the angels proclaiming that we need have no fear, for henceforth you shall be with us in Christ, your begotten. We give thanks for your gift of salvation and hope.

We glorify and praise you for making your will known to us. You have opened the gates of heaven to pilgrims such as we. From Jesus we have caught sight of your righteousness and truth. By him we have been taught your commandments and been called to follow in the way of justice and service. You have not forsaken us when we have strayed from his paths of obedience. Through him we give thanks for your forbearance and forgiveness.

On this day when all the earth is bathed in the dazzling light of your presence, we give thanks for your Holy Spirit, who continues to guide us. When we are confused, you grant us clarity. In the midst of ambiguity, we can discern the direction you would have us take. When perplexed, you empower us to rise above those forces that would subdue us. Your gifts are immeasurable and will endure when all else fails.

You are the cause of joy that abounds, the source of our righteousness, and the author of hope that dispels shadows of lingering doubt. With the multitude of the heavenly host, we praise you, saying, "Glory to God in the highest, and on earth peace among those whom God favors."

1ST SUNDAY AFTER CHRISTMAS (A)

Isaiah 63:7–9; Psalm 148
Hebrews 2:10–18; Matthew 2:13–23

Three times an angel of the Lord appears to Joseph and each time requires the family to move. They do what they are told and finally settle in the district of Galilee where they make their home in Nazareth. Joseph knows that to follow the Lord requires attentiveness to God's Word however it appears, the willingness to go where God's voice directs whenever it's heard, and to do what the Spirit suggests as the moment occurs. All the while those who believe know of God's continuing love and care.

Call to Worship   Isaiah 63

Leader: I will recount the gracious deeds of the Lord, the praiseworthy acts of God most high.
People: Because of all that the Lord has done for us, according to the abundance of God's love.
Leader: It was your presence that saved the house of Israel, your love and pity redeemed them.
People: We join with them as your people, O God, your children who sing you our praises.
Leader: Let us worship God!

Prayer of Praise and Adoration

We praise the name of the Lord, O God; the heavens praise you and the waters above the heavens. You commanded and they were created; you established them forever and ever. Mountains and all hills, fruit trees and all cedars, wild animals and all cattle, creeping things and flying birds all praise you. Young men and women alike, old and young together exalt your name. Your glory is above earth and heaven and yet you have chosen to live amongst us. In the name of Jesus of Nazareth we praise your name.

Litany of Affirmation

Leader: It was fitting that God, should make the pioneer of our salvation perfect through sufferings.
People: For the one who sanctifies and those who are sanctified all have one Father.
Leader: For this reason Jesus is not ashamed to call them brothers and sisters.
People: For the one who sanctifies and those who are sanctified all have one Father.

17

Leader:	Since, therefore, the children share flesh and blood, he himself likewise shared the same things.
People:	For the one who sanctifies and those who are sanctified all have one Father.
Leader:	Therefore he had to become like his brothers and sisters in every respect.
People:	For the one who sanctifies and those who are sanctified all have one Father.
Leader:	Because he was tested, he is able to help those who are being tested.
People:	For the one who sanctifies and those who are sanctified all have one Father.

Prayer of Dedication

Great Shepherd of the sheep, you feast our soul with abundance and satisfy your people with goodness. We dine on your mercy and are filled by your grace. Having received your gift of Christ our Redeemer, we no longer languish in barrenness but are full of new life. Accept these gifts that we bring you in response to the love you have shown us in Christ.

Prayer of Thanksgiving and Supplication

As we cross the threshold into the new, we take time in our journey to give you thanks, O God. You have accompanied us through the year that has passed. We have been clothed and fed by your gifts. When fear has engulfed us, or we have faced the unknown, Christ our high priest has interceded on our behalf. Faced with decisions, we have been enlightened by your Spirit, and enlivened through your abiding presence. Those who have passed from our presence we have entrusted to your care. Compassion has yoked us with those ill and in pain. You are the source of all comfort and the judge of all that is done. As your commandments have served to direct our path, your discipline has kept our eyes focused on your way.

As we offer you thanks for past mercies, we seek your guidance for future tasks. In a land that abounds with resources, there are still many who are poor and without hope. Let the prophet's vision of promised abundance become real to them through our ministry. The claims of those who have compete for our attention and zeal; it is easy to forget those who have not. Keep us firm and insistent that it is you whom we serve and you alone. When decisions are to be made, let us first seek your will. When we are met by challenges, stay by our side. When we enter the unknown, be our confidence and strength. And wanting for nothing, may we serve others with the fullness of new life you have promised in Christ's name.

18

2ND SUNDAY AFTER CHRISTMAS (YEAR A B C)

Jeremiah 31:7–14; Psalm 147:12–20
Ephesians 1:3–14; John 1:(1–9) 10–18

What a wonderful gift when the Word becomes flesh and dwells among us! As Ecclesiastes reminds us, "That which is, already has been; that which is to be, already is; and God seeks out what has gone by" (*Eccl. 3:20*). Jesus Christ, the eternal Word of God, was in the beginning, is now, and evermore shall be. It is a comforting thought to realize that God's presence, "Emmanuel," abides with us as God's grace, mercy, and strength continue to embrace us in all that we do.

Call to Worship
Jeremiah 31

Leader: Hear the word of the Lord, O nations, and declare it in the coastlands far away.

People: They shall come and sing aloud on the height of Zion; they shall be radiant over the goodness of the Lord.

Leader: I will turn their mourning into joy; I will comfort them, and give them gladness for sorrow.

People: For thus says the Lord: proclaim, give praise, and say, "Save, O Lord, your people, the remnant of Israel."

Leader: Let us worship God!

Prayer of Praise and Adoration

It is good to sing you our praises, O God, for you are gracious and a song of praise is fitting. You heal the brokenhearted and bind up their wounds. You determine the number of stars and give them their names. Your greatness abounds and your understanding is beyond measure. We will sing to you hymns of thanksgiving and make melody with songs of praise. As you take pleasure in those who hope in your steadfast love, be pleased with our worship as we lift our voices in glad adoration.

Prayer of Confession

Unison: Gracious God, you chose us in Christ before the foundation of the world to be holy and blameless, yet we do not love our brothers and sisters as he taught. You destined us for adoption as your children through Jesus Christ, yet we take our status for granted and fail to obey Christ when he calls us to follow. With all wisdom and insight you have made known to us the mystery of your will, yet we stubbornly refuse to study your Word. Forgive our sin, O God, and help us set our hope on Christ that we may live for the praise of his glory.

Assurance of Pardon

Leader: In Christ, when we heard the word of truth, the gospel of our salvation, and believed in him, we were marked with the seal of the promised Holy Spirit. This is the pledge of our inheritance toward redemption as God's own people, to the praise of his glory. In this promise lies our assurance, in Jesus Christ we are forgiven.

Prayer of Dedication

As in Christ we have obtained an inheritance, having been destined according to your purpose, O God, we seek to live now for the praise of your glory. Accept these gifts we bring as symbols of our renewed commitment to Christ's will for our lives. Use them to enhance your kingdom beyond the walls of this sanctuary and bring a sense of your presence to all that they benefit. Make us ever mindful of those who are needy and more diligent in our use of the means of your grace.

Prayer of Thanksgiving and Supplication

O God, you who are Alpha and Omega, the beginning and the end, we greet the dawn of redeeming grace with its radiant beams from Christ's holy face. We have passed through the night of doubt and no longer fear that you will forsake us. The One who was with you when you blessed all creation has come as our Savior full of your grace and truth. Through him you have assembled those who were scattered, "the blind and the lame, the woman with child and her who is in travail." We gather as those empowered to become your children and give you thanks for this grace upon grace.

There are those for whom each new day is threatening, whose fear block out the vision of your grace. We pray for them: the unemployed and homeless who find no sense of fulfillment. Their days are spent awaiting the call that does not come. Help us to stand with them and be their companions. May we lessen their travail through our support and encouragement. Fill us with resolve to change a society that denies work and the means of life.

Some spend their days in aimless wandering; they cannot remember where they have been or where they are going. We pray for those whom society casts aside. Make us impatient ambassadors for your truth and justice, unwilling to tolerate systems that neglect your children.

You are the beginning of goodness and the end of all our striving. In you abides a hope that cannot be denied. You have assembled us as your children; now dismiss us as your agents. You have caused light to shine in our lives; help us to lead others to that light, so that their day may dawn brightly.

EPIPHANY OF THE LORD (YEAR A B C)

Isaiah 60:1–6; Psalm 72:1–7, 10–14
Ephesians 3:1–12; Matthew 2:1–12

The heavens proclaim a birth in Bethlehem. Following a star, three Magi journey to see what has occurred. They carry with them gifts appropriate for a ruler: gold, frankincense, and myrrh. Upon arrival at the scene, they observe a mother and child, God's heavenly glory on earth to bring light to the nations. Proclaiming God's praise, they fall down and worship. The radiance of God's love evokes wonder and awe.

Call to Worship

Isaiah 60

Leader: Arise, shine; for your light has come; and the glory of the Lord has risen upon you.
People: Lift up your eyes and look around; sons and daughters gather together, they come to you.
Leader: Then you shall see and be radiant; your heart shall thrill and rejoice.
People: They shall bring gold and frankincense, and shall proclaim the praise of the Lord.
Leader: Let us worship God.

Prayer of Praise and Adoration

Merciful God of deliverance, we praise you for sending Jesus as Light for the nations. He is the glory and radiance of your compassion and care. Our eyes behold the brightness of your promised righteousness; you illumine our darkness with the hope of your justice. As generations before us, we stand in awe of your splendor; we bow down to worship you, lifting our voices in praise of your goodness and giving heed to your instruction.

Prayer of Confession

Unison: Source of salvation and Bringer of light, we fail to sense the mystery of your love. We bear grudges against our neighbors, while it is your nature to forgive. We hold tightly to our possessions, while Christ blesses the poor. In him you have spoken peace, yet we live in turmoil. We care little for this planet, which you in goodness created for our habitation. In mercy forgive us, and help us to amend our ways.

Assurance of Pardon

Leader: God is righteous and just, and forgives the iniquity of all who repent. Like "rain that falls on the mown grass, like showers that water the earth," God's goodwill overflows toward us in the Babe of Bethlehem. Through that child, who is our risen Lord, we plead for forgiveness and claim God's mercy and assurance of pardon.

Prayer of Dedication

O God, as wise rulers of old brought gifts and worshiped a newly born baby, so also we bring offerings in praise of him whom you sent. The star that we follow is the light of Christ's teachings, calling us to be faithful in service to all in need. Accept what we earn, the products of our creative energy and talent. Let this be the gold, frankincense, and myrrh that we bring. By our gifts may a sad and needy world be enriched and comforted.

Prayer of Thanksgiving, Supplication, and Intercession

Eternal God of manifold wisdom, we give you thanks that through the gift of Jesus you have given us a glimpse into your plan of creation. He shows us how you rule the nations, bringing hope of justice to those in need, and deliverance to all captives. In him we see the promise of new life if only we follow his will for our lives.

Your infinite mercy is always before us, granting us haven from storm-tossed seas. We give you thanks that Jesus walked this earth, suffered more pain than we shall ever endure, and sits by your side to intercede for us. You know our needs before we voice them. Make your presence felt among us during our times of trial, and give us courage to face the suffering that will test our faith.

Let your all-encompassing presence be with those who, for whatever reasons, are in need of your loving care. Help them sense your healing power at work to ease their pain, shield them from the demonic powers of this world that seek to undermine their spirit, and protect them from any aggravation that might weaken them further.

We pray particularly for those in institutions who seem to be forgotten, those disturbed in mind and spirit. Bring wholeness to them, and a sense of your companionship in the midst of their loneliness. Let us not cast aside any who dwell among us, whether they be the simple, the slow, or the impaired. Rather, help us to see in them a special gleam of the light that Jesus brought to the world. We give you thanks for a righteousness that is all-inclusive, a hope that is ever sure, a deliverance that knows no limits, and a promise of life that is eternal, through Christ, whose going forth we celebrate today.

BAPTISM OF THE LORD (A)

Isaiah 42:1–9; Psalm 29
Acts 10:34–43; Matthew 3:13–17

Jesus is baptized in order to fulfill all righteousness. When priorities are askew and directions misleading, he shows the way of God's kingdom. When neighbors are in conflict, the Spirit descends like a dove with the hope of peace for all God's people. The baptism of Jesus portrays God's promise to set aright the creation.

Call to Worship   Psalm 29

Leader: Ascribe to the Lord, O heavenly beings; ascribe to the Lord glory and strength.

People: Ascribe to the Lord the glory of God's name; worship the Lord in holy splendor.

Leader: The voice of the Lord is over the waters; the voice of the Lord is full of majesty.

People: May the Lord give strength to God's people! May the Lord bless the people with peace.

Leader: Let us worship God!

Prayer of Praise and Adoration

O God of all power and majesty, you created the heavens and stretched them out. You spread forth the earth and what comes from it. You give breath to the people and spirit to those who walk on the face of the earth. You are our Lord: glory is due your name. The former things have come to pass; we now await the new things you shall bring forth. We do indeed cry "Glory!" as we gather to worship your name.

Prayer of Confession

Unison: You have given Christ as a covenant to the nations, O God, yet your people continue to live at war. Your prophets proclaim justice and peace, yet we dwell amid hostility and oppression. You judge your people with fairness; we implore you to have mercy upon us. Give sight to eyes that are blind to your truth. Enlighten our darkness, that we may behold you even in the midst of our enemies. Free us from seeking your own grandeur, so that in humility we may live at peace with your people.

Assurance of Pardon

Leader: The promises of God are with us still. As the prophet foretold, a Servant is sent. A bruised reed he will not break, and a dimly burning

23

wick he will not quench. He knows our weakness. Trust the promises of God in Jesus Christ: we are forgiven.

Prayer of Dedication

We acknowledge our baptism, O God, and the call to become members of Christ's body. Accept our gifts, that others may be led into your way. Help us so to arrange our priorities that we may seek first your will for us and prepare ourselves to follow where Christ may lead us. May the offering we bring be a sign and symbol of our commitment to answer his call to "come, follow me."

Prayer of Thanksgiving, Supplication, and Intercession

Eternal God of manifold wisdom, we give you thanks that through the gift of Jesus you have given us a glimpse into your plan of creation. He shows us how you rule the nations, bringing hope of justice to those in need, and deliverance to all captives. In him we see the promise of new life if only we follow his will for our lives.

Your infinite mercy is always before us, granting us haven from storm-tossed seas. We give you thanks that Jesus walked this earth, suffered more pain than we shall ever endure, and sits by your side to intercede for us. You know our needs before we voice them. Make your presence felt among us during our times of trial, and give us courage to face the suffering that will test our faith.

Let your all-encompassing presence be with those who, for whatever reasons, are in need of your loving care. Help them sense your healing power at work to ease their pain, shield them from the demonic powers of this world that seek to undermine their spirit, and protect them from any aggravation that might weaken them further.

We pray particularly for those in institutions who seem to be forgotten, those disturbed in mind and spirit. Bring wholeness to them, and a sense of your companionship in the midst of their loneliness. Let us not cast aside any who dwell among us, whether they be the simple, the slow, or the impaired. Rather, help us to see in them a special gleam of the light that Jesus brought to the world. We give you thanks for a righteousness that is all-inclusive, a hope that is ever sure, a deliverance that knows no limits, and a promise of life that is eternal, through Christ, whose going forth we celebrate today.

24

2ND SUNDAY IN ORDINARY TIME (A)

Isaiah 49:1–7; Psalm 40:1–11
1 Corinthians 1:1–9; John 1:29–42

John bears witness to Jesus as the one upon whom the Spirit descends. Henceforth he is known as "the Lamb of God, who takes away the sin of the world." Water is known for its cleansing power. The Spirit is recognized as the source of new life. The lamb is a symbol of innocence and faith. Rejoice in your baptism and receive anew God's merciful gifts!

Call to Worship
Psalm 49

Leader: When I waited patiently for you, O God, you bent down to me and heard my cry.

People: You put a new song in my mouth, a song of praise to our God

Leader: I have told the glad news of deliverance in the great congregation; I have not restrained my lips, as you know, O Lord.

People: Do not, O Lord, withhold your mercy from me; let your steadfast love and faithfulness keep me safe forever.

Leader: Let us worship God!

Prayer of Praise and Adoration

You have called us before we were born, O God, and named us in our mother's womb. You have made our mouths like sharp swords, and hid us in the shadow of your hand. You have made us polished arrows and kept us safe in your quiver. In Christ you have called us to be your servants, to be a light to the nations, and to herald your goodness to all. Now our heads are lifted up and we will offer you our sacrifices with shouts of joy.

Prayer of Confession

Unison: Our desire is to do your will, O God; your law is in our hearts. But when misfortunes beyond counting press from all sides, and iniquities overtake us, our sight fails. When we are tempted by the vain promises of a life full of ease, our courage forsakes us and we submit to their charm. When enemies overpower us and mock our faith, we shrink back in disgrace and abandon what Christ taught. O God, we are poor and in need. You are our help and salvation. Come to our aid, and make no delay.

Assurance of Pardon

Leader: Grace and peace is given to you in Jesus Christ. All who call upon his name he claims as his own. God will keep you firm to the end, without reproach on the Day of our Lord Jesus. It is God who called you to share in the life of God's Son, Jesus Christ. God keeps faith and forgives our sin.

Prayer of Dedication

As the Lamb of God takes away the sins of the world, we remember that we are baptized as a sign of new life. Accept these gifts, O God, which we offer as we recommit ourselves to ministry in Christ's name. May your Spirit empower us for the tasks that await, and the waters refresh us as we go forth to serve.

Prayer of Thanksgiving and Intercession

Redeemer of your people Israel, and our Redeemer, you sent your servant as a light to the nations. His salvation reaches to the ends of the earth. He taught as one with authority; his wisdom enlightens our way. He was bruised for our sakes and intercedes on our behalf. He served others as a sign of your love; he offers hope to all who are in need. You are God forever, benevolent, compassionate, and full of purpose. What you create, you leave not alone. When you judge, it is with loving concern. Those you call you also empower. Wondrous God, we come to you with thanksgiving. Incline your ear to our prayer, and look with favor on our requests.

We pray for those who are beset with burdens too heavy to bear. Draw them up out of the pits of desolation and depression, and set their feet again on solid ground. May they find in Jesus Christ a sure foundation for their lives. We pray for those who face death, and for those encumbered with sorrow at the loss of one held dear. May they rest in the conviction that in Christ life shall not end. We pray for the sick and those weakened by pain. As Jesus worked wonders, making persons whole, may we in Christ's name surround the infirm with healing ministries of comfort and care. Let our comfort convince them that they do not suffer alone. Let our care provide for their dignity despite their disabling condition.

We pray for ourselves and for those offering prayers on behalf of others. Put a new song in our mouths and your praise on our lips. We delight to do your will; may your law remain in our hearts. As we speak of your faithfulness before all of your people, continue to multiply your wonderful deeds in our midst.

3RD SUNDAY IN ORDINARY TIME (A)

Isaiah 9:1–4; Psalm 27:1, 4–9
1 Corinthians 1:10–18; Matthew 4:12–23

With a call for repentance, Jesus bids others to follow him. The message is urgent: the kingdom of heaven is at hand. His invitation includes the offer to make them fishers of others. The sought-for response is unconditional and unequivocal: "Immediately they left their nets and followed him." The kingdom involves action.

Call to Worship

Psalm 27

Leader: The Lord is my light and my salvation; whom shall I fear?

People: The Lord is the stronghold of my life; of whom shall I be afraid?

Leader: One thing I asked of the Lord, to live in the house of the Lord all the days of my life.

People: "Come," my heart says, "seek the face of the Lord." Your face, Lord, do I seek.

Leader: Let us worship God!

Prayer of Praise and Adoration

"The people who walked in darkness have seen a great light; those who lived in a land of deep darkness, on them light has shined. You have multiplied the nation, you have increased its joy." We rejoice now before you as the yoke of our burden and the bar across our shoulders you have broken as on the day of Midian. As those numbered to walk in the light of the Christ who names us in our baptism and washes us with the waters of new life, we gather now in his name to give you all praise and glory.

Prayer of Confession

Unison: If we claim to have fellowship with Christ, yet walk in darkness, we are liars. If we claim to possess the light, but hide it under a bushel, of what use is such wisdom to the world? If we rest secure in our abundance, while all about us others go hungry and their lives are imperiled, what has become of our call to share the good news? You know our inmost selves, O God. We cannot hide from you. Forgive our betrayal of your Son, and restore us to fellowship with him.

Assurance of Pardon

Leader: Jesus said, "I am the light of the world." Whoever follows the Christ will not walk in darkness, but will have the light of life. He has come as light into the world, so that whoever believes in him may not remain in darkness. Come now to that light, for in him we are restored and forgiven.

Prayer of Dedication

Christ, you invite us to follow and become fishers of others. You equip us with talents and gifts for our venture. We humbly respond to your gracious invitation and place our gifts at your disposal. As we go out to serve, receive the results of our efforts in your name. Turn them to good where we have erred. Shed light on our path as we seek to abide in your way.

Prayer of Supplication

God of the covenant, your people who walk in darkness have seen a great light. Upon those who dwell in the night of their lives a new day has dawned. For the long-awaited Christ, whom you promised, has entered the world to illumine our way. The radiance of your glory cannot be hidden from our eyes. When we seek to live in the shadows of doubt, you reveal the folly of our ways. If the darkness of gloom overtakes us, you dazzle us with the luster of your kingdom. Our flickering faith is matched with the brilliance of your plan for creation. We bow before you, bathed in the light of your love and aglow with the gift of your grace.

In your light may we see light, and so lead others to greater clarity of vision. Where perceptions are distorted through mistrust of Christ's message, may our lives make clear what he taught. When others are captive to seeing things only one way, let our openness provide them a choice. If because of our silence others know not what we think, give us courage of conviction and a willingness to confer. When leaders make decisions with which we do not agree, make us bold in dissent and reconciling in spirit.

Deliver us from pretension in the truth we hold; open our eyes to what others may reveal. Keep us attuned to the diversity of voices in the church, as they reflect upon your message in varied tones and accents. Lift our horizons so that we may glimpse the full scope of your covenant love. Let us dare to be astonished by the grandeur of your providence and grace.

4TH SUNDAY IN ORDINARY TIME (A)

Micah 6:1–8; Psalm 15
1 Corinthians 1:18–31; Matthew 5:1–12

Blessings abound for the people of God! The poor in spirit are rich; theirs is the kingdom of heaven. The meek inherit the earth; the merciful obtain mercy. Peacemakers are children of God, imitating their heavenly parent. And those who search for righteousness find fulfillment in their quest. In spite of persecution and slander, gladness and joy are proclaimed. For such is the nature of God's reign in our midst.

Call to Worship

Psalm 15

Leader: O Lord, who may abide in your tent? Who may dwell on your holy hill?

People: Those who walk blamelessly, and do what is right; and speak the truth from their heart.

Leader: Those who do not slander with their tongue, and do no evil to their friends.

People: Those who do these things shall never be moved.

Leader: Let us worship God!

Prayer of Praise and Adoration

Gracious God, you have brought our ancestors up from Egypt, and redeemed them from the house of slavery. You have sent before them Moses, Aaron, and Miriam to guide them along their journey of faith. You have taught us, O God, what we should bring you. You do not want our burnt offerings, thousands of rams, or ten thousands of rivers of oil. What you expect from us is to do justice, to love kindness and to walk humbly with you in all that we do. We humbly enter your sanctuary to give you all glory and honor.

Litany of Confession

Leader: When the cross appears as folly instead of God's power;

People: Let those who boast, boast of the Lord.

Leader: When some demand signs and others seek wisdom;

People: Let those who boast, boast of the Lord.

Leader: When the favored of the world claim the favor of God;

People: Let those who boast, boast of the Lord.

Leader: We despise the weak and long to be strong;

People: God's foolishness is wisdom; God's weakness is strength.

29

Leader:	We despise the ignorant and seek to be wise;
People:	God's foolishness is wisdom; God's weakness is strength.
Leader:	We despise the lowly and struggle for status;
People:	God's foolishness is wisdom; God's weakness is strength.

Assurance of Pardon

Leader: Blessings abound for the people of God! The poor in spirit are rich; theirs is the kingdom of heaven. The meek inherit the earth; the merciful obtain mercy. Peacemakers are children of God, imitating their heavenly parent. And those who search for righteousness find fulfillment in their quest. In spite of persecution and slander, gladness and joy are proclaimed. Such occurs when Christ intercedes on our behalf!

Prayer of Dedication

We offer but a portion of the bounty that you bestow, O God. Receive our gifts as we seek to walk in your way. Where justice is sought, use these gifts to bring Christ's liberating word. Where there is pain, may they bring the healing of Christ's love. Where there is want, let them assure others that you know of their needs before they are voiced. Continue to enhance what we give to you, as we become more obedient to Christ's will for our lives.

Prayer of Thanksgiving and Supplication

O God, we enter your gates with thanksgiving and come into your courts with praise. You have brought your people out of Egypt and redeemed them from bondage. You sent Moses, Aaron, and Miriam to make known your will. In Jesus Christ you portrayed the extent of your love, as he gave his life as a ransom for many. He has shown us, O God, how to do justly, love kindness, and walk humbly with you.

We are taught by the psalmist how we are to walk blamelessly, do what is right, speak the truth from our hearts, do not slander with our tongues, and do no evil to our friends. May we be as diligent in our search for such goodness as we are attentive to our own desire for well-being.

We are also taught to commit our way unto you, since you will make our virtue clear as the light and our integrity as bright as the moon's glow. When greed or desire lessens our goodness, temper our wants with more moderate tastes. When our honesty is threatened by our lack of truth, make us sure of your presence so that we stand fast in our faith.

Again we are taught to wait patiently and be still, that you may speak. Quiet our longing to be like others and make us content with the word that Christ calls us as we are.

5TH SUNDAY IN ORDINARY TIME (A)

Isaiah 58:1–9a (9b–12); Psalm 112:1–9 (10)
1 Corinthians 2:1–12 (13–16); Matthew 5:13–20

With a taste of salt and a glimmer of light, food is enhanced and the darkness dispelled. With life in the Spirit and the discipline of faith, neighbors are served and Christ is proclaimed. Let life find its savor in service among others, as the light of the gospel becomes a beacon of hope. Then good works shall be made manifest and God's name shall be given the glory.

Call to Worship   Psalm 112

Leader: Praise the Lord! Happy are those who fear the Lord, who take great delight in God's commandments.

People: Their descendants will be mighty in the land; the generation of the upright will be blessed.

Leader: They rise in the darkness as a light for the upright; they are gracious, merciful, and righteous.

People: For the righteous will never be moved; they will be remembered forever.

Leader: Let us worship God!

Prayer of Praise and Adoration

Merciful God, what no eye has seen, nor ear heard, nor the human heart conceived, you have prepared for those who love you and revealed to us through the gift of your Spirit. You have sent us in Christ not only the spirit of the world, but the Spirit that comes from you, that we may know and understand the bountiful gifts you give us. Hear now our worship as we interpret spiritual things to those who are spiritual.

Prayer of Confession

Unison: The path that you choose for us, O God, is: to loose the bonds of injustice, to undo the thongs of the yoke, to let the oppressed go free, to share our bread with the hungry, to bring the homeless poor into our houses, to cover the naked, and not to hide ourselves from our own kin. Break forth the light of dawn to dispel our darkness when we disobey you and let the glory of the Lord shine through when we do. For then when we cry for help you shall answer and say, "Here I am."

Assurance of Pardon

Leader: "If you offer your food to the hungry and satisfy the needs of the afflicted . . . the Lord will guide you continually . . . so that you shall be like a watered garden, like a spring of water, whose waters never fail. . . . Take delight in the Lord and God will make you ride upon the heights of the earth; God will feed you with the heritage of your ancestor Jacob, for the mouth of the Lord has spoken."

Prayer of Dedication

You flavor our actions, O God, and illumine our minds. May the fruits of our labors nourish others. May the wisdom you give us lead others to know the living Christ. May our lives be seasoned by service, and the light of our good works bring glory to your name. We have received an abundance of your grace and mercy. Accept now our offerings as we go forth to serve you. In all that we accomplish let us give you the honor your name is due.

Prayer of Adoration and Supplication

You are all wise and all knowing, O God. You know our thoughts before the words leave our lips. You impart wisdom and offer us the gift of new life in your Son, Jesus Christ. We have been touched by your Spirit and given a glimpse of your glory. We approach you with reverence and awe, mindful of your grace and your mercy. Look with favor upon us and grant us now a portion of your goodness so that what we do may be your will, what we say may be good news, and who we are may be in accordance with Christ's call to be your children.

As we go forth to serve in your name, let our days reflect the brightness of your light that breaks forth like the dawn. Use us to loosen the fetters of injustice upon those oppressed by poverty, harassment, or abuse. Let us take their yoke upon us, that we may share in their burden and lighten their load. Give us the goodness to divide our plenty with those who are hungry. Free us from our love of goods and comforts so that we can take the risks and endure the rigors of service to a needy world.

Be our vanguard when opponents lie in wait before us. As Christ spoke with authority and not as the chief priests or scribes, may our witness ring true as we face the world. Save us from shrinking when we meet the slick arguments of the defenders of the status quo. Be our rearguard when we become fearful and our footsteps lag. As Christ drew away by himself when besieged by the crowds, give us the good sense also to withdraw, that we may find refreshment and rest. With the assurance that when we call you answer, and when we cry you hear us, we commit our way to you.

6TH SUNDAY IN ORDINARY TIME (A)

Deuteronomy 30:15–20 or Sirach 15:15–20; Psalm 119:1–8
1 Corinthians 3:1–9; Matthew 5:21–37

To look with lust violates relationships. To swear an oath disguises God's mercy. The law of the God is a pattern against pretense. It affects how we perceive others, the relationships that we enter, and what comes forth from our mouths. The lesson is twofold: let how we behave be obedient, and let what we say have integrity.

Call to Worship   Psalm 119:1–8

Leader: Happy are those whose way is blameless, who walk in the law of the Lord.

People: Happy are those who keep the decrees of the Lord and walk in God's ways.

Leader: O that my ways may be steadfast in keeping your statutes!

People: Then I shall not be put to shame, having my eyes fixed on all your commandments.

Leader: Let us worship God!

Prayer of Praise and Adoration

Great is your wisdom, O God. You are mighty in power and wondrous in your love for us. Your eyes are fixed on those who put their trust in you; you know all that we do. You command no one to be wicked nor give anyone permission to sin. In all that we do you seek obedience from us and send us your Spirit that we may know of your will. We come now before you with hearts that are upright and voices singing your praise.

Prayer of Confession

Unison: God of compassion, have mercy upon us. You have given us statutes, but we follow our own desires. We know of your laws, yet we try to justify our own way. You desire obedience, we practice rebellion. You offer blessing, we search for scapegoats. Make us mindful of how we disorder your intentions. Set us aright in accord with your design for us.

Assurance of Pardon

Leader: "And the Holy Spirit also testifies to us, for after saying, 'This is the covenant that I will make with the house of Israel after those days, says the Lord: I will put my law within them, and I will write it on their hearts. . . . I will forgive their iniquity and remember their sin no more.'

Where there is forgiveness of these, there is no longer any offering for sin" (*Heb. 10:15–17*).

Prayer of Dedication

Accept the gifts that we offer, O God, as we go seeking reconciliation with our brothers and sisters. In them we seek to love you with all our hearts, souls, and minds. May the reconciliation we pursue reflect our love for neighbor as for ourselves. We pray in the name of the Christ who allows us to present ourselves blameless before you.

Prayer of Intercession and Supplication

O God, you are just and you treat your people with fairness. From our foremothers and forefathers we have learned your commandments: how you desired love of neighbor and not empty praise; how you called for justice and mercy rather than rites and rituals; how in our search for your justice we should show kindness, not a spirit of reprisal. We learned of Jesus, whom you sent to show us your perfect way. As he went about healing, his disciples learned of love. As he taught in the Temple, his followers heard of your promise of new life. And in his death the world would know that you are a God of infinite love. That same Jesus, whom you raised from the dead, is our chief priest, and intercedes on behalf of us all. We are strengthened by that knowledge.

We still have a distance to go in our quest of commitment and growth. Help us to learn from children what it means to have faith. May we not be afraid of dependence when it comes to trusting in you. Let us learn from our enemies what it means to forgive. May we not be so sure of ourselves that we condemn others whom you also save. Let us learn from the foreigner what it means to dwell in a strange land, and offer hospitality to the rootless, the homeless, and the estranged of this world.

Continue to nourish and sustain us, so that we may mature according to your design for our lives. We are your agents in bringing others to faith. May our lives be for them an example of the confidence and endurance that come from the assurance of Christ's love. May our care of and compassion toward them be a constant reminder of your abiding presence. And may our ministry to them be evidence of the fruit of an obedient life.

7TH SUNDAY IN ORDINARY TIME (A)

Leviticus 19:1–2, 9–18; Psalm 119:33–40
1 Corinthians 3:10–11, 16–23; Matthew 5:38–48

The ways of God's kingdom demand endurance and patience. It takes endurance to resist one who is evil. Patience is needed when praying for those who would persecute. The scope of God's kingdom is pervasive and whole. As the sun rises on evil, so rain falls on the just. Let that which we offer be in response to God's mercy, and let what we do be dependent on God's grace.

Call to Worship   Psalm 119:33–40

Leader: Teach me, O Lord, the way of your statutes, and I will observe it to the end.

People: Give me understanding that I may keep your law and observe it with my whole heart.

Leader: Turn my eyes from looking at vanities; give me life in your ways.

People: See, I have longed for your precepts; in your righteousness give me life.

Leader: Let us worship God!

Prayer of Praise and Adoration

O God, you confirm us in your promise. With the coming of Christ you have implanted your Word within us, sealing the covenant once and for all. We gather to give you all praise and thanksgiving. Impart to us the fullness of your truth. Lead us along the paths of righteousness in the name of Jesus, the Word made flesh, whom with you we adore.

Prayer of Confession

Unison: We pour out our hearts before you, O God; you are our refuge and strength. Waves of doubt beat against us, weakening our faith. Tremors of discord shake our foundation. The winds of temptation drive us from our course. Too often we rely on ourselves when wisdom is sought. Still the storms in our souls! Provide in Christ a haven of hope for our troubled and distracted spirits.

Assurance of Pardon

Leader: Scripture declares that Christ is "a sure and steadfast anchor of the soul." He is able for all time to save those who draw near to God through him. He lives to make intercession for all. In Christ, our high priest, abides the assurance of the haven we seek.

Prayer of Dedication

O God, through your grace the foundations of faith have been laid. Christ, the cornerstone, has once and for all been set in place, and you have called us to be your building in whom the Spirit dwells. Each of us is a builder, too; in the Day of Christ our work will be revealed. Accept what we do and the gifts that we bring. May they fit your design and prove enduring.

Prayer of Thanksgiving

O God, truly you are our rock of salvation. You are the source of strength that lifts us from the depths of our own cares and concerns. We give thanks that you set our feet upon solid ground, and give us courage to face the day. The mountains you have raised as a sign of your majesty. Spring waters flow to assuage our thirst. Highways spread before us as we seek to follow your way. The cities teem with the people you have called us to serve.

We remember that you have sent us Christ as the seal of your promise. He went about healing and teaching in response to your will. When questioned by others, he relied upon you as the source of his power. Beset with doubts and fears, he was not afraid to call out your name. He withdrew from the crowds to find direction through prayer. We give you thanks that when tempted, he withstood his accuser, teaching his followers to be confident and endure.

The Holy Spirit abides with us still as a sign that you will not leave us alone, comforting and consoling us when we are distressed or in pain. The spirit brings strength to the weak, and to the sick hope for new health. For the dying there is hospice to ease their passage into your eternal realm. The Spirit cajoles us when we are lax, and conjures up visions of your destiny for us. We give you thanks that the Spirit restores our enthusiasm and harmonizes our attempts to obey your will.

You are indeed a God of compassion and solace. We confess again and again our trust in your merciful attention to our needs. Renew us by the testimony of your enduring indulgence, and empower us through your continuing charity. With the hosts of those who have gone before us, may we go forth from this place singing your praise. We proclaim to those all about us that you are our rock of salvation!

8TH SUNDAY IN ORDINARY TIME (A)

Isaiah 49:8–16a; Psalm 131
1 Corinthians 4:1–5; Matthew 6:24–34

Today's Gospel lesson speaks to all who fret. They are told not to worry. It will add nothing to the span of one's life. Comfort comes when they realize that God knows their needs. It is God who has draped the fields with raiment more splendid than even the court of Solomon can rival. The goal remains to fasten one's focus on the kingdom of God and God's righteousness, "and all these things will be given to you as well."

Call to Worship
Isaiah 49

Leader: Thus says the Lord: In a time of favor I have answered you, on a day of salvation I have helped you.

People: Sing for joy, O heavens, and exult, O earth; break forth, O mountains, into singing!

Leader: I have kept you and given you as a covenant to the people. I have inscribed you on the palms of my hands.

People: Sing for joy, O heavens, and exult, O earth; break forth, O mountains, into singing!

Leader: Let us worship God!

Prayer of Praise and Adoration

We do not need to lift our hearts far, O God, for you are always near us. You bring your greatness down to our level. Your marvel is manifest wherever we look. You calm our souls through the gift of your Spirit. Not a day passes without a reminder that you care for our needs. All we need do is be attentive to the signs of your righteousness and the bounty of your kingdom will pervade all that we do. Heed our prayers of praise and thanksgiving as we place ourselves before your throne of grace.

Prayer of Confession

Unison: You call us to be servants of Christ and stewards of your mysteries, O God. Yet, we resist the basin and towel of discipleship and hesitate to wash others with the waters of our baptism. We shy away from the mysteries of the gospel and settle for comfortable truths. We know it is required of stewards that they be found trustworthy, yet we are seldom worthy of the trust you place in us. Bring to light the things now hidden in darkness as in Christ you forgive us our sin.

Assurance of Pardon

Leader: Paul reminds us that it is the Lord who judges us. "Therefore do not pronounce judgment before the time, before the Lord comes, who will bring to light the things now hidden in darkness and will disclose the purposes of the heart. Then each one will receive commendation from God." In that commendation lies our assurance of pardon.

Prayer of Dedication

O God, you rule over all. The sun rises on the just and the unjust. You care for all. Let that which we offer be in response to your incredible mercy. Let that which we do be dependent on your grace. Accept what we bring as signs of our endurance in faith. Lead us forth with persistence, that your way shall be known.

Prayer of Intercession

O God, you have set forth your law; we seek to obey your commandment. You have set apart a people and called them holy. We endeavor to respond to your grace, and to proclaim your glory. In Christ's name you have commissioned us to be stewards of your mysteries, bringing justice to bear where injustice prevails. We strive to serve you as ambassadors of good news, offering our labors in love to restore others to life.

Hear us as we pray for our neighbors in need. Then give us the courage to transform our words into actions. We pray for the poor, the homeless, and those who live on the streets. Protect them from those who would prey upon them, and use us to find ways to shelter and feed them. Grant that we shall not take them lightly, since you call them blessed.

We pray for those who feel they must steal to survive. Lead us as we seek ways for society to share, so that all may live. Where systems keep persons out of work, impel us to change those systems. As we chain our doors for our protection, may we also change our ways, so that peace and security may abide in the land. We pray for those in homes, institutions, and jails. Be with those who serve them, performing their duties. Be with those who miss them, keeping their vigils of hope. Be with us who intercede on their behalf. May we seek dignity for them in spite of their condition.

O God, we will not squander your goodness or take lightly your grace. As you commission us in Christ, so empower us with the Holy Spirit that we may show ourselves trustworthy to have been set apart for your praise.

TRANSFIGURATION OF THE LORD
(SUNDAY PRECEDING LENT) (A)

Exodus 24:12–18, Psalm 2 or Psalm 99
2 Peter 1:16–21; Matthew 17:1–9

Jesus took Peter, James, and John to a high mountain, and he was transfigured before them. As the season of Lent approaches, Christians remember the trial of Jesus, the meaning of his death and the implications of his resurrection. It is a time for reflection, the season to renew commitment, and an interval when discipline may become a habit.

Call to Worship   2 Peter 1:13–16

Leader·   Prepare your minds for action; discipline yourselves; set all your hope on the grace that Jesus Christ will bring you.
People: As he who called you is holy, be holy yourselves in all your conduct.
Leader: For it is written, "You shall be holy, for I am holy."
People: Trust in God who raised him and gave him glory, so that your faith and hope are set on God.
Leader: Let us worship God!

Prayer of Praise and Adoration

We come with reverence to praise and adore you, O God. You have given your beloved Son for our salvation, and made the nations his inheritance, the ends of the earth his possession. You call us to be part of your household, and therein to partake of your promise. We gather as your people, attentive to your word and ready to do your bidding.

Prayer of Confession

Unison: We seek you on the mountaintop, O God, for we fear to face the city. We would rather by dazzled by your splendor on some Sinai than obey your commands in the urban wilderness. We find it easier to worship the wonder-working Jesus than to follow the Christ, who was obedient unto death. Merciful God, forgive our shallow ways. Help us to find you wherever you choose to dwell, and to serve you wherever you choose to send us.

Assurance of Pardon

Leader: "Since, then, we have a great high priest who has passed through the heavens, Jesus, the Son of God, let us hold fast to our confession. . . . Let us therefore approach the throne of grace with boldness, so that we may receive mercy and find grace to help in time of need."

Prayer of Dedication

As the transfigured Christ revealed a life offered for the sake of us all, receive our offerings for the sake of others. Transform, O God, money into the hope for justice, time into signs of service, talents into acts of ministry, and ourselves into expressions of faithfulness.

Prayer of Supplication

You are all-wise and majestic, O God. We approach you with awe. You set our sights on lofty heights; you stoop to hear our cries and our pleas. You spoke through your servant Moses, delivering your commandments etched out of stone. You have come with power in your Son, Jesus Christ, bringing redemption to all who believe.

We are your people, O God, called by you and commissioned to serve. We still grope for guidance in understanding our tasks. In the midst of the decisions we face, you seem so distant and removed from the scene. We need the assurance of your presence and the memory of Jesus Christ to illumine our way.

We declare our faith in the Christ as your Son with whom you are pleased. At times those words seem so empty; hearts are still hardened, and society goes its own way. Yet we cling to your promise. Help us to believe without seeing and to endure for Christ's sake even when our efforts seem fruitless.

You have sent us the Holy Spirit as our guide. We desperately need your Spirit of wisdom and truth. Help us to move with love as we seek to meet particular concerns, and to listen as long as it takes to do what is appropriate in our tangled world. May the decisions we make lead to changes that are in accordance with your will. May the care we give to our tasks reflect the care you have for your creation.

Our journey in faith goes on without ceasing. Save us from complacency with what we have done, and from fear of what you expect us yet to do. As you give meaning to our past, order and direct our present, so that the future may be shaped by your action in our lives today.

ASH WEDNESDAY (YEAR A B C)

Joel 2:1–2, 12–17 or Isaiah 58:1–12; Psalm 51:1–17
2 Corinthians 5:20b-6:10; Matthew 6:1–6, 16–21

Matthew offers some house rules on how Christians ought to behave: don't practice piety with pretense; don't go public with the alms you give; when you pray, it's best to do so privately; and when you fast don't look dismal! All in all it's best to keep the faith a matter between yourself and God. The bottom line? It's God we serve and it's God who will ultimately determine if our piety is sanctimonious or sacred.

Call to Worship   Psalm 51

Leader: Have mercy on me, O God, according to your steadfast love;
People: Purge me with hyssop, and I shall be clean; wash me, and I shall be whiter than snow.
Leader: Create in me a clean heart, O God, and put a new and right spirit within me.
People: The sacrifice acceptable to God is a broken spirit; a broken and contrite heart, O God, you will not despise.
Leader: Let us worship God!

Prayer of Praise and Adoration

You do, indeed, have mercy upon us, O God, and fashion us according to your benevolent design. You instill within us the seeds of your righteousness and foster our growth through the gift of your Son. You enhance our efforts when we seek to be faithful and hinder us when we stray from your will. As you open our lips our mouths will declare your praise. As you bring us the word we will worship your name.

Litany of Confession

Leader: We entreat you on behalf of Christ, be reconciled to God.
People: We confess that when we practice our piety we want others to know it.
Leader: We urge you also not to accept the grace of God in vain.
People: We confess the propensity to focus on how much we give of ourselves.
Leader: For our sake God made him to be sin who knew no sin.
People: We confess our prayers lack sincerity unless there is something we want.
Leader: So that in him we might become the righteousness of God.

People: The sacrifice acceptable to God is a broken spirit; a broken
and contrite heart, O God, you will not despise.

Assurance of Pardon

Leader: Paul reminds us that "We are the temple of the living God; as
God said, 'I will live in them and walk among them, and I will be their
God and they shall be my people. Therefore come out from them and be
separate from them, says the Lord, and touch nothing unclean; then I will
welcome you, and I will be your father, and you shall be my sons and
daughters, says the Lord Almighty.'"

Prayer of Dedication

We dare not come with pretense before you, O God, for you discern the
thoughts of our minds and the desires of our hearts. We can only humbly
bring you that which you have already so abundantly given to us. Accept
our gifts of praise and thanksgiving and be pleased with these tokens of
our faith and conviction. Use them to further the ways of your kingdom
amongst us as in Christ others come to know of your love.

Prayer of Petition

Let no fault be found with our ministry, O God, and see to it that we put
no obstacle in anyone's way. For now is the acceptable time; now is the day
of salvation. As we enter into this season of Lent we offer ourselves anew
as disciples of the living Christ. Help us recommit ourselves to the one who
says, "Come, follow me!" Help us discern the ways of discipleship that do not
call attention to ourselves but in all things give you the glory and the honor.

As Paul writes, "We are treated as impostors, and yet are true; as
unknown, and yet are well known; as dying, and see—we are alive; as
punished, and yet not killed; as sorrowful, yet always rejoicing; as poor,
yet making many rich; as having nothing, and yet possessing everything,"
all thanks to your grace and mercy. By your power and through the gift of
the Holy Spirit, continue to enable us to pursue our piety without pretense,
give of ourselves without thought of gratification, pray without ceasing,
and sacrifice our wants on behalf of those who are in need.

In our baptism you have named us and marked us with the sign of the
cross. Renew within us the vows that we took, or were taken on our
behalf, to place our ultimate trust in your governing goodness. Help us to
be ambassadors for Christ, so that we do not forsake the one you made to
be sin who knew no sin. Make us aright with Christ so that we may be
right with the brothers and sisters who walk with us and ultimately with
you, our Righteous Redeemer.

1ST SUNDAY IN LENT (A)

Genesis 2:15–17; 3:1–7; Psalm 32
Romans 5:12–19; Matthew 4:1–11

Out in the wilderness Jesus is tempted. Challenged to turn stones into bread, he replies that strength comes only from God. Charged to resist the natural laws of creation, he responds that God is not to be put to the test. When invited to worship the devil in return for worldly kingdoms, he answers that God alone shall be served.

Call to Worship   Psalm 32

Leader: Let all who are faithful offer prayer to you; at a time of distress, the rush of mighty waters shall not reach them.

People: You are a hiding place for me; you preserve me from trouble; you surround me with glad cries of deliverance.

Leader: I will instruct you and teach you the way you should go. I will counsel you with my eye upon you.

People: Be glad in the Lord and rejoice, O righteous, and shout for joy, all you upright in heart.

Leader: Let us worship God!

Prayer of Praise and Adoration

In times of distress you do not forsake us, O God. Amid the intrusions of life you comfort your people. When we find ourselves in whatever wilderness we wander, your Spirit is there to guide us correctly. Your eye is ever upon us as a mother watches over her brood. In Christ's name we gather as those you have made righteous. Hear our shouts of joy with our hearts made upright!

Prayer of Confession

Unison: When confronted by temptations, we are easily overcome. They allure us with promises we find hard to resist. We harbor fantasies of how our lives might have been. Our dreams become pervasive, hiding the truth of your love. Gracious God, have mercy upon us; enable us to discern deception when it appears. Enlighten us to your genuine renewal in Christ.

Assurance of Pardon

Leader: "It was fitting that God, for whom and through whom all things exist, in bringing many children to glory, should make the pioneer

43

of their salvation perfect through sufferings. . . . Because Christ himself was tested by what he suffered, he is able to help those who are being tested." Therein lies our assurance that Christ intercedes on our behalf. Live as those made righteous in him!

Prayer of Dedication

God of compassion, you minister to us in our wilderness. When barren wastes surround us, you hear our prayers of petition. In times of want, you ease our plight with mercy. In times of plenty all that we have comes from your grace. In bringing our gifts to you, we return what is already yours. May these gifts be used to bring all your people into the Promised Land.

Prayer of Supplication

O God, we stand before you shorn of all pretense and pride. If we boast, it is because of your grace. What goodness we have, you have bestowed upon us. You created us and gave us our name. As a fine potter works the clay, so have you fashioned us. You shape us and mold us to fit your design. Out of the depths we cry unto you, our Maker; hear our voice and be attentive to our supplication.

When we are cast into the wilderness and alone with ourselves, keep us from temptation beyond what we can endure. As in the garden you provided all that man and woman needed, so now let us rely on your goodness to protect us from harm. We are tempted to turn your blessings into means to gratify ourselves. Money, status, and power seduce us. Teach us the mind of Christ, who emptied himself and took the form of a servant. And when others treat us with disdain, and their taunts wound us and weaken our resolve, keep us firm in our confession that it is your favor we seek. When success comes our way, and friends speak well of us, help us to receive these gifts as the ministry of your angels, and praise your name without ceasing.

Bring us back from times alone better equipped to serve the needs of others. In Jesus Christ the free gift of your righteousness has come to us. Use us in turn to set upright those lives that are askew. Empower us to bring comfort to those who mourn, wholeness to those who are sick, the bread of life to the hungry, and the cup of salvation to the oppressed. Help us to give from the abundance of the blessings you bestow, so that others may abound in your promise of new life.

2ND SUNDAY IN LENT (A)

Genesis 12:1–4a; Psalm 121
Romans 4:1–5, 13–17; John 3:1–17

John's Gospel speaks of rebirth and new life. Both are required to enter God's kingdom. Rebirth occurs as one is baptized, receiving God's Spirit. New life is received through the gift of God's Son. It is time to put the old order aside in order that God's will may be known. Baptism and repentance remain points of departure for life lived in faith.

Call to Worship   John 3

Leader: No one can enter the kingdom of God without being born of water and spirit.

People: Truly I tell you, we speak of what we know and testify to what we have seen.

Leader: Everyone who believes in the Son of God may not perish but have eternal life.

People: God sent not the Son into the world to condemn the world, but that the world might be saved through him.

Leader: Let us worship God!

Prayer of Praise and Adoration

You keep your eye upon us, O God; you protect us as a shield. You give us hope in spite of the disquiet that lingers within us. You lift our spirits and make us glad. All creation sings your praise; we your people laud your name. Hear us as we worship, and speak to us as we gather. For we seek to be filled with your Spirit and made alive by your abiding Word.

Prayer of Confession

Unison: You call us to become pilgrims, to follow you in a journey of faith. We would find it easier to follow when not so much is at stake. But you promise that you will be with us and that our needs will be met. We cling to our possessions, trusting in them for security. You lead us into unfamiliar places, asking that we trust in your will. O God, your way is challenging when we choose to be complacent. You make great demands; we are anxious and uncertain. Have mercy upon us and forgive our hesitant steps toward the promise.

Assurance of Pardon

Leader: "For the sake of the joy that was set before him Jesus endured the cross, disregarding its shame, and has taken his seat at the right hand

45

of the throne of God." Our faith depends on him from start to finish, and he unceasingly intercedes on our behalf. Therein abides our hope and our assurance.

Prayer of Dedication

O God, you have sent your Son into the world, that we may have life. As we go forth from your sanctuary, may we offer that life in Christ's name to our neighbor. Use our talents to build up Christ's body. Use the money that we give to bring healing for his sake. All that we give is in response to your benevolent care.

Prayer of Supplication

You reckon us righteous, O God, in accordance with your covenant made long ago and fulfilled in Jesus Christ. You promised to the descendants of Abraham and Sarah the righteousness that comes by trusting your will. You have sent Jesus Christ as the guarantor of our hope, since he was faithful to you in all ways. You seal our inheritance at baptism in Christ's name, as a sign of our cleansing by your grace. In company with all those whom, down through the ages, you have called as the people of faith, we give you thanksgiving and the honor due your glorious name.

As we continue our journey in quest of your promised land, send your Spirit to accompany us as a source of guidance and strength. We fear to leave the security we have gained. Decisions are not easy when our own comfort is at stake. Send your Holy Spirit to give us courage and the clarity we need. We carry with us a heavy burden of past failure and present guilt. Send your Holy Spirit to assure us of your acceptance and forgiveness in Christ, so that, relieved of our own burden, we may ease the burden of others. The demands of the gospel lead us into paths unknown; we fear the risk. Our hope quickly fades; our confidence wanes. May the Holy Spirit give us the boldness we need.

Abraham, Sarah, and Lot left their homeland, as you bade them to do. We follow their example as your children called by Christ. Look with favor upon us as we seek to walk boldly in faith. May our journey be charted according to your design, and the course that we follow be in line with the path Jesus walked for our sake.

3RD SUNDAY IN LENT (A)

Exodus 17:1–7; Psalm 95
Romans 5:1–11; John 4:5–42

True worship is not confined within the walls of a sanctuary; nor is it limited to certain times and seasons. Jesus speaks of worshiping God in spirit and in truth. God's people bear witness to the indwelling Spirit in all that they do. The truth that guides them is substantiated through acts of forbearance and love. May all that is done praise God's name.

Call to Worship

Psalm 95

Leader: O come, let us sing to the Lord; let us make a joyful noise to the rock of our salvation!

People: We shall come into your presence with thanksgiving and make a joyful noise unto you with our songs of praise!

Leader: O come, let us worship and bow down; let us kneel before the Lord our Maker!

People: For we are your people, the flock that you shepherd. We will know of your power as we listen for your voice!

Leader: Let us worship God!

Prayer of Praise and Adoration

We do indeed bow down before you and sing you our praises, O God; you are the shepherd who tends to our needs. You gather us from among different races and cultures and blend us into a people who radiate your love. You show deference toward us as you stoop to hear both our pleas and our praise. We wear proudly the mantle of your grace and mercy and as we worship you humbly in thought, word, and deed.

Prayer of Confession

Unison: Do not harden our hearts, O God, to the sound of your voice. We confess we don't listen to the word that you send. You give us Jesus, the Word of Life in our midst. We confess our delay in obeying the direction he brings. You promise the Holy Spirit, a source of counsel and power. We confess ignoring such guidance, since we do not respond. Forgive us our sin, and help us through Christ to enter the rest you have promised.

Assurance of Pardon

Leader: "Therefore, since we are justified by faith, we have peace with God through our Lord Jesus Christ, through whom we have obtained access to this grace in which we stand. . . . But more than that, we even boast in God through our Lord Jesus Christ, through whom we have now received reconciliation." Brothers and sisters, in Jesus Christ we are forgiven!

Prayer of Dedication

Just as our worship of you, O God, is not confined to this place, so also our praise is not limited to certain times or seasons. Accept the offerings that we bring as a witness to your Spirit, who dwells in all that we do. May our acts of forbearance and love testify to Christ's truth pervading our lives. Use what we give so that others may come into your presence with joyful songs of hope and thanksgiving.

Prayer of Thanksgiving and Petition

O God, at Horeb you caused water to come forth from a rock. At Sychar, Jesus came to drink from Jacob's well. When throats have been dry or your people have felt parched, you have led them to streams of your kindness, bringing refreshment and new life. We have taken that water and set it apart in Christ's name, knowing that in him we need not ever thirst again. Cleansed of our sin and justified by Christ's faith, we receive the promise of your grace. Given new hope of sharing your glory, we come before you with thanksgiving, as the source of our having been washed and set apart as Christ's church.

Hear our prayers for all those who feel pain; may they persevere with greater patience and strength. May our arms enfold them as we support them in their trials. May our presence be of comfort as we bear with them their disease. We have heard that endurance develops character. May we, through our mutual forbearance as brothers and sisters, learn what it means to trust in your love. Having sent us your Son, who himself agonized with death, you have shown us to what extent you will go to relieve estrangement and distress. With our lives attuned to your purpose and will, may we be of some hope to those needing your word. And may that word be one of reconciliation as they are enabled in Christ to find peace in your care.

Give us faith, O God, like that of Moses at Horeb. Let us not be among those who would put you to the test. Rather, trusting in Jesus who invites us to drink from the well of eternal life, may we draw from that source as we offer the cup to our neighbor in need.

4TH SUNDAY IN LENT (A)

1 Samuel 16:1–13; Psalm 23
Ephesians 5:8–14; John 9:1–41

The man blind from his birth receives sight as a gift. Arguments occur concerning the cause of his healing. Did Jesus profane the Sabbath? Was the man's blindness due to his birth in utter sin? In the midst of the turmoil the man believes and worships the Christ. Truly, there are those who see but behold not the truth. Christ comes that all may discern God's mercy and grace.

Call to Worship   Psalm 23

Leader: The Lord is my shepherd, I shall not want.
People: You prepare a table before me in the presence of my enemies.
Leader: You anoint my head with oil; my cup overflows.
People: Surely your goodness and mercy shall follow me all the days of my life.
Unison: And I shall dwell in the house of the Lord my whole life long.

Prayer of Praise and Adoration

Shepherd God, you caused your Spirit to come mightily upon David. You promised your children your comforting presence and direction. You sent Jesus as the light of the world to remove the scales from our eyes. We behold your grandeur and offer the praise due your name.

A Litany of Confession

Leader: For once you were darkness, but now you are light in the Lord.
People: May Christ give us the light, that we may awaken to his truth.
Leader: Walk as children of light as you pursue what is good, right, and true.
People: May Christ give us the light, that we may awaken to his truth.
Leader: Take no part in works of darkness but try to learn what is pleasing to God.
People: May Christ give us the light, that we may awaken to his truth.

Assurance of Pardon

Leader: Jesus has said, "As long as I am in the world, I am the light of the world. . . . I came into this world for judgment so that those who do not see may see, and those who do see may become blind. As we confess our sins to God in Christ's name, he intercedes on our behalf as we are awakened from death to the hope of new life.

Prayer of Dedication

As you pray for us in spite of our wayward behavior, O Christ, so also we intercede for others with the assurance of new life for them. Translate now our prayers into acts of charity and peace as we offer these gifts. Let us not be content with our giving while others live a life less than fulfilled.

Prayer of Supplication

You are, O God, the Good Shepherd, who leads your people along still waters. You have sent your Son, Jesus Christ, into the world as the lamb who redeems your people from their sin. He has become the light that illumines the darkness, allowing us to learn what is pleasing in your sight. You know the thoughts of our hearts before we speak. Hear us then as we utter this prayer.

As you lead us along paths of righteousness, give to us the clarity of vision to discern the way we should go. Our spirits are eager to be faithful in Christ's name. The problems that confront us impel us to act. When we hold back for fear that we will fail, may your Spirit infuse us with the courage to proceed. The issues that face us often do not lend themselves to simple solutions. May your rod and staff comfort us with the promise of your presence. There are many that hunger for sustenance, and thirst after their own redemption from the demons that enslave them. May we take from your table the bread that will nourish them with the truth of your gracious salvation; may we lift to their lips the cup that holds the promise of new life.

Your goodness and mercy dwell with us throughout our lives. As members of your household we inherit the promise of your rest. Help us in times of reflection to discover the truth, and in times of action to be more decisive and deliberate. As we pass through valleys that await us, may we be led by your radiance and refreshed by the promise that you shepherd us still.

5TH SUNDAY IN LENT (A)

Ezekiel 37:1–4; Psalm 130
Romans 8:6–11; John 11:1–45

Lazarus is dead, and Jesus weeps with compassion. Approached by Martha and Mary, he translates concern into action. He goes to the tomb, and from thence Lazarus steps forth. The one who was dead is unbound and set free. Jesus' ministry abounds with accounts of those likewise freed from bondage. He was and continues to be a merciful high priest on behalf of God's people.

Call to Worship   Psalm 130

Leader: Out of the depths I cry to you, O Lord. Lord, hear my voice! Let your ears be attentive to the voice of my supplications!

People: If you, O Lord, should mark iniquities, Lord, who could stand? But there is forgiveness with you, so that you may be revered.

Leader: Hope in the Lord! For with the Lord there is steadfast love, and great power to redeem.

People: I wait for the Lord, my soul waits; and in the word of the Lord I hope.

Leader: Let us worship God!

Prayer of Praise and Adoration

You are merciful and just in the deliverance of your people, O God. You draw us up out of the depths of distress; you incline your ear as we call on your name. Our souls rest in you and in the promise of Christ's redeeming love. Lay now your hand upon us, and draw us out by your Spirit, that we may sing praises to your name.

Prayer of Confession

Unison: You called us to life in the Spirit, yet we seek to satisfy the flesh. We call you gracious, yet we practice greed. We praise you with our lips, O God, yet we do not honor you in our lives. Discontent consumes us as we yearn for still more things. We know that to live by your grace promises inheritance of new life. Redeem our enslavement to corruptible desires, that we may be worthy to be called righteous in Christ.

Assurance of Pardon

Leader: Paul declares that if the Spirit of God dwells in us, the one who raised Christ Jesus from the dead will give life to our mortal bodies through God's Spirit which dwells in us. For all who are led by the Spirit of God are children of God. Believe this word of promise and walk in newness of life.

Prayer of Dedication

O God, as Jesus released Lazarus from the hands of death, may our ministry give to others the promise of new life. Accept the gifts that we offer to proclaim your love. Use our talents in ways that will set others free. May the liberating truth of Christ's gospel be heard anew in the land.

Prayer of Thanksgiving and Petition

O God, you rob death of its sting; you cause graves to set free their captives. You assemble and enliven dry bones strewn amid barren fields. Through the grace of the Holy Spirit sent forth in Christ, our mortal lives are aflame with your presence and redeemed by your love. You hear the voice of our supplications, inclining your ear to our needs. We give you thanks for your indulgence, your kindness and care. We owe our lives to your righteous salvation in the gift of your Son. We are the people of your compassion, your judgment, and your justice. You are our God and we give you the praise due your name.

Hear our prayer for those bones that have become brittle and dry. We pray for the aging, those in our midst whose movements are not so swift as they once were. May the breath of life that you give them be for us an abiding source of inspiration and wisdom! Give to us patience to listen to what they say, and may our presence be to them a comfort as they meet each new day.

Hear our prayer for those muscles that lack sinew and are no longer pliable or tight. We pray for the lazy and those who are overly cautious when called upon to act. Give to them discipline that will train them in faith, and may we show them boldness tempered with patience and care. Hear our prayer for those whose flesh is different from ours because of pigment and race. We pray for sisters and brothers of all colors who give radiance to Christ's church. Assemble our diverse gifts in a vivid display of our common baptism in Christ, and set ablaze the unity of our witness with the Holy Spirit, who binds us as one. So breathe on us, Breath of God, and fill us with life anew, that we may love what you love, and do what you would do.

PASSION/PALM SUNDAY (A)

Palm: Matthew 21:1–11; Psalm 118:1–2, 19–29
Passion: Isaiah 50:4–9a; Psalm 31:9–16; Philippians 2:5–11; Matthew 26:14–27:66 or Matthew 27:11–54

Garments and branches were spread on the road. The way was prepared, fulfilling the promise of Scripture. The king indeed came "on a colt, the foal of an ass." Amid shouts of "Hosanna" and blessings, the prophet of Nazareth entered Jerusalem, acclaimed as a king. As the streets were cleared and the cheering subsided, a drama unfolded that even today grips the hearts of the crowds.

Call to Worship   Psalm 31

Leader: In you, O Lord, I seek refuge; do not let me ever be put to shame; in your righteousness deliver me.
People: Incline your ear to me; rescue me speedily. Be a rock of refuge for me, a strong fortress to save me.
Leader: I trust in you, O Lord; I say, "You are my God."
People: Let your face shine upon your servant; save me in your steadfast love.
Leader: Let us worship God!

Prayer of Praise and Adoration

You give us tongues to speak comforting words to those who are weary. Each morning you awaken us to the words of new life. Throughout the day your graciousness accompanies each step that we take. When we retire we reflect on your mercy and how it sustains us. As we sleep you nurture us with your untiring care. We are borne aloft with your unbridled benevolence and come now to praise you and worship your name.

Prayer of Confession

Unison: O God, we confess our distress when afflicted with pain. We often avoid those encounters that will cause us discomfort. It is easier to hide from distress than to be exposed to forms of misery and grief. Yet we believe in Christ, who was sacrificed for all. Help us to trust in him when he calls us to bear abuse on his behalf and show more compassion on others for whom pain is so constant.

Assurance of Pardon

Leader: Our assurance of pardon is in Jesus, "who, though he was in the form of God, did not regard equality with God as something to be exploited, but emptied himself, taking the form of a slave . . . and became obedient to the point of death . . . on a cross." Through his obedience we are freed from whatever bondage enslaves us.

Prayer of Dedication

Blessed is the one who comes in the name of the Lord. Blessed are the gifts that are received in Christ's name. We come before you, O God, with the many blessings that you have bestowed upon us. Accept them as in Christ you accept us. Use what we bring, so that others can shout, "Hosanna, Christ reigns!"

Prayer of Thanksgiving and Petition

O God, we give thanks for your Son Jesus, whom we confess as our Lord. You sustain us by his word when we grow weary in faith. You have caused your commandments to pervade his life, giving focus and direction to our attempts to obey your will. When we stumble and fall, it is he who intercedes on our behalf. He is our righteousness and redeemer, our source of hope, and the anchor of our assurance. He suffered rejection and endured the cross. We approach you with boldness, with acceptance through his promise of new life. He is indeed the name above every name, the one who enables and frees our tongues to confess, to give you all glory as God of our lives.

May our thanksgiving breed endurance as we offer our lives to others in Christ's name. There are those whose energies are sapped by sorrow, whose bodies are bent with grief. Imbued with your Spirit, we seek to infuse them with hope. There are others who are scorned by their neighbors, cast aside as being inferior or of no use. We are encouraged by the forgiveness you give us in Christ; let our words of acceptance offer them asylum and rest. We hear whispers of gossip, and are witnesses to plots that will repay still others for wrongs that they have done. Let us at those times be emboldened to speak the word of reconciliation and peace.

Keep us from compounding the pain that is inflicted on your people by whatever cause. Christ made the sacrifice once and for all. May we in Christ's name have compassion on all those who suffer abuse, joining with them in the one hope that makes all things new.

MAUNDY THURSDAY (YEAR A B C)

Exodus 12:1–4 (5–10) 11–14; Psalm 116:1–2, 12–19
1 Corinthians 11:23–26; John 13:1–17, 31b–35

Jesus teaches the true meaning of discipleship as he drapes a towel around his loins, pours water into a basin, and prepares to wash the disciples' feet. Since then the basin and towel have reminded Christians of their call to be attentive to the needs of others, to humble themselves in service to sisters and brothers everywhere, and to use the waters of baptism daily in the common tasks they are called upon to perform. Jesus concludes the lesson: "By this everyone will know that you are my disciples, if you have love for one another."

Call to Worship   Psalm 116

Leader: I love the Lord, because God has heard my voice and my supplications.
People: You have inclined your ear to me; therefore I will call on you as long as I live.
Leader: What shall I return to the Lord? I will lift up the cup of salvation and call on your name, O God.
People: I will pay my vows to the Lord in the presence of all God's people.
Leader: Let us worship God!

Prayer of Praise and Adoration

No God can compare with you, O Lord; your works are awesome. Nations bow down before you. They glorify your name. Your greatness penetrates each moment of our day. Through the night you care for us. As the day dawns your splendor fills the heavens. As we arise and give you glory, you empower us to serve you in all we do. Not a breath passes our lips that we do not know of your presence. We enter now the gates of your temple to sing you our praises. Be pleased with our worship as we honor your name.

Prayer of Confession

"By this everyone will know that you are my disciples, if you have love for one another." We are not always that willing to love one another, especially when others have wronged us for whatever reasons. We hold grudges rather than confront our aggressors. We talk *about* them rather than *to* them. As Judas betrayed Jesus we continue to deceive the risen

Christ. As we partake of the Lord's Supper the table is not yet spread with good will. Forgive our reluctance to humble ourselves and wash us anew with the waters of new life.

Assurance of Pardon

Leader: As Jesus washed the disciples' feet, we are washed anew with the waters of our baptism. As we have died with Christ in a death like his, we shall arise to new life in a resurrection like his. Therein lies our assurance, in Jesus Christ we are forgiven!

Prayer of Dedication

Gracious God, we drape the towel about us and fill the basin with the waters of our baptism. As we call Jesus our teacher we will strive to bring others the good news of his grace poured out for all peoples. As we name him Lord of our lives we will follow his commandment to love one another as he has loved us. Receive these offerings we bring you as symbols of our renewed commitment to serve as his faithful disciples.

Prayer of Thanksgiving and Petition

As you passed through the land of Egypt and spared those whose blood of the lamb graced the doorposts of their homes, you have continued to grace us with your presence throughout this Lenten season. You have brought us to this time and place when we can gather in Christ's name to break bread with those who journey with us on our pilgrimage of faith. We thank you for their comforting presence along the way that only reflects your encompassing love for all of us.

We thank you for the guidance of your Holy Spirit. During times of quiet reflection, we can count the ways the Spirit has led us and kept us from peril. When our judgments might have been hasty, the Spirit kept us from taking premature action. When our foresight was hindered by hindsight that was confusing, the Spirit gave us a moment to put things into perspective. When our vision was clouded by our desires as opposed to your will for us, the Spirit hindered our egos from taking control.

We pray, O God, that as Christ has loved us, we also might love one another. Help us to bring to his table compassion, forgiveness, and humility, that we may break down any walls of hostility that divide and fracture his body. Amid our diversity help us to celebrate the unity of our common baptism that binds us together, and combine our unique talents into a composite of effectiveness that may better meet the needs of our people. As we go forth to serve you, enhance our efforts that we may become Christ's faithful disciples.

GOOD FRIDAY (YEAR A B C)

Isaiah 52:13–53:12; Psalm 22
Hebrews 10:16–25 or Hebrews 4:14–16; 5:7–9; John 18:1–19:42

As Jesus faces the tribunal Peter is outside warming himself by the fire. When asked if he was a disciple of Jesus he denies any involvement with the accused man. Jesus alone will carry the cross to Golgotha and be hanged on the garbage dump of the city. Little do we know that at that moment he will henceforth sanctify even the lowliest existence on the face of creation and bring hope to the most downtrodden among us.

Call to Worship
Psalm 22

Leader: My God, my God, why have you forsaken me?
People: Yet, you are holy, enthroned on the praises of Israel.
Leader: In you our ancestors trusted; they trusted, and you delivered them.
People: To you they cried, and were saved; in you they trusted, and were not put to shame.
Leader: Let us worship God!

Prayer of Praise and Adoration

Great God of the covenant, in you we have confidence to enter the sanctuary by the blood of Jesus, in the new and living way he opens to us through his sacrifice on our behalf. With true hearts in full assurance of faith, sprinkled clean from an evil conscience, and our bodies washed with pure water, we hold fast to our confession of hope. You have promised new life and you can be trusted! We cross the threshold and enter the sanctuary to sing you our praises. Be pleased with our worship as we honor your name.

A Litany of Assurance

Leader: Since, then, we have a great high priest who has passed through the heavens, let us hold fast to our confession.
People: We have one who in every respect has been tested as we are, yet without sin.
Leader: Let us therefore approach the throne of grace with boldness, so that we may receive mercy and find grace to help in time of need.
People: We have one who in every respect has been tested as we are, yet without sin.

Leader:	In the days of his flesh, Jesus offered up prayers and supplications, and he was heard because of his reverent submission.
People:	We have one who in every respect has been tested as we are, yet without sin.
Leader:	Although he was a Son, he learned obedience through what he suffered and became the source of eternal salvation for all who obey him.
People:	We have one who in every respect has been tested as we are, yet without sin.

Prayer of Dedication

O sacred Head now wounded, your sacrifice is the source of our salvation. Your dying for us breeds in us undying devotion. We can never repay you for what you have done for us. We can only offer ourselves in humble submission to your will. Take these gifts as symbols of our commitment to honor your sacrifice on our behalf. May we become worthy of the love you poured out with unmeasurable mercy.

Prayer of Thanksgiving and Supplication

We do indeed approach your throne of grace with boldness, O God, and there receive mercy and find grace to help in time of need. We give you thanks for Jesus, who throughout his life offered up prayers and supplications on behalf of the least of those among your people. He suffered and died amid the city's garbage and made of that filth sacred ground. Henceforth nothing within your creation can be considered off limits of your care and concern.

You heed the calls of those who are aimless and lost. They feel forsaken and are anxious of what awaits them. Provide them with your providence that will point them toward safe havens, where they can rest from their tensions, gain strength to pursue further their journeys, and find directions toward beneficial destinies.

There are those imprisoned within walls of their own making and confinements over which they have had no control. As Jesus descended into Sheol to rescue those caught in the throes of their own hell, so send your sacrificial Son as their source of salvation. Help them to find in your comforting Spirit the assurance that you continue to care for them and the promise that you will consider their plight.

Those whom the world considers little more than garbage henceforth hold a hallowed place in your heart. Help us likewise not to forsake them, but follow the example of our high priest who is able to sympathize with all of our weaknesses. Make us bold to reach out to them, consider them sisters and brother in covenant with Christ, and henceforth pledge ourselves to walk with them toward dignity and self worth. For in so doing, we shall ourselves bear that cross Jesus bore on behalf of us all.

RESURRECTION OF THE LORD/EASTER (A)

Acts 10:34–43 or Jeremiah 31:1–6; Psalm 118:1–2, 14–24
Colossians 3:1–4 or Acts 10:34–43; John 20:1–18 or Matthew 28:1–10

Mary's Easter Day was a mixture of discovery, sadness, and awareness. With her discovery she runs quickly to tell the others. In her sadness she finds comfort among the angels. When made aware of Jesus' presence she calls him "Rabbouni," teacher. Easter continues today as a time to relate the good news, to find comfort, and to confess Christ as the source of new truth.

Call to Worship

Leader: Christ is risen!
People: Christ is risen indeed!
Leader: This is the day that the Lord has made;
People: Let us rejoice and be glad in it.

Prayer of Praise and Adoration

This is indeed the day that you have made, O God, a day of gladness and rejoicing. You cause new life to burst forth with great beauty and fragrance. You adorn the creation with splendor and grandeur. You give your people a taste of your righteousness as we worship the Christ, the cup of new life. Be with us now as we enter the gates of your temple, and hear us as we give you thanksgiving and praise.

A Litany of Assurance

Leader: With the stone rolled away came emptiness
People: Of a tomb that held captive the Crucified,
of the space that was once filled with death,
of the cross that now pointed to greater truth
of God's love in spite of ourselves.
Leader: With the stone rolled away came questions
People: From those whose world lay shattered,
from those who would demand living proof,
from those who were seeking a sign of promise
breeding confidence, assurance and trust.
Leader: With the stone rolled away came light
People: To illumine the darkness of suspicion and fear,
to dispel the shadows of distrust, anxiety, insecurity,
to radiate with the beams of new hope and understanding
the life about to be lived.

Leader:	With the stone rolled away comes a future
People:	With a truth that outshines the wisdom of ages,
	with space to be filled with the kingdom of God,
	with the company of those who through history confess
	Jesus Christ is risen today, Alleluia! Amen.

Prayer of Dedication

Bountiful God, we come with our offerings in response to your love. With the new life in Christ, we give ourselves in service to others. With the energy bestowed by the Spirit, we seek to inflame all your people with a zeal for your way. Receive the work we do, and the gifts we bring, that they may become a blessing in your sight.

A Prayer of Thanksgiving

All honor, praise, and glory are due your name, O God. You cause the breath to fill our lungs, our eyes to see, and our lips to proclaim your merciful name to all the nations. You awaken us this day with the dawn of a new age, with the sun rising on friend and foe alike, and the truth of Christ's redeeming resurrection ablaze across the heavens. Christ is risen indeed to bring fullness of life to all your people.

We give you thanks that in Christ Jesus you reveal to us your Word. As prophets listened to your voice, make us likewise attentive to the Word that became flesh, and thereby empowered to speak the truth of your love.

We give you thanks that in Christ Jesus you have opened the way for all to approach you in prayer. As he offered himself as a sacrifice that was pleasing in your sight, we yearn for the day when all that we do will be in praise of your name. We confess Christ as the cornerstone of the church. As we seek to respond to his call, may our conviction breed courage, and our charity challenge others to approach you with hope.

We give you thanks that even now in Christ Jesus we taste the new wine of the gospel. Already the past is finished and gone. We gather this day as the community of witnesses to the meaning of Jesus for all human life. Fill us with the Spirit of resurrection as we seek to become your redemptive society.

2ND SUNDAY OF EASTER (A)

Acts 2:14a, 22–32; Psalm 16
1 Peter 1:3–9; John 20:19–31

"The peace of the Lord be with you." Jesus died that all may henceforth have life. "The peace of the Lord be with you." He sent forth his people to serve. "The peace of the Lord be with you." Jesus said his people would receive God's Spirit. The truth of the gospel is contained in the peace of God.

Call to Worship   Psalm 16

Leader: I say to the Lord, "You are my Lord; I have no good apart from you."

People: I bless the Lord who gives me counsel; in the night also my heart instructs me.

Leader: Therefore my heart is glad, and my soul rejoices; my body also rests secure.

People: You show me the path of life. In your presence there is fullness of joy.

Leader: Let us worship God!

Prayer of Praise and Adoration

Source of our refuge and strength, as we enter your sanctuary you guide the way our footsteps should go. You protect us from paths that often imperil us; you shield us from situations we should not pursue. As we pause to ponder your bountiful goodness, may your comforting presence precede us this day. Hear our words of praise and thanksgiving as we respond to your counsel and care.

A Litany of Assurance

Leader: By God's great mercy we have been born anew to a living hope through Christ's resurrection from the dead.

People: This Jesus God raised up, and of that we are all witnesses.

Leader: We have an inheritance that is imperishable, undefiled, and unfading.

People: This Jesus God raised up, and of that we are all witnesses.

Leader: By God's power we are guarded through faith for a salvation to be revealed in the last time.

People: This Jesus God raised up, and of that we are all witnesses.

Leader: The trials you may suffer are so that your faith may prove

itself worthy of all praise, glory, and honor when Christ is
revealed.

People: This Jesus God raised up, and of that we are all witnesses.

Leader: As the outcome of your faith you obtain the salvation of
your souls.

People: This Jesus God raised up, and of that we are all witnesses.

Prayer of Dedication

You promise your peace through the gift of your Son. Alive with your
Spirit, O God, we are sent forth to serve. We offer you now the first fruits
of our labor. Accept them and use them in accordance with your desires.

Prayer of Thanksgiving and Petition

All blessing and honor is due unto you, O God; by your unending love
we have been born again to a life full of freedom and hope. You have
caused the bonds that enslaved us to be loosened through your forgiveness
offered in Christ Jesus. You have opened our eyes through his vision of
your gracious will. We see now what it means to care for our neighbor.
With his sacrifice made once and for all, you broke down the walls of
enmity and strife. We are able to cross lines of hostility, seeking reconciliation and peace. For all that we thank you, as we offer this prayer.

We thank you for the life full of freedom and hope. We pray that what
we do will be worthy of your covenant that Christ sealed on the cross. We
thank you for forgiveness that opens our eyes to your gracious will. We
pray that you will pour out your Spirit freshly upon us, and kindle us anew
with the flame of your desires. We thank you for neighbors, and for showing us what it means to care. We pray that as we prophesy, you will give
us commitment to act within your society. We thank you for breaking
down the walls of enmity and strife. Let us not be content with the way
things are, when so many are suffering without some sign of hope. We
thank you for the ability to cross lines of hostility, seeking reconciliation
and peace. As we see visions of what ought to be done, make us not afraid
to speak out on behalf of those whose voices are not heard. We thank you
for Christ who suffered on behalf of us all. When our faith is put to the
test, and we face the trials that obedience demands, fill us with boldness
to proclaim just what new life may mean.

3RD SUNDAY OF EASTER (A)

Acts 2:14a, 36–41; Psalm 116:1–4, 12–19
1 Peter 1:17–23; Luke 24:13–35

Two men on the road to Emmaus encounter another who appears to be a stranger. They relate to him what has happened, how Jesus was tried and sentenced to death. In response he tells them how it was necessary to accomplish what the Scriptures foretold. At table that evening his identity was revealed as he took bread and blessed it. The extent of God's love becomes known each time bread is broken and shared. The truth of God's mercy remains; Christ has risen indeed!

Call to Worship   Psalm 116

Leader: I love the Lord, because God has heard my voice and my supplications.

People: Because you inclined your ear to me, therefore I will call on you as long as I live.

Leader: I will lift up the cup of salvation and call on the name of the Lord.

People: I will pay my vows to the Lord in the presence of all God's people.

Leader: Let us worship God!

Prayer of Praise and Adoration

We enter your courts with praise, O God; we come into your house with thanksgiving. In Christ you give us the cup of salvation; in him we receive the bread of life. To you indeed our vows are to be made; you shall hear our confession of faith. So be with us now as we gather, and be pleased with the homage we bring.

A Litany of Affirmation

Leader: You know that you were ransomed from futile ways with the precious blood of Christ.

People: That word is the good news preached to us.

Leader: He was destined before the foundation of the world but was made manifest at the end of all times for your sake.

People: That word is the good news preached to us.

Leader: Through him you have confidence in God, who raised him from the dead and gave him glory.

People: That word is the good news preached to us.

64

Leader:	Having purified your souls by your obedience to the truth, love one another earnestly from the heart.
People:	That word is the good news preached to us.
Leader:	You have been born anew, through the living and abiding word of God.
People:	That word is the good news preached to us.

Prayer of Dedication

We bring our gifts to you in response to good news. Christ is risen indeed and abides in us still. May all that we do be in response to new life. As you accept who we are, O God, receive what we offer, and transform all of our being to confirm with your will. Extend your grace through us so that others hear of the salvation you bring.

Prayer of Thanksgiving and Petition

O God, we are a people of promise, thanks to your abiding grace. Through the gift of your Son Jesus we are born anew. You do not forsake us when we stray from your way. You have sent us the Christ, who shows us your will. In our distance from you he has redeemed us from exile, and been by our side. He brings us the light to illumine your desires, and shows us our error when we disobey you. In him we have confidence that you will set things aright. For all that you do for us, we thank you through Christ.

We pray for all who have their own Emmaus to reach, whose eyes have not seen that Christ lives in their midst. We pray for those who fear losing control of who they shall be. Help us to show them what it means to be filled with the Spirit. We pray for those seeking to cope with the pressures they face. Help us to guide them to submit to your will. We pray for those who fashion idols of what Christ ought to be. Help us to teach them how to obey his commands. Help us to guide them to take that first leap of faith. May they discover through their trust that you do not leave them alone.

There are others who have heard the good news and now wonder what it means. They are new to Christ's church and eager for faith. They are tempted to be overzealous and expect results beyond their means to accomplish. Help us, O God, to surround them with care. While we partake of their zeal, may we temper their desires, and together grow in fulfilling Christ's call. While our hearts burn within, open the Scriptures to us.

4TH SUNDAY OF EASTER (A)

Acts 2:42–47; Psalm 23
1 Peter 2:19–25; John 10:1–10

Jesus teaches his disciples what it means to be shepherd and sheep. Hearing his voice, they will follow. Trusting in him, they will be led to new pastures. Obeying him, they will be less prone to fight, even finding themselves abundantly sustained. With Jesus as the door, entrance into the faith is prepared. Do not flee from the quest, for the promise remains firm.

Call to Worship   Psalm 23

Leader: Even though I walk through the darkest valley, I fear no evil; for you are with me; your rod and your staff—they comfort me.
People: You prepare a table before me in the presence of my enemies; you anoint my head with oil; my cup overflows.
Leader: Surely goodness and mercy shall follow me all the days of my life.
People: And I shall dwell in the house of the Lord my whole life long.
Leader: Let us worship God!

Prayer of Praise and Adoration

Christ is the door by which we enter your new order, O God; he is the source of our comfort and the anchor of our faith. Through him you have shown us the way unto the land of your promise, where peace is eternal and grace has no bounds. As we enter the courts of your sanctuary may we know you are with us, and give you all honor due your glorious name.

A Litany of Assurance

Leader: When you do right and suffer for it patiently, you have God's approval.
People: We are healed by Christ's wounds.
Leader: For to this you have been called, that you should follow in Christ's steps.
People: We are healed by Christ's wounds.
Leader: He himself bore our sins in his body on the tree, that we might die to sin and live to righteousness.
People: We are healed by Christ's wounds.
Leader: For you were straying like sheep, but have now returned to the Shepherd and Guardian of your souls.

People:	We are healed by Christ's wounds.
Leader:	The Lord is my shepherd; I shall not be in want.
People:	We are healed by Christ's wounds.

Prayer of Dedication

We hear the voice of Jesus the Shepherd, O God, and seek to follow his course for our lives. We bring our gifts now before you as results of our search. Accept them and use them so that others may join in the quest. Bring others to the gates of your promised land, and let them hear you calling them to come, enter in.

Prayer of Thanksgiving and Intercession

Merciful God, you are the source of all life. All goodness and beauty flow from the depths of your being. You have caused the mountains to form and rise up; their valleys you clothe with blossoms, like a fine carpet woven with design. You give the birds freedom of flight; the fish search the depths of your oceans. The fields are fertile with the seeds of the harvest. Cities teem with your people of many races and languages. You are the Great Designer who delights in creating. We give you thanks that you have placed us at the pinnacle of your plan. We are humbled by the honor you give and awed by your affirmation of us. May our service to others confirm our confession that you are God of our lives.

We pray for all who suffer this day from pains that are caused by others and those that are self-inflicted. Hear us, O God, as we intercede for sisters, brothers, and strangers who are wounded and long to be made whole. Bless doctors and nurses and all who support them as daily they minister to the sick and infirm. May clinics, hospitals, and places of convalescence be sources of hospice, giving hope to your people. May those who dispense drugs, and those who take them, do so in order to reduce disorders and disease. May those facing death retain dignity and be graced with the assurance that Christ lives in their midst. For those plagued by phobias that hinder their freedom, illumine their dark places by the light of your guidance. Fill the afflicted with the same Spirit that in Christ drove out demons. Since Jesus bore in his body on the tree all that grieves us, let us die to sin and live as those who are healed and forgiven.

5TH SUNDAY OF EASTER (A)

Acts 7:55–60; Psalm 31:1–5, 15–16
1 Peter 2:2–10; John 14:1–14

As in God's house many rooms are to be found, so also in Christ's church many tasks are to be done. Jesus says that he is "the way, and the truth, and the life." Service among others is the way he portrays. The truth of the gospel is that God's people are free. The life that Christ offers removes the bondage to sin.

Call to Worship
Psalm 31

Leader: In you, O Lord, I seek refuge; do not let me ever be put to shame.

People: Incline your ear to me, rescue me speedily. Be a rock of refuge for me, a strong fortress to save me.

Leader: You are indeed my rock and my fortress; for your name's sake lead me and guide me.

People: Into your hand I commit my spirit; you have redeemed me, O Lord, faithful God.

Leader: Let us worship God!

Prayer of Praise and Adoration

You are cause for rejoicing, O God, and the source of our gladness. You know what afflicts us; you can sense our distress. You remove whatever net will ensnare us; you give our feet firm places to stand. In Christ you have brought us deliverance. For all your mercies we praise your name and worship you now as our refuge and strength.

A Litany of Assurance

Leader: Come to Christ, the living stone, chosen and precious in God's sight.

People: We are a chosen race, a royal priesthood, a holy nation, God's chosen people.

Leader: Like living stones, be built yourselves into a spiritual house.

People: We are a chosen race, a royal priesthood, a holy nation, God's chosen people.

Leader: Offer spiritual sacrifices acceptable to God through Jesus Christ.

People: We are a chosen race, a royal priesthood, a holy nation, God's chosen people.

Leader:	Declare the wonderful deeds of Christ who called you out of darkness into his marvelous light.
People:	We are a chosen race, a royal priesthood, a holy nation, God's own people.
Leader:	Once you were no people but now you are God's people; once you had not received mercy but now you have received mercy.
People:	We are a chosen race, a royal priesthood, a holy nation, God's own people.

Prayer of Dedication

As Jesus is the way, the truth, and the life, O God, may we find in him the source of our strength. As we carry gifts to you, empower our hands to lift others to Christ. As we offer our praise, place on our lips the good news of your love. As we hear your word spoken, lead us to new wisdom to impart the truth of the gospel; your people are free! Accept all that we do in the name of the Christ who makes all things new.

Prayer of Supplication

You open our eyes to your glory, O God; we see the Christ who stands by your side. He allows us to come into your presence and intercedes for us when we know not what to say. By his sacrifice he tore down the curtain that kept you at a distance because of the disobedience of your people. He showed us how much you love us and how you desire that we be kept near. In him you restore our confidence; you will not forsake us, or cast us away. So we approach you with assurance and boldness.

You have called us a chosen race, O God. Keep us mindful that you chose us for service and that it is your will we must heed. When we are arrogant, let the needs that surround us make us humble, so that your commandments may be obeyed. You have ordained us your royal priesthood, set apart for ministry. Help us to use the talents you give us, so that others may feed on the bread of life.

You have named us a holy nation. We plead your forgiveness when we forsake your redemptive society for our own patriotic zeal. Guide us as we take seriously our citizenship in your sacred order. Help us to exercise our electoral rights to the benefit of all those who remain powerless and without voice. You bestow a title upon us as we inherit in Christ the name of your people. Let us not look askance at the honor or take lightly the task it implies. The Spirit empowers us to respond with obedience, and by that guidance we seek to be faithful.

6TH SUNDAY OF EASTER (A)

Acts 17:22–31; Psalm 66:8–20
1 Peter 3:13–22; John 14:15–21

With the promise of the Counselor comes an abiding sense of God's presence. Jesus has said that he will not leave us alone. His followers will know that as God is in him, so will he dwell in them. As the assurance is given, a task is assigned. Christ's commandments are at hand and they are to be kept. He is made manifest as his will is fulfilled.

Call to Worship   Psalm 66

Leader: Come and hear, all you who fear God, and I will tell what the Lord has done for me.
People: Truly God has listened and given heed to the words of my prayer.
Leader: You are blessed, O God, because you have not rejected my prayer, or removed your steadfast love from me.
People: I will come into your house and pay you my vows, those that my lips uttered and my mouth promised when I was in trouble.
Leader: Let us worship God!

Prayer of Praise and Adoration

Truly you have listened and given heed to the words of our prayers. You have kept us among the living and have not let our feet slip. You have tested and tried us, laid burdens on our backs, and let people ride over our heads. We have gone through fire and through water; yet you have brought us into a spacious place. We enter into the courtyard of your sanctuary and offer you hearty thanksgiving. Be pleased with our worship that we lay now before you and give heed to our voices as we sing you our praises.

A Litany of Assurance

Leader: Now who is there to harm you if you are zealous for what is right? Have no fear of them, nor be troubled.
People: For Christ also died for sins once and for all, that he might bring us to God.
Leader: Keep your conscience clear, so that those who revile your good behavior in Christ may be put to shame.
People: For Christ also died for sins once and for all, that he might bring us to God.

Leader:	Baptism now save you, as an appeal to God for a clear conscience, through the resurrection of Jesus Christ.
People:	For Christ also died for sins once and for all, that he might bring us to God.
Leader:	Christ has gone into heaven and is at the right hand of God, with angels, authorities, and powers subject to God.
People:	For Christ also died for sins once and for all, that he might bring us to God.

Prayer of Dedication

We come with assurance, O God, since you do not leave us alone. Your presence continues to guide us as we pursue the paths of discipleship. All that we have is a gift of your grace. As we offer our gifts to you, accept them as signs of our commitment to Christ. May all that we do be in praise of your encompassing care.

Prayer of Thanksgiving and Supplication

Gracious God, you neither need our praise nor want our burnt offerings. You have created the universe and all that therein dwells. All that we have or will become is an outpouring of your gracious care. You are God, with compassion and redemption flowing from the core of your being. You have sent us the Christ to set us aright. You allot the boundaries of our existence as his body the church. You determine the times for our ministry in his name. Apart from your mercy, we wander aimlessly through life. Yet you have looked with favor upon your people and for that we laud you with thanksgiving. In you we live, move, and have our being, and with that assurance we dare to give you all praise.

We look to your Spirit to fill us with counsel and guidance. Help us to learn what it means to be called your people. As the eight were saved through water in the covenant made with Noah, cleanse our conscience through the sacrifice of Jesus made once and for all. Fill us with zeal for the fulfillment of your commandments. Give us endurance and patience when the waters are troubled. May we tread bravely the way of the cross. As Christ has subjected all authorities and powers, rendering them mute upon hearing your word, attune us to your wisdom, to learn from the Scripture what you would have us do. You hide not yourself from us; our ignorance you do not overlook. Accept therefore our repentance through Jesus Christ, and fill us anew with the promise he lived and died to proclaim. As the Spirit pervades us, may we live in Christ to your eternal glory.

7TH SUNDAY OF EASTER (A)

Acts 1:6–14; Psalm 68:1–10, 32–35
1 Peter 4:12–14; 5:6–11; John 17:1–11

Jesus prays to God with an outpouring of love on behalf of his people; that they will know God as the only true God; and that Christ may be glorified in God's presence as his words are made manifest among his disciples. May we strive to be one as Christ is at one with the only true God—that God's truth may be known.

Call to Worship   Psalm 68

Leader: Let the righteous be joyful; let them exult before God; let them be jubilant with joy.

People: We ascribe you all power and majesty, O God, and sing you our praises.

Leader: Awesome is God in the sanctuary, the same God of Israel who gives power and strength to the people.

People: We ascribe you all power and majesty, O God, and sing you our praises.

Leader: Let us worship God!

Prayer of Praise and Adoration

We sing praises to you, O God; we raise a psalm in your honor. You clothe us in all goodness; we are draped in accordance with your design. As you have sent Jesus Christ to make your will known, you promise your Holy Spirit to guide us along your path. As your holiness fills our halls, hear us as we worship your name.

A Litany of Assurance

Leader: Rejoice in so far as you share Christ's sufferings, that you may be glad when Christ's glory is revealed.

People: To God be the dominion for ever and ever.

Leader: Humble yourselves under God's mighty hand, that in due time God may exalt you.

People: To God be the dominion for ever and ever.

Leader: Cast all your anxieties on God, for God cares about you.

People: To God be the dominion for ever and ever.

Leader: Be sober, be watchful. Your enemy the devil prowls around seeking some one to devour.

People: To God be the dominion for ever and ever.

Prayer of Dedication

You pour out your love upon us, O God; you give us eternal life. As your mercy is made manifest in Jesus, may thanksgiving be shown by our gifts. Accept what we offer as signs of our humble gratitude for all that you do on our behalf. Make us useful servants of Christ in bringing your sons and daughters to a greater sense of your glory.

Prayer of Supplication

You put a song in our hearts, O God; our lips praise your name. The ordeals we face are nothing compared to the blessings you have in store for your people. If we are cast down, let it be because we seek to follow your way. You have sent Jesus Christ into the world to make known your will. He calls us and names us as your chosen people. Made right by his atoning sacrifice, we face boldly the tasks assigned to us. Give us courage as we translate our confession into acts of reconciling love. Let us not be afraid to follow the example he set before us, but be encouraged by his intercession on our behalf. We submit our lives to you, yoked in harmony with what you command us to do. May our actions be an outburst of praise to your name, and our thoughts be in tune with the harmony you seek among the nations.

We yearn to be filled with the embracing presence of your Spirit. With our senses dulled by decisions that demand our attention, we need to be focused on what you want us to do. Give us some discipline to determine your desire, and equip us to fulfill your expectations of us. Our hands droop at times when they should reach out to support others, and knees become weak when our feet seek your straight path. Jar us out of our listless ways and enliven us with your quickening power. When we are short-sighted or misuse your grace, chasten our choices by your judgment, and replace our schemes with your design for our lives. Deliver us from the undue need to control our own destiny, and from anxiety when our fate is uncertain. Prepare us to be responsive to the counsel of your Spirit, and thereby be led to new ventures of faith. May we who are your flock find our dwelling in your goodness, O God, and, secure in your love, find boldness to serve others.

THE DAY OF PENTECOST (A)

Acts 2:1–21 or Numbers 11:24–30; Psalm 104:24–34, 35b
1 Corinthians 12:3b–13 or Acts 2:1–21; John 20:19–23 or John 7:37–39

Remember your baptism! Those are appropriate words for this day. Believers in Christ are cleansed with living water. The Spirit bestows the truth of God's grace. The community, called the church, surrounds the baptized, as one is engrafted into the body of Christ. Pentecost is the day of one's birth into God's kingdom. Come, let us celebrate!

Call to Worship   Psalm 104

Leader: O Lord, how manifold are your works! In wisdom you have made them all; the earth is full of your creatures.
People: I will sing to the Lord as long as I live; I will sing praise to my God while I have being.
Leader: May my meditation be pleasing to you, O God, for I rejoice in the Lord.
People: Bless the Lord, O my soul. Praise the Lord!
Leader: Let us worship God!

Prayer of Praise and Adoration

We sing psalms of adoration, O God, we gather in praise of your name. You send your Spirit into our midst filling us with the promise of new life. We are aglow with the light that Christ shines on the new day, dispelling the darkness of the night that has passed. Be among us to gather our words of devotion and be in us as we seek to obey your will.

Prayer of Confession

Unison: With new life all about us, O God, we still cling to old ways. In spite of your promises we seek self-assurance. You send the Holy Spirit to enliven our existence. The darkness of doubt dispels the new light the Spirit brings. We are afraid to admit what it might mean if we surrendered our selves. So we continue to pursue our flights of fancy, and pretend that we can go it alone.

Assurance of Pardon

Leader: God has mercy upon us and hears our confession. In Christ we have the assurance that we dwell not alone. All who approach God with a desire for wholeness will be filled with living waters, which the Spirit gives. Be refreshed in your quest to do what is faithful, and be alive with the promise of God's guidance and care.

Prayer of Dedication

With many voices we praise you, O God; in different ways we serve you. Take our diversity and mold it into a common theme of thanksgiving. Weave these gifts that we bring into a whole cloth of service that will blanket the world with your love as we announce with one accord your truth which sets us free.

Prayer of Thanksgiving

With many voices we give you thanks, O God. By your Spirit blend our utterances into a symphony of praise worthy of your name. You have stretched out the heavens and set the earth on its course. You have raised up the mountains; the valleys you laid low. The trees you cause to rise toward the sun; their branches provide a haven for birds. You bring the rain in its season to water the earth. You prepare the fields for the harvest. Silos are filled with the yield you occasion, and our tables are spread with your bounty. You place the moon over us by night, the sun above us to warm our day. The tides ebb and flow in response to your bidding, and the winds blow as you direct them. You are God, who is above us and below us, before us and behind us, watching over us and caring for us, directing the way we shall go.

We give you thanks for the Holy Spirit, who guides us, and gives us gifts by which to respond to your will. Some among us utter wisdom and knowledge; we give you thanks for their minds. May they be led to further their thinking, that we may become more enlightened with increasing truth. Some in our midst have gifts of healing; we give you thanks for their compassion and patience. In their search to ease the suffering of others, may they help overcome the causes of pain. Some work with their hands or fashion fine art; we give you thanks for their imagination and skill. May their creations be tributes that honor your name, and reminders to us that we serve you alone. There are some with good business sense, others with talents they volunteer; we give you thanks for their discipline and service. Help us to learn from them how to use our time wisely, to apportion our talents so that others rejoice. You amaze us, O God, with the breadth of your love. You continue to fill us with the breath of your Spirit. For all your mercies we give you thanks.

TRINITY SUNDAY (A)

Genesis 1:1–2:4a; Psalm 8
2 Corinthians 13:11–13; Matthew 28:16–20

The disciples went to Galilee, and there met the risen Christ on the mountain. We are told that they worshiped him, even though some doubted. Christ spoke with authority and gave them a task. Since then, people have ventured into all nations, teaching what Jesus commanded. As people continue to labor in the shadow of Christ's cross, others are enabled to delight in the radiance of its glory.

Call to Worship

Psalm 8

Leader: O Lord, our God, how majestic is your name in all the earth!
People: When I look at your heavens, the work of your fingers, what are mortals that you care for them?
Leader: Yet you have made them a little lower than God and crowned them with glory and honor.
People: O Lord, our God, how majestic is your name in all the earth!
Leader: Let us worship God!

Prayer of Praise and Adoration

We do indeed stand in awe of you, O God. We rejoice that you have chosen us to be your own. By your word the heavens were made; your loving kindness fills the whole earth. By the bounty of your mercy we have been born to new life. Hear now what fanfare we give you as we lift our voices in praise of your name.

Prayer of Confession

Unison: O God, when we are put to the test we do not quickly respond. If called upon to decide, we lack the courage of faith. Confessing commitment, we confuse your will with our own. Seeking security, we turn to devices that we control. Your voice comes from heaven to chasten and discipline. Your commandments Jesus proclaimed as the course we should take. Forgive us when we deviate from the truth you deliver, and increase our trust in you.

Assurance of Pardon

Leader: As Jesus met his disciples on the mountain, he is with us today, even to the close of the age. With authority he commissions us to service; with redeeming love he sets us aright when we fall. All who humbly approach him seeking forgiveness for their sins can live with assurance, since Christ died for us all.

Prayer of Dedication

You call us to labor, O God, and to be about the tasks you design. You equip us to serve you, and care for all of our needs. The gifts that we offer are but a portion of the treasures you heap on us. May the work that we do be worthy of your name. Take what we bring and all that we are and fashion our responses to meet your standards for faith.

Prayer of Thanksgiving and Petition

O God of promise and fulfillment, you called Abraham and Sarah and promised to make of them a mighty nation. In them all the families of the earth would be blessed. As they journeyed by faith you never forsook your promise. They in turn called on your name and learned to believe in you. We give you thanks for these foremothers and forefathers who are our family in faith.

You sent your Son Jesus to redeem us from sin. He was tempted and suffered, yet remained obedient even unto death. The grave could not hold him, for he stands by your side. We give you thanks that he atones for our sins and intercedes on our behalf. As he calls us into his household, help us to obey him through the guidance of your Spirit. Inflame us with zeal for devotion to your way. Order our thinking and our acting, so that our total behavior accords with what you command.

We pray for those who serve Christ's household in other lands. We give you thanks for their courage, which remains a badge of their boldness. We hold high their vision of wholeness, as they go about teaching and healing your people. They have remembered their baptism, and thereby revealed the gifts of your new order. When we despair of our dwindling vitality, inspire us by their talk of renewal. If we are prone to be parochial, hold them as a testimony to your universal love. As your disciples went to Galilee, and there met Christ on the mountain, let your world be our arena and that same Christ be our source of strength. As your people everywhere labor in the shadow of Christ's cross, may we bathe in the radiance of your unending glory.

9TH SUNDAY IN ORDINARY TIME (A)

Genesis 6:9–22, 7:24; 8:14–19; Psalm 46
Romans 1:16–17; 3:22b–28, (29–31); Matthew 7:21–29

The question is, Where do you want to build your house of faith, on the rock of commitment or the sands of idleness? The rock of commitment leads to stability, firm assurance, solid acts of obedience to the risen Lord and building blocks of trust in God's will. The sands of idleness, on the other hand, lead to a hesitation to witness to Christ's way for us, a hindrance to act decisively to bring peace, love and justice on earth, and a commitment that crumbles when adversity and doubt appear. Choose the rock!

Call to Worship

Psalm 46

Leader: God is our refuge and strength, a very present help in trouble.

People: Therefore we will not fear; though the earth should change, though the mountains shake in the heart of the sea.

Leader: Be still, and know that I am God! I am exalted among the nations; I am exalted in the earth.

People: The Lord of hosts is with us; the God of Jacob is our refuge.

Leader: Let us worship God!

Prayer of Praise and Adoration

Your are our refuge and our strength, O God, a very present help in trouble. Before the sun rises, the birds have sung your praises. The hours that follow are a witness to your countless deeds of grace and mercy. As evening falls the sun sets as a reminder that you continue to watch over us. With darkness comes the promise that you will be with us as e greet the new day. Throughout each moment you hear the faintest cries of those who call to you and heed their heart's yearnings through good times and bad. You are indeed in the midst of all that we do and for that we give you all glory and praise.

Prayer of Confession

Unison: O God, we confess that all of us sin and fall short of your glory. We are idle when we should be active. We listen to gossip more than we listen to the gospel. When called to serve we have excuses rather than excitement. We hesitate rather than hasten to do what you ask. Time is short for we know not when you will call us to judgment. Help us to be mindful of how precious each moment is and be quick to fill them with deeds of discipleship in response to your will.

Assurance of Pardon

Leader: As Paul reminds us, O God, you gave us Jesus Christ to show your righteousness, because in your divine forbearance you passed over sins previously committed. Now you have proven that you yourself are righteous and you justify the one who has faith in Jesus. So, we can say with assurance, "In Jesus Christ we are forgiven!"

Prayer of Dedication

Moment by moment your arms embrace us, O God, with the bountiful gifts of your grace and mercy. We are mindful each day of how you care for our needs. Be pleased with our worship of praise and thanksgiving and receive now our offerings we gratefully bring. May they be used to further the mission Christ brought to the nations and enhance his efforts to bring peace, love and justice on earth.

Prayer of Thanksgiving and Petition

Gracious God, our Rock and Redeemer, you are indeed our source of stability on the storm-tossed seas of life. When the waves of doubt wash over us, the light of Christ's love provides a beacon that can lead us to safe havens. During times of dread, the Spirit continues to comfort us and direct us toward your will for us. You have been with your people Israel from the days of Abraham and Sarah and walked them safely through the waters of the Jordan. In the days of Noah you promised, "As long as the earth endures, seedtime and harvest, cold and heat, summer and winter, day and night, shall not cease" (*Gen. 8:22*). The rainbow reminds us that you will abide by your promise.

We thank you for the waters of our baptism. They remind us yet again that as we have died with Christ in a death like his we shall also be raised with him in a resurrection like his. With such assurance we can go forth boldly to serve, knowing that in Christ, "there is no longer Jew or Greek, there is no longer slave or free, there is no longer male and female; for all of (us) are one in Christ Jesus" (*Gal. 3:28*). May we continue to break down whatever dividing walls continue to hinder our showing such hospitality to those who remain estranged to that promise.

We thank you for the bread and the grape on the Lord's Table. They remind us again how Christ is our bread of life and cup of salvation. May the Table remain the symbol of our unity amidst our diversity and the place we can gather despite whatever differences we have with our brothers and sisters. Help us make it inviting to strangers that they may come to know the love of Christ. May we go forth from the Table to give bread to the hungry, hope to those who despair and bring comfort to whoever is anxious. In that way we will help them to learn of your all-encompassing love.

10TH SUNDAY IN ORDINARY TIME (A)

Genesis 12:1–9; Psalm 33:1–12
Romans 4:13–25; Matthew 9:9–13, 18–26

Others judged those at table with Jesus unworthy of such honor. Mercy is often misunderstood in this way. Those who think they deserve it are seldom receptive to others being included. The ones invited in spite of their faults often bring little to commend such distinction. Mercy provides a place at the table, where those who hunger for righteousness may be fed.

Call to Worship   Psalm 33

Leader: Rejoice in the Lord, O you righteous. Sing to the Lord a new song.
People: Your word is upright, O God, the earth is full of your steadfast love.
Leader: Let the earth fear the Lord; let all the inhabitants of the world stand in awe of your presence.
People: Happy is the nation whose God is the Lord, the people you have chosen to be your own.
Leader: Let us worship God!

Prayer of Praise and Adoration

It is right to give you praise and honor, O God, for your love endures forever. As your people gather to give your name glory, they shall come from east and west, from north and south. We are assembled together as those redeemed by your Son; may what we say be a blessing worthy of your hearing, and what we do a service befitting your glory.

Prayer of Confession

Unison: O God, you spread your table before us and invite us to dine. We judge some as unworthy to partake of your feast. You call us to faith in the Lord Jesus Christ. We close the doors of your household to those we deem unfit to come in. You desire mercy, not sacrifice, as a response to your grace. We expect others to be thankful that we accept them at all. Forgive us our arrogance in response to your love. Make us mindful of those whom you also hold dear.

Assurance of Pardon

Leader: Jesus said: "Those who are well have no need of a physician, but those who are sick. Go and learn what this means, 'I desire mercy, not sacrifice.' For I have come to call not the righteous but sinners." If we are honest and confess our sins before God, we inherit the righteousness of faith revealed in Jesus Christ.

Prayer of Dedication

O God, you crown us with distinction and honor. You lavish us with gifts in abundance. You spread your mercy before us as a host preparing a banquet. What we offer, you have already given to us. What we do with our hands is a gift of the life you breathe into us. We give you but your own, a legacy of your love and concern.

Prayer of Thanksgiving

Nations are formed according to your design, O God. People are gathered to suit your purpose. You call us together and give us our names; you set us apart and fix our boundaries. You have peopled the world with many colors and features: many languages are spoken and different customs are observed. You are like one who weaves a rich tapestry with fine cloth, where each thread is important to the blend you desire. We rejoice in the splendor of the mix you have created, and offer our thanksgiving for the composite you intend us to be.

We give you thanks for the vision that those of faith have brought to this land. For the Native Americans who were here long before. They taught us to live at peace with your earth. Remind us by their presence how dependent we are on your created order. We thank you for those who left homelands and ventured across seas. They came with dreams of new beginnings and built a country rich in opportunity. May the diversity of our ethnic origins serve as a composite that brings wholeness and health. We thank you for men and women of color; those who came shackled and bound. They have given us a legacy of hope and determination. Let them not flag in their zeal for a society free of bigotry and hate. We give you thanks for the freedoms we enjoy. For the freedom of religion; all praise be unto you. We praise you for the freedom of the press; help our search for the truth to accord with your will. We praise you for freedom from want; serving Christ, we commit ourselves to overcome injustice and greed. And we praise you for the freedom to assemble; may our gatherings bring peace, not discord.

Once nations are formed they also need to mature. O God, you are our strength and deliverance. For your mercy, patience, comfort, and grace, we give you thanks and applaud your design.

11TH SUNDAY IN ORDINARY TIME (A)

Genesis 18:1–15 (21:1–7); Psalm 116:1–2, 12–19
Romans 5:1–8; Matthew 9:35–10:8 (9–23)

Jesus had compassion on the helpless and infirm. The disciples were sent to heal and to cleanse. Wherever they went, the kingdom of heaven was proclaimed in their midst. The harvest is still plentiful, and laborers continue to be in demand. There are the sick for whom health care is needed. The hungry still wait to be fed. Go forth to your fields of labor.

Call to Worship   Psalm 116

Leader: What shall we return to you, O God, for all of your bounty to us?

People: I will lift up the cup of salvation and call on the name of the Lord.

Leader: O Lord, I am your servant, the child of your serving girl. You have loosed my bonds.

People: I will give you thanksgiving and call on your name in the presence of all the people.

Leader: Let us worship God!

Prayer of Praise and Adoration

Gracious God, you shelter your people amid their distress; you provide them a haven of security and rest. You bring comfort to those with affliction, and hear the pleas of the persecuted. You cause your mercy to flow like living water; your benevolence stretches to the ends of the earth. We come in praise of all your goodness and lift our voices with thanks for your care.

A Litany of Assurance

Leader: We boast in our hope of sharing the glory of God.

People: Therefore, since we are justified by faith, we have peace with God through our Lord Jesus Christ.

Leader: We also boast in our sufferings, knowing that suffering produces endurance.

People: Therefore, since we are justified by faith, we have peace with God through our Lord Jesus Christ.

Leader: Endurance produces character and character produces hope, and hope does not disappoint us.

People:	Therefore, since we are justified by faith, we have peace with God through our Lord Jesus Christ.
Leader:	Because God's love has been poured into our hearts through the Holy Spirit that has been given to us.
People:	Therefore, since we are justified by faith, we have peace with God through our Lord Jesus Christ.

Prayer of Dedication

You urge us to travel lightly and proclaim your peace. Relieve us of whatever hinders our mission, and give to us sustenance for the journey. The gifts we offer are symbols of our commitment; by whatever peace we foster, help us to heal antagonisms that divide your people; and may our actions provide hospitality even in the midst of hostility.

Prayer of Thanksgiving

As you appeared to Abraham and Sarah by the oaks of Mamre, we give you thanks, O God, for your continued presence in the gift of your Son, Jesus Christ. As Abraham promised the visitors some water, we give you thanks for our baptism which sets us apart. As Abraham sought to bring bread to refresh them, we thank you for the Lord's Table around which we may gather. As he prepared the feast and set it before them, we give thanks that we may approach your throne of grace during this service of worship.

You caused a son to come forth from Sarah. You continue to grace our lives through the many blessings you provide. We thank you for our families with whom we travel through this journey of faith. We thank you for the children you entrust to our care. We thank you for friends who keep vigil with us through the good times and bad times. We thank you for the strangers we meet and how we might entertain angels unawares.

When we read that Sarah laughed at the Lord, we are reminded of how you continue to surprise us through the gift of your Holy Spirit. When we think we are most in control of our lives you startle us into awareness that your will shall be done. When we walk through the valleys of our own darkness and despair you provide the light of the Gospel to guide us to safe havens.

We give you thanks that you have promised you will never forsake us. You have been constant through history in your care for that which you created. You have given us the covenant through the risen Christ which assures our future salvation. We can now live more boldly obeying your will. As we go forth into your world, help us to be at peace, to render no one evil for evil and in all that we do to give you the honor and the glory your name is due.

12TH SUNDAY IN ORDINARY TIME (A)

Genesis 21:8–21; Psalm 86:1–10, 16–17
Romans 6:1b–11; Matthew 10:24–39

There need be no fear among those called God's people, since there is nothing still hidden from God. What was covered is now revealed; what was secret is made known, and the message earlier whispered is now shouted. Two sparrows are worth merely a penny, yet God is aware of their fate. How much more will God know of your needs, when even the hairs of your head are numbered.

Call to Worship
Psalm 86

Leader: You are my God; be gracious to me, O Lord, for to you I cry all day long.

People: For you, O Lord, are good and forgiving, abounding in steadfast love to all who call on you.

Leader: For you are great and do wondrous things; you alone are God.

People: Teach me your way, O Lord, that I may walk in your truth; give me an undivided heart to revere your name.

Leader: Let us worship God!

Prayer of Praise and Adoration

You incline your ear to hear us, O Lord, when we cry to you. You are a God of compassion who gently cares for our needs in times of distress. In Christ you teach us your ways that we may walk in your truth. Your Spirit directs the way we shall go. As we discern your word we hear how you are a God who can be trusted. Through the years you have never forsaken those who called on your name. Hear us now as we offer our praise and thanksgiving. May they be worthy of your gracious care.

Prayer of Confession

Unison: Gracious God, in Christ Jesus, have mercy upon us. We are not quick to proclaim Christ as our savior. We have our own desires that demand our devotion. Other people have power over us that we dare not deny. We sometimes confuse Christ's will and our own. At times it is awkward to confess him the source of new life. With compassion he suffers, aware of our plight. O God, hear our confession, and through Christ keep us upright.

Assurance of Pardon

Leader: Paul reminds us how we also must consider ourselves dead to sin and alive to God in Christ Jesus. "For if we have been united with him in a death like his, we will certainly be united with him in a resurrection like his." In Christ we may live anew, with the assurance of Jesus Christ that in him we are forgiven.

Prayer of Dedication

O God, we have been led to acknowledge Christ Jesus as the source of new life. With Hagar we have come to observe the wellsprings of your love. As you have called us to be your people, accept now the offerings we bring you. Use them to spread your message from east to west and from south to north, so that those who come after us may be led to proclaim you God of their lives.

Prayer of Thanksgiving and Petition

You open the gates of heaven, O God, and we catch sight of your eternal order. Your way of righteousness and peace is made known in Jesus, who announces the dawn of a new age. You invite us as citizens of your holy city, where justice and order prevail. Your commandments become our guide and direction in how to discern your will. Jesus has shown us what it means to obey; he has made what was hidden now known. As the light he illumines our way, and makes common what once we feared. We thank you that as we face that which lies ahead, we can approach you with assurance that our past is forgiven. You know of our needs before we announce them; by your grace we greet the new day. As we continue to dwell in your mercy, we thank you for that sustaining presence. Through the guidance of the Holy Spirit as our counselor, we seek to fulfill what you expect us to be.

We pray for our nation and the role we perform as citizens. Help us to take responsibility for our actions so that others become able to respond. Keep us from ignoring those who are in need, either because we are greedy or we think them inferior. Guide us to measure our own generosity by the magnitude of your benevolence. When we read of issues that confront us, keep us from complacency and apathy. May we not abrogate our inherent right to speak, out of fear that our voices will go unheard. Help us to assist those who have been elected to office, those we have entrusted to govern. Participating with them in the process, help us to provide them with the benefit of our thoughts. We pray for the leaders of our country and other nations as well. Give to them a sense of humility amid the power they exercise. May they foster more humane ways of making decisions than with threats and the instruments of war. Endow within them respect for each other, so that all your people can dwell in the hope that the peace you ordain does in fact prevail.

13TH SUNDAY IN ORDINARY TIME (A)

Genesis 22:1–14; Psalm 13
Romans 6:12–23; Matthew 10:40–42

A cross is heavy and burdensome to carry. It takes most of the energy that one can muster. It limits peripheral vision, keeping one's eyes fixed straight on the road. To lay it down in order to rest creates problems; it will need to be lifted again. To set it aside and ignore it would be easiest. But then Christ wasn't given that option. To follow means bearing a cross.

Call to Worship   Psalm 13

Leader: I trust in your steadfast love, O God; my heart rejoices in your salvation.
People: I will sing praises unto you, O Lord, because you have dealt bountifully with me.
Leader: Let us worship God!

Prayer of Praise and Adoration

Our hearts leap with joy at the sight of your goodness; you are the bountiful source of compassion and care. You deal bountifully with us in our goings and comings; you are attuned to our needs before we utter a word. Your wisdom is vast; we cannot comprehend it, yet you send Christ who makes your will known. As we sit now at the feet of your glory open our ears to hear of your faithfulness and our mouths to sing you our praises.

Prayer of Confession

Unison: Righteous Judge and Benevolent Ruler, hear us as we confess our sin. We are prone to punish those who offend us. We hasten to harm the image of those with whom we disagree. In the midst of diversity we are quick to determine who shall be saved or condemned while claiming that you alone discern all goodness and truth. Help us to hear again how Christ died to save all of humanity, and hinder our efforts to decide who will enter your kingdom.

Assurance of Pardon

Leader: Paul writes, "But now that you have been freed from sin and enslaved to God, the advantage you get is sanctification. The end is eternal life. For the wages of sin is death, but the free gift of God is eternal life in Christ Jesus our Lord." Therein lies our assurance that in Jesus Christ we are forgiven!

Prayer of Dedication

"In the cross of Christ I glory, towering o'er the wrecks of time; all the light of sacred story gathers round its head sublime." As we glory in the cross of Christ, O God, so we also seek to serve the cause for which he died. Accept the gifts placed before you as symbols of our commitment. May the light of your sacred story shine forth for all to see.

Prayer of Thanksgiving

As the angel of the Lord called, "Abraham, Abraham!" and he answered "Here I am," the angel said, "Do not lay your hand on the boy or do anything to him; for now I know that you fear God." From that day forth Abraham named the place, "The Lord will provide," and so it is that as we gather we continue to give you thanks as you have provided for the needs of your people throughout history.

We give you thanks for Christ Jesus, whose name we now bear through baptism. He went about teaching what it means to obey. He fulfilled your law as he served all those in need. By his death he atoned for the sins of your people. He interceded for all as he was hung on a cross. But death could not keep him, and he lives now in our midst.

We give you thanks for the Holy Spirit, who guides us today. The Spirit serves as assurance that you do not leave us alone. The Spirit instills in us zeal, so that we perform tasks in accord with your will. By the Spirit we are led to people in want, confronted by thorny issues, and prodded to enlarge our horizons.

We give you thanks for the Scripture that bears witness to your presence. The words leap from the pages and challenge our timid ways. Keep us mindful, O God, of those who have gone before us and of the history in which stand.

14TH SUNDAY IN ORDINARY TIME (A)

Genesis 24:34–38, 42–49, 58–67
Psalm 45:10–17 or Song of Solomon 2:8–13
Romans 7:15–25a; Matthew 11:16–19, 25–30

Whereas each person alone must bear a cross, a yoke is worn jointly. When Christ commands the one, at the same time he promises the other. Our labor is faithfully to follow Christ's way. Our hope is his word that he will teach us the path. Our rest is the assurance that he knows of our burdens. The task is to join him in the venture called faith.

Call to Worship   Psalm 45

Leader: Your throne, O God, endures forever and ever. You love righteousness and hate wickedness.

People: I will cause your name to be celebrated in all generations; therefore the peoples will praise you forever and ever.

Leader: Let us worship God!

Prayer of Praise and Adoration

You are our guardian and shield, O God, our protector who keeps us from falling. You surround us with righteousness that wards off evil forces; in Christ is the assurance to withstand ways that may tempt us. You shower us with your mercy that cleanses wrongdoing. You temper your judgment with compassion. We stand in adoration and in praise of your name.

Litany of Confession

Leader: There is therefore now no condemnation for those who are in Christ Jesus.

People: I do not understand my own actions. For I do not do what I want, but I do the very thing I hate.

Leader: There is therefore now no condemnation for those who are in Christ Jesus.

People: But in fact it is no longer I that do it, but sin that dwells with me.

Leader: There is therefore now no condemnation for those who are in Christ Jesus.

People: I can will what is right, but I cannot do it.

Leader: There is therefore now no condemnation for those who are in Christ Jesus.

People: Miserable creature that I am! Who will rescue me from the body of death?

Leader: God alone through Jesus Christ our Lord!

People: Thanks be to God.

Prayer of Dedication

Gracious God, as we are in ministry with sisters and brothers through-out the world, collectively and individually we seek obediently to answer Christ's call. Use the gifts that we offer to enhance our work to your glory. Let them provide guidance for the venture called faith. Link us as partners and unite us to serve you wherever we dwell.

Prayer of Thanksgiving and Petition

O God of Rebekah and Isaac, God of birth who conceives the nations, you have brought forth a people as a mother delivers a child. You have suckled them with the milk of kindness, holding them close and away from harm's door. You have nurtured them with your wisdom, while cleansing them at the font of living waters. You have chastised them and cajoled them when their obedience has waned. Your judgment has not been wanting when they strayed from your ways. You have caused Christ to come forth, conceived by your Spirit of reconciling love. He grew up with stature in accordance with your will. Submissive to your command-ments, he was vulnerable to the needs of others. He stooped to lift the weak out of their depths of despair. His authority you gave to him, his des-tiny you designed, his death you determined on behalf of us all. We live with hope because of your care. We inherit the promise of new life because of your compassion.

With such a witness of your sustaining indulgence before us, help us to show sympathy to others. Send us forth to labor in the name of Christ Jesus. Equip us with tongues to proclaim to them your word. Give us keen minds to detect the causes of injustice and oppression. Make us resource-ful in devising means to expose and eliminate persecution. Help us to stand in rapport with the downtrodden, as we accompany them through the gates of your redeemed society.

We pray for the sick and those shut in for whatever reason. Give cheer to our voices as we greet them in the name of Christ Jesus. May our arms embrace them with your encompassing care. Open our hearts to their plight, as with our hand we seek to lift them to a sense of their dignity. As we are able to lead them to wholeness we laud your benevolent support for all your children, and thank you for kindness by which you hear this our prayer.

15TH SUNDAY IN ORDINARY TIME (A)

Genesis 25:19–34; Psalm 119:105–112
Romans 8:1–11; Matthew 13:1–9, 18–23

When seeds are sown along various routes, the results can be precisely predicted. If no thought is given to their nourishment, they will be snatched and taken away. If they are fed for a time, then forgotten, their life will be fleeting at best. When their care is sporadic, other growth will get in their way. It is best to tend them with care; then their growth and their yield will be great.

Call to Worship
Psalm 119

Leader: Your word is a lamp to my feet and a light to my path.

People: Accept my offerings of praise, O Lord, and teach me your ordinances.

Leader: Your decrees are my heritage forever; they are the joy of my heart.

People: I incline my heart to perform your statutes forever, even unto the end.

Leader: Let us worship God!

Prayer of Praise and Adoration

Your word is a lamp to our feet and a light to our path. Like a beacon you lead us to safe havens. Like a laser you discern the thoughts of our hearts. You enlighten our darkness and clarify our confusion. You, indeed, rescue us when we are bewildered and lost. Accept now our offerings of praise and thanksgiving as we open your word and learn of your ways.

A Litany of Assurance

Leader: The law of the Spirit of life in Christ Jesus has set you free from the law of sin and of death.

People: There is therefore now no condemnation for those who are in Christ Jesus.

Leader: For God has done what the law, weakened by the flesh, could not do.

People: There is therefore now no condemnation for those who are in Christ Jesus.

Leader: Be sending his own Son in the likeness of sinful flesh, and to deal with sin, God condemned sin in the flesh.

People: There is therefore now no condemnation for those who are in Christ Jesus.

| *Leader:* | So that the just requirement of the law might be fulfilled in us, who walk not according to the flesh but according to the Spirit. |
| *People:* | There is therefore now no condemnation for those who are in Christ Jesus. |

Prayer of Dedication

As you delivered Rebekah from her barrenness so also you fill our lives with your blessings. Send us in Christ's name into the world to sow your seeds of righteousness and peace. We offer ourselves to your service with the prayer that we become receptive to your command. Nourish us with the gift of your Spirit that we may grow more pleasing in your sight. We pray that the fruit of our faith shall lead others to you.

Prayer of Thanksgiving and Supplication

O God our refuge and strength, as you deliver your people from the oppressor, you accompany them on their journeys. You give them bread to sustain them and the fruit of the vine to make glad their hearts. You cause the earth to nourish the seeds, the wheat and the corn to flower and yield grain in abundance. The comb fills with honey from nectar you have hidden in the blossoms; the pine bears its cones to feed your friends in the forest. You are God of all living things; you designed the creation with an eye for beauty. We partake of your splendor, and give thanks for your grandeur. Grant us humility as we offer our prayer.

We are sojourners in our quest to be faithful. Help us to be more receptive to the seeds of your love. As your word is delivered, there are those who distort it and purge it of meaning. They render it innocuous with impact impaired. Give us the insight to discern your message, and the courage to confess trust in your truth. At times our hearts are hardened by the trials that confront us. Tribulation tempts us to turn away from you. We build idols and monuments to support our security; they are shorn of your wisdom and do not weather the storm. Give us the hindsight to learn from past deeds, and the foresight to depend on your word.

At times we choke on consumption of society's goods. We take a fancy to gadgets and entrust our well-being to them. Surrounded by such objects, we still yearn for stability. Temper our desires with your compassion, and help us to surrender ourselves to your protective care. May our understanding and obedience be in accordance with what you desire, so that in our quest to be faithful the yield of our labor may be pleasing in your sight.

16TH SUNDAY IN ORDINARY TIME (A)

Genesis 28:10–19a; Psalm 139:1–12, 23–24
Romans 8:12–25; Matthew 13:24–30, 36–43

The wheat and the seeds represent the way of God's kingdom in the midst of the world. False doctrine and misplaced allegiance exist alongside God's truth and God's will. When the harvest occurs there will be judgment. What bears good fruit will be gathered and stored. The useless will be cast aside. Jesus reminds those who hear to take note.

Call to Worship
Psalm 139

Leader: O Lord, you have searched me and known me. You discern my thoughts from far away.

People: You search out my path and my lying down, and are acquainted with all my ways.

Leader: Where can I go from your spirit? Or where can I flee from your presence?

People: Search me, O God, and know my heart. See if there is any wicked way in me and lead me in the way everlasting.

Leader: Let us worship God!

Prayer of Praise and Adoration

Gracious God, you have searched us and known us. You, indeed, discern our thoughts from afar. You lead us in the way everlasting as we gather to bless you for your bountiful mercy, for the compassion and care you extend to us. You surround us with a mantle that protects us from danger; our breastplate is your righteousness fulfilled in Christ Jesus. You are our shield and defender, our hope and our comfort. We give you all praise as we assemble in Christ's name.

Prayer of Confession

Unison: We confess, O God, that our lives are a mixture of weeds and good seeds. The weeds choke us and limit our will to respond. We admire the good seeds and want to nourish them. When the harvest comes, we know that the good seed will be kept and all else will be judged unfit for your realm. Christ have mercy upon us as we learn of your will. Give us guidance and determination as we obey your command. Forgive our misplaced allegiance when we settle for weeds. May we broadcast the landscape with the good seed of your Word.

Assurance of Pardon

Leader: Paul writes of our assurance when he says: "We know that the whole creation has been groaning in labor pain until now; and not only the creation, but we ourselves, who have the first fruits of the Spirit, groan inwardly while we wait for adoption, the redemption of our bodies. For in hope we were saved."

Prayer of Dedication

As the wheat is gathered into the barns, O God, so the fruits of our labors are brought into your house. Through the purging fire of your judgment, render our gifts acceptable in your sight. Set them aside as worthy, so that Jesus Christ, the bread of life, may nourish others.

Prayer of Thanksgiving

You are God of Abraham and Sarah, Isaac and Rebekah, Jacob, Leah and Rachel, Joseph and Asenath, Moses and Zipporah. From them have come a mighty people you have chosen to call your own. You have spoken through your prophets; your priests have taught your people how to worship your name. With wisdom scribes have delivered your word; with poetry writers have penned praise in your honor. Nations have been brought to submission in the face of your judgment. History has recorded testimony of your mercy that has withstood the ages. What are we compared to your grandeur and grace?

Yet, in love you sent us your Son Jesus Christ. He walked among your people and taught them your will. He enlightened his followers to the sense of your commandments. He stooped to hear the plight of the stranger and cast out demons from those who were oppressed. He suffered the shame of the cross for the sins of all your people, and even now pulls us from the pit of our own disgrace and shame. The grave cannot contain your righteous deliverance; he lives as our mediator and guide.

We give you thanks, O God, for this perspective on your providence. It sheds light on the sufferings that we endure in our time. You surround us with hope as we seek to be faithful; you give a glimpse of your glory as we groan in travail. Make us mindful of all who are part of the household of God. Let the legacy that they bequeath be a source of inspiration as with confidence we interpret your will for our time.

17TH SUNDAY IN ORDINARY TIME (A)

Genesis 29:15–28; Psalm 105:1–11, 45b or Psalm 128
Romans 8:26–39; Matthew 13:31–33, 44–52

The kingdom of heaven is like a treasure of great value. Much will be sacrificed in order to possess it. Its worth is so obvious that its presence is protected. In order to retain its purity the superfluous is cast aside. Christ died that all may have life. God sends the Spirit so that God's truth may be known. When Jesus calls us to discipleship he bids us to forsake former ways.

Call to Worship

Romans 8

Leader: The Spirit helps us in our weakness, for we do not know how to pray as we ought.

People: We know that all things work together for good for those who love God.

Leader: What then are we to say about these things? If God is for us, who is against us?

People: You, who did not withhold your own Son, will you not also give us all things through him?

Leader: Let us worship God!

Prayer of Praise and Adoration

We do not know how to pray as we ought, but as Christ intercedes on our behalf we are emboldened to come before your throne of grace. You make us mindful of your bountiful care as each morning we arise to greet the dawn of a new day. As we enter the sanctuary we behold your countenance in the eyes of sisters and brothers. As your Word is read and proclaimed we hear how you have been faithful throughout the ages. Be pleased with our offerings of praise and thanksgiving as we respond to your goodness in thought, word, and deed.

Prayer of Confession

Unison: Gracious God, have mercy upon us as we make our confession. We question your judgment when your will conflicts with our own. We are reluctant to follow the course you prescribe. Our patience grows thin when you intrude in life's journey, causing us to veer from the path we pursue. We seek to be faithful and obey your directions, but our own desires delay us in fulfilling your will. Have mercy upon us and deliver us from self-deception.

Assurance of Pardon

Leader: Paul assures us that the Spirit helps us in our weakness, and intercedes for us according to God's will. In Jesus Christ, God calls us, and God conforms us to Christ, so that in him we receive the promise of new life. As we dwell in the Spirit let us also rest assured in the promise. In Jesus Christ we are forgiven!

Prayer of Dedication

Treasures lose their luster, and riches are easily spent, but your kingdom endures forever. We approach you, O God, trusting your will for our lives. You give us assurance of your abiding presence. You provide us with confidence as we follow Christ's call. Accept now the gifts that we offer, so that your truth may be known throughout the land.

Prayer of Thanksgiving and Supplication

We know you as God who is and shall be, one who with might performs wonders and with graciousness bestows manifold blessing. You speak and the heavens thunder with the sound of your voice. You stretch forth your hand and even the sparrows find safe lodging. In Christ Jesus you chose to walk among your people, revealing in him your marvelous love. As your Holy Spirit breathes fresh upon us, we are filled with the sense of your presence everywhere. You choose not to leave us alone, but to guide us; for all your mercies we give you our thanks.

Your heavenly order conditions our decisions, O God, determining the present and future course of our lives. Your commandments ordain how we should respect other people; your judgment controls us when we seek to rebel. We pray for a recurring sense of revelation, an intrusion of perception that will enlighten our vision. We know of the Christ, how he calls us to follow. We ask for direction in our quest to obey. He calls us to struggle on behalf of your righteousness; keep us from complacency that hinders response. When we wrestle with forces that would dehumanize our neighbors, help us to be specific on what needs to occur. Give us those extraordinary glimpses of your purpose, and grant us strength to obey your will.

Help us not to be unduly anxious, when the results of our actions are not readily known. Add to our need for security a level of your providence that you promise in Christ. Chasten our desires to control our own destiny, and give us the freedom to take risks for your sake. When we stumble, set us securely once again on your path. When we take detours, keep us safe until we regain our bearings. You know who we are and where we are going. With that assurance, we shall be on our way.

18TH SUNDAY IN ORDINARY TIME (A)

Genesis 32:22–31; Psalm 17:1–7, 15
Romans 9:1–5; Matthew 14:13–21

The compassion of Jesus included healing the sick and feeding the crowds. Both are a necessity in order to make others whole. While sickness attacks the body and renders it incapable of enjoying full life, hunger deprives it of nourishment so that the self is unable to grow. The size of the crowds didn't matter. With Christ the gifts of God's grace are available to all.

Call to Worship   Psalm 17

Leader: Hear a just cause, O Lord; attend to our cries; give ear to prayers from lips free of deceit.
People: I call upon you, for you will answer me, O God; incline your ear to me, hear my words.
Leader: Wondrously show your steadfast love, O savior of those who seek refuge from their adversaries at your right hand.
People: As for me, I shall behold your face in righteousness; when I awake I shall be satisfied, beholding your likeness.
Leader: Let us worship God!

Prayer of Praise and Adoration

You do hear the prayers of your people, O God, and give heed to their supplications. Your faithfulness spans generations and nations, as a cloak of protection sewn with benevolent care. You promise your presence as your Spirit abides in our midst. We bow down before you, as our ancestors have done before us, in praise and adoration of your gracious name.

Prayer of Confession

Unison: Merciful God, you teach us compassion, and we practice bigotry. You implore us to trust you, while we create idols. You send Christ as a witness that you will not forsake us; yet we fret over matters as though you cared not at all. Forgive our compulsion to control our own destiny. Look kindly upon us when we fear for our future. Have mercy upon us when we mismanage your grace. We are your people; help us to dwell in your promise.

Assurance of Pardon

Leader: "For I am convinced that neither death, nor life, nor angels, nor rulers, nor powers, nor things present, nor things to come, nor powers, nor

97

height, nor depth, nor anything else in all creation, will be able to separate us from the love of God in Christ Jesus our Lord." Therein lies our assurance of pardon.

Prayer of Dedication

Gracious God, your compassion brings wholeness, and your forgiveness brings promise of new life. Through Christ the gifts of your grace are available to all. We place ourselves before you as recipients of your mercy; we make our offerings to you in response to Christ's call. Accept them as tributes to your glory as we dedicate ourselves anew to Christ's service.

Prayer of Thanksgiving

God of the past, the present, and the ages to come, you set the seasons and cause the sun to rise and fall, numbering our days. The earth is yours, for you have made it. The heavens declare your handiwork; they are crafted according to your design. Streams gush from their sources to refresh us with clear waters; mighty rivers flow on their courses, as you have decreed. The seas ebb and flow and tides are determined; waves dash against the shores of the land you created. You place us amid your ordered universe, O Creator, and unceasingly reveal your providential intention. If we will but dwell in the midst of your mercy, we may be assured of your benevolent protection.

So what can befall us to hinder thanksgiving? You wrestled with Jacob and he prevailed. When he asked you gave him a blessing, and called his name Israel. He called the place Peniel, "for I have seen God face to face and yet my life is preserved." The covenant that you made with him you have never broken. You sent Jesus Christ as a sign of your love. You did not spare him when he was subjected to scorn. When he died for our sins he made us the victors. When the grave could not hold him we were granted new life. He knows of our plight and how we might suffer. He prays for our well-being so that we can rejoice.

Who or what then can separate us from your love? We shall continue to endure persecution. In faithfulness to Christ, we persevere in our struggle against injustice and greed. Yet even when distress or peril confronts us, we are upheld by his redeeming grace. For all you have been, are, and will continue to be, we give you thanks as we abide in your love, in the name of Christ Jesus.

19TH SUNDAY IN ORDINARY TIME (A)

Genesis 37:1–4, 12–28; Psalm 105:1–6, 16–22, 45b
Romans 10:5–15; Matthew 14:22–33

Christian life is often like a storm-tossed sea. Risking the waves, we venture forth, seeking to be faithful to Christ. As he bids us to follow, the wind rises and we panic. Doubts emerge like clouds, hiding the horizon and with it the hope of reaching a haven. Then a hand reaches out with a grip of security, and assurance is given: "Have no fear."

Call to Worship   Romans 10

Leader: The word is near you, on your lips and in your heart
People: If we confess with our lips that Jesus is Lord and believe in our hearts that God raised him from the dead, we will be saved.
Leader: For one believes with the heart and so is justified, and one confesses with the mouth and so is saved.
People: Everyone who calls on the name of the Lord shall be saved.
Leader: Let us worship God!

Prayer of Praise and Adoration

O God, we gather to hear of the mighty acts you perform, of how you deal justly with your people. You have led them from peril and delivered them from persecution. By the hands of Christ you lift us up to safe places, and give us a vision of how we may dwell secure in your love. Hear us now as we give thanks for your providence and praise for your mercy.

Prayer of Confession

Unison: O God, when trials beset us it is natural to fear. Called to be courageous, we find our faith lacking. When asked to take risks, we confess our complacency. By ignoring injustice, we hope that it will subside. You have shown us how you are a God to be trusted. Leading your people, you have stayed by their side. Even Christ overcame his enemies as he hung on the cross. Forgive our reluctance to believe in your guidance, and grant us the wisdom to seek refuge in Christ.

Assurance of Pardon

Leader: As God has driven the sea back by a strong east wind, dividing the waters and making of the sea a dry land, so now in Christ, God gives us a rock upon which to stand. Today, know that Christ is merciful and intercedes on our behalf. He is our redeemer in whom we rest forgiven.

Prayer of Dedication

O God, we go forth to serve you, wherever Christ calls us. Bless our endeavors to make his name known. May all that we do be unto your glory, the talents we offer are the gifts of your love. As you accept us in Christ, so also acknowledge our efforts. Use what is of value to further his teachings, and what is inadequate enhance with your grace. Hear this our prayer, O God of benevolence!

Prayer of Thanksgiving and Petition

O God of liberation, who releases the captives, hear our prayer of thanksgiving for the freedom you offer. You caused the king to send for and release Joseph, who became lord of the house and ruler of the possessions, instructed the officials at his pleasure, and taught the elders wisdom. When turbulent waves almost engulfed Christ's disciples, you sent your son Jesus to calm their fear. He walked on the waters upheld by your hands and tempered their fright sustained by your mercy.

We recall how Peter would walk out to greet him. He would show boldness in the midst of the tempest, only to lose heart when the seas became rough. We give you thanks for this abiding witness, which testifies to your trust in your people in spite of their doubt. We owe our very existence to your pardon, which lets us dwell in your favor. We acknowledge your safekeeping that is the bedrock of faith.

There are times when Christ calls us to take perilous journeys, to venture amid uncharted terrain in response to your will. We pray for your presence, that it will sustain us, and for your guidance, that we may not lose heart. Our cities teem with people whose lives are in torment; we need to stand with them in their trial. Jails and prisons hold countless others whose acts have been judged. We fear for our safety when we are near them, yet they, like us, are dependent on your care and in need of forgiveness. Help us to work for those measures of reform that will bring order and justice to our society. Let us speak on behalf of the defenseless, remembering Christ, who intercedes even for us. O God, forbid that we should take your freedom for granted, as though we have license to boast. Instead, let freedom release us to serve you with fervor, to show others that boldness which Christ taught on the cross.

20TH SUNDAY IN ORDINARY TIME (A)

Genesis 45:1–15; Psalm 133
Romans 11:1–2a, 29–32; Matthew 15:(10–20) 21–28

A woman's daughter is healed because a mother has faith. Since the woman is a Canaanite, she is labeled a dog and unworthy of the bread of new life. Yet she is even willing to take the crumbs that happen to fall on the floor. Those who hunger and thirst after righteousness, earnestly pursuing their quest for the truth, will find adequate food to sustain them, turning to Christ in faith.

Call to Worship   Psalm 133

Leader: How very good and pleasant it is when families live together in unity!

People: It is like precious oil on the head, running down upon the beard of Aaron.

Leader: It is like the dew of Hermon, which falls on the mountains of Zion.

People: For there the Lord ordained the blessing upon us, life forevermore.

Leader: Let us worship God!

Prayer of Praise and Adoration

We broadcast your glorious deeds, O God, and spread abroad the good news of the gospel. You have not forsaken your people, but promise your presence through the gift of your Spirit. In Christ you redeem us from a past that enslaves us, and free us for a future of life lived in your love. Hear us now as we sing your praises and fill us with wisdom as we learn of your way.

Prayer of Confession

Unison: Our Source of Deliverance, Christ, calls us to faith, while we seek our own security. He teaches us to trust him, yet we don't take that risk. He expects total commitment, and we think in terms of percentage. Time after time we turn our backs on your grace, serving our idols and forsaking our Christ. We rely on your promise in him to redeem us. We are dependent on him who can intercede for us. O God, in Christ have mercy upon us.

Assurance of Pardon

Leader: As God gave manna to the Israelites during their time in the wilderness, we now receive Christ as the bread of life. As God went before the Israelites as a pillar of fire, we now receive the Holy Spirit as a source of comfort and presence. God is consistently in love with those called God's people. As Christ numbers us among those chosen, we have assurance of God's grace and forgiveness.

Prayer of Dedication

There are those who would be glad with the crumbs from your table, O God; we have received your gifts in abundance. Make us mindful of those who are needy, as we bring you our tithes and our offerings. Use them to ease the pain of those who are suffering. As we serve others, use us to fulfill your will.

Prayer of Thanksgiving and Petition

O God of abiding presence, you stoop to hear the murmuring of your people. You do not desert them in the midst of their fears. You see that they are continually fed, and promise that they will always be led. You provide substance in the evening to sustain them through the night. With the dawn comes the promise of abundance that will last them throughout the day. We are your people, called by Christ to the banquet. You heap your mercies upon us and surround us with care. We thank you for how you watch over your children and seek to meet their every need. Through Christ we inherit your promised deliverance and entrust our lives to you. Hear our prayers as we make our entreaties; feed us the bread of life that Christ brings. Help us to arise refreshed with the dawn, ready to meet what awaits us.

We pray for those who are hungry, O God, those for whom the lack of food is real. The wilderness exists in their stomachs. They murmur and long to be fed. Help us to share what we have in abundance, to be good stewards over what you place in our care. Keep us from greed that inhibits our obedience, and give us compassion to respond to their needs.

We pray for those whose quest is for righteousness, who thirst after the cup of new life. They would be nourished by the commandments from heaven, and be filled by your promised redemption. Help us to tell them the good news of the gospel, how Christ died for their freedom. As we teach them what it means to obey you, let them join with us in service.

O God, keep us from taking your blessings for granted, as though we were entitled to all you give. We have what surrounds us because of your grace. In Christ's name we unceasingly praise you for your unending mercy and care.

21ST SUNDAY IN ORDINARY TIME (A)

Exodus 1:8–2:10; Psalm 124
Romans 12:1–8; Matthew 16:13–20

Peter confesses that Jesus is the Christ, and henceforth is known as the rock upon which the church will be built. Confession has continued as a means of the faith being passed from one generation to another. It occurs during our baptism, and when we are gathered around the Lord's Table. It is a source of instruction, renewal, and commitment. It provides a solid foundation.

Call to Worship   Psalm 124

Leader: If it had not been the Lord who was on our side—let the people now say,

People: If it had not been the Lord who was on our side, when our enemies attacked us,

Leader: The flood would have swept us away, the torrent would have gone over us;

People: We have escaped like a bird from the snare of the fowlers; our help is in the name of the Lord, who made heaven and earth.

Leader: Let us worship God!

Prayer of Praise and Adoration

We give you all praise, O God of salvation. We come with devotion to you, O Christ our redeemer. We honor you, O Holy Spirit, our source of encouragement; one God who sustains us with your love and your presence. Hear our words of reverence as we bow down before you. Grace us with your presence, that we may learn of your way.

Prayer of Confession

Unison: Gracious God, forgive us for allowing living water to be fouled. There are times when we blame you for all our troubles, and cast upon you the waste in our lives. Our wants are insatiable through misuse of your mercy; we tap your good graces with unending requests. We let the waters of our baptism become barren and stagnant; new life cannot flourish when we don't do your will. Cleanse us through Christ, in whose name we confess to you, and bathe us with mercy to give us fresh hope.

Assurance of Pardon

Leader: The words of Scripture remind us that "baptism now saves you, not as a removal of dirt from the body but as an appeal to God for a clear conscience, through the resurrection of Jesus Christ." Being baptized into Christ, we may approach God with assurance that Christ intercedes on our behalf, and we may hear once again that in Jesus Christ we are forgiven!

Prayer of Dedication

Great Shepherd of the sheep, we confess faith in your mercy as we bring you our offerings. Use them to further your work. May our talents be useful in serving your people, and our time filled with obeying your will. The money we give is in response to your graciousness. Accept it as part of renewed commitment to Christ.

Prayer of Thanksgiving and Supplication

Who can probe the depths of your wisdom, O God, and who can attain the height of your vision? Your goodness surrounds us like the waters of the ocean. Your mercy envelops us as the sun warms our days. The gentle breezes hint of your tenderness; the claps of thunder remind us of your fierce judgment. You bring order out of chaos, command discipline in the midst of faithfulness, and offer forgiveness with the promise of new life.

You stoop to us as a mother bends to lift up her child. You lend an ear to our needs, and hear our supplications. You rejoice at the sounds of our thanksgiving, and are warmed with the songs of our praise. You leave us not alone during times of temptation, but assure us that you will be with us when put to the test. Your Spirit comforts us in our distress, and goads us to action when our commitment wanes. In Jesus you bestow on us the worth we possess; we owe all our successes to his love. He endured persecution for our sakes; he came into the world to enlighten our way.

Giver of compassion and mercy, make us mindful once again of the water that cleanses. As the water that sprang from a rock soothed the parched throats of the Israelites, enliven our faith as we recall our baptism. May our confession of Christ as our redeemer and savior sustain us as we thirst for salvation. Lead us to offer to others the cup of hope that brings refreshment and rest. Fill our lips with the story of Christ's deliverance from evil, how he thwarted oppression with embracing love and concern. Let others through us taste your goodness, draw from the well of your wisdom, and come to confess Christ as the source of their lives.

22ND SUNDAY IN ORDINARY TIME (A)

Exodus 3:1–15; Psalm 105:1–6, 23–26, 45c
Romans 12:9–21; Matthew 16:21–28

The economy of the kingdom may seem topsy-turvy to some. Something that is saved is claimed to be lost. What is forfeited on behalf of another is said to be found. What is given freely is said to be more credible than that which is earned. What is stored for tomorrow may be consumed overnight. Indeed, to follow Christ does tend to change perceptions.

Call to Worship   Psalm 105

Leader: We will give thanks to you, O Lord, and call on your name.
People: We will make known your deeds among the peoples, sing you our praises and tell of all your wonderful works.
Leader: Glory in God's holy name! Let the hearts of those who seek the Lord rejoice.
People: Praise the Lord!
Leader: Let us worship God!

Prayer of Praise and Adoration

As we mention your name, O God, our hearts are glad. We dare come before you with praise and thanksgiving. You have been there for us during times of trial and hardship. You have brought us through many a crisis and care. We owe it to you each time we act wisely, for every thought that promotes goodness and each deed that helps others. Hear us now as we sing you our praises. Be pleased with our worship as we call on your name.

Prayer of Confession

Unison: You say to hate evil, yet we seek to get even with those who hurt us. We are to love one another, yet we choose some over others. When it comes time to serve you we are not that zealous to act. We do not pray as we ought, nor do we seek your guidance often enough. Forgive us, O God, our wayward behavior and help us to live in harmony with one another. Thereby through your grace and mercy may we live peaceably with all.

Assurance of Pardon

Leader: Do not be overcome by evil, but overcome evil with good. Rejoice in hope, be patient in suffering, persevere in prayer, contribute to the needs of the saints and extend hospitality to strangers. For in so doing you will live the new life promised by the Risen Christ and show forth the love of God in whom abides the assurance, in Jesus Christ you are forgiven!

Prayer of Dedication

O God, we offer those gifts you bestow abundantly upon us. Take them and blend them into a composite of commitment. Empower our hands to reach out to others. Enlighten our minds to perceive clearly your will. May the money we offer support the church's endeavors, as in Christ's name we seek faithfully to respond to your will.

Prayer of Thanksgiving

You are the great I Am, the God of Abraham and Sarah, Isaac and Rebekah, Jacob, Leah and Rachel, Joseph and Asenath, Moses and Zipporah. From them have come a mighty people you have chosen to call your own. You have spoken through your prophets; your priests have taught your people how to worship your name. With wisdom, scribes have delivered your word; with poetry, writers have penned praise in your honor. Nations have been brought to submission in the face of your judgment. History has recorded testimony of your mercy that has withstood the ages. What are we compared to your grandeur and grace?

Yet, in love you sent us your Son Jesus Christ. He walked among your people and taught them your will. He enlightened his followers to the sense of your commandments. He stooped to hear the plight of the stranger and cast out demons from those who were oppressed. He suffered the shame of the cross for the sins of all your people, and even now pulls us from the pit of our own disgrace and shame. The grave cannot contain your righteous deliverance; he lives as our mediator and guide.

We give you thanks, O God, for this perspective on your providence. It sheds light on the sufferings we endure in our time. Surround us now with hope as we seek to be faithful, give us a glimpse of your glory as we groan in travail. Make us mindful of all who are part of your household. Let the legacy they bequeath to us be a source of inspiration for us as with confidence we interpret your will for our time.

23RD SUNDAY IN ORDINARY TIME (A)

Exodus 12:1–14; Psalm 149
Romans 13:8–14; Matthew 18:15–20

When at least two come together in God's name, God is in their midst. When they gather, there are rules for appropriate conduct. One rule deals with relationships when conflict occurs. In the church it is better to let conflict be known. There, listening occurs in the context of God's love. Perceptions may change, causing different behavior. As a result Christ's body is strengthened.

Call to Worship   Psalm 149

Leader: Praise the Lord! Sing to the Lord a new song; give praise in the assembly of the faithful.

People: For the Lord takes pleasure in the people and adorns the humble with victory.

Leader: Let us praise God's name with dancing, making melody with tambourine and lyre.

People: Let the faithful exult in glory; we will sing for joy and let the high praises of God be in our throats.

Leader: Let us worship God!

Prayer of Praise and Adoration

May the words of our mouths and the meditations of our hearts be acceptable to you, O Lord. Day by day you guide us; every breath we take is a gift of your mercy. You strengthen our knees to serve you. You lift our hands to give you all praise. We come before you in the company of sisters and brothers to give you the worship due your wonderful name. May our words be worthy of the trust you place in us and our meditations mindful of your benevolent care.

Prayer of Confession

Unison: With the dawn comes awareness that we are to serve you in all that we do. Yet we turn our backs on you when called on to act. Our eyes deceive us when we lust after others. While we may not murder we do not hesitate to harm. It is so easy to covet when others have what we want. We fail to love neighbors as Christ taught us to do. We hear how a new day awaits us, to put on the armor of light. We confess our unworthiness to wear your mantle of love.

Assurance of Pardon

Leader: Paul reminds us how "it is now the moment . . . to wake from sleep. For salvation is nearer to us now than when we became believers; the night is far gone, the day is near." We may then lay aside the works of darkness and put on the armor of light, for in Jesus Christ we are forgiven!

Prayer of Dedication

We know whatever we bind on earth will be bound in heaven; whatever we loose on earth will be loosed in heaven. We seek to bind ourselves to you, O God, and bring your heavenly kingdom here amongst us. May what we offer be a sign of our commitment to offer our finest for the sake of your mission. Use our gifts as firstfruits of our entrance into your heavenly realm.

Prayer of Thanksgiving and Intercession

O God, you have chosen to speak through the mouths of your servants; by them your word has become known. The heavens shake with the roar of thunder, but you are not in the claps that are heard. The skies are lighted with bolts of lightening, but you are not in the arcs that are seen. The air is filled with pillars of billowing smoke, but you are not found in their density. No, you are known by the voices of those whom you have sent to serve you, who speak with the authority you give them.

We give thanks for all those who have faithfully studied your words, who through the years have made known your will. You summoned Moses and Aaron to the top of the mountain, and unto them you delivered the law. We give thanks for the prophets and poets, for the people of vision and the voices of praise. They were not afraid to take heed of your judgment, and they did not shrink from giving you the glory you are due. We give thanks for those who have taught us, the mothers and fathers, sisters and brothers, teachers and leaders who have gone before us. We stand on their shoulders for a glimpse of your way.

In Christ your Word became flesh and dwelt among us. It is in his name you call us to walk. We now seek to be faithful for his sake, as you enlist us to serve you in the decisions we make. We pray on behalf of those in authority, for leaders and representatives we have chosen to rule. Give to them proper standards for judgment and a measure of wisdom in the choices they make. Make their voices credible as they speak on behalf of the people; make their rulings in accord with what you command. You have entrusted to us the care of creation. We assign legislators to assist us as custodians of that legacy. Help them and us in Christ's name to discern your word for our day.

24TH SUNDAY IN ORDINARY TIME (A)

Exodus 14:19–31; Psalm 114 or Exodus 15:1b–11, 20–21
Romans 14:1–12; Matthew 18:21–35

The Lord's Table puts forgiveness in perspective. Christ invites God's people to dine. Around the table, dividing walls of hostility are breached. The peace of Christ is passed among sisters and brothers, and all partake of the bread of heaven and the cup of salvation. As the Table remains a sign of God's reconciling love on behalf of us all, let us go forth to forgive others their debts.

Call to Worship   Psalm 114

Leader: In the presence of God the sea shall flee, the mountains shall skip like rams and the hills like lambs.

People: We are bold to approach you and call you our God. We come into your presence with singing and into your courts with praise.

Leader: Let us worship God!

Prayer of Praise and Adoration

You are worthy of all praise, O God, more than could ever flow from our mouths. The birds sing of your glory; the day's sun rises to honor you. The mountains owe their grandeur to your design for creation; the seas have their depth, as you have decreed. We blend our voices with all of your creatures, and join with your people in praising your name.

Prayer of Confession

Unison: We are mindful that each time we come into your presence how willing you are to forgive seventy times seven. Yet when people betray us we bear grudges and think ill of them. We are quick to anger when we feel we've been wronged. We do not hasten to seek reconciliation even when we would rather things were less stressful and tense. Forgive us when we hesitate to emulate your example and help us to seek the peace Christ taught us to practice.

Assurance of Pardon

Leader: Paul writes how we do not live to ourselves alone. "If we live, we live to the Lord, and if we die, we die to the Lord; so then, whether we live or whether we die, we are the Lord's. For to this end Christ died and lived again, that he might be Lord of both the dead and the living." To be at one with Christ is to live in assurance that our sins are forgiven!

Prayer of Dedication

"We gather together to ask the Lord's blessing; he chastens and hastens his will to make known." We do gather before you, O God, and ask that you will bless the fruits of our labor. Hasten to make your will known among us, so that all that we do shall be to your glory. Accept the gifts that we offer for the furtherance of your peace; in Christ's name we pray.

Prayer of Thanksgiving and Petition

O God of liberation, who releases the captives, hear our prayer of thanksgiving for the freedom you offer. You delivered the Israelites from the hands of the Pharaoh; you parted the seas for them to pass through. You made them aware of your presence in the pillar of fire; they knew you were near as clouds moved in the sky. You focus for us the ways of your kingdom, how forgiveness reigns no matter the cost. We hear of the slave who is released of a debt that he could never repay, only to inflict on others the same guilt from which he is freed. As Christ stands at the door and knocks, as he invites us to open the door, that he may come in and dine with us and we with him, help us open our lives to him and practice the same forgiveness God gives us so abundantly. We owe our very existence to your pardon, which lets us dwell in your favor. We acknowledge your safekeeping that is the bedrock of our faith.

There are times when Christ calls us to take perilous journeys, to venture into uncharted terrain in response to your will. We pray for your presence, that it will sustain us, and for your guidance, that we may not lose heart. Our cities teem with people whose lives are in torment; we need to stand with them in their trial. Jails and prisons hold countless others whose acts have been judged. We fear for our safety when we are near them, yet they, like us, are dependent on your care and in need of forgiveness. Help us to work for those measures of reform that will bring order and justice to our society. Let us speak on behalf of the defenseless, remembering Christ, who intercedes even for us. Forbid, O God, our taking your freedom for granted, as though we have license to boast. Instead, let freedom release us to serve you with fervor, to show others that boldness which Christ taught on the cross.

25TH SUNDAY IN ORDINARY TIME (A)

Exodus 16:2–15; Psalm 105:1–6, 37–45
Philippians 1:21–30; Matthew 20:1–16

Laborers are sent into the vineyard and are told what they will be paid. The amount is the same regardless of the hours that are worked. The gifts of God's kingdom are likewise equally allotted. They never depend upon how much one produces. The emphasis remains upon how willing we are to approach God's tasks, and not so much upon what we are due because we responded.

Call to Worship   Psalm 105

Leader: Give thanks to God who spread a cloud for a covering and gave fire to light the night!

People: Who opened the rock and water gushed forth and flowed through the desert sands.

Leader: Seek the Lord and the strength only God can give, a presence that continually abides.

People: We will remember the wonderful works God has done, the miracles, and the judgments God made.

Leader: Let us worship God!

Prayer of Praise and Adoration

O Lord, it would take forever to tell of your deeds, an eternity of boasting how great you are. The heavens could not contain our bountiful expressions of your grace and mercy. The seas would flood ashore with the expanse of your love. Yet, we are bold to bring you our praise and thanksgiving. We delight to remember how you care for us all. Be pleased with our offerings of unbridled devotion and accept our attempts to give you the worship you are due.

Prayer of Confession

Unison: Like our ancestors before us, we complain when things do not go our own way. We want abundance of everything rather than what is sufficient to sustain us. We would rather be elsewhere than where we are at the moment. When things do not go our way we ask, where are you? We would rather you serve us than be accountable ourselves. You gave manna and quail to those before us, yet we still doubt you will be there for us. Forgive our lack of trust in your goodness and grant us forgiveness, we humbly pray.

111

Assurance of Pardon

Leader: As Paul reminds us, let us live our lives in a manner worthy of the gospel of Christ, standing firm in one spirit, striving side by side with one mind for the faith of the gospel. As we focus our minds on the goodness of God we will have the assurance that in Christ Jesus we are forgiven.

Prayer of Dedication

O God, you give us tasks to perform. You equip us with strengths and abilities beyond what we deserve. In Christ you call us to faithfulness, to exercise obedience, to be deliberate in our discipline. We come now offering you the results of our labors. Use them as a means to further your work in Christ's name.

Prayer of Thanksgiving

Provider of quail in the evening and manna in the morning, we give you all praise and thanksgiving. You did not desert our ancestors in the wilderness, but saw to it their every need was met. When they wished they had never left Egypt you helped them to focus on your plan for their lives. In time they became a people and are now a great nation. We thank you for the legacy of faith and endurance they have passed on to us. Help us as nations to celebrate each other's culture and history and blend together our blessings into a composite of praise.

In Christ you have called us to be responsible disciples, to do work that befits your redemption. Our vineyards are the scenes of diverse tasks in our churches and communities. In halls and assemblies where decisions are debated, in libraries where study occurs, on pavements that resound with footsteps and movement, your people are alert to your call to obey. Enhance our efforts that aid the well-being of our sisters and brothers, and frustrate those that go against your will.

Throughout this new week bless our eyes that we may see the needs that exist. Bless our mouths that we may speak with conviction. Bless our perceptions that we may analyze how best to resolve issues and tensions that exist. With our hands let us embrace one another in common endeavors, and may our feet not be afraid to stand for what we believe. Help us all to remember how our bodies are temples of the grace, mercy, and strength you give us each day, and thereby use the gifts you give us to your glory and honor.

26TH SUNDAY IN ORDINARY TIME (A)

Exodus 17:1–7; Psalm 78:1–4, 12–16
Philippians 2:1–13; Matthew 21:23–32

Followers of Christ are sent to work in the vineyard. Will they respond or evade the call? If they say yes, then action is implied. Christ offers repentance to those who hold back, while those who say yes, but then fail to act, are judged. Relationship with Christ demands that our actions match our intentions.

Call to Worship   Psalm 78

Leader: Give ear, O my people, to my teaching; incline your ears to the words of my mouth.

People: We will tell to the coming generation the glorious deeds of the Lord and the wonders that God has done.

Leader: How in the daytime the Lord led them with a cloud, and all night long with a fiery light.

People: He split rocks open in the wilderness, and gave them drink abundantly as from the deep.

Leader: Let us drink deeply of the Lord's goodness as we come into God's courts with praise!

Prayer of Praise and Adoration

O God, your grandeur towers above the highest peaks; your strength can make them tremble and fall. Your love is deeper than the valleys of the oceans, and as encompassing as the water that covers the earth. In Christ Jesus you call us your children and through him your word is forever made known. Be with us now as in Christ's name we gather. Accept our praises as we confess him Redeemer and Lord.

Prayer of Confession

Unison: God of compassion, have mercy upon us as we make our confession. How often we do not do what we intended! What we confess is not how we act. We hear your word preached and we give our assent, but faith is found wanting when it comes time to obey. We are confronted by conflict; decisions are called for. Our desires are at odds with what you command and we do not do what you wish. O God, have mercy upon us and in Christ forgive us. Give us the strength to do your will.

Assurance of Pardon

Leader: Again, hear the words of Paul when he writes that God has bestowed on Christ "the name that is above every name, so that at the

113

name of Jesus every knee should bend . . . and every tongue confess that Jesus Christ is Lord, to the glory of God the Father." As we make our confession we have the assurance that the exalted Christ intercedes on our behalf.

Prayer of Dedication

As we are called to be faithful in our work, O God, accept our gifts as we seek to respond. May our hearts be as willing as your grace is reassuring. May our faith be as firm as your forgiveness that frees us. May our decisions be as deliberate as your righteousness that delivers us. You have called us your own, O Christ. We confess you as Lord of all that we have and all that we are.

Prayer of Thanksgiving

O God, you are not hidden from us, but cause yourself to be known. With your direction Moses struck the rock of Horeb and water flowed to refresh your people. He called the place Massah and Meribah, because they quarreled amongst themselves and asked if you were among them or not. There is not a day that goes by when you fail to reveal your wishes. You provide us with mercy and your grace gives us hope.

We give you thanks for all those who surround us. They reveal your love as they offer their guidance. Their hands reach out to lift us from our depths of despair. They are not hesitant when we ask for assistance. Their voices are soothing as they speak words that encourage us.

We give thanks for those moments when we are made aware of your kindness. You temper your judgment with patience. You give us the cup to refresh our bodies; you give us bread daily to nurture our growth. Our baptism is a sign that we are heirs of the covenant. All our senses are made aware of your grace.

We give you thanks for Christ Jesus, whose Spirit abides with us constantly. Even when we would hide from you we are left not alone. We are assured of your presence when we face danger; you give us wisdom that keeps us from falling. Our days have new meaning since Christ intercedes for us. We dwell with a confidence that we receive by Christ's call.

O source of the waters that continue to refresh us, make known your will in the decisions that face us. Surrounded by such a significant witness, may we not shrink from our commitment to serve. We confess anew that in you alone abides our hope of salvation. With Christ to guide us we set forth on our tasks.

27TH SUNDAY IN ORDINARY TIME (A)

Exodus 20:1–4, 7–9, 12–20; Psalm 19
Philippians 3:4b–14; Matthew 21:33–46

The stone, which the builders rejected, becomes the corner upon which the structure is built. Stones from the past have a way of providing foundations in the present. Even those at first rejected are appreciated in time. Confessions and creeds, which have withstood the ages, may be tempered and worn; but they likewise remain as foundations of our faith.

Call to Worship   Psalm 19

Leader: The law of the Lord is perfect, reviving the soul;
People: The decrees of the Lord are sure, making wise the simple;
Leader: The precepts of the Lord are right, rejoicing the heart;
People: The commandment of the Lord is clear, enlightening the eyes;
Leader: The fear of the Lord is pure, enduring forever;
People: the ordinances of the Lord are true and righteous altogether.
Unison: Let the words of my mouth and the meditation of my heart
             be acceptable to you, O Lord, my rock and my redeemer.

Prayer of Praise and Adoration

As we look at the heavens, the stars shine forth to herald your presence. The sun exudes the warmth of your love. The vastness reminds us we cannot escape from your presence. You are above and beyond us, yet you choose to dwell with us. In Christ you promise you'll be with us throughout whatever befalls us. You will strengthen us in whatever needs we may have. As your voice goes out through all the earth and your words to the ends of the world, may our voices resound now as we give you all thanks and praise.

Prayer of Confession

Unison: You whose voice extends to the ends of the world, have mercy upon us as we confess our sin. We live as enemies of the cross when we crave earthly things, glory in the weakness of others, yearn above all for satisfaction for ourselves, and serve only those gods who do what we want. Having attained the prize of your mercy in Jesus, help us to obey him as the source of new life.

Assurance of Pardon

Leader: As the Gospel reminds us, "The very stone that the builders rejected has become the cornerstone; this was the Lord's doing and it is amazing in our eyes." Christ is our foundation; God's will in him cannot be shaken. Our redemption is sure; we are forgiven!

Prayer of Dedication

We rely on your promise, O God, that you will not forsake us; our pledge to you is that we will be faithful. As we stand on the shoulders of those who have gone before, give us a vision of what commitment can mean. Accept the gifts that we place here before you, as we in our day make our response. Let what we do be an example for others so that future believers learn of Christ and his way.

Prayer of Thanksgiving

Your commandments, O God, are like the refiner's fire. They temper our judgment, melting down our resistance to your all-embracing will. They mold us into the people you would have us become. They reflect the brilliance of your pervasive compassion, casting shadows on our errant behavior when we stray from your path. You have taught us how we ought to behave. Your commandments revive us and set our hearts to rejoicing. They radiate the warmth of your love.

You do not leave us alone in our attempts to be faithful. We give you thanks for Christ Jesus, who shows us the way. He was tempted as we are, yet did not falter. His life was blameless, his commitment complete. As he hung on the cross on our behalf and because of our sin, the fires of sacrifice were no longer needed. He died once and for all, that we may all live. Now he intercedes for us as we offer our prayers. Through him you hear us as we dwell in his grace.

The fire that could consume us with judgment instead kindles our spirits as we stand here before you. We give you thanks for the Holy Spirit, whose counsel we seek. Through the Spirit you promise us a foretaste of heaven. We are comforted and led along paths of discipleship. Whatever decision we are called on to make, your Spirit awaits to guide and direct our thoughts. By that same Spirit we are enlivened for action and filled with the desire to serve you alone.

In Christ you have taught us the meaning of obedience. May all that we do be done for his sake. Help us to extend to others the warmth of the gospel, the good news that in Christ your people are freed. Let us seek the renewal of our common life, loosing the bonds that hold millions in poverty's grasp. Set aflame in us the prophet's passion for justice so that the aim of your commandments may be fulfilled: life for all!

28TH SUNDAY IN ORDINARY TIME (A)

Exodus 32:1–14; Psalm 106:1–6, 19–23
Philippians 4:1–9; Matthew 22:1–14

The wedding feast was prepared; the invitations had been sent. But some guests could not come. Others made light of the feast by insisting they were too busy, or otherwise engaged. When the Lord's Table is spread, the call is extended. All those are welcome who confess their faith in Jesus Christ. God's chosen people shall partake of the heavenly banquet.

Call to Worship   Psalm 106

Leader: Praise the Lord! O give thanks to the Lord, who is good, and whose steadfast love endures forever.

People: Who can utter the mighty doings of the Lord, or declare the praise God is due?

Leader: Happy are those who observe justice, who do righteousness at all times.

People: Remember me, O Lord, when you show favor to your people; help me when you deliver them.

Leader: Let us worship God!

Prayer of Praise and Adoration

Whatever is true, whatever is honorable, whatever is just, whatever is pure, whatever is lovely, whatever is gracious, all, O God, are gifts of your grace. We gather to sing you our praises and to tell of your virtues in the midst of our neighbors. Your commandments are just; they give us direction. Your covenant encompasses us and in Christ knits us together. We give you all honor as we rejoice in your glory!

Prayer of Confession

Unison: O Christ, we confess that we, too, make light of your invitation. We are reluctant to come when the feast is made ready. Our time is committed; business is pressing. We are afraid we will be with the wrong people. At times dissension hinders our response. We are not at peace with those likewise invited. We are in need of forgiveness to heal our divisions, and a measure of mercy to partake of your grace.

Assurance of Pardon

Leader: Scripture reminds us that the bread of God is that which comes down from heaven and gives life to the world. Jesus has taught that he is the bread of life. Whoever lives and believes in Jesus Christ as the bread of life has eternal life. Therein abides our assurance of pardon and renewal.

Prayer of Dedication

Gracious God, you call us to be agents of Christ's way. We accept the commission as we confess faith in his will. What we now offer reflects our commitment. Accept our labors as befitting your righteousness. Enhance our endeavors by sending your Spirit. May our obedience be worthy of your continuing trust.

Prayer of Thanksgiving and Petition

Gracious God, you know our inmost thoughts before the words cross our lips. Your wisdom embraces the seen and the unseen. Your judgment probes to the core of our being. Your love extends beyond the farthest reaches of the oceans. The highest peaks of the mountains do not approach the heights of your compassion. You are God whose anger is kindled by injustice, whose heart is touched by the suffering of a child. Your grace extends to those who bow down and worship your name; you have sent Christ as a means of salvation to all who believe. We give you thanks, O Lord, that in him you look with favor upon us. Cleanse the thoughts of our hearts by the inspiration of your Holy Spirit, that we may be found acceptable in your sight, our strength and redeemer.

We pray that we shall stand firm in the face of tribulation. May our conviction not waver as we witness in Christ's name. When we are tossed to and fro by the trials that beset us, give us clear heads and open hearts that we may hear what you are saying. As we confront contemporary demons that tempt us from your way, keep us resolute in Christ's own triumph over the destructive power of evil.

We pray for boldness to risk greater ventures, to take specific steps in response to your love. Give us the sense to recognize evil and the courage to oppose it. As Christ was released from the tomb that bound him, may we, too, be freed from powers that impede us. Lift us to the heights where we can gain a vision of your eternal order; then set us in the midst of those who need a glimpse of your peace.

29TH SUNDAY IN ORDINARY TIME (A)

Exodus 33:12–23; Psalm 99
1 Thessalonians 1:1–10; Matthew 22:15–22

The distinction is made between what is God's and what is Caesar's. The decision remains, who shall be served? If it is God, then God's will shall be done. If it is Caesar, then Caesar shall reign. Idolatry occurs when the distinction is blurred. When put to the test, Jesus simply asks the question: To whom will allegiance be given?

Call to Worship   Psalm 99

Leader: You are the Lord; let the peoples tremble! You sit enthroned upon the cherubim; let the earth quake!

People: You are exalted over all the peoples. Hear us as we praise your great and awesome name. You indeed are holy!

Leader: Lover of justice, you have established equity; you have executed justice and righteousness in Jacob.

People: We will extol you, O Lord our God, and worship at your footstool.

Leader: Let us worship God!

Prayer of Praise and Adoration

All of our lives are full of your mercy, O God; wherever we turn you are sure to be there. If we are found in the depths of depression, you lift up our spirits with the hope of new life. When we bound to the heights of ecstasy, you rejoice with us and make our feet light. You surround us with your Spirit who knows our needs before we announce them. We give you all praise, O God of all life.

Prayer of Confession

Unison: Lover of justice, distinctions becomes blurred when we are called on to serve you. We have been taught that to serve you is to obey you. At times fidelity to others gets in our way. Societal pressures appeal to that sense of security that speaks to our welfare. Mores and customs become mandates; higher loyalties are put aside. We confess our mixed allegiance. Have mercy upon us as we face obligations, and reclaim us from error when we obey not your will.

Assurance of Pardon

Leader: Remember the words of the prophet Jeremiah when he wrote: "Behold, the days are coming, says the Lord, when . . . I will put my law within them, and I will write it upon their hearts; and I will be their God, and they shall be my people . . . for I will forgive their iniquity, and I will remember their sin no more." Therein lies our assurance.

Prayer of Dedication

O God, we hear about the cost of discipleship. Nothing less than our whole life is required. We dedicate these gifts in response to Christ's call, and offer ourselves in full commitment. Take us and mold us according to his will. We pray that who we are may be acceptable, what we do may find favor, and that which we give will reflect your love.

Prayer of Intercession

Source of comfort and rest, you showed your glory to the people of Israel. You made your goodness known and proclaimed before them your graciousness and mercy. You have heard the weeping of those sorely afflicted and have felt the need of those too weak to speak. We give you thanks, O God, for your tender compassion, how you watch over your people with care. We give you thanks that in Christ you have shown us your love for us; filled with his Spirit we make our needs known before you. Hear us now as we intercede on behalf of those who have no advocates. Be with them in their time of tribulation.

We pray for all those imprisoned for whatever cause. As Christ broke the fetters of death that closed in about him, may those who are confined be freed by his love. Let us care enough to work for humane systems of justice, to advocate means whereby healing occurs. Keep us, O God, from making too hasty judgments, from casting aside as unwanted those Christ came to redeem.

We pray on behalf of those for whom hope is a fantasy, the forlorn and forgotten who now seem so alone. Comfort those who through deaths have lost a loved one, or for reasons unknown could never count on a friend. Help us to reach out to them in their plight, and to embrace them in tenderness. As Christ was quick to lift the wounded, may we, too, be instant in transmitting his kindness.

We pray on behalf of those who hunger and thirst after righteousness, for whom society seems like an alien place. May they through Christ find dignity, and learn of his reign, which offers new life. Help us, O God, to declare to them as to us the day of deliverance. Help us to offer the bread and the cup by which we are nourished as a source of sustenance for all those who yearn for a taste of your mercy.

30TH SUNDAY IN ORDINARY TIME (A)

Deuteronomy 34:1–12; Psalm 90:1–6, 13–17
1 Thessalonians 2:1–8; Matthew 22:34–46

Obedience to God is both a gift and a task. The heart has been given the ability to love. The soul has been freed from the finality of death. The mind has been granted the inspiration of God's Spirit. God has bestowed means whereby we may return God's love. Our task is to place ourselves, so endowed, in service to others—that they too may know of God's mercy and grace.

Call to Worship   Psalm 90

Leader: Lord, you have been our dwelling place in all generations.

People: Satisfy us in the morning with your steadfast love, so that we may rejoice and be glad all our days.

Leader: Before the mountains were brought forth, or ever you had formed the earth and the world, from everlasting to everlasting you are God.

People: Let the favor of the Lord our God be upon us, and prosper the work of our hands—O prosper the work of our hands!

Leader: Let us worship God!

Prayer of Praise and Adoration

The works of our hands are gifts of your mercy, O God, and everything we have is a sign of your love. If we have strength, it is because you uplift us; when we have joy, it is on account of your grace. We praise you when you comfort us. We are afraid when you judge us in anger. With Christ to intercede, accept now our worship. May it be worthy of the care you show us.

Litany of Confession

Leader: We are taught to love you, O God, with all of our heart.

People: We confess that our allegiance is less than complete.

Leader: We are taught to love you, O God, with all of our soul.

People: We confess that we long to have our own way.

Leader: We are taught to love you, O God, with all of our mind.

People: We confess that our thoughts are seldom so pure.

Leader: We are taught to love our neighbors, as we love ourselves.

People: We confess preference for ourselves being first.

Leader: God have mercy upon us as we make our confession.

People: Christ have mercy upon us and forgive our sin.

Assurance of Pardon

Leader: In Christ the "fullness of God was pleased to dwell, and through him God was pleased to reconcile . . . all things, . . . making peace through the blood of his cross." Know that in Christ you have been reconciled so that through him you are presented holy and blameless to God. Therein lies our assurance of pardon.

Prayer of Dedication

O God, you call us as stewards to take care of your creation. As we till its soil, help us also to replenish and nurture the earth. As we sow seeds for tomorrow's crops, teach us the meaning of patience and hope. As we reap the harvest, guide us to see that all your people are fed.

Prayer of Thanksgiving and Supplication

Source of steadfast love in the morning, in you we may rejoice and be glad all our days. With your favor upon us the work of our hands prospers to your honor and glory. The fruits of your goodness have made glad your people; gleanings of the harvest have reflected your grace. When with fear and trembling your followers have faced an unknown future, you have sent forth your Spirit to comfort their plight. We thank you, O God, that your presence abides with us. We rejoice in the truth that Christ died to make known. We pray with the assurance that you know of our needs before we utter the words.

We pray for patience when we experience conflict. Help us take the time necessary to discern your will. When we are hemmed in on every side, and we must decide, give us boldness to act, and a clear sense of your guidance as we begin to act.

Control our tempers, O God, when we feel put down. As once and for all Christ died to redeem us, may we save others from suffering disgrace. Keep us humble in the face of our enemies, armed with the conviction that your love abides. Help us to honor their need for well-being, and work toward forgiveness, reconciliation, and peace.

We pray for courage in declaring the gospel. Help us not to hide the faith we confess. May others see sincerity in how we seek solutions, and honesty in our confrontation with forces that oppose your will. As you call us in Christ's name to specific tasks of ministry, give us strength to respond with insight and hope. Send the Spirit to guide us as we go forth to serve.

31ST SUNDAY IN ORDINARY TIME (A)

Joshua 3:7–17; Psalm 107:1–7, 33–37
1 Thessalonians 2:9–13; Matthew 23:1–12

"Whoever exalts himself will be humbled, and whoever humbles himself will be exalted." To exalt or humble is to position one's self in relationship to another. Christ calls his followers to be servants since there is only one master. Let us then be in a position to serve the other person. For then the other's needs and concerns will be raised above our own and Christ will be faithful in meeting our needs.

Call to Worship

Psalm 107

Leader: We give you thanks, O Lord, for you are good; your steadfast love endures forever.

People: We have cried to you in times of trouble; you delivered us from our distress.

Leader: We thank you, O Lord, for your steadfast love; your wonderful works abound about us.

People: You know of our needs before we utter your name; you indeed are to be praised!

Leader: Let us worship God!

Prayer of Praise and Adoration

You have built your house on a rock, O God, and have sent us the Christ as its cornerstone. We praise your name for the assurance Christ gives us, and rejoice in the hope that his presence provides. Bring now your Spirit into the midst of our gathering and bless our endeavors as we follow Christ's call. May our voices be blended into one of thanksgiving and our actions united into one of great praise.

Prayer of Confession

Unison: You bring justice upon us and give us compassion, have mercy upon us as we make our confession. So often what we preach is not what we practice. We ourselves do not bear the burdens we impose on others. We expect commendation for our acts of benevolence; we like others to see us and how well we behave. Titles and honors are worn with pride, sometimes with envy, when others about us seem to be getting ahead. O God, forgive our craving to be exalted; help us to be humble in the knowledge that we live by grace alone.

Assurance of Pardon

Leader: Remember Jesus Christ, "who, though he was in the form of God, did not count equality with God a thing to be grasped, but emptied himself, taking the form of a servant." He bore our sins on a cross that we might die to sin and rise to life anew. In Christ we boast of the good news of God's love.

Prayer of Dedication

You are witness, O God, to the work we do for the sake of Christ Jesus. To your name all honor is due. Help us to raise the needs of others above those of our own and, thereby, be more faithful in our commitment and faith. Take the gifts that we bring, and enhance our endeavors. Make us ever bolder in our love for neighbors and use us to lead others to the truth of your gospel.

Prayer of Thanksgiving and Supplication

Source of all wisdom, the truth of your love is like a rare treasure; its value exceeds comprehension and its scope is beyond the farthest limits of our imagination. To grasp it for a moment is to be lifted high above whatever may threaten us; to be nurtured by it is to be held in an embrace that protects us from ultimate harm. Your truth leads us along the way of life that develops discipleship, challenging our self-centered vision and helping us to focus on your commands and desires. It breeds acts of compassion, causing us to take steps that will bring justice to light. It holds within it hope for tomorrow, and puts in perspective the toil of today.

We give you thanks for Christ Jesus, who makes your love known. It is through him that we claim our inheritance, and participate in the promise of a day without end. As he taught his disciples what it means to serve others, so also we learn how we ought to live. As he sacrificed himself on the cross for our salvation, so also we know that we may suffer abuse. As the grave could not hold him, since he dwells by your side, so also our foes will not harm us, since we abide by your grace.

O God, as we reaffirm our confession in Christ our redeemer, help us to pass on to others the truth of your love. May we be for them a treasure trove of understanding and acceptance, so that they can discover the wealth of your blessings. We pray for guidance as we act out Christ's gospel, for each individual has a particular need to be met. Help us to treat your people as unique sisters and brothers. Help us to make the most of unexpected opportunities to share your benevolent mercy and care, so that others are led to confess you as their God.

32ND SUNDAY IN ORDINARY TIME (A)

Joshua 24:1–3a, 14–25; Psalm 78:1–7
1 Thessalonians 4:13–18; Matthew 25:1–13

As we approach the season of Advent, we read, "Keep awake therefore, for you know neither the day nor the hour." How strange, when everyone knows the date of Christmas! May our calendars, however, not limit our preparation for the usual, nor our anticipation of the day rule out God's surprises.

Call to Worship   Psalm 78

Leader: Give ear, O my people, to my teaching; incline your ears to the words of my mouth.

People: We will tell of your glorious deeds, O Lord, and the wonders that you have done.

Leader: Tell your children and your children's children that they should set their hope in God.

People: And not forget your works, O God, but keep your commandments.

Leader: Let us worship God!

Prayer of Praise and Adoration

We incline our ears to the words of your mouth and will tell of your glorious deeds, O Lord. Your righteousness is like streams of goodness washing our soul. You purify the thoughts of our minds by the inspiration of your Holy Spirit, and sanctify our actions by the gift of your Son Jesus Christ. We appear now before you as children renewed by your mercy, to give you all praise in response to your grace.

Prayer of Confession

Unison: Far be it from us that we should forsake you, O Lord, to serve other gods. Yet, we confess our allegiance is not what it should be. You brought our ancestors out of Egypt, yet we do not always trust you to hear of our needs. You protected them all along the way that they went; yet we wonder if you hear us when we cry to you. We hear you are a jealous God and will not forgive our transgressions or our sins, yet we are bold to lay them before you and implore you, have mercy upon us and give us your grace.

Assurance of Pardon

Leader: Paul delivers words of comfort when he writes, "May the God of peace . . . sanctify you entirely; and may your spirit and soul and body

125

be kept sound and blameless at the coming of our Lord Jesus Christ." God who calls you is faithful and in Christ we hear again the words of assurance, we are forgiven!

Prayer of Dedication

Wherever we look we see your grandeur about us. All that we have is a gift of your grace. You fill each day with bountiful blessings and keep us mindful of how you care for our needs. We return to you now what you have already provided; may it be a symbol of our thanksgiving and love. Enhance their effectiveness and multiply our efforts, so that Christ's mission may spread to wherever there is need.

Prayer of Thanksgiving

God of infinite mercy, we offer thanksgiving for your goodness. You have not forsaken your people. When our tables are laden, it is due to your grace. Our lungs are filled with the life you breathe into us; our limbs move with purpose because of the strength you impart. When anxieties engulf us, you hide not your compassion. If we are afflicted with pain, you comfort us with your presence.

We give you thanks for Christ Jesus, who fulfills all that you promised. In him we have confidence that you accept who we are. It is he who redeems us in spite of our rebellion, and offers salvation when we stray from your will. He tempers your judgment with his intercession, and stays your anger as he acts on our behalf. We can approach you with assurance that in Christ you will hear us, and we take heart that we still dwell in your favor.

We give thanks for our loved ones who are at rest now with you. Their faith in Christ Jesus helped transform our lives. We thank you as well for prophets and saints of all ages. Their journeys taken in obedience have inspired us to pilgrimage. We thank you for all those who have shown us how to seek justice and kindness. By their example our lives have perspective, and because of their commitment, we too have had faith. As we continue our own quest to be obedient, help us to remember your presence throughout history.

33RD SUNDAY IN ORDINARY TIME (A)

Judges 4:1–7; Psalm 123
1 Thessalonians 5:1–11; Matthew 25:14–30

The parable of the talents is a classic reminder that we are stewards of all the creation. We are not to hoard its goods, nor hurt and destroy. It is ours to return when the landowner comes to settle accounts. What we have to give will depend upon how we care for it, multiply its fruits, and sustain its yield. To be faithful even over a little is to be given responsibility for much.

Call to Worship   Psalm 123

Leader: To you I lift up my eyes, O you who are enthroned in the heavens!
People: As the eyes of a maid look to the hand of her mistress, so our eyes look to you, Giver of every good gift.
Leader: Have mercy upon us, O Lord, have mercy upon us.
People: Look with favor upon us, O Lord, and be pleased with our praise and thanksgiving.
Leader: Let us worship God!

Prayer of Praise and Adoration

Gracious Creator, your day draws near with deliberate haste. We prepare ourselves for the providence that you promise to us in Christ. As we gather in this place to give you all praise and glory, fill us so with the Holy Spirit that we may discern your will. May we thereby be led to worship you in all that we do, with thanksgiving to Jesus who shows us the way.

Prayer of Confession

Unison: O God, have mercy upon us as we confess our sin. Christ calls us stewards, but we squander your gifts. He gives us tasks to perform, yet we do as we please. He sends us to minister on behalf of those suffering; we are slow to respond until our own needs are met. He expects us to praise you in all that we do; we take all the credit for those things we do well. Forgive us and help us to be more obedient.

Assurance of Pardon

Leader: Paul reminds us: "Since we belong to the day, let us be sober, and put on the breastplate of faith and love, and for a helmet the hope of

127

salvation. For God has destined us not for wrath but for obtaining salvation through our Lord Jesus Christ." Therein lies our assurance of pardon.

Prayer of Dedication

O God, you endow us with talent beyond what we earn or deserve. You seek from us service to you in all that we think, yearn for, and do. As we bring our gifts and offerings before you, may they reflect a wise investment of your trust in us. May their yield continue to abound as the work that we do spreads your will farther.

Prayer of Thanksgiving and Supplication

O God of all times and seasons, great and wonderful are all your works. You set the sun in the heavens to give warmth to our days. The moon and the stars you cause to light up the night. We spend our days surrounded by your abiding presence; our nights are filled with the assurance that you care for the whole of creation. When we awake, we arise refreshed from the sleep that you grant us. When we retire, we rest secure in the comfort that you provide.

As shadows lengthen and daylight hours grow shorter, praise of your name still comes forth from our mouths. You are God for all seasons of our lives. When winter chills us, you warm us with your love. With the appearance of springtime, you cause new life to abound. The long days of summer you fill with times of recreation and leisure. During the fall, we thank you for the yield that comes forth from the earth.

Teach us, O God, so to number our days that all that we do may be done in response to your grace. As you sent us the Christ to redeem us from darkness, may we live in obedience to your will as the children of light. Give us the insight to discern your work, and the conviction to act according to what Christ commands us to do.

As you send us the Spirit as proof of your abiding goodness, may we be courageous in how we care for creation. May the love we show our sisters and brothers open their eyes to the dawn of new life. Help us in the midst of trials to be made bold by the confession that Christ stands with us. May we rise above everyday living to catch sight of your wonderful works and never fear the involvement that a new day can bring. You are God of the harvest; we offer ourselves in response to your providence.

34TH SUNDAY IN ORDINARY TIME
(REIGN OF CHRIST OR CHRIST THE KING) (A)

Ezekiel 34:11–16, 20–24; Psalm 100
Ephesians 1:15–23; Matthew 25:31–46

God judges obedience by how well the needs of others are met. Whey they hunger and thirst, where is the bread of new life? When they are outcast or imprisoned, what has become of Christ's compassion and care? When they are sick or alone, how are they told of the miracles Jesus performed? As the least of God's people are raised to behold the hope of the gospel, God's will is done.

Call to Worship   Psalm 100

Leader: Make a joyful noise to the Lord, all the earth. Worship the Lord with gladness; come into God's presence with singing.

People: Know that the Lord is God. You have made us and we are yours; we are your people and the sheep of your pasture.

Leader: Go through the gates with thanksgiving, and into the courts with praise. Give thanks and bless God's name.

People: You are good; your steadfast love endures forever, and your faithfulness to all generations.

Leader: Let us worship God!

Prayer of Praise and Adoration

Great Shepherd of the sheep, you have given us Christ who shepherds the church. He is the host when the table is spread. We praise your name for all the goodness you give us, the mercy that, like oil, anoints all of our lives. As we dwell secure in the sanctuary of your salvation, open to us the truth of your word. Lead us to serve you more faithfully as in Christ you have called us to do your will.

Prayer of Confession

Unison: Even as we have done it unto one of the least of these, your children, we have done it unto you. When they hunger and thirst we are not quick to offer them the bread of life and the cup of salvation. When they are outcast or imprisoned we seldom go out of our way to visit them. When they are sick or alone we are not quick to keep vigil at their side. We know you are in our midst and await our response. Forgive us when we do not go out of our way to be there for you.

Assurance of Pardon

Leader: Paul reminds us that God raised Jesus Christ from the dead and seated him at God's right hand in the heavenly places and has put all things under his feet. With Christ thus seated, there to intercede on our behalf, we can dwell with the assurance that in him we are forgiven!

Prayer of Dedication

O God, may your will be done as the least of your children are led to behold the hope of the gospel. Take our lives and let them be consecrated to obeying what Christ commands. Take our gifts and use them as means of hope to those who hunger and thirst after righteousness. Take our time and fill it with a sense of your abiding Spirit, that others may learn of your redeeming grace.

Prayer of Thanksgiving and Petition

Shepherd God of Israel, who sent Jesus to be the shepherd of the church, we thank you for his love that guides and nurtures your people. He cradles us in his arms and brings us back to the fold and to safety. He leads us to pastures where quiet streams flow. In the waters of baptism we are made members of his fold. In the breaking of bread we are strengthened; the cup passed among us is the sign of new life. The old find consolation; the young are granted visions.

We thank you that we are numbered as the flock of Jesus the Good Shepherd. He names us as he calls us to walk with him. He leads us on the journey our life will take as his followers; he teaches us what it means to obey. By his judgment we will know when we have strayed; by his mercy we will be saved from foolish ways.

By your mercy, teach us the meaning of true righteousness. Help us to know what it means to serve your people in need. Where there is hunger, let us be the ones to offer bread. When others thirst, let us offer the cup of cold water in Christ's name. Through us may the stranger find a place to stay, and the tattered and the naked be clothed. May our ministry serve as the keys to your pasture, unlocking the gates so that your people enter the sheepfold. There may all find shelter and grow in faith and obedience as followers of Christ who fulfilled all of your will.

THANKSGIVING EVE/DAY (A)

Deuteronomy 8:7–18; Psalm 65
2 Corinthians 9:6–15; Luke 17:11–19

"Come ye thankful people come, raise the song of harvest home: All is safely gathered in, ere the winter storms begin; God, our Maker, doth provide for our wants to be supplied: Come to God's own temple, come, raise the song of harvest home." We do indeed gather with thanksgiving for the bountiful mercies God bestows on us day by day as we set apart this time to give God our grateful praise.

Call to Worship   Psalm 65

Leader: Praise is due to you, O God, for you answer our prayer.
People: We shall be satisfied with the goodness of your holy temple.
Leader: By awesome deeds you answer us with deliverance.
People: You are the hope of all the ends of the earth and of the farthest seas.
Leader: Let us worship God!

Prayer of Praise and Adoration

You are the Lamb at the center of our very existence and the Shepherd who guides us to the springs of the water of life. You are a God who wipes away every tear from our eyes and opens them to your splendor and care. Blessing and glory and wisdom and thanksgiving and honor and power and might be unto you, our God, forever and ever! We bow down before the throne of your greatness and worship you now within your temple.

Prayer of Confession

Unison: See what love the Lord has given us that we should be called the children of God. Yet, we so easily forsake our high calling. We make a mockery of God's greatness when we don't render ourselves thankful for all God's goodness and grace. We squander the bountiful assets God entrusts to us when we don't care for the gifts God provides. We turn our attention inward, rather than humbly attending the throne of God's greatness, when we worship ourselves and proudly boast of our gains. Forgive us, O Christ, and intercede for us.

Assurance of Pardon

Leader: Beloved, we are God's children now; what we will be has not yet been revealed. What we do know is this: when Christ is revealed we will be like him, for we will see him as he is. And all who have this hope in him purify themselves, just as he is pure. Let us abide in that purity with the assurance that, in Jesus Christ, we are forgiven.

Prayer of Dedication

We come laden with the bounty of your benevolence, O Gracious Creator, as the recipients of all your nurture and care. You cause the earth to spring forth abundantly with harvests that nourish us. Not a day passes without your providence providing the necessities to sustain us throughout our earthly journey. May the offerings we now bring you continue to spread abroad the good news of your bountiful mercy.

Prayer of Thanksgiving

Great Potter of the universe, how good it is to give you thanksgiving and praise for your design and fashion of this wonderful life you created us to be. Wherever we look we see your handiwork and stand in awe that you stoop to heed our every need. The grandeur of mountain peaks are the heights of your ecstasy when we abide in your love. The depths of the seas are the extent to which you will go to assist us. The speed of the mightiest rivers attests to your ability to empower us to reach levels of greatness. You have fashioned us in your image and made us a little less than the angels; we give you thanks for the inheritance to which we are born.

We thank you for the heritage of this nation, and its diversity of people. It is a sign of your encompassing goodness that we can live at peace with one another across the miles that stretch from ocean to ocean and from farmlands to large cities teeming with people. It is a tapestry of many colors, blended with threads from many countries, compiled into a fabric that has worn well throughout the years. We will seek to keep fresh the many hues and shadings, since they only reflect the richness of your creative energy.

We thank you for the democracy by which we govern ourselves, how it is possible for even the least of voices to be heard. From those we elect to represent us to those who place themselves in public service, there is a composite of influence on the spectrum of opinion that enhances the ability of everyone's needs to be met. We will seek to insure that all are franchised and exercise their influence when decisions are made.

We thank you for the bounty of the harvest and the care that is given to those who still hunger and thirst for justice and their share of well-being. As we feed the hungry, clothe the naked, visit the imprisoned and welcome the stranger, we know that we walk in the shadow of the one who did likewise on our behalf, even Jesus the Christ, in whose name we pray.

ALL SAINTS' DAY (A)

Revelation 7:9–17; Psalm 34:1–10, 22
1 John 3:1–3; Matthew 5:1–12

Blessings abound for the people of God! The poor in spirit are rich; theirs is the kingdom of Heaven. The meek inherit the earth; the merciful obtain mercy. Peacemakers are children of God, imitating their heavenly parent. And those who search for righteousness find fulfillment in their quest. In spite of persecution and slander, gladness and joy are proclaimed. For such is the nature of God's reign in our midst.

Call to Worship   Psalm 34

Leader: O magnify the Lord with me, and let us exalt God's name together.

People: When I sought you, O God, you answered me, and delivered me from all my fears.

Leader: Look upon God's countenance and be radiant; so your faces shall never be ashamed.

People: O taste and see that the Lord is good; happy are those who take refuge in you, O God.

Leader: Let us worship God!

Prayer of Praise and Adoration

Praise passes easily from our lips when it comes time to worship you. You are the source of all goodness as you bestow upon us bountiful mercy. When we feast our eyes upon your countenance our faces radiate the glow of your glory. We lay before you now our offerings of praise and thanksgiving. Be pleased with our tokens of commitment to Christ who calls us, and may your Spirit enhance our efforts as we worship your name.

Prayer of Confession

Unison: It is easy to judge those poor in spirit a failure and not a blessing. We often ask those who mourn to call us if they need something rather than keep vigil by their side. We consider the meek weak and too often ignore them; those who hunger and thirst often take too much of our time. We hear how we are to be merciful and pure in heart, and how we are to make peace with our neighbors, yet we harbor resentments that keep us apart. Forgive our failure to live your beatitudes and in Christ give us your blessing as we confess our sin.

Assurance of Pardon

Leader: Sisters and brothers, John reminds us how we are the children of God. When the great revelation occurs we shall know ourselves as created in that divine image. As Christ sits at God's right hand and intercedes on our behalf, we have hope that we are purified through such loving testimony and may dwell in the assurance of the pardon God gives us in Christ.

Prayer of Dedication

This day we stand on the shoulders of those who have gone before us. They have taught us of your love, O God. By their example we have learned what it means to commit ourselves to Christ, how the Spirit guides us daily, and to dedicate our lives to your glory and honor. May these offerings we bring symbolize that commitment and continue the heritage of the saints gone by.

Prayer of Thanksgiving

Blessing and glory and wisdom and thanksgiving and honor and power and might be to you, O God, forever and ever. You have welcomed our elders into their heavenly dwelling place; they have donned their white robes and washed in the waters of their baptism, and they now abide secure in the countenance of your love forever. For this reason they are before your throne and worship you day and night within your abiding temple, sheltered by the Lamb of God, even Jesus Christ our Lord. They will hunger no more and thirst no more. The sun will not strike them by day nor the moon by night, "for the Lamb at the center of the throne will be their shepherd, and he will guide them to springs of the water of life," as you wipe away every tear from their eyes.

We thank you for memories of those who continue to comfort us. How thoughts of them will enter our streams of consciousness like serendipitous moments of grace that bring them close to us. Those moments remind us yet again of your assurance of eternal life through the living Christ and teach us yet again how in life as in death we belong to you. We continue to hear their laughter, see the gleam in their eyes and tell their stories we hold dear to us. We thank you that for them death is past and pain is ended and their time is now your time, unbounded and unbridled by earthly fetters.

As we continue our earthly journey we thank you for the path they trod. How they made our sojourn one of sure footing for their having walked this way before us. May we treasure the time they took with us and make our commitment to you a lasting tribute to the faith they taught us. Help us now to impart their heritage to the generations that will come after us and thereby continue the lineage you have nurtured throughout the years.

Year B

1ST SUNDAY OF ADVENT (B)

Isaiah 64:1–9; Psalm 80:1–7, 17–19
1 Corinthians 1:3–9; Mark 13:24–37

Advent is a time of expectant watching, watching for the One who like a potter molds us and shapes us in accordance with God's will. The people are told to be ready, for they know not when the hour will come. They are to be about their tasks, performing functions appropriate to the gifts they have received. It is a time of anticipation and preparation, of being alert to God's presence among us. Watch!

Call to Worship   Psalm 80

Leader: Give ear, O Shepherd of Israel. Stir up your might and come to save us!
People: Restore us, O God; let your face shine, that we may be saved.
Leader: Let your hand be upon us that we may be made strong for yourself.
People: Then we will never turn back from you; give us life, and we will call on your name.
Leader: Let us worship God!

Prayer of Praise and Adoration

O Shepherd of Israel, you open our lips; our mouths give you praise. You shepherd your flock, gathering us from our wanderings, assembling us in Christ's name to learn of your will. Your covenant names us, your law guides us. The prophets attest to your promise that we shall not be forsaken. With great expectation we watch for your unfolding plan of salvation. Be present with us and guide us toward the truth in Christ's name.

Prayer of Confession

Unison: Almighty God, "we have all become like one who is unclean, and all our righteous deeds are like a polluted garment. We all fade like a leaf, and our iniquities, like the wind, take us away." We fail to call on your name; we don't stir to take hold of your plan for us. Yet you are our God. "We are the clay, and thou art the potter." May all that we do be the work of your hand.

Assurance of Pardon

Leader: Hear the words of Paul when he writes: "God is faithful, by whom you were called into fellowship of God's Son, Jesus Christ." By

God's grace you will be sustained to the end, and through Christ's mercy you will be found guiltless in the day of our Lord Jesus Christ. To God be all praise and glory.

Prayer of Dedication

God of unchanging truth, your promise is eternal, your benevolent care spans the ages. We come with our gifts to be molded in accordance with your purposes. We offer ourselves to be shaped by your will. Fill us with wisdom, and make us vessels of your truth. Make all that we do an outpouring of your goodness, spreading compassion on the afflicted and care to all who may be in need.

Prayer of Thanksgiving and Supplication

O God our Redeemer, by your grace you enrich us in speech and knowledge. We can pray with all confidence that through Christ you hear us. You fill our days with the presence of your Holy Spirit; we receive guidance for the decisions we must make. Waking or sleeping, we are enfolded with your protection.

You bid us watch for signs of your reign. Open our eyes to behold your presence in all parts of our lives. Keep us from putting you on the fringe of existence, from turning to you only when we are in need. Keep us forever aware that you accompany us in all our journeys; help us to make you preeminent in all that we do. Let others see in us the firstfruits of goodness and mercy, and they themselves brought to know you through deeds of goodwill.

You tell us through Christ to be ready, since we know not when the hour will come. Keep us from putting off until another time the discipline that will make us better disciples. Make us willing to break the comfortable routine and dare to start ventures that will test our obedience. Surround us with those who have made a similar commitment, so that they may teach us. Help us to seek their assistance and to learn of their ways.

You send us out to be about our tasks. Go before us to guide us, and stay behind us to prod us. Live within us as God who fashions our being, as Christ who keeps us from falling, and as Holy Spirit in whose name we can do all things.

2ND SUNDAY OF ADVENT (B)

Isaiah 40:1–11; Psalm 85:1–2, 8–13
2 Peter 3:8–15a; Mark 1:1–8

A message is sent to prepare the way. The tone is set for what will be involved. John comes, crying in the wilderness, "Make straight the way of the coming Messiah." There shall be baptism with water; Jesus will baptize with the Holy Spirit. There shall be confession of sins; Christ will himself be the means of repentance. Heralds proclaim what is to come, offering a foretaste of what to expect.

Call to Worship

Psalm 85

Leader: Let me hear what you will speak, O God, for you will speak peace to your people.

People: Surely your salvation is at hand for those who fear you, that glory may dwell in our land.

Leader: Yea, God will give what is good, and our land will yield its increase.

People: In God's righteousness let us worship, that we may walk in the Lord's way.

Prayer of Praise and Adoration

O God of peace, your way is sure and leads to salvation. You send your Son, the promise of life eternal; your Holy Spirit guides us to truth. We hear your heralds proclaim the path of obedience, and receive your abounding grace, making firm our footsteps; we know that all is made ready to follow you faithfully. We praise you in thought, word, and deed. By your mercy, affirm your unending love for us, and in our worship make us alive in your promise.

Prayer of Confession

Unison: O God of forgiveness, with our tongues we speak evil against our sisters and brothers. By our actions, we disobey your commandments. Hostility is bred through our suspicion and envy; anger continues in spite of Christ's peace. You open our eyes to his righteousness, yet we remain blind to the truth of his reconciling presence. Forgive our deliberate misuse of your mercy, and in Christ hear our prayer.

Assurance of Pardon

Leader: Isaiah speaks of God's comfort, of God's pardoning of iniquity, and of the coming One who shall level uneven ground and make a

141

plain of the rough places. All the earth shall know that God's judgment is tempered by Christ's presence and peace on our behalf. In him we have assurance of pardon.

Prayer of Dedication

O God of our righteousness, in whose sight a thousand years are as one day, we come this day offering our gifts. Use them to spread the news that Christ comes so that all may dwell in peace. Help us to break down whatever hostility divides our sisters and brothers, and hear us as we dedicate ourselves anew to becoming your agents of reconciliation.

Prayer of Thanksgiving and Intercession

Herald of good tidings and Proclaimer of peace to the nations, we thank you for all those who bring a foretaste of your righteousness. Your word is a beacon that illumines your goodness, bringing hope to a world that is weary of strife. The message has gone out throughout all of history that you will judge the nations with fairness; you will lead your people to a more glorious day. We yearn for the time when our days are more tranquil. Be with all those who still dwell amid tension. Ease suspicion that breeds hostility, leading brothers to speak out against brothers, and sisters to mourn the death of those who are victims. Make us impatient with mere words that speak of peace. Help us to substitute words with actions, and to take those first steps to heal divisions and reconcile differences.

We give thanks for leaders who boldly proclaim the end to warfare and strife. Give them courage to match their convictions, and firm resolution to remain steadfast in their commitment. Give us determination to acquaint ourselves fully with the issues, and keep us from making hasty judgments in complex situations.

We pray for those whose very lives depend upon decisions made elsewhere. Give them some sense of justice and dignity. Let us who are the church of your Word, Jesus Christ, join with them in their plight and their promise, uniting to bring about a new day. Enlarge our world to include them in the decisions we make. Make us more sensitive to the truth that how we live determines whether others survive. Bring closer the time when the way of love shall be recognized as your way, and the nations shall confess that you alone are God.

3RD SUNDAY OF ADVENT (B)

Isaiah 61:1–4, 8–11; Psalm 126 or Luke 1:47–55
1 Thessalonians 5:16–24; John 1:6–8, 19–28

The call to repentance is the start of discipleship. Passing through the waters, the believer emerges with newness of life. The waters of baptism symbolize that rite of passage whereby old ways are forsaken in favor of a commitment to God's justice and righteousness. John baptizes in the wilderness, bearing witness to the Light that illumines God's will, even Jesus Christ, the way of justice and peace.

Call to Worship   Isaiah 61

Leader: I will greatly rejoice in the Lord, my whole being shall exult in my God.

People: For you have clothed me with the garments of salvation, you have covered me with the robe of righteousness.

Leader: For as the earth brings forth its shoots, and as a garden causes what is sown in it to spring up.

People: So the Lord God will cause righteousness and praise to spring up before all nations.

Leader: Let us worship God!

Prayer of Praise and Adoration

Your spirit is upon us, O God, because you have anointed us to bring good news to the oppressed, to bind up the brokenhearted, to proclaim liberty to the captives and release to the prisoners; to proclaim the year of the Lord's favor and to comfort all who mourn. This is all your doing and it is wonderful in our sight. As we pass through the portals of your sanctuary we come bringing our hymns of praise and thanksgiving. Be pleased with our worship as we bless your name.

Prayer of Confession

Unison: O God of the Covenant, have mercy upon us as we make our confession. The afflicted await good tidings. The brokenhearted would have their wounds bound. The captives still yearn for freedom, and those who mourn remain to be comforted. Forgive us who fail to follow Christ's call to faithful ministry; restore us and make us worthy to serve in his name.

Assurance of Pardon

Leader: Brothers and sisters, hear what Paul writes concerning the assurance we have in Christ: "May the God of peace . . . sanctify you entirely; and may your spirit and soul and body be kept sound and blameless at the coming of our Lord Jesus Christ. The one who calls you is faithful, and will do it."

Prayer of Dedication

God of peace, in Christ you bring light to illumine the nations. He makes your will known to all who believe. We come in response to his call to us, seeking to follow and fulfill his commands. Accept the gifts we offer as symbols of our commitment; sanctify them wholly, that they may be used as you desire. Mold us and use us as instruments of your will. May all that we do be in accord with the gospel of him you have sent.

Prayer of Thanksgiving and Supplication

Eternal God of grace, you comfort those who mourn, heal the afflicted, deliver the captives, and bring hope to those who despair. You are a God who bends to the needs of your people, surrounds them with tenderness, and lifts them out of despair. We give you thanks for sending us Jesus, who walked this earthly way and himself was tormented and afflicted with pain. Through him we can face those trials that await us, and reach out to others with words of good cheer. We give you thanks for your Holy Spirit, who continually guides us, inspiring us to greater service on behalf of all your people. We are frail and prone to weakness, yet you remain our source of inspiration and strength.

Clothe us in the garment of Christ's promised salvation and send us out to proclaim renewed hope to your people. Make us bold to witness to the truth of your righteousness, and fearless in the face of our adversaries. Protect us from accusations against us, and help us to counter charges intended to weaken our resolve. Keep firm our commitment to act on behalf of your justice, so that the weak can themselves receive courage to stand.

Garb us with the splendor of your Spirit, and renew our spiritual core. Make us faithful in our study of Scripture, disciplined in prayer, and wholly abandoned in our response to the gifts that you give us. Deliver us from the frenzied pace of the world about us, so that we may find time to reflect on your will for our lives. Arm us with your mercy and strengthen us by your grace, so that we can be truly free to obey Christ, whom we serve.

4TH SUNDAY OF ADVENT (B)

2 Samuel 7:1–11, 16; Luke 1:47–55 or Psalm 89:1–4, 19–26
Romans 16:25–27; Luke 1:26–38

Mary finds favor in God's sight. Filled with God's Spirit, she will conceive and bear a Son. He will be called holy, and his reign will be everlasting. He will call people to obedience, to a life of witness on behalf of God's will. In him the fullness of God's revelation will reach culmination, as he teaches his followers the extent of God's love. Mary carries within her the embodiment of God's promise and is blessed with the living presence of God's grace.

Call to Worship   Psalm 89

Leader: I will sing of your steadfast love, O Lord, forever; I will proclaim your faithfulness to all generations.
People: I declare that your steadfast love is established forever; your faithfulness is as firm as the heavens.
Leader: You said, "I will establish your descendants forever, and build your throne for all generations."
People: Let the heavens praise your wonders, O Lord, your faithfulness in the assembly of the holy ones.
Leader: Let us worship God!

Prayer or Praise and Adoration

Your steadfast love endures forever, O God; your name is heralded throughout the land. Songs of rejoicing are heard in your sanctuary as hymns of praise proceed from our mouths. You fill your people with the gift of your Holy Spirit; you send forth a Savior with the promise of new life. You are our God, and great are your wonderful deeds. We worship you now in great adoration.

Prayer of Confession

Unison: O God of compassion, have mercy upon us. You send forth your Spirit, yet we ignore your counsel. Christ dwells among us, yet we fail to obey him. We sing of peace on earth, yet hostility continues. Angels herald good tidings, yet we commit evil deeds. Forgive our deliberate and indirect misuse of your graciousness, and make us worthy to receive Christ in our lives.

Assurance of Pardon

Leader: God, who is just and gracious, has sent Jesus Christ into the world to redeem us from sin. As we turn to God with contrite hearts, Christ intercedes on our behalf. So with assurance I can say to you, in Jesus Christ we are forgiven.

Prayer of Dedication

Source of life and Bringer of light to the nations, you provide for all our needs. We bring our gifts in response to your goodness. We thank you for sending Christ into our midst. Use what we offer, to enlighten all people to the truth of his salvation, and bless all our endeavors as we seek faithfully in Christ's name to do your will.

Prayer of Thanksgiving and Supplication

Eternal God of the covenant, whose faithfulness endures from age to age, we pray knowing that you will not forsake us. You have come to us as a child born of Mary, full of promise and grace. Through the power of the Holy Spirit, this Holy One, Emmanuel, reveals forevermore the depth of your wisdom and the wonder of your salvation. As we commit our lives to him and learn of his will, we give you thanks for your manifold gifts, which embrace all of life.

We pray that by your compassion you will sustain the lonely, give hope to the despairing, and fill the fainthearted with courage. Help us to comfort, encourage, and strengthen others as we minister in Christ's name. Make our very presence a source of solace, and the assistance we offer a means of succor.

May your patience become an example to those who struggle for righteousness and await the results, and may your sending the Prince of Peace be an incentive to us and all people who yearn for peace. Fill us with the vision of the prophet Isaiah, who proclaimed release to the captive, liberty to the oppressed, and good news to the poor.

Let your wisdom sustain all who worship you, providing counsel and guidance as your children mature in the faith. Broaden our vision to behold how we may serve you more obediently amid the complexity of our world. Keep us attuned through our own study to your enduring revelation.

Your salvation comes in an infant born of a woman. We give thanks for Jesus Christ, that he calls us to be members of his household of commitment. Empower us to respond obediently to those tasks set before us, and make us worthy to be called his disciples in all that we do.

CHRISTMAS EVE/DAY (B) — *See Year A*

1ST SUNDAY AFTER CHRISTMAS (B)

Isaiah 61:10–62:3; Psalm 148
Galatians 4:4–7; Luke 2:22–40

Simeon, a righteous and devout old man blessed with the gift of God's Holy Spirit, meets Jesus, a child called "Emmanuel," full of promise for all God's people. Simeon sees salvation in the child, God's revelation that will bring light and glory to all who believe. Having held the child, Simeon may depart in peace. God's promise of eternal life remains for all who receive with open arms God's hope of salvation, Jesus of Nazareth.

Call to Worship   Psalm 148

Leader: Praise the Lord! Praise the Lord from the heavens; praise God in the heights!
People: All the shining stars praise you, O God, for you commanded and they were created.
Leader: Praise the Lord from the earth, young men and women alike, old and young together!
People: Let everyone praise the name of the Lord, for your glory is above earth and heaven.
Leader: Let us worship God!

Prayer of Praise and Adoration

Eternal God of the covenant, you have clothed your people with the garments of salvation, and covered them with the robe of righteousness. We praise your name for your work of redemption, sending us Jesus as the promise of peace. Hear our rejoicing as we sing hymns of thanksgiving; hear our prayers as we give voice to our inmost thoughts. Fill us with the presence of your living Spirit, and give us wisdom to live in the light of your gifts.

Prayer of Confession

Unison: God of compassion, have mercy upon us as we make our confession. The year is soon spent. What we ought to have done still awaits action, while we commit acts not in accord with your will. We think of ourselves before others; we serve our own needs. We keep for ourselves the gifts of your graciousness. The new life you offer is not yet proclaimed in the land. Forgive us our sins and make us more faithful. Help us to use our time wisely as we follow Christ's way.

Assurance of Pardon

Leader: Hear Paul's words of assurance: "If we have died with Christ, we believe that we shall also live with him. . . . The death he died he died to sin, once for all, but the life he lives he lives to God. So you also must consider yourselves dead to sin and alive to God in Christ Jesus." In Christ we are forgiven.

Prayer of Dedication

Eternal God of redemption, you bless your creation and it springs forth with beauty. You judge your people with righteousness and new life abounds. We bring you now the fruits of our labors. Bless the work of our hands, so that what we do reflects the radiance of your love. Fill us with your Holy Spirit; so that what we say proclaims to all people the new hope in Jesus.

Prayer of Thanksgiving and Intercession

Bringer of hope to the nations, glory be to you. We thank you that through the gift of your Son, Jesus, we can now be called heirs of your righteousness and children of the covenant. By your grace we bear the name Christ and are members of Christ's household of faith. We thank you for his call to ministry and for the empowerment of your Spirit, which enables us to respond.

We pray that our ministry may be more effective in the new year that awaits us. We thank you for watching over us in the days that have passed. Take the good that we have done, and by your grace increase it to the glory of your holy name. We are sorry for those actions of ours that have frustrated your design for creation. Forgive our failures, and keep us from compounding useless endeavors.

We pray for those we have overlooked for whatever reasons: the lonely, the sick, the maligned, and the forgotten. Give us compassion to reach out to comfort them, and bestow in us a sense of your Holy Spirit, which can make them whole. Increase our vision to see clearly the causes of anger, hurt, and resentment, and where it is within our power to act, save us from hesitation.

We pray that nations may heed the word of peace that Christ proclaims. Be with all that suffer as a result of human hostility, and, through Christ, break down the walls that keep us apart. Fill leaders with wisdom; bring humility to rulers. Make us effective witnesses to the hope of Christ's salvation, and give us firm resolution to proclaim him Redeemer of all.

2ND SUNDAY AFTER CHRISTMAS (B) — *See Year A*

EPIPHANY OF THE LORD (B) — *See Year A*

BAPTISM OF THE LORD (B)

Genesis 1:1–5; Psalm 29
Acts 19:1–7; Mark 1:4–11

Jesus is baptized and proclaimed "beloved," chosen for a ministry that will condition his life. Full of God's Spirit, he will himself be tempted, but he will endure. He will call others to follow, and they will be led to obey. He will teach with wisdom that surpasses all earthly knowledge. He will perform acts of healing that reveal God's mercy. Christian ministry begins with baptism, which marks believers as God's chosen people.

Call to Worship   Psalm 29

Leader: Ascribe to the Lord, O heavenly being, ascribe to the Lord glory and strength.

People: Ascribe to the Lord the glory of God's name; worship the Lord in holy splendor.

Leader: The voice of the Lord is powerful; the voice of the Lord is full of majesty.

People: May the Lord give strength to God's people! May the Lord bless God's people with peace!

Leader: Let us worship God!

Prayer of Praise and Adoration

You speak, O God, and the oceans tremble; their waters crest in waves that dash upon the shore. You speak the heavens open; thunder signals the rain that freshens the earth. You breathe and the leaves shudder; the trees of the forest bow to your majesty. You speak and the Spirit descends on your people; we ascribe to you all glory as we worship your name.

Prayer of Confession

Unison: We come as your baptized believers, O God, confessing our sins. You send forth your Spirit, yet we do not respond to your presence. You set us apart as water is poured over us, yet our behavior in faith does not match our unique status. Christ calls us to follow; yet we disobey his commandment. Evidence of your goodness surrounds us, yet we ignore your gracious ways. Have mercy upon us, and in your love uphold us. Above all, teach us the meaning of repentance.

Assurance of Pardon

Leader: Hear the good news! God said to Jesus, "You are my Son, the Beloved; with you I am well pleased." We have a high priest who is able to sympathize with our weakness, who has been tempted as we are, yet is without sin. In Christ's name we may draw near with confidence to the throne of grace, and there find mercy and grace to help in time of need.

Prayer of Dedication

Source of eternal renewal, we come before you full of new life. We hear Christ's call to follow, and seek to obey. We yearn to be faithful as his baptized believers. Accept these offerings as signs of our commitment, and use us to lead others to repentance. We pray in the name of him who calls us his own.

Prayer of Thanksgiving and Intercession

God of all creation, whose voice causes oceans to tremble, you lighten our darkness, give form to the void within, and send your Spirit as comfort and hope. We thank you for visiting us with mercy. Your goodness overwhelms us. We can look to you in times of need, rely on you to drive away our doubt, depend on your judgment to curb our folly, and live in the hope that one day Jesus shall reign.

There are those in our midst whose days are filled with uncertainty. Invade their gloom with the warmth of your loving care. Give them the sense that you are there. Lift them from feelings of futility, and enable them to grasp your abiding concern. Give us a measure of the compassion that Jesus showed. Help us to be open to all in need, that we may become instruments of your mercy.

We pray for those whose days lack luster, who wander aimlessly. Give to them a sense of your will for their lives, the strength to pursue it, and the discipline to do what you would have them do. Erase from us our need to be critical of those who do not conform to our standards. Teach us forbearance as they seek to discern your intentions.

Make this day and all our days a celebration of our baptism. Fill us anew with your Spirit, and cleanse us of past sins, which estrange us from Christ and from one another. Send us forth as Christ's disciples, abounding in the hope of new life and proclaiming good news to aid the afflicted. Give us your blessing, O God of all creation.

2ND SUNDAY IN ORDINARY TIME (B)

1 Samuel 3:1–10 (11–20); Psalm 139:1–6, 13–18
1 Corinthians 6:12–20; John 1:43–51

John's Gospel lesson today is about "finding," and "seeing." Jesus found Philip and said to him, "Follow me." Philip found Nathanael and said to him, "We have found him. . . . Come and see." When Jesus saw Nathanael he told him how he had seen him under a fig tree. Soon, the time would come when Nathanael would see greater things. "You will see heaven opened and the angels of God ascending and descending upon the Son of Man." When Jesus finds us our eyes are opened and we see things more clearly.

Call to Worship   Psalm 139

Leader: O Lord, you have searched me and known me. You discern my thoughts from far away.

People: Even before a word is on my tongue, O Lord, you know it completely.

Leader: I praise you, for I am fearfully and wonderfully made. Wonderful are your works.

People: How weighty to me are your thoughts, O God! I try to count them—they are more than the sand.

Leader: Let us worship God!

Prayer of Praise and Adoration

You are the rock of our salvation, O God, the source of our strength. You are the fountainhead from which flow living waters. When our souls thirst after righteousness, your justice sustains us. In need of encouragement, we behold your power and glory. We lift our hands in the sanctuary; with our lips we praise you. We raise our voices in the company of believers and call on your name. Fill us now with your Holy Spirit, and nourish us by your presence.

Prayer of Confession

Unison: O Lamb of God, you take away the sin of the world; have mercy upon us as we make our confession. We grow lax in our discipline, and we disobey Christ. Our faith is flabby when put to the test; our courage vanishes in the face of temptation. Our joints stiffen when we are called to act. We profess loyalty, while our bodies deny commitment. Have mercy upon us and forgive us our sin.

Assurance of Pardon

Leader: Hear Paul's words when he writes: "Do you not know that your body is a temple of the Holy Spirit within you, which you have from God, and that you are not your own? For you were bought with a price." Christ mercifully paid the price for our sin. Through him we may approach God with our temples made clean.

Prayer of Dedication

O God, you nourish us by the outpouring of your love. You strengthen us with your enlivening Spirit. Our bodies are sustained by your goodness and power. You are the source of every good act we perform and of every talent we possess. These gifts are but a portion of what you give us in abundance. Accept them as signs of our thanksgiving.

Prayer of Thanksgiving and Intercession

Incarnate Word of life, eternal and unchanging, you call us to discipleship, and we seek to follow. Your will surpasses all earthly wisdom; you are known to us amid our dreams and our deliberations. Sleeping or waking, we cannot hide from your presence. You are around us and within us; you direct us and watch over us. We give you thanks for your incarnate grace.

Soften those who resist your truth. Surprise them with the message of new life that awaits their response. Turn them from making themselves their only source of value, and show them how your mercy can transform their worth.

Surround and nourish the young in faith, the newly baptized, whose commitment has not been tested. Keep them from trials beyond their capacity to endure, yet help them take risks that will strengthen their resolve to stand firm in Jesus Christ. Build up their confidence through the gift of your Holy Spirit. Enable us in the family of faith to be a source of assurance and support to them.

Startle those who have grown complacent, whose commitment to Christ has become a leisure-time activity. Intrude in our lives with the transforming revelation of your judgment, and astonish us with a sense of your awesome power. Keep us from seeking comforts above discipleship, and make of us faithful witnesses to your eternal and incarnate Word.

3RD SUNDAY IN ORDINARY TIME (B)

Jonah 3:1–5, 10; Psalm 62:5–12
1 Corinthians 7:29–31; Mark 1:14–20

Jesus calls the disciples to follow. No bargaining occurs; conditions are not discussed; there isn't even much time given to decide. Mark's Gospel makes the whole episode quite matter-of-fact. To follow Jesus is both a command and a promise. The command involves forsaking one's past in an act of obedience. The promise implies that as one makes the decision, the future will be revealed. The disciples immediately leave their nets and follow.

Call to Worship
Psalm 62

Leader: For God alone my soul waits in silence, for my hope is from the Lord.

People: God only is my rock and my salvation; I shall not be shaken.

Leader: Trust in the Lord at all times, O people; pour out your heart before God.

People: Our trust is in the Lord. We worship God's name.

Leader: Let us worship God!

Prayer of Praise and Adoration

You are our rock and our strength, O God, and in you rests our deliverance. You defend us in the midst of adversity; you protect us from ultimate harm. You humble the mighty with acts that manifest your transcendent power; the lowly you comfort with your tender embrace. We gather this day, saved by your mercy. Hear now our praises as we herald your greatness.

Prayer of Confession

Unison: God of compassion and mercy, hear us as we make our confession. Christ preaches repentance; we do not heed his call. Your new day is proclaimed; we dwell on the past. We turn not from our evil ways, nor do we sacrifice those treasures that give us status. We say we obey you, but our deeds betray us. By your grace renew us, and cleanse us of sin.

Assurance of Pardon

Leader: Hear the good news: "The time is fulfilled, and the kingdom of God is at hand; repent, and believe in the gospel." God is merciful and just, and Jesus Christ promises redemption to all that believe. As we turn from our old ways and respond with faith to Christ's call, we receive the assurance that we shall be saved.

Prayer of Dedication

Eternal Source of refuge and trust, our days are filled with your abiding presence. We awaken with the dawn of new life. We labor with assurance that you bless the work of our hands. We sleep at peace in the promise of your protection and care. All that we are and all that we do are signs of your benevolent deliverance. Accept now the gifts we bring you as tokens of our unending devotion.

Prayer of Thanksgiving and Supplication

O God of Jonah, of Jesus, of Paul and the disciples, throughout the ages you have called your people to repentance. We give you thanks for your saving grace shown to Nineveh, that you withheld your wrath because of their repentance. We give you thanks for the promise of Jesus, that those who turn from their evil ways and follow him are assured of life anew. We give you thanks for all the disciples who testified to your faithfulness. In spite of their trials, they persevered, and left us a legacy of what it means to repent.

Have mercy upon us as we join this host of witnesses. Save us from your anger as we turn to you with contrite hearts, imploring your forgiveness. You know our inmost thoughts, hidden desires, and everything we do in betraying your will. We rely on your goodness to overcome our weakness, and your endless mercy to redeem us from sin.

Strengthen within us the resolve to be faithful. Give us the needed discipline to let go of old forms of security and to risk putting our trust in your will. As we take our first few halting steps of faith, encourage us with the vision of your reign on earth. Lift us from a sense of defeat when we stumble and fall.

O God of deliverance, make of us beacons of light to show others the way. By our examples of faithfulness, bring them to a greater sense of your justice and righteousness. By our claims of obedience, lead them to be willing to practice their faith. Support us with your Holy Spirit as we surround them with our care and concern. Help us make a fresh witness to your saving grace.

4TH SUNDAY IN ORDINARY TIME (B)

Deuteronomy 18:15–20; Psalm 111
1 Corinthians 8:1–13; Mark 1:21–28

The authority of Jesus is cause for amazement. His teachings are not what the people expected. Even demons obey him; their power is dissolved. The crowds are astonished by what he accomplishes. God's order has a way of upsetting the prevailing state of affairs. What is taught provides a new vision of what ought to be. What is done testifies to the unlimited scope of God's goodness and love.

Call to Worship   Psalm 111

Leader: I will give thanks to the Lord with my whole heart. Praise the Lord!

People: Your work is full of honor and majesty, and your righteousness endures forever.

Leader: The works of your hands are faithful and just; all your precepts are trustworthy.

People: The fear of the Lord is the beginning of wisdom; all who practice it have good understanding.

Leader: Let us worship God!

Prayer of Praise and Adoration

Great God of the universe, whose wisdom pervades all creation, we gather before you to give you all praise and honor. Wonderful and majestic are your works; righteousness is seen in all that you do. You make a covenant and call us as heirs of its promise. You establish your law, showing all people that you are to be trusted. In company with the redeemed of all ages, we lift our voices to acclaim your worth.

Prayer of Confession

Unison: God of mercy, show compassion as we make our confession. You command us to tell of your mighty deeds, yet we remain silent. You call us to act faithfully, yet we are slow to respond. We claim to be wise, but we know not your law. Our allegiance is divided, for we worship false gods. Help us to obey Christ, to whom we owe our existence, and to love our neighbors, whom we are commanded to serve.

Assurance of Pardon

Leader: Paul reminds us, "There is one God . . . from whom are all things and for whom we exist, and one Lord, Jesus Christ, through whom are all things and through whom we exist. . . . If one loves God, one is known by God." As we confess our sin before God, God is faithful and just, and in Jesus Christ, through whom we exist, God forgives us our sin.

Prayer of Dedication

Most merciful and gracious God, the good that we do we owe to your righteousness. Whatever honor we receive is due to your redeeming love in Christ Jesus. All that we have is a gift of your grace. You call us, you name us, you watch over us with care. We bring now our gifts in response to your goodness. Use them and us to further the work of your eternal benevolence, through Jesus Christ, whom we seek to obey.

Prayer of Thanksgiving and Intercession

O Holy One, whose righteousness endures forever, we give you thanks for the prophets who faithfully spoke your word. We give you thanks for Jesus Christ, who obediently performed acts of mercy on behalf of those who suffered. We give you thanks for the apostle Paul, who taught what it means to take into account the needs of others. Through Christ, who intercedes when our words are not adequate, hear our prayer as we speak on behalf of those who concern us.

We pray for those in the thrall of false gods. Give to them a sense of your majesty that cannot be limited, your wonder that spans the universe, and your goodness that cares for even the smallest creature of nature, your comforting Spirit that hears the faintest cry. Let them find no satisfaction in their closets full of goods that wear out with age. Lead them to your Word that endures through the ages, even Jesus Christ, who makes known your merciful deeds.

We pray for those whom the world calls wise. Give them a sense of humility, and grant them perspective to accompany their vision. May they not mistake power for justice or order for well-being. When they are called upon to make decisions, hold them particularly close to you and make them instruments of your peace.

Give to the weak a sense of your blessing, and help us support them in their search for life's meaning. Let us see them as partners in this venture of faithfulness, and together help us grow closer to righteousness, in Jesus Christ, who endures forever.

5TH SUNDAY IN ORDINARY TIME (B)

Isaiah 40:21–31; Psalm 147:1–11, 20c
1 Corinthians 9:16–23; Mark 1:29–39

The compassion of Jesus has a healing effect! The crowds bring to him those who are sick and possessed. He lays his hands on them, comforts them, lifts them out of their misery, and heals them. Throughout his ministry, he remains aware of the source of his healing power, for he will withdraw and be in prayer with God. Compassion, healing, and being at one with God are marks of Jesus' ministry.

Call to Worship

Psalm 147

Leader: It is good to sing praises to our God. God is gracious and a song of praise is fitting.

People: Great is the Lord, and abundant in power, whose understanding is beyond measure.

Leader: Sing to the Lord with thanksgiving; make melody to our God with the lyre.

People: You take pleasure in those who fear you and hope in your steadfast love.

Leader: Let us worship God!

Prayer of Praise and Adoration

Great God of the universe, you set the stars on course in the heavens; the earth radiates your glory and honor; the rain never falls without your knowing it. The fields produce their harvest according to your design. We admire the strength by which you rule the nations. We bow down in adoration at how you care for your children. We gather gladly to herald your encompassing acts of goodwill. Hear us as we respond by giving you praise.

Prayer of Confession

Unison: O God, you heal the brokenhearted; save us from sin when we inflict pain on our neighbors. We bear grudges against those who deceive us. We seek revenge on those who hurt us. Some we judge inferior, since they don't meet our standards. Others we deem unworthy of our respect and support. Jesus had compassion upon all who were afflicted. Forgive us, O God, when our hearts are hardened against neighbors in need.

Assurance of Pardon

Leader: The assurance of our pardon resides in Christ, "who, though he was in the form of God . . . emptied himself, taking the form of a slave."

157

Today, he intercedes on behalf of human weakness before the great throne of God. Therefore, let every knee bow, and let every tongue confess that Jesus Christ is Lord. Therein lies our assurance that we are forgiven!

Prayer of Dedication

You are worthy, O God, of more honor than mere humans can hope to bestow on you. You are God of all creation, and the source of all goodness. We dare to approach you with our gifts of thanksgiving. Receive them as symbols of our wholehearted praise. Transform what we bring you to harmonize with your wishes, and convert all our actions to accord with your will.

Prayer of Thanksgiving and Intercession

O God of sympathy and tenderness, who surrounded Job when he was despondent and sent Jesus to bind the wounds of the afflicted, we give you thanks that you take pity upon us and nurse us to wholeness when we are distressed and forlorn. We give you thanks that even when despair so easily overtakes us, you send your Spirit to comfort our fears.

Hear us as we pray for those confined by illness. In the midst of their infirmities, help them to sense your healing presence, which brings peace of mind. Give to them that patience which allows their bodies to draw upon those sources of regeneration so necessary to health and vigor. When the days are full of fretting, and nights prolong the anxiety over a new dawn of suffering, hold them in your bosom and grant them peace.

Hear us as we pray for those who despair. When earthly hope seems to elude them, grant them a vision of your boundless mercy. Appear to them in the sadness of their darkest moments, and make real for them the victory of Christ's resurrection. Help them to hear the good news that transforms light out of darkness, and may they henceforth have confidence in your loving care.

Hear us as we pray for those blessed with sound minds and well bodies. Help them to care for those temples of your grace. Keep them from abusing what you so intricately created, and give them discipline to look after themselves. We give you thanks for the countless mercies we take for granted: for movement, for strength, for our minds and our senses. Help us, O God, to take heed of our health as a gift freely given, and never cease to praise you for the grace it reflects.

6TH SUNDAY IN ORDINARY TIME (B)

2 Kings 5:1–14; Psalm 30
1 Corinthians 9:24–27; Mark 1:40–45

Jesus seeks obedience in response to his ministry. He shows genuine compassion for people. He cares for them, cleansing them of their infirmities. Yet he does not want to be known only as a worker of miracles, so he teaches those he heals to give God the glory, and faithfully to follow God's commands. But the people are thinking more about what Jesus can do for them than about what they can do for him.

Call to Worship   Psalm 30

Leader: Sing praise to the Lord, O you faithful one, and give thanks to God's holy name.

People: Hear, O Lord, and be gracious to me! O Lord, be my helper!

Leader: You have turned my mourning into dancing; you have clothed me with joy,

People: So that my soul may praise you and not be silent. O Lord, my God, I will praise you forever.

Leader: Let us worship God!

Prayer of Praise and Adoration

Eternal God, we come rejoicing with gladness of heart, singing your praises and adoring your wondrous gifts of love. You cause the darkness of night to steal away with the dawn. You bring us promise of new life in the gift of Jesus our Savior. We arise refreshed from the rest you give, and wait for your Spirit to fill us with the hope of the gospel. Come, Creator Spirit, and dwell here among us. Hear our songs of thanksgiving as we seek to worship you in thought, word, and deed.

Prayer of Confession

Unison: Merciful God, hear our confession as we pray in Christ's name. We claim to be faithful, but we obey not your commandments. We boast of our hope, yet we dwell not in faith. We gather security about us while others go hungry. We arm ourselves mightily as though we could buy peace of mind. We hear Christ's words of assurance, but we live not in his promise. Forgive our ambivalence, as in Christ we repent.

Assurance of Pardon

Leader: Our help is in God. "It is God who justifies. . . . It is Christ Jesus, who died, yes, who was raised, who is at the right hand of God, who indeed intercedes for us. Who will separate us from the love of Christ?" Know that as we confess our sin, God is just. Through Jesus Christ, who intercedes on our behalf, we have assurance that God forgives us.

Prayer of Dedication

God of all grace and goodness, throughout the ages you have looked after the needs of your children; we thank you for your mercy. Bless the words we speak, that they may proclaim your greatness. Look with favor on those acts we perform, that we may show others your tender love. Make us responsive to the high calling of Jesus, as we offer you gifts in his name.

Prayer of Thanksgiving and Supplication

God of healing and wholeness, we give thanks for the prophets, who proclaimed your power to cleanse the afflicted and restore them to health. We give you thanks for your Savior, the Christ, whose touch cured those in need. We give thanks for Paul's vision of what it means to obey you. Help us, we pray, to run the race of faith, that we may seize the goal of our calling, and obtain the prize of deliverance Christ promises to all.

We pray that you will renew our drooping spirits and give us fresh hope. Sustain our confidence during those times of trial that encroach on our sense of well-being. Keep us from submitting to temptation, and uphold us with your commandments, which show us your will. When our energy wanes, or we lack the discipline to press on with commitment, enthuse us and enliven us through the gift of your Holy Spirit.

We pray that you will restore in us a new sense of the gospel. Help us regain the excitement of when we first came to have faith. Let the teachings of the Scripture sound afresh to our listening ears, and help us recall those initial confessions we made to follow the Christ. As we remember our baptism, strengthen our resolve to live in the light of your cleansing pardon, alive to dawn of your redeeming grace.

We pray that you will remake us in the image of those prophets, apostles, and disciples who gave their lives in utmost devotion. Make of us witnesses of what it means to believe. Keep us from being satisfied with our current level of devotion, consigned to the present as though our responses were sufficient. Rather, like Paul, urge us to run the good race with unflagging zeal, aiming to please you in all that we do.

7TH SUNDAY IN ORDINARY TIME (B)

Isaiah 43:18–25; Psalm 41
2 Corinthians 1:18–22; Mark 2:1–12

Jesus forgives sins and alarms the authorities. The scribes think it blasphemy to forgive sins. The friends of the paralytic have faith that Jesus can heal him. The crowds are amazed and give God the glory. Similar scenarios will be repeated throughout the ministry of Jesus. As Jesus proclaims God's will, many will question his authority, some will have faith. In the end, God will be glorified.

Call to Worship   2 Corinthians 1:18–25

Leader: All the promises of God find their Yes in Christ.
People: That is why we utter the "Amen" through him, to the glory of God.
Leader: But it is God who establishes us with you in Christ, and has commissioned us.
People: God has put the seal of Christ upon us and given us the Spirit as a guarantee.
Leader: Let us worship God!

Prayer of Praise and Adoration

God of promise and fulfillment, hear our resounding "Amen" to your glorious deeds. You caused Christ to come to earth as our redeemer and the giver of new life. You sent forth your Holy Spirit to guide us with counsel and might. You commissioned us as your people, sealed by your covenant and empowered by your grace. We laud your manifold deeds of mercy, and say "Amen" to the glory of your holy name.

Prayer of Confession

Unison: Eternal God, have mercy upon us, for we burden you with our sins. We do not bring you our offerings; we seldom make sacrifices. Praise of your glory is not often heard; we are dedicated to seeking our own fortunes. We live not by faith but by our own resources. Forgive our reluctance to accept your promises. Forgive our human quest for security at all costs, and help us to commit our lives to you alone.

Assurance of Pardon

Leader: Hear the words of assurance as the prophet Isaiah records them: "Do not remember the former things, or consider the things of old.

161

I am about to do a new thing; now it springs forth, do you not perceive it? I will make a way in the wilderness and rivers in the desert. . . . I am the Lord who blots out your transgressions for my own sake, and I will not remember your sins." In Christ God remains faithful and forgives us our sins.

Prayer of Dedication

Eternal God of the covenant, you call us, commission us, and fill us with your Holy Spirit. We gather as Christ's people in response to your call. We seek to be faithful to your commission to make disciples of all nations. Filled with your Spirit, our hearts beat with joy as with our voices we sing you our praise. You are the God of our faith—just, true, and righteous. Accept now our offerings in response to your love.

Prayer of Thanksgiving

Merciful God, it is good to give thanks for your manifold gifts of love. For gracious acts shown in countless ways, we praise your name. We stand in line with generations that have gone before, as we consider your blessing to us. You called us as those worthy to bear the name of your chosen people. You included us within the boundless love of your covenant, and saw fit to seal our eternal future in the person of Christ. He bore our sins on the cross. We give thanks that you remove our transgressions for his sake.

We give you thanks that he intercedes on our behalf. In Christ we know that you stoop to hear the cries of the suffering; you comfort the lonely, and the needy you send not away. We are grateful that all manner of human want is within the embrace of your encompassing care for all of creation. We can dwell in peace, since you are faithful and you forget not your own.

We give you thanks that you send forth your Spirit to dwell amid the frenzied pace of our daily lives. As the paralytic was lowered through the roof to face Jesus, so we descend through the barriers of our defenses to confront your healing presence. Enabled by the indwelling gift of your redeeming forgiveness, we can confidently face whatever challenges await us.

Help us count each day an occasion to greet you with our songs of thanksgiving. Grant that we may number each hour a moment to be filled with praise of your name. We give thanks to you for your countless gifts of love.

8TH SUNDAY IN ORDINARY TIME (B)

Hosea 2:14–20; Psalm 103:1–13, 22
2 Corinthians 3:1–6; Mark 2:13–22

There is talk of a new day. Prior perceptions will no longer be adequate; old forms will not be suitable; past practices will no longer suffice. Jesus prepares his followers for what is to come. The bridegroom dwells among them and is no longer awaited. They are to be filled with the new wine of the gospel. They are to put on the cloth of righteousness and greet the new day!

Call to Worship

Psalm 103

Leader: Bless the Lord, O my soul. With all that is within me I will bless your holy name.

People: Bless the Lord, O my soul. You forgive our iniquity and heal our diseases.

Leader: The Lord is merciful and gracious, slow to anger and abounding in steadfast love.

People: So great is your love toward all those who fear you. Bless the Lord, O my soul.

Leader: Let us worship God!

Prayer of Praise and Adoration

Holy God, merciful and gracious, slow to anger, and abounding in steadfast love, we greet you with praise on our lips and thanksgiving in our hearts. You take pity upon us and shower us with your blessings, satisfying our every need and renewing our strength. You lift us above all earthly cares, and grant us a vision of your eternal salvation. We bow in reverence before you and rise to praise you. You are the God of new life.

Litany of Confession

Leader: I will remove the names of Baals from your mouths.

People: Forgive us, O God, for we worship false gods.

Leader: I will make for you a covenant with the beasts of the field, the birds of the air, and the creeping things of the ground.

People: Forgive us, O God, when we despise your creation.

Leader: I will abolish war, and make you to lie down in safety.

People: Forgive us, O God, since we do not seek peace.

Leader: I will betroth you to me in righteousness.

People: Forgive us, O God, for we love not our neighbor.

Leader: I will betroth you to me in faithfulness, and you shall know the God of Israel.

People: Forgive us our sin, O God, and grant us your pardon.

Assurance of Pardon

Leader: The Lord is merciful and gracious, slow to anger and abounding in steadfast love. The Lord does not deal with us according to our sins, nor repay us according to our iniquities. For as the heavens are high above the earth, so also does Christ sit at God's right hand and intercede on our behalf. With that assurance I can say, in Jesus Christ we are forgiven!

Prayer of Dedication

O God of new life, you restore us with the hope of the gospel; you bind up our wounds and make us whole once again. You enliven us with the gift of your Spirit and empower us to serve you in thought, word, and deed. Accept now the gifts we bring, transform their worth and enhance their effectiveness to accord with your will.

Prayer of Thanksgiving and Supplication

Ruler of all creation, in Christ Jesus you have written the new covenant indelibly upon the hearts of humankind; we give you thanks for your grace, mercy, and favor. You do not hold our sins against us, but deal with us as a loving parent who bears with rebellious and errant children. You withhold not your love, but continually shower us with blessings beyond our hopes and desires. Your patience extends beyond the farthest reaches of the horizon; your care probes the very depths of creation. You are God of the great beyond and the immediate moment, of the unknown future and the recorded past. There is nowhere we can go to escape your dominion. We give you thanks that you have seen fit to crown us with your glory and in Christ call us your own.

Renew these earthen vessels we call our bodies. Enable us to become fit receptacles for the new life in the Spirit. When cracks appear from the countless pressures upon us, keep us from being content with just mending the tear. When our energies wane because of over-commitment, or conflict saps our strength to pursue peaceful negotiations, keep us from relying upon worn-out solutions.

Make us worthy to carry the banner of your redeeming grace to all people here on earth. Invest us with the truth of Christ's reconciling love, so that we become instruments of your peace rather than weapons of hostility. Awaken within us the contagion of forgiveness, so that we can henceforth act out your justice and dwell in your mercy.

TRANSFIGURATION OF THE LORD
(SUNDAY PRECEDING LENT) (B)

2 Kings 2:1–12; Psalm 50:1–6
2 Corinthians 4:3–6; Mark 9:2–9

Jesus leads his three disciples up a high mountain and there is transfigured before them. The light of the gospel will henceforth shine on the darkness of the world. A cloud appears, and they hear a voice proclaim, "This is my beloved Son; listen to him." No longer can anything on earth or in heaven separate God's people from the love Christ came to reveal. The glory of Christ shone in order that God's will would be known.

Call to Worship   Psalm 50

Leader: The Mighty One speaks and summons the earth from the rising of the sun to its setting.

People: Keep not your silence before us, O God, but let the heavens declare your righteousness.

Leader: "Gather to me my faithful ones, all you who have made a covenant with me."

People: We offer you our sacrifices of praise and thanksgiving as we call on your name.

Leader: Let us worship God!

Prayer of Praise and Adoration

Morning by morning you awaken us, O God; day by day you show us your wondrous love. The words of your commandments fall fresh upon our listening ears; we heed your wisdom and are renewed by your word. You surround us with countless acts that tell of your majesty; we are struck by your goodness as we are refreshed in your Spirit. Come, dwell among us, and through Christ let us praise you. You are the God we worship and adore.

Prayer of Confession

Unison: God of compassion, have mercy upon us as we confess our sin. In Christ you bring light, yet we still dwell in darkness. Your Word offers guidance, but we choose to ignore your counsel. You promise renewal, but we heed not your wisdom. We bow to the gods of this world, choosing to hide from your truth. Speak to us again from beyond the clouds of our sinfulness; dazzle us anew with the light of Christ's love. Restore and forgive us.

165

Assurance of Pardon

Leader: Hear the good news. God is light, and in God there is no darkness. "If we say that we have fellowship with him while we are walking in darkness, we lie and do not do what is true; but if we walk in the light as he himself is in the light, we have fellowship with one another, and the blood of Jesus his Son cleanses us from all sin." God is faithful and just, and in Jesus Christ forgives us our sin.

Prayer of Dedication

Redeeming God, you hide not your radiance, neither hold back your word. You come to us in love, fresh as the morning. We are sustained by your mercy and renewed through your grace. You have sent us your Spirit to freshen our day. All that we are we owe to you. Accept our gifts and bless our endeavors, so that all we do may accord with your will.

Prayer of Thanksgiving and Supplication

Great Source of light, wisdom, and truth, you make all things new by the radiance of your transforming love. We give thanks for the Christ who leads us to the mountain and there sets before us your plan for creation. We give thanks that you speak from behind the clouds that surround us, sending forth hope that we may travel your path of new life. We give you thanks for your Spirit who dwells among us, encouraging us to follow your call for justice and peace.

Continue to enlighten us with your Word, that we may ever be faithful to what you would have us be and do. Dispel the shadows of doubt that hover in spite of Christ's intercession on our behalf. In the face of conflict, we shrink from standing firm in the truth. Confronted with the pain of those who suffer, we lack confidence in our ability to comfort them. Envelop us in the truth that you can do all things through those who believe in you.

Spread your wisdom abroad in a land whose leaders so often lack direction. We speak of peace while the thunder of war is heard in distant corners of the earth. You command us to love neighbors, but we are prisoners of self-interest and greed. Cries for justice fall on deaf ears. Bring order to our chaos, O God, and restore us through a vision of your care for all.

As we descend the mountain, accompany us on our journey of faithfulness. In the wilderness, help us to know that you will not forsake us. In the city's streets, direct us to the needy. Show us that wherever we go you are with us.

ASH WEDNESDAY (B) — *See Year A*

1ST SUNDAY IN LENT (B)

Genesis 9:8–17; Psalm 25:1–10
1 Peter 3:18–22; Mark 1:9–15

A trilogy of dramatic events in Mark's Gospel involves Jesus' baptism by John, his testing in the wilderness, and his preaching the gospel. Each event is significant because of what it implies for us. Those who follow Jesus will be cleansed of their past. They will be filled with the Holy Spirit, and sustained when put to the test. They will dwell in God's time, a time of new life. The message rings clearly: Repent and believe; God's reign is at hand!

Call to Worship   Psalm 25

Leader: To you, O Lord, I lift up my soul. Lead the humble and teach them your way.
People: Make me to know your ways, O Lord; teach me your paths.
Leader: For you are the God of my salvation; for you I wait all the day long.
People: Your paths are steadfast love and faithfulness for those who keep your decrees.
Leader: Let us worship God!

Prayer of Praise and Adoration

Your paths are straight and true, O God; they guide all who seek the way of salvation. By your mercy you instruct your children how to pursue steadfast love and faithfulness. Upheld by your covenant and enlightened by your testimony, we live securely in your goodness and truth. Hear us now as we lift our souls in praise to you. Accept our glad adoration, and teach us your will.

Prayer of Confession

Unison: Have mercy upon us and hear our prayer, O God. We have failed to live in the light of your covenant. You set your rainbow above us, yet clouds of unbelief darken our days. Distrust wells within us; fear, not hope, is our watchword. Your beloved bids us follow, but we are slow to obey. Without your grace, we are fruitless and inert. In mercy renew us and bring us to life, through Jesus Christ.

Assurance of Pardon

Leader: Remember that Christ died for sins once and for all, that he might bring us to God cleansed of unrighteousness. "Baptism . . . now saves you—not as removal of dirt from the body, but as an appeal to God for a good conscience, through the resurrection of Jesus Christ." Remember your baptism and live in new life, assured of forgiveness through Christ, who intercedes on our behalf.

Prayer of Dedication

God of our hope and salvation, your covenant names us, your grace sustains us. Your Chosen One calls us, and in our baptism sets us apart. We are a people called to minister, and equipped through your mercy to perform deeds of compassion and love. Accept our offerings as tokens of our faithfulness; enhance their effectiveness in accordance with your will. May all that we do be a clear sign of our willingness to respond to the call of Christ.

Prayer of Thanksgiving and Supplication

O God of the covenant, who turned the waters from a cause of death to a source of life, we praise you for our baptism received in Christ's name. We give thanks that through him you saw fit to set us apart for ministry. You gave us the rainbow as a sign of your covenant, an everlasting promise that you will never separate yourself from us. You have given your Spirit to rest upon us and dwell within us, so that we are empowered for service. Truly, in you we live, and move, and have our being. You are the Alpha and the Omega, the beginning and the end of our existence. By you alone we are sustained and upheld.

Continue to make your presence known as we face the barren times of life. Help us to see in the creation the manifold signs of your care for us. Instill within us confidence to trust in you, courage to face the powers that threaten us, and boldness to praise your name despite all difficulty. Set your covenant rainbow above us as the sign of your faithfulness, and beyond us as the beckoning light of your righteous love.

When Christ bids us come, give us strength to forsake all earthly ties and follow him. Help us to catch the vision of what you would have us do; give us signs of assurance that assist us to obey. Frustrate our efforts when we are headstrong and ignorant. Keep us faithful to our baptism and open to the leading of your Spirit, as fit recipients of your covenant. In grace sustain us as we respond.

2ND SUNDAY IN LENT (B)

Genesis 17:1–17, 15–16; Psalm 22:23–31
Romans 4:13–25; Mark 8:31–38

Peter is rebuked because he misunderstood what it meant to follow Jesus. Jesus must suffer, even be put to death. To be his disciple means sacrifice as well. Such a thought was difficult for Peter, just as it is for us today. To lose one's life for Christ's sake is to put self behind and serve others without thought of reward.

Call to Worship   Psalm 22

Leader: I will tell of your name to my brothers and sisters, and lead them in praise.

People: You did not despise the afflicted nor turn a deaf ear when they cried to you.

Leader: All the ends of the earth shall turn to you, O God; all families shall worship the Lord.

People: We will tell of your deeds to those who follow, and proclaim your deliverance to all.

Leader: Let us worship God!

Prayer of Praise and Adoration

We glory in your holy name, O God; we marvel at your wondrous works. You gathered a nation around you and called it blessed. You spared not your own Son, but sent him in the midst of a people to redeem them from sin. We gather this day to bear witness to your majesty. Our hearts rejoice in the promise of your covenant of love; our souls are cleansed by your mercy. Our bodies rise to bless your name; our voices sing your praises.

Prayer of Confession

Unison: God of compassion and mercy, look with favor upon us as we confess our sins. Our faith is weak in the face of crisis. Our hope collapses when we are threatened or maligned. We seek our own safety and abandon those you love. We trust in objects we can create and control. We speak much and risk little. But you, O God, have given your promise that you will never forsake us. Forgive our failure to take you at your word.

Assurance of Pardon

Leader: God's promises rest on grace and guaranteed to all who believe in Christ. "I will establish my covenant between me and you, and your

169

offspring after you throughout their generations." "It will be reckoned to us who believe in him who raised Jesus our Lord from the dead, who was handed over to death for our trespasses and was raised for our justification." Trust the promises of grace, and accept the righteousness of God bestowed in Christ.

Prayer of Dedication

Source of all goodness, what can we give that has not already been given to us? Surely no gift of ours can repay Christ's gift of love. Therefore we offer ourselves, with thanksgiving for new life in the Spirit, and place before you what we have in response to your love. Use us in ways that fulfill your plan for creation, and bless what we give, so that others may learn of your ways.

Prayer of Thanksgiving

Gracious God, whom we trust in childlike faith, we give you thanks for setting apart Abraham and Sarah as parents in faith. We draw courage from their example of obedience. From them we gain confidence that you will never forsake us. What to us is beyond belief, in you becomes possible, O God. We trust the promise and await your call to pilgrimage.

We thank you for Jesus, who taught what it means to be obedient unto death. In his earthly ministry, he showed the way of discipleship; we are heirs of his words and example. We give thanks that you have revealed your wisdom and continue to involve us in your reign of righteousness and truth. Christ's faith abides forever as our means of deliverance. We walk in the light of your judgment, ever thankful for the living Word.

We praise you for the Holy Spirit, who sustains us amid doubts and trials. When earthly pressures weigh upon us and we are near despair, your Spirit brings release, giving encouragement to lighten our burden. You alone are the assurance that strengthens, the light that illuminates, the truth that dispels disbelief. You are the source of all hope, O God of the covenant. We can endure if you abide with us as you have promised.

You are indeed a God for all seasons. We give you thanks that you see fit to look with favor on us in this time and place. For Christ who nourishes and the Spirit who sustains, we give you all praise and bless your name!

3RD SUNDAY IN LENT (B)

Exodus 20:1–17; Psalm 19
1 Corinthians 1:18–25; John 2:13–22

The tables are turned on the moneychangers! Jesus was angered by their disregard for the Temple. God's house was never intended to be merely a trading place. However, more than the tables get turned, for in his prophecy Jesus predicts how true worship will occur. He points to his resurrection, when believers will worship him in spirit and in the truth of new life. No longer will God's praise be confined so some building.

Call to Worship   Psalm 19

Leader: The law of the Lord is perfect, reviving the soul; the decrees of the Lord are sure, making wise the simple.

People: The precepts of the Lord are right, rejoicing the heart; the commandment of the Lord is clear, enlightening the eyes.

Leader: The fear of the Lord is pure, enduring forever; the ordinances of the Lord are true and righteous altogether.

People: Let the words of my mouth and the meditation of my heart be acceptable to you, O Lord, my rock and my redeemer.

Leader: Let us worship God!

Prayer of Praise and Adoration

O Holy One of Israel, in Christ you call us to dwell in your favor; we gather to praise you and worship your name. You are the rock that keeps us from falling, the redeemer who can save us from sin. You set us upon the sure foundation of your commandments; you cleanse us from all unrighteousness through the gift of your Son. Accept our words as we honor your judgment and be pleased with our worship as we respond to Christ's call.

Prayer of Confession

Unison: Gracious God, you set us within the temple of your grace and mercy, hear us now as we confess our sin. We still carry our business into your sanctuary. As we enter our motives are not just to worship your name. We want our needs met rather than Christ's will that calls us. We seek our own satisfaction before we can turn to your ways. As Christ got angry and overturned the tables, keep us from receiving what may be our due. Rather hear our confession and forgive us our sin.

171

Assurance of Pardon

Leader: Our assurance is this: "There is therefore now no condemnation for those who are in Christ Jesus. . . . For God has done what the law, weakened by the flesh, could not do." God sent the Savior, who redeems us of all unworthiness.

Prayer of Dedication

O God of justice and mercy, your way commands our obedience; your grace gives us encouragement. We can do nothing apart from the blessing you bestow. Alive with the presence of your indwelling Spirit, we are bold to offer what we have as signs of our devotion. Accept what we bring, and multiply its effectiveness, for the sake of Jesus, your gift to us.

Prayer of Thanksgiving and Supplication

Eternal Source of guidance and direction, what you require you also reveal, and what you ask of us you also enable. There is nothing good that we do apart from your making it possible. You are the author and the finisher of our faith. We give thanks for Christ Jesus, who fulfills on our behalf all that you could possibly want us to be. We give thanks for Scripture, which sets forth your will and way for your chosen people. We give thanks for the Holy Spirit, who encourages us in every way.

We pray that our worship may be in accordance with the spirit and truth of our new life in Christ. Hear us this day as we give thanks for countless blessings from your hand. When we awake, remind us of Christ's resurrection. As we gather for worship, hear our intercessions on behalf of others, and strengthen us to serve them in appropriate ways. Help us to draw apart for moments of quiet and rest during the day. Discipline us to recall how Christ spent time alone, refreshing himself through meditation and prayer. When evening comes and the shadows lengthen, make us mindful of your sustaining grace.

With your Spirit to guide us, and our worship rehearsing for us how you are never far from us, help us become the disciples Christ would have us be. Attune our lives to the intent of your commandments, that we may come to love you with soul, mind, and body and be enabled to love our neighbors as ourselves. We pray in the name of Jesus, who makes possible such love.

4TH SUNDAY IN LENT (B)

Numbers 21:4–9; Psalm 107:1–3, 17–22
Ephesians 2:1–10; John 3:14–21

As with God's mercy and grace, so also with God's love—it reveals God as the One who cares for creation. God's mercy gives hope to the weary. God's grace gives new life to all who believe. God's love gives light to the world. In Jesus Christ the fullness of God is made known once and for all. So hope in Christ that you may be strong; have faith and receive the gift that is eternal; live in love and let the light shine. "For God so loved the world . . ."

Call to Worship   Psalm 107

Leader: We give you thanks, O God, for you are good; your steadfast love endures forever.
People: When we cried to you with our troubles, O Lord, you saved us from our distress.
Leader: We give you thanks, O God, for your wonderful works to all of humanity.
People: Hear now our offerings of praise and thanksgiving, as we tell of your deeds with songs of joy.
Leader: Let us worship God!

Prayer of Praise and Adoration

God of infinite goodness and mercy, we cannot escape your presence. Your promise remains with us in every situation. When we are desolate, your Spirit comes to comfort us. Amid our tribulation, your Chosen One remains our firm hope. We can sing your song in whatever land we find our abode. We shall forever give thanks for the gift of your grace. You are God who never forsakes us. To you be glory and praise now and forever.

Prayer of Confession

Unison: O God, in Christ Jesus you proclaimed your love for all creation. Have mercy on us as we confess our sin. We have overpopulated the earth and violated its goodness. We have depleted nature of its vital resources. Pollution besets us, waters lie stagnant. We care not for ourselves as temples, nor for communities as building not built with hands. We plead for forgiveness and ask for your guidance. Help us to be disciplined in taking care of your gifts, lest in neglecting them we lose them forever.

Assurance of Pardon

Leader: Know that God is rich in mercy. Even though we are dead through our trespasses, God's great love for us makes us alive through Jesus the Christ. We are thus saved by God's grace. Live in the assurance that, as we confess our sin, through Christ's intercession on our behalf we are forgiven.

Prayer of Dedication

O God of boundless love, you restore our strength through faith in your goodness. You look with favor upon us and through Christ redeems us. You take not yourself from us, but promise your presence through the gift of your Spirit. You come from behind to push us, and go before us as our guide. Accept now what we bring you in response to your encompassing care of us.

Prayer of Thanksgiving and Intercession

O God of light and life, through the ages your messengers have proclaimed that your day is at hand. Creation has spoken of your care and benevolent love. You sent the Christ into the midst of humanity, so that there could be no denying your concern for our wellbeing. You are God who restores that which your people destroy. You mend brokenness and bring wholeness in the midst of fractured relations. You make wars to cease, and establish peace among all nations. We hear your word for our time, and give thanks for your unending pursuit of righteousness. Send forth your light so that all may inherit your eternal life.

Reform those who disregard how creation depends on your grace. Give them a sense of how all things ought to cohere. You have instilled in us such awesome power; grant us humility to acknowledge your gift and exercise it humanely. Make us aware of how fragile life is, that any one part cannot be abused without affecting the whole. Help us work toward a rightly ordered creation, whatever our role or status.

We pray for those whose relationships are in disarray. Keep us from premature or harmful judgments that only enhance the pain. Help us to offer reconciling suggestions when they can be helpful, and make our presence beneficial in overcoming the incipient loneliness. You have taught us what it means to love one another. You have shown how interdependent all creation ought to be. Keep us mindful of the mutual support we can offer one another, and make us willing to bear another's burden as though it were our own. Let us thereby shed some light on what it means to love others, as you so love the world.

5TH SUNDAY IN LENT (B)

Jeremiah 31:31–34; Psalm 51:1–12 or Psalm 119:9–16
Hebrews 5:5–10; John 12:20–33

The old passes away, the new emerges. The grain of wheat falls to the earth and dies. From it springs the stalk that in time produces much fruit. Death's sting is tempered by the promise of new life. Do not cling to old ways that hinder your ability to realize the hope of the gospel. Rather, let what you glean from the past lead to fresh insight, so that you may mature in faith.

Call to Worship   Psalm 51

Leader: O Lord, open my lips, and my mouth will declare your praise.

People: Purge me with hyssop, and I shall be clean; wash me, and I shall be whiter than snow.

Leader: The sacrifice acceptable to God is a broken spirit; a broken and contrite heart, O God, you will not despise.

People: Restore to me the joy of your salvation, and sustain in me a willing spirit.

Leader: Let us worship God!

Prayer of Praise and Adoration

O God, who fashioned the covenant and sealed it with the promise of life everlasting, we praise you for mercies that are boundless and sure. Your ways are just, your grace is unending. You have sent us the Christ in whom lies your promise that all things will be made new. We come before your throne of grace with the assurance that you will meet us as we call on your name. Hear us now as we give our oblations and be pleased with our efforts, as we respond to Christ's call.

Prayer of Confession

Unison: O God of forgiveness, we pray for new life as we confess our old ways. We hear of your promise amid our own sense of self-doubt. Hope is proclaimed, yet we seek guarantees. Christ calls us to obedience, but we set conditions. When called on to follow, we ask to what end. We applaud commitment, but we treasure our comfort. Forgive our reluctance to walk in newness of life.

Assurance of Pardon

Leader: Although he was as we are, Jesus "learned obedience through what he suffered; and being made perfect he became the source of eternal salvation to all who obey him." Today, as we come before God confessing our sins, Jesus the high priest is our source of forgiveness. Trust in the word of Christ and be forgiven.

Prayer of Dedication

Most giving and forgiving God, you provide for our every need. You open our lips to offer you praise. You strengthen our hands to respond to Christ's call. With hearts, hands, and voices renewed by your Spirit, we place now before you our commitment to serve. Use us in ways that will benefit others, and accept what we offer as a sign of our faith.

Prayer of Praise and Supplication

Great God of the universe, you open our lips to give you praise. We thank you for the psalmist of old who sings of deliverance. The words lift our spirits as we hear of your faithfulness. We praise you for the prophets who foresaw your promise. They teach us to obey you with total allegiance. We praise you for Christ Jesus, our source of salvation. Through him we are able to approach you in prayer. We praise you for the Holy Spirit, who gives a glimpse of your glory. We receive counsel and guidance to go forth and serve.

Deliver us from all that prevents us from singing your song: from bitterness toward others who hurt or take advantage of us, from fear and insecurity when the future confronts us with a sense of the unknown, from thinking of ourselves so highly that we fail to notice those who need us, from failure to speak out on behalf of those whom society no longer heeds, and from despair when our acts amount to very little when the needs are so great.

As Jeremiah proclaimed allegiance written on the hearts of humanity, let us be diligent in discerning the hope of your salvation. Turn bitterness into understanding, and make us willing to care about even those who would hurt us. Replace our fear with the assurance that you know of our needs. Help us to find comfort in Jesus, who endured the cross for us. Give us humble hearts, so that we hear the cries of our neighbors, and give us soothing voices to speak comforting words to them.

We seek to please you, O God of all glory. What we offer, you have implanted within us. What springs forth from our efforts, you have nourished and allowed to blossom. All praise be unto you for that Seed of salvation, Christ Jesus, who puts the song of new life on our lips.

PASSION/PALM SUNDAY (B)

Palm: Mark 11:1–11 or John 12:12–16; Psalm 118:1–2, 19–29
Passion: Isaiah 50:4–9a; Psalm 31:9–16; Philippians 2:5–11; Mark 14:1–15:47 or Mark 15:1–39 (40–47)

Jesus prepares to enter Jerusalem. He will enter majestically, hearing cries of "Hosanna in the highest!" His sights are set on what he must do; his intentions are faithful to God, who sustains him. Soon the crowds will disperse, to be replaced by tormentors. Adulation will cease, and he will be faced with betrayal. Humiliation and obedience lead to death so that life may abound to God's glory.

Call to Worship
Psalm 118

Leader: This is the day that the Lord has made; let us rejoice and be glad in it.
People: I thank you that you have answered me and have become my salvation.
Leader: Blessed is the one who comes in the name of the Lord.
People: We bless you from the house of the Lord.
Leader: Let us worship God!

Prayer of Praise and Adoration

We praise you, O God, for your faithfulness through the ages. You are with us as we greet the dawn of a new day. Your word guides us as we seek to be obedient. You comfort us during times of distress, and judge us according to your righteousness. As you sent Jesus to fulfill your promise, you fill us with your Spirit that we may know of your will. As we enter the gates of your sacred space, hear now our voices as we sing you our praise.

Prayer of Confession

Unison: Eternal God of mercy, hear us as we confess our sin. Daily we awaken to the new life you give us, yet we fail to be thankful for the rest we have received. Moments await our decision to serve you, yet time passes away as we think only of ourselves. Our routine affords us the chance to minister to others, yet we are absorbed with our own self-improvement. The day is soon passed; it has been much the same as the others. Forgive us for casting aside the precious time you give us each day.

Assurance of Pardon

Leader: Hear these words of assurance: Even though Jesus was in the form of God, he "did not regard equality with God as something to be

177

exploited." Rather, "he humbled himself and became obedient to the point of death—even death on a cross." He died for us, so that we might have life and approach God's throne of judgment cleansed of our sin. In Christ we are forgiven!

Prayer of Dedication

O God of wisdom, you open our eyes to behold the wonder of your mighty acts. You free our tongues to proclaim as good news Christ's suffering for us all. We sing, "Hosanna in the highest!" Christ has entered our lives. Accept now these offerings as our garlands of welcome, and hear our shouts of praise as we seek to follow him.

Prayer of Thanksgiving and Supplication

O God of the prophets and the psalmist, of Mark and of Paul, we thank you for their testimony to your abiding presence. Through times of trial you accompany your people. For those who seek wisdom, you enlighten the mind. You loosen the tongue of the one who stammers, and open the eyes of those whose vision is dimmed. Amid the clamor of noisy parades, you are in the excitement and laughter. When the gathering disperses and your people are lonely, your voice quiets their fears.

Be with us now when we face our trials. Let them not be so overpowering that we succumb to their force. Give us the strength to withstand the pressure, and courage to face boldly those times when our faith is tested. Confronted by those seeking our counsel, we implore your Word to illumine our guidance. Help us to offer appropriate options, and to assist our brothers and sisters to choose wisely as they make decisions.

Let us not be reserved in proclaiming Christ's gospel. Keep us free from the fear of embarrassing ourselves. Give us the joy that makes constraint inappropriate, the assurance of new life that makes us willing to take risks. Set us in the midst of those who are seeking salvation. Help us to stand with them long enough to trust us, so together we can learn how Christ sets people free.

Give us patience to sit with the lonely, those for whom crowds pose an unpleasant threat. If they seek comfort, open our arms to embrace them. If they need assurance, free our tongues from stammering, so we can offer them words of confidence. If their sense of well-being is plagued by unseen foes or forces, let our words of witness rehearse how Christ disarms the demons. Through times of trial, you do indeed accompany your people. We sense your Spirit moving among us as we go forth to serve others in Christ's name.

MAUNDY THURSDAY (B) — *See Year A*

GOOD FRIDAY (B) — *See Year A*

RESURRECTION OF THE LORD/ EASTER (B)

Acts 10:34–43 or Isaiah 25:6–9; Psalm 118:1–2, 14–24
1 Corinthians 15:1–11 or Acts 10:34–43
John 20:1–18 or Mark 16:1–8

The women bring spices to anoint the body of their slain leader. Instead, they are told, "He has risen," and gone on to Galilee as foretold. God has rolled back the stone, the covering cast over all peoples, the veil spread over all nations. Death is swallowed up forever. Henceforth there shall be gladness and rejoicing. Christ reigns eternally, so that all may have life.

Call to Worship   Psalm 118

Leader: Christ is risen!
People: Christ is risen indeed!
Leader: This is the day that the Lord has made.
People: Let us rejoice and be glad in it.

Prayer of Praise and Adoration

O God who was, is, and evermore shall be; to you belong all praise and glory. Angels in heaven announce the dawn of your eternal order; trumpets herald Christ's victory as the stone is rolled away; our mouths are opened to proclaim your mercies. We lift up our hearts to you, our Judge and Redeemer.

Litany of Affirmation

Leader: Truly I perceive that God shows no partiality, but in every nation any one who fears the Lord and does what is right is acceptable.
People: By the grace of God I am what I am.
Leader: God raised Jesus on the third day and made him manifest to those God chose, who ate and drank with him after he rose from the dead.
People: By the grace of God I am what I am.
Leader: God commanded us to preach to the people, and to testify that Christ is the one ordained by the Lord to be judge of the living and the dead.

People:	By the grace of God I am what I am.
Leader:	To him all the prophets bear witness that everyone who believes in him receives forgiveness of sins through his name.
People:	By the grace of God I am what I am, and his grace toward me was not in vain.

Prayer of Dedication

O God, Giver of life, who sends the dawn and fills us with hope, we come now before you, bringing our gifts. We cannot repay you for your undying mercy; our gestures are feeble compared to your love. As we commit our days to proclaiming Christ's gospel, accept these offerings as a pledge of our faith. Today is the first day of the rest of our lives.

Prayer of Thanksgiving

Most merciful God, we come before you with all praise and honor, giving thanks for your faithfulness in raising Christ Jesus from the dead. You have set our feet upon the sacred ground of your holy mountain and flung wide the doors of your holy temple. The curtain is rent and we behold your glory, the glory of your only begotten Son, who now intercedes for us.

We give you thanks that, because he lived, died, and rose again, we have gained a vision of your eternal order. Because he stooped to minister to the least of your people, we too have hope that can lift our spirits out of despair. Since he taught us how to love our neighbor, dividing walls of hostility may no longer keep us apart. When the angels proclaimed his coming to bring peace among nations, we gained a glimpse of your promise that swords shall be beaten into plowshares.

We give you thanks that through Christ your law is written indelibly within us. No longer can we claim that you hide yourself from us. As we seek to serve others, your Holy Spirit is with us. When we face troubled times, you are the source of our comfort and strength. Christ calls us and teaches us what it means to follow your will for us; in our search for maturity, your wisdom prevails.

We give you thanks that all our days can now be lived with assurance, with confidence that in Christ we may dwell in your favor. Remove all hesitation as we step out to greet the dawn of your endless Easter. Fill us with hope as we behold Christ's resurrection. Let us view from your mountain how deserts spring forth with blossoms, how valleys are uplifted and high places made low. We enter your temple to dine with our risen Savior, to break the bread that sustains us and to drink the cup of new life.

2ND SUNDAY OF EASTER (B)

Acts 4:32–35; Psalm 133
1 John 1:1–2:2; John 20:19–31

Jesus appears and offers peace to the disciples. He shows them his hands and his side, sends them forth into the world, and gives them the gift of the Holy Spirit. With God's grace to guide them they witness to Christ's resurrection, sharing their gifts with those who are in need. The truth of God's love has brought light to the world. Let all who have seen that light strive to live in it, so that Christ's promise of peace may dispel the darkness of need.

Call to Worship

Psalm 133

Leader: Behold, how good it is when brothers and sisters live together in unity!
People: It is like the precious oil on the head, running down over the collar of Aaron's robes.
Leader: It is like the dew of Hermon, which falls on the mountains of Zion.
People: For there the Lord ordained God's blessing, life forevermore.
Leader: Let us worship God!

Prayer of Praise and Adoration

Infinite wisdom, you bring the dawn of each new day. We praise your name for sending Christ with the promise of new life. You scatter the clouds of darkness so that our eyes can behold the truth of your love. You replace the finality of death with an affirmation of life without ending. You burst upon our being with each ray of sunlight, bringing light to illumine our world with the presence of your redeeming grace. As we stand on the threshold of your magnificence be pleased with our worship as we utter your name.

Litany of Affirmation and Assurance

Leader: That which was from the beginning, which we have heard and seen with our eyes concerning the word of life, we proclaim to you.
People: God of light, in whom is no darkness, we praise you.
Leader: The life was made manifest, and we testify to it.
People: God of light, in whom is no darkness, we praise you.

Leader:	If we say we have fellowship with God while we walk in darkness, we lie and do not live according to the truth.
People:	God of light, in whom is no darkness, we praise you.
Leader:	If we confess our sins, Jesus Christ is faithful and just, and will forgive our sins and cleanse us from all unrighteousness.
People:	Jesus Christ is the expiation for our sins, and not for ours only but also for the sins of the whole world.

Prayer of Dedication

Source of life, who raised Christ from the dead, all that we have reflects your eternal love. As those in the infant church in Jerusalem brought gifts for those in need, so we too bring offerings as a sign of our commitment and concern. Accept them as our testimony to Christ's resurrection, and cause them to be distributed so that others may live.

Prayer of Thanksgiving and Supplication

Loving God, you dry the tears of those who weep and bring hope and comfort to all who mourn. We give you thanks for the peace of Christ and the signs of his sovereignty over life. We cannot hide from your presence, O Holy One; you know all of our needs. We are an open book to the One who created us. You have sent Jesus to be our intercessor and redeemer. We give you thanks that through him we can approach you with trust and confidence.

We give thanks for your providence and care for creation. You reign supreme in spite of suspicion, destruction, and greed. Implant within us the peace that Christ bestowed upon his frightened disciples. Send us forth in the Spirit, with wisdom to resolve differences, grace to pray for those who hate us, and vision to strive for harmony in the midst of discord and strife.

We give thanks for the forgiveness offered freely to all through Christ's resurrection from the dead. From now on we can live confident of your grace. Help us to awaken to the assurance of Easter, and to be more attuned to the mercy you bestow. Deliver us from bondage to limits both real and imagined, from principalities and powers that seek to crush us. Let the light of Christ dispel the shadows, making bright the pathway you would have us walk. You are the source of our sanctuary, the haven to whom we turn in times of distress. You are the judge of our decisions and actions. We give you thanks for your abiding forbearance as promised in Christ.

3RD SUNDAY OF EASTER (B)

Acts 3:12–19; Psalm 4
1 John 3:1–7; Luke 24:36b–48

Jesus proclaims the fulfillment of God's covenant, and the disciples are helped to understand the words of Scripture. The lame walk, sins are forgiven, the hungry are fed, the promise of wholeness abides in Christ's purifying atonement. Henceforth, those who believe will be clothed with power to perform acts of compassion and mercy, ministering to other in the name of Christ, who died that all may live!

Call to Worship   Psalm 4

Leader: O God, be gracious to me and hear my prayer.
People: Know that God has set us apart and hears us when we call.
Leader: O God, lift up the light of your countenance upon us.
People: O God, be gracious to us and hear our prayer.
Leader: Let us worship God!

Prayer of Praise and Adoration

Author of life, you have given us breath to praise you, eyes to behold your mercy, and words to proclaim your abiding love. You have set apart a people to worship you in thought, word, and deed, and through Christ you have numbered us in the midst of them. We sleep with the assurance that you will never forsake us and we awaken each day to the glory of your creating goodness. Breathe upon us the promised Holy Spirit, that our minds may be opened to your wisdom and our tongues boldly declare that you alone are God.

Litany of Affirmation

Leader: See what love God has given us that we should be called God's children.
People: What God foretold by the mouths of the prophets, God fulfilled.
Leader: It does not yet appear what we shall be, but we know that when God appears we shall be in God's likeness.
People: What God foretold by the mouths of the prophets, God fulfilled.
Leader: Every one who thus hopes in God is made pure, as God is pure.
People: What God foretold by the mouths of the prophets, God fulfilled.

Leader:	Whoever does right is righteous, as God is righteous.
People:	What God foretold by the mouths of the prophets, God fulfilled.

Prayer of Dedication

Giver of eternal gladness, Fountain of life from whom flow endless blessings, all that we have is a gift of your love. Accept now these offerings of thanksgiving, symbols of our grateful response to Christ's sacrifice for us. Use our gifts to spread the good news of repentance and forgiveness of sins. May they bring times of refreshment as results of Christ's presence.

Prayer of Thanksgiving and Supplication

O God of Abraham and Sarah, our ancestors in faith, by your grace we have been made, with them, a part of your family. You call us your children, and so we are. You watch over our coming and going; you nurture our growth with sustaining wisdom. You send your Spirit as a guide for our wanderings, and give the promise of Christ's redeeming love to rescue us from waywardness.

We thank you for the innocence of children, and their trusting natures. Teach us that same love and trust as we look to you for aid. Their dependence leaves them vulnerable to those in whose care they are placed; may they remind us of the obedience of Christ to the One who sent him into the world. Help our children to teach us what it means to be dependent on another, and give us some measure of their humility as we seek to be faithful.

We thank you for curiosity that leads to learning, for the willingness to move beyond what is already known. Use the spirit of inquiry to prod us out of complacency, and make us impatient to know more of your truth. By the gift of your Spirit, give us an insatiable longing to see your will accomplished. Guide us to the scriptures in search of wisdom, and give us the discipline to pursue the quest.

We thank you for trials that test our allegiance, and the brokenness within that is the prelude to new growth. When we shy away from suffering, confront us with the courage of Jesus, who endured on our behalf. When we avoid sacrifice, chasten us with your judgment and fill us anew with zeal for your righteousness. You have called us your children and made us members of your household. Help us to grow as faithful brothers and sisters in response to your trust.

4TH SUNDAY OF EASTER (B)

Acts 4:5–12; Psalm 23
1 John 3:16–24; John 10:11–18

The stone rejected by the builders has become the head of the corner. God in Jesus Christ has established the household of believers, who will henceforth be known as the church. As a shepherd cares for the sheep, so also will Christ watch over his followers. As they enter the household, they will be fed, protected, cared for, and led to ventures in faith. A solid foundation and benevolent care are the marks of God's sacrificial love.

Call to Worship   Psalm 23

Leader: The Lord is my shepherd; I shall not be in want.
People: You spread a table before me in the presence of my enemies.
Leader: You anoint my head with oil, my cup is running over.
People: Surely your goodness and mercy shall follow me all the days of my life.
Unison: And we shall dwell in the house of the Lord forever.

Prayer of Praise and Adoration

All praise be unto you, O God, Great Shepherd of the sheep. You gather your people as lambs to your bosom; you enfold them with your all-embracing love. You refresh us like a stream flowing freely with living waters; you nourish us like a host whose table is heavy laden. We gather to hear your refreshing word of promise and direction, to honor your name as our guardian and hope.

Litany of Affirmation

Leader: Little children, let us love not just in word or speech but in deed and in truth.
People: All who keep God's commandments abide in God, and God abides in them.
Leader: by this we shall know that we are of the truth, for God knows everything.
People: All who keep God's commandments abide in God, and God abides in them.
Leader: Beloved, if our hearts do not condemn us, we have confidence before God.
People: All who keep God's commandments abide in God, and God abides in them.

Leader:	This is what God commands: believe in the name of Christ Jesus and love one another.
People:	And by this we know that God abides in us, by the Spirit which God has given us.

Prayer of Dedication

Source of healing, Bringer of wholeness, you enter the world and cause the light to shine, the lame to walk, the sins of all to be forgiven. Whatever we bring you is a gift of your graciousness. All that we offer, you have poured out upon us. Use us and mold us to conform to your will for all people. Take our talents and apply them to spread the truth of your love.

Prayer of Thanksgiving and Supplication

God of the universe and all that dwells therein, great is your name. You are worthy of all our praise. You sent Jesus of Nazareth to redeem us from sin. You raised him from the dead, and seated him at your right hand. He knows our inmost thoughts, our fears and rejoicing. He walked this earth as we do, yet without straying from the course you designed. As a shepherd, he watches over us even at this moment.

We pray for all those who wander this day in the wilderness of broken covenants and confused goals. Give them an awareness of your presence amid their faltering steps, and a sense of direction that will lead them to safety. Keep us from judging them as somehow weak or inferior because they appear aimless or lost. Help us to lend them our understanding as they seek to find their way. Remind us of our own wanderings and our constant need for guidance from you.

We pray for all those entrapped by whatever snare restrains them. Loose them and make them free, as Christ was free, to do your will. You sent your Word, Jesus Christ, to show what humanity was intended to be; send now your Spirit to form in us that new creation.

Our Savior promised to search for the stray, give guidance to the aimless, and direct the course of those who are lost. We pray for the Shepherd's encompassing care as we in Christ's name commit ourselves to do likewise.

5TH SUNDAY OF EASTER (B)

Acts 8:26–40; Psalm 22:25–31
1 John 4:7–21; John 15:1–8

To bear fruit is both a gift and a responsibility. Nourishment flows through
the vine, bringing gifts of beauty as leaves and buds appear. Cultivation
and care coax the fruit to maturity in time for the harvest. There is both
promise and judgment as Christ calls his disciples to go and bear fruit.
With the promise of God's sustenance, believers will be judged by the
gifts of love they produce.

Call to Worship   Psalm 22

Leader: From you, O God, comes my praise in the great congregation.

People: My vows I will pay before those who fear the Lord.

Leader: All the ends of the earth shall remember and turn to the
Lord.

People: And all the families of the nations shall worship you, O God,
our Lord and our Redeemer.

Leader: Let us worship God!

Prayer of Praise and Adoration

Ruler of nations, you have dominion over all the earth. We praise your
name and bow down before you. You bring pride to the humble, and cause
the boastful to be brought low. The afflicted find hope through your
mercy; the comfortable you challenge and chasten. As your wisdom led
our fathers and mothers throughout the ages, make us receptive to the testimony of your love, for we pray in the name of Christ Jesus, the Word
made flesh.

Litany of Affirmation

Leader: Beloved, let us love one another; for love is of God, and
whoever loves is born of God and knows God.

People: If we love one another, God abides in us.

Leader: In this the love of God was made manifest among us, that
God sent Jesus Christ into the world.

People: If we love one another, God abides in us.

Leader: In this is love, not that we loved God but that God loved us
and sent Jesus to be the expiation for our sins.

People: If we love one another, God abides in us.

187

| Leader: | Beloved, if God so loved us, we also ought to love one another. |
| People: | If we love one another, God abides in us and God's love is perfected in us. |

Prayer of Dedication

Your love, O God, is perfected in us through the gift of your chosen one, Christ Jesus. All that we have reflects a measure of his atoning sacrifice poured out on behalf of us all. Accept what we give to you as we respond to Christ's loving-kindness, and enhance what we do, so that others may experience your tenderness. Cultivate us to bear more fruit to the glory of your name.

Prayer of Thanksgiving and Supplication

Eternal God, we thank you for Jesus, who brought hope to the distressed, promise to the despairing, and healing to the afflicted. In him there is the gift of life eternal to all who believe. We thank you for your Holy Spirit, who calls us to labor. As Christ is the vine, you name us the branches and send us forth to bear much fruit.

Let love lead us to be more forgiving, and add to love the discipline to be a reconciling force in the world. When enemies taunt us, assure us of your presence as we seek patience and inner strength. Amid tensions caused by misunderstanding, suspicion, or lack of trust, send your Spirit of insight and hope. Help us make the first move toward those we have offended, forsaking our pride in seeking peace.

Let love lead us to be more daring. Give us the boldness to speak out on behalf of the voiceless. Let us not be afraid to venture into dark places, or into situations in which we are not in control. Fill us with the confidence that you will not desert us, the assurance that what we do is in accord with your will. Keep us from becoming frustrated by the many faces of evil, and set our sights on those injustices that we can overcome.

Let love lead us to be more trusting. Give us the faith to make Christ supreme in our lives. Help us translate our words of confession into acts of compassion, our desire to be faithful into deeds of obedience. Your love does indeed work wonders. Work now in us, so that others may behold your love.

6TH SUNDAY OF EASTER (B)

Acts 10:44–48; Psalm 98
1 John 5:1–6; John 15:9–17

Filled with joy, Jesus' disciples are no longer called servants but friends. Jesus has laid down his life for his followers, so that their life may be complete in his love. As friends of Jesus, they are to go and do as he commands, baptizing others in the name of Jesus Christ and performing acts of love.

Call to Worship   Psalm 98

Leader: Make a joyful noise to the Lord, all the earth; break forth into joyous song and sing praises.

People: We will sing praises to the Lord with the lyre and the sound of the horn.

Leader: Let the sea roar, and all that fills it; the world and those who live in it.

People: We will sing you a new song, O God, for the marvelous things you have done.

Leader: Let us worship God!

Prayer of Praise and Adoration

O God of power and majesty, as the sea roars, your name is praised. Waves pounding the shore remind us of your grandeur. By your creative design birds fly, fish swim, and creatures in the forests and meadows leap and run. All creation chants in praise of your plan for them. As you make our joy complete in the gift of your Son, Christ Jesus our Savior, we worship you with hearts, hands, and voices in songs of glad adoration.

Litany of Affirmation

Leader: Every one who believes that Jesus is the Christ is a child of God, and every one who loves the parent loves the child.

People: For this is the love of God, that we keep God's commandments.

Leader: By this we know that we love the children of God, when we love the Lord and obey God's commandments.

People: For this is the love of God, that we keep God's commandments.

Leader: For whatever is born of God overcomes the world; and this is the victory that overcomes the world, our faith.

People: For this is the love of God, that we keep God's commandments.

Leader: Who overcomes the world? Those who believe that Jesus is
the Christ.

People: For this is the love of God, that we keep God's commandments. And God's commandments are not burdensome.

Prayer of Dedication

O God, as the Holy Spirit fell on all who heard your word, so fill us as
we come before you in response to Christ's gift of love. By your Spirit,
enable us to bear fruit and overcome the world with our faith. Accept our
gifts as the first signs of a bountiful harvest, and our commitment to labor
on behalf of all your children. Through our work, may they be led to
believe in your word.

Prayer of Thanksgiving and Intercession

O God of righteousness and equity, you speak and the earth responds
with sounds of thanksgiving; you act and the nations attest to your victory.
We thank you for your word that teaches us to trust in you. We thank you
for your actions and the promises you fulfill: for Christ Jesus, whose sacrifice restores us to goodness because of your mercy; for the Holy Spirit,
whose guidance enables us to seek justice, to love kindness, and to walk
humbly with you.

We pray for those who wonder when justice will come to them. They
cry out for equity, but their pleas go unheard. As you brought vindication
to the Israelites when the hosts rose up against them, bring a sense of your
justice to those who are wronged and misused. Give us compassion to
stand with them, courage to speak on their behalf, and commitment to work
for change in those systems that work against them.

We give thanks for all those who show kindness without thought of
their own gain. They are the saints of Christ's household who glide grace-
fully from chore to chore. Bestow upon them a measure of strength to
match their diligence; reward them with a sense of accomplishment equal
to their level of patience. Forbid, O God, that we should ever take them
for granted.

We pray for all brothers and sisters who seek to walk humbly with you.
Help us to support one another in the quest to live simply; guide us to note
afresh the many blessings you give us. In all that we do together, hear our
shouts of thanksgiving!

7TH SUNDAY OF EASTER (B)

Acts 1:15–17, 21–26; Psalm 1
1 John 5:9–13; John 17:6–19

Jesus prays for his followers, that they may be kept safe. They are sent into the world armed with God's Word and sanctified in the truth. For their sake Christ consecrates himself. The world may hate them, but there is no escape from involvement within it. Henceforth Christ's followers will go into all nations, proclaiming the truth of God's love and radiating the joy of new life. They are given the assurance of God's protection as Christ intercedes on their behalf.

Call to Worship   Psalm 1

Leader: Happy are those who take delight in the law of the Lord.
People: They are like trees planted by streams of water. In all that they do they prosper.
Leader: For the Lord watches over the way of the righteous.
People: May God number us with the righteous as we worship the Lord.
Leader: Let us worship God!

Prayer of Praise and Adoration

To meditate upon your law, O God, is to learn of your love and know of your righteousness. You are a God of tender mercy, whose benevolent care protects our children and all creation. We gather to worship you, as creatures of righteousness, made whole by the redeeming love of Jesus the Christ. Open our hearts to sing of your goodness, our minds to explore your wisdom, and our lips to give you all praise.

Litany of Affirmation

Leader: The testimony of God is greater than human testimony. God's testimony has borne witness to Jesus, the Christ.
People: Whoever receives the Word of God has life.
Leader: Whoever believes in the One whom God sent has God's testimony.
People: Whoever receives the Word of God has life.
Leader: The testimony is this: God gave us eternal life, and this life is in Jesus Christ, God's Anointed One.
People: Whoever receives the Word of God has life.

Leader: I proclaim this to you who confess the name of Jesus Christ, that you may know that you have eternal life.

People: Whoever receives the Word of God has life.

Prayer of Dedication

Armed with the truth of your love, O Shield and Defender, you send us into the world to radiate the joy of new life. Accept our efforts, and make them productive in fulfilling your will. Enhance our gifts with the empowerment of your Holy Spirit. In all that we do, challenge us to be obedient to the call of Jesus Christ, to walk in faithfulness, and to respond to the tasks you assign us.

Prayer of Thanksgiving and Supplication

God of wisdom, power, and majesty, who are we that you should look with favor upon us? Yet you have written your law upon our hearts, that we may know of your righteousness. You have sent the prophets; they teach us obedience. Your Spirit guides us. We have assurance that you will never forsake us. Christ Jesus reveals all that we know of you. We give you thanks for his redeeming love in spite of our wayward behavior. We claim the benefits of his sacrifice on our behalf.

Help us to be still, so that we can hear you speak. Amid the babble of human speech, give us ears to listen to your voice. As demands are made and pressure mounts, put us at ease and sustain us by your presence. As we meditate on the love of Jesus, may the hope he gives be a haven of rest and renewal.

Help us to find the discipline to be more faithful. Time passes quickly, and our tasks are undone. Translate our desires into commitment; keep us from putting off decisions that demand energy and effort. Send your Holy Spirit to guide us when the way seems unsure, and instill within us that measure of confidence that will enable us to act.

Enlighten us with your wisdom. Awaken us to the abiding testimony of your covenant; illumine the dark places of our nagging doubts. By your power, make us bolder and better disciples. Give us the courage to forsake the easy life and risk personal security so that others may learn of your love. In your majesty keep us ever conscious of our dependence on you, and ready to give you praise.

DAY OF PENTECOST (B)

Acts 2:1–21 or Ezekiel 37:1–14; Psalm 104:24–34, 35b
Romans 8:22–27 or Acts 2:1–21; John 15:26–27; 16:4b–15

The gift of the Holy Spirit brings guidance to humanity, glory to Christ, and clarity of God's righteousness to the believer. Henceforth God's people shall be led to behold the extent of God's truth. Christ's name is to be praised in all that they do. He intercedes on behalf of their weaknesses, and promises to uphold them when judgment occurs. With the gift of empowerment, all things are now possible, so long as they occur in God's name.

Call to Worship Psalm 104

Leader: O Lord, how manifold are your works! The earth is full of your creatures.

People: I will sing to the Lord as long as I live; I will sing praise to my God while I have being.

Leader: May my meditation be pleasing to you, O God, for I rejoice in the Lord.

People: Bless the Lord, O my soul. Praise the Lord!

People: Let us worship God!

Prayer of Praise and Adoration

Give thanks to God, O my soul, and all that is within me praise God's holy name. We come, O God, to give you honor and glory. We gather to bless you for your countless gifts. Alive with your Spirit and made whole by Christ's love, we praise your name. The heavens portray the extent of your wisdom; the earth is full of your handiwork. We join in creation's song, lauding your name with the glad praises we bring.

Prayer of Confession

Unison: O God, like bones in the desert our faith is dried up and lifeless. The winds of false doctrine sear our spirit; the heat of conflict saps our strength. We seek an oasis to escape your judgment; we wander aimlessly in search of direction. Have mercy upon us, and fill us anew with your Spirit. Give us counsel and guidance, and forgive us our waywardness.

Assurance of Pardon

Leader: The prophet Joel declares that in the last days God's Spirit will be poured out upon all flesh. "All it shall be that whoever calls on God shall be saved." Know that as you call on God's name, Christ intercedes on your behalf to deliver you in his righteousness, blameless before God.

Prayer of Dedication

O God of deliverance, with a right spirit within us we pour out our gifts in your presence. Take us and use us as you see fit. Where speaking can bring a sense of your righteousness, we offer our voices to proclaim your will. Where our efforts can free others from bondage, we offer our strength to help in time of need. We bring ourselves to be used for Christ's sake. Show us the way, and we will respond.

Prayer of Thanksgiving and Supplication

Almighty God, you speak and the heavens tremble. You move and the leaves of the trees shiver with delight. The babble of waters on their course to the sea attests to your wisdom and plan for creation. A child does not cry without your hearing it; as a parent you brood over young ones and watch their coming and going. No one and no thing can evade your watchful presence. We give you thanks that you see fit even to dwell in our midst.

We are amazed by your love for us, and moved that you should send your Son to atone for our sins. We give you thanks that he walked this earthly life, suffered as we do yet remained steadfastly obedient. Give us a measure of his faithfulness. Lend us the necessary commitment to be his disciples. Grant that our decisions and actions may be in accord with his will for us. Frustrate us when our involvement departs from his path.

We are in awe of the wisdom you continually give us, how you fill us with the Holy Spirit, who offers counsel and guidance. You share our concerns, accompany us amid the routines of the day, and comfort us during times of great anxiety. When our spirits radiate joy, you rejoice with us. Make us grateful to hear your word of discipline, and ready always to return you thanks. Help us to be mindful of your presence with us, and to reflect your indwelling Spirit in all that we do.

Guide now our movements and course of our actions. May we care for others as you care for us. Bring life to our spirits and a sense of joy to our living. Let our days be full of witness to your overwhelming goodness in Christ.

TRINITY SUNDAY (B)

Isaiah 6:1–8; Psalm 29
Romans 8:12–17; John 3:1–17

Jesus teaches what it means to be born of the Spirit. It means being baptized as a sign of God's grace; it means life unlimited by the frailties of the flesh; it means that those believing in Christ are no longer condemned. Salvation comes as a gift of God's love. Nicodemus asks Jesus for clarity; what he gets is much more. Jesus invites him to believe that life in the Spirit is eternal life.

Call to Worship
Psalm 29

Leader: Ascribe to the Lord, O heavenly beings, ascribe to the Lord glory and strength.

People: Your name is above every name, O God, we will worship you in the splendor of holiness.

Leader: The voice of the Lord is powerful; the voice of the Lord is full of majesty.

People: May the Lord give strength to your people, O God, may the Lord bless your people with peace.

Leader: Let us worship God!

Prayer of Praise and Adoration

Holy, holy, holy God, all the earth is full of your majesty. The lightning flash is a sign of your creative voice. Thunder resounds with the magnitude of your power and strength. The rains fall as a reminder of your gentle refreshment. The sun shines in testimony to the warmth of your love. All creation is your temple; none can hide from you. Exposed to your grandeur and led by your Spirit, we give you all praise and honor, God of our lives.

Prayer of Confession

Unison: Source of redeeming grace and infinite goodness, bear us as in Christ we pray for forgiveness. While you reach out to us in fellowship, we turn from you in shame. We do not do what you command. We proclaim not your love, since we seldom serve others. We confess Christ as Savior, yet obey him indifferently, if at all. Our discipleship suffers, for we heed not your guidance. We are in need of repentance as we confess our sins. Have mercy upon us, and grant us your pardon.

Assurance of Pardon

Leader: After Isaiah had confessed his uncleanness, a seraph flew to him, carrying a burning coal from the altar. The seraph touched Isaiah and said, "Now that this has touched your lips, your guilt has departed and your sin is blotted out." The sacrifice of Christ at the altar of God's eternal grace has touched our lives, and we too can rest in the assurance of God's pardon.

Prayer of Dedication

You beckon us to follow you, O Christ, and to proclaim our salvation to all people everywhere. We are like Isaiah, hearing God's voice and responding, "Here am I! Send me." We offer ourselves at the threshold of your sanctuary, to be sent forth in ministry, as the Holy Spirit will guide us.

Prayer of Thanksgiving

O God of revelation, who chose not to remain apart from your people but sent Jesus into the world to enlighten us, we give thanks that in Christ we can know you, and through him find favor as we worship you in thought, word, and deed. By Christ we are taught what it means to obey you: He remained faithful in spite of persecution at the hands of his enemies; he sacrificed his own life, so that those who believe in him might inherit your promise of life everlasting. Give us such courage and conviction, so that in his name we can act with compassion.

In Scripture the witness of those who have sought to be faithful leads us. We give you thanks for their testimony to the truth of your presence. You spoke through the scribes as they recorded the commandments. You filled the poets with inspiration as they penned their songs of praise and thanksgiving. You gave the prophets dreams of eternal salvation and visions of your awesome judgment as they called the chosen people to account for their actions. We stand in succession with men and women of all generations: prophets, priests, disciples and teachers, parents and guardians, who testify to your truth.

Through the Holy Spirit, we are convinced that you will eternally guide us along your path of righteousness. The goodly heritage awaits us, thanks to your abiding encouragement. As you warm our hearts, our arms will embrace strangers. As you guide our thinking, our mouths will proclaim your love. As you redeem us from futility, our whole being will be cleansed of impurity. We give thanks for your revelation, which frees us to serve.

9TH SUNDAY IN ORDINARY TIME (B)

1 Samuel 3:1–10 (11–20); Psalm 139:1–6, 13–18
2 Corinthians 4:5–12; Mark 2:23–3:6

Jesus upsets the authorities with his unorthodox behavior. When the disciples pluck grain on the Sabbath, Jesus reminds the authorities that David ate the bread of the Presence. When Jesus himself heals the man with the withered hand, he asks them if it is harmful to do good on the Sabbath. Do not clutter the day with binding regulations that inhibit the possibility of giving God praise.

Call to Worship   Psalm 139

Leader: O Lord, you have searched me and known me. You discern my thoughts from afar.
People: You search out my path and are acquainted with all my ways.
Leader: Even before a word is on my tongue, O Lord, you know it completely.
People: Where can I go from your spirit? Or where can I flee from your presence?
Leader: Let us worship God!

Prayer of Praise and Adoration

God our protector and comforter, our shield and defender, hear our glad praises as we boast of your goodness. We gather as witnesses to your redeeming graciousness. We worship in response to your encompassing love. The birds start to sing before the sun even rises, proof that you promise the dawn of new life while it is yet dark. Let your light now shine on our darkness, that we may discern your will for us, giving you the honor due your glorious name.

Prayer of Confession

Unison: O God, hear our confession, for we still dwell in darkness. We are afflicted and crushed by a sense of inadequacy. When perplexed, we despair that there may be no hope. Persecution leaves us feeling forsaken. When foes strike us down, we assume we're destroyed. We hear that Christ resides like a treasure within us. Transform our whole being so that we live in that truth.

Assurance of Pardon

Leader: Do not lose heart! God is merciful and just and forgives us our sins. Renounce disgraceful, underhanded ways. Refuse to practice cunning or to tamper with God's word. Be open to the truth of God's graciousness. In Jesus Christ, we are forgiven.

Prayer of Dedication

O God, you anoint us with the oil of your blessing. You set us apart as Christ calls us to serve. You fill us with the Spirit of righteousness. We are vessels of your holiness, prepared to do what you command. Be pleased with our sacrifices, and take delight in our victories. Enhance all our efforts, and multiply their effectiveness. Help us rise to the level of your trust in us, as we dedicate our gifts in response to your goodness.

Prayer of Thanksgiving and Supplication

Creator God, who set aside one day a week as holy, a day of rest for our re-creation, we give you thanks for the liberating message of Jesus, which affirms the day and keeps us from becoming enslaved by it. Save us when we tend to bind ourselves with countless regulations. May Christ speak to us too, with authority, and set us free to praise you at all times and in all ways.

Help us to model all our days on this one you call holy. As the disciples plucked heads of grain, give us the bread we need to sustain ourselves. Keep us from wanton craving after an ever-increasing list of goods, things that weigh us down and in time demand so much attention. Help us to be satisfied with the simple necessities of life, and enable us to share our abundance.

As Jesus healed the man with a withered hand, cleanse us from the sin that limits our ability to do good. Remove the scales from our eyes that allow us to see only our own needs. Open our ears, so that we may hear Christ's commandment to forsake all and follow him. May our hearts beat with joy at the thought of self-giving service. Give us the good sense to use our time wisely.

As the Pharisees held counsel on how to destroy Jesus, so there are those today who would prefer to have us out of the way. Nevertheless, make us the goads who call others to righteousness, the alarms that sound when the rights of others are disregarded. Help us to ferret out injustice, and make us quick to praise goodness whenever it occurs. On this holy day, re-create in us a sense of urgency to be about your business.

10TH SUNDAY IN ORDINARY TIME (B)

1 Samuel 8:4–11 (12–15) 16–20 (11:14–15); Psalm 138
2 Corinthians 4:13–5:1; Mark 3:20–35

A covenant community is a gathering of individuals with a common experience of being called by God and given a purpose. It is characterized by a common loyalty to God and a shared sense of purpose in the world. In the covenant community, the members are related to one another as organs of the body. When one suffers, all are in pain. The body functions best when all members are present and functioning.

Call to Worship   Psalm 138

Leader: I give you thanks, O Lord, with my whole heart; before the gods I sing your praise.

People: I bow down before you and give thanks for your steadfast love and faithfulness.

Leader: On the day I called, you answered me and increased the strength of my soul.

People: You steadfast love, O Lord, endures forever. Do not forsake the work of your hands.

Leader: Let us worship God!

Prayer of Praise and Adoration

Our souls awake, O God, to the thrill of your splendor. With our voices we praise you from dawn unto dusk. We greet the new day warmed by your love for us; we rest secure in the night, comforted by the light of your Spirit. Each hour you give us is a moment of blessing, a time to rejoice and abound with new life. We exalt your name to the heavens, O God, as your glory is seen over all the earth.

Litany of Affirmation

Leader: Since we have the same spirit of faith as he had who wrote, "I believed, and so I spoke," we too believe, and so we speak.

People: So we do not lose heart. Our inner nature is being renewed every day.

Leader: Knowing that God who raised the Lord Jesus will raise us also with Jesus and bring us with you into God's presence.

People: So we do not lose heart. Our inner nature is being renewed every day.

Leader: For is it all for your sake, so that grace, as it extends to more and more people, may increase thanksgiving, to the glory of God.

People: So we do not lose heart. Our inner nature is being renewed every day.

Prayer of Dedication

You call forth eternal hope within us, O God. Our faith abounds, because of your redeeming grace. With hearts uplifted by the truth of your mercy, and spirits cleansed with the fullness of your indwelling blessing, we come before you, ready and eager to serve. Continue to fashion us until we conform to your will for us. Equip us and through Christ make us useful as agents of your all-embracing love.

Prayer of Thanksgiving

Tender and loving God, you bear our afflictions as though they were your own. We give you thanks for our refuge in Jesus, our haven and shelter. In him we see your care for us when we are attacked or aggrieved. In him we see your anger with forces that hinder our obedience. In him we see your compassion for our weakness, and your clear call to rise above our doubts and misgivings. In him we see your firm resolution that nothing shall ultimately separate us from your promised salvation.

We give you thanks for David, and all those whose music dispels gloom and makes hearts lighter. Their harmony brings resolution and accord amid the dissonant sounds of competing forces vying for our attention. Their discipline reminds us of our own need to attune ourselves to your will through obedience and skillful practice. Their melody teaches us to blend our talents with those about us, composing a unison refrain in which all can join. Their gaiety keeps us from taking our efforts and ourselves too seriously, since it is ultimately to you that we sing our praises.

We give you thanks for brothers and sisters, mothers and fathers, and all those who are family to us in the venture of faith. Upon them we rely for nurture and sustenance, support and guidance, and understanding and forgiveness as we search for your truth. We give thanks that we can trust them when all else around us is threatening, and rely on them without feeling ashamed. The household of faith abounds with signs of your tenderness and mercy. We give thanks for Jesus who is the cornerstone, for David who taught us to sing, and for each other, upon whom we rely to show us your love.

11TH SUNDAY IN ORDINARY TIME (B)

1 Samuel 15:34–16:13; Psalm 20
2 Corinthians 5:6–10 (11–13) 14–17; Mark 4:26–34

The mystery of the kingdom of God is like a seed planted. It grows, and we know not how. Sometimes it is helped by our efforts. At other times it is hindered by what we do. It is best for us to remember that it is always God's kingdom and we are its agents. Let what we do be to God's glory, so that the kingdom may spread and all may taste the fruits of the harvest.

Call to Worship   Psalm 20

Leader: May the Lord answer you in the day of trouble, and may the name of the God of Jacob protect you!
People: May the Lord remember all of our offerings and regard with favor our sacrifices of praise.
Leader: May the Lord grant you your heart's desire, and fulfill all of your plans.
People: Our pride is in the name of the Lord who hears us when we pray and answers our needs.
Leader: Let us worship God!

Prayer of Praise and Adoration

God of our refuge, what have we to fear? You are a very present help in times of trouble, a source of comfort during distress. There is no matter so small that you are not aware of it, no problem too great that we cannot share it with you. You who move mountains and set streams on their courses, within your providence you take care even of us. We praise you and honor you, God of Creation; you are indeed our refuge and strength.

Litany of Affirmation

Leader: So we are always confident.
People: For we walk by faith, not by sight.
Leader: We know that while we are at home in the body we are away from the risen Christ.
People: For we walk by faith, not by sight.
Leader: We do have confidence, and we would rather be away from the body and at home with the risen Christ.
People: For we walk by faith, not by sight.
Leader: So whether we are at home or away, we make it our aim to please him.

People:	For we walk by faith, not by sight.
Leader:	For all of us must appear before the judgment seat of Christ, so that each may receive good recompense for what has been done in the body, whether good or evil.
People:	Let us then continue to walk by faith, not by sight.

Prayer of Dedication

O God, your goodness surrounds us, your grace sustains us, your mercy redeems us; by your love we are saved. We come before you, offering our praise for your indwelling Spirit and giving you thanks for Christ Jesus, who sends us new life. Placing before you the fruits of our labors, we confess anew our trust in your goodness. We rely on your grace. We are in the hands of your mercy as we seek to love others as you command.

Prayer of Thanksgiving and Petition

O God, our refuge and strength, we give you thanks that when we appear before the judgment seat of Christ we can have courage, since he intercedes on our behalf. His Spirit chides us out of complacency and goads us away from unfaithful behavior. In spite of our rebellion and betrayal, we can in repentance put ourselves at your mercy.

We give thanks for your covenant, which spans generations. Through Scripture we hear again the promise that you will not forsake us. Those who have gone before now dwell with assurance of your eternal presence. We trust that those who come after us will inherit your favor. We stand in succession of those called your people, redeemed and forgiven, thanks to your grace.

Through Christ's intercession, we are encouraged to pray for your wisdom and guidance. Help us to learn from the struggles of history that weapons are no substitute for feeding the hungry. Make us as eager to help others shape their own destiny as we are zealous in protecting our rights. We need to hear again how to beat swords into plowshares, and spears into pruning hooks, for the mighty keep falling, and threats of war do not cease.

Make us agents of your peace. When we stand before the judgment seat, grant that we shall have acted to ease pain, given refuge to those who needed shelter, and helped the oppressed live with dignity. Through our faithful response, may the naked have been clothed, the sick made well. Your encouragement makes us bold. Christ's intercession gives us hope. O Refuge and our Strength, we give you thanks.

12TH SUNDAY IN ORDINARY TIME (B)

1 Samuel 17:(1a, 4–11, 19–23) 32–49 and Psalm 9:9–20
or 1 Samuel 17:57–18:5, 10–16 and Psalm 133
2 Corinthians 6:1–13; Mark 4:35–41

There is calmness that comes with faith. When the winds blow and waves threaten the ship of life, we trust in One who will tend our needs. Such care awed the disciples, as Jesus rebuked the wind and ordered the sea to be still. So we too may turn to Jesus in the midst of the perils of life and hear his "Peace! Be still."

Call to Worship   Psalm 9

Leader: Those who know your name put their trust in you, O Lord.
People: For you, O Lord, have not forsaken those who seek you.
Leader: Sing praises to the Lord, who dwells in Zion.
People: We will declare your wonderful deeds among all the people.
Leader: Let us worship God!

Prayer of Praise and Adoration

You are great, O God, and deserving of praise. Your works attest to your grandeur; your love exceeds comprehension. Wherever we look, we see signs of your splendor; the good that we do is a result of your grace. You fill your sanctuary with the presence of your Holy Spirit; you send your Word, Jesus, to dwell in our midst. We are surrounded by testimony to your loving goodness; we bow down before you and give you our praise.

Litany of Affirmation

Leader: We are putting no obstacle in anyone's way, so that no fault may be found with our ministry.
People: Now is the acceptable time; now is the day of salvation!
Leader: As servants of God we have commended ourselves in every way, through truthful speech and the power of God.
People: Now is the acceptable time; now is the day of salvation!
Leader: We are treated as impostors, and yet are true; as unknown, and yet are well known.
People: Now is the acceptable time; now is the day of salvation!
Leader: We are treated as dying, and see—we are alive; as punished, and yet not killed.
People: Now is the acceptable time; now is the day of salvation!

Leader:	We are treated as sorrowful, yet always rejoicing; as poor, yet making many rich.
People:	Now is the acceptable time; now is the day of salvation!
Leader:	We are treated as having nothing, and yet possessing everything.
People:	Now is the acceptable time; now is the day of salvation!

Prayer of Dedication

O God, as Christ calls us, your Spirit empowers us. We accept your charge to be his ambassadors for peace. Reconciled by Christ to your loving judgment, we will seek to work righteousness through acts of goodwill. Accept our efforts when they please you, and frustrate our attempts when they do not serve you. Lead us in Christ to become worthy disciples, as, filled with your Spirit, we respond to his call.

Prayer of Thanksgiving and Supplication

O God, if you build the house, who can destroy it? If you establish a covenant, who can defeat your purpose? If you turn against your people in righteous judgment, who can withstand your anger? Yet you have assembled a people and called them your own. You have built mighty temples for your people and accepted their praise. You have set your sign in the heavens that you will never withdraw your blessing, and you have sent Christ as the eternal seal of your love. Nothing can separate us from your redeeming graciousness.

We thank you that you call and name us Christ's church. Make us worthy servants in his name. Set us apart, so that we can witness to your commandment, your reconciliation, your righteousness, and your peace. Help us to build a society where justice reigns, where the weak are empowered, not exploited. Give us a sense of what is right, so that what we do is in accord with Christ's will.

Still within us those turbulent fears of our own making, and those inflicted upon us. When thoughts of inadequacy grip us, remind us of Christ, who hung on the cross that we might live. When we are attacked in pursuit of your righteousness, surround us with the armor of your impenetrable Spirit. When all around us there is evidence of suffering, and when cries of injustice arise from those seeking a sign of compassion, keep us attuned to your call to be ambassadors for Christ and ministers of reconciliation.

13TH SUNDAY IN ORDINARY TIME (B)

2 Samuel 1:1, 17–27; Psalm 130
2 Corinthians 8:7–15; Mark 5:21–43

Faith makes a woman whole. Faith raises a father's daughter who all feared was dead. Believing in Jesus, the woman touches his garment as he passes. She feels a healing power within her, and she is well again. The child's father too believes in Jesus' miraculous power and intercedes for her. Jesus goes to the little girl and touches her, and she regains consciousness. Faith involves reaching out for help. It also involves hope despite impossible situations. Jesus taught how to reach out and hope in God.

Call to Worship   Psalm 130

Leader: Out of the depths I cry to you, O Lord. Lord, hear my voice.
People: Let your ears be attentive to the voice of my supplications!
Leader: If you, O Lord, should mark iniquities, Lord, who could stand?
People: But there is forgiveness with you, so that you may be revered.
Leader: I wait for the Lord, and in your word I put my hope.
People: My soul waits for the Lord more than those who watch for the morning.
Leader: Let us worship God!

Prayer of Praise and Adoration

O God of all creation, the earth is yours and the fullness thereof. You touch the leaves with the dew of the morning; you send the breezes to cool the night. The trees are laden with fruit because of your blessing; fields produce crops because of your care. As you watch over your people and fill all their needs, now send forth your Spirit and be present among us. We lift up our heads and give you praise in Christ's name.

Prayer of Confession

Unison: God of forgiveness, grant us your favor as we make our confession. You call us to excellence; we fall short of your confidence in us. You grant to us grace; we abuse your gift. You expect our decisions to match your desires, our love to be genuine in obeying your will. Yet we trust our appetites rather than rely on your goodness. We look to our comfort rather than to our neighbor's need. In Christ, have mercy on us and forgive us our sin.

Assurance of Pardon

Leader: Paul assures us of God's reconciling graciousness when he writes, "You know the generous act of our Lord Jesus Christ, that though he was rich, yet for your sakes he became poor, so that by his poverty you might become rich." In Christ we may dwell in the richness of God's favor, and may rest assured in the fullness of God's redeeming forgiveness.

Prayer of Dedication

Great God, you called a people and in Christ you named us to serve you. We present ourselves in response to your mercy. Magnify your name through our thoughts and actions, so that we may reflect your goodness in all that we do. Let the seal of our baptism be your stamp of approval, so that engrafted into Christ's body we can respond to his will.

Prayer of Thanksgiving

O God of the covenant, we give you thanks that Christ has lifted the gates to eternity through his death and resurrection. Your Holy Spirit opens the doors of the sanctuary, wherein we may dwell with assurance of new life. Even as David treasured the Ark of the Covenant, the symbol of your presence, and carried it to Jerusalem, so we treasure your word in Scripture and give you thanks for its guidance.

As we hear how your promise led the people to rejoice, and learn of the richness Christ's sacrifice bestowed, we give thanks for the Scriptures that continue to guide us. Their words meet our needs as we heed what they say. We confess that we are not diligent in seeking their direction. Our own desires conflict with what we read therein. Yet we are heartened as we learn afresh of your forgiveness, and trust Christ to lead us as we repent.

We give thanks for the Holy Spirit, who continues to touch us with your everlasting presence. Allow us to experience the healing power of Christ's seamless garment as we face daily the trials that test our faith. The abiding witness of those whose courage continues to uphold them in spite of their suffering consoles us. We are led to have hope ourselves, as we give thanks for their trust.

We praise you that not even death itself can erase your promise of life eternal. The memories of those departed attest to the truth that Christ has indeed opened the portals to your heavenly reaches. We hold our heads high and with our voices sing your blessings. Your covenant never ceases, and for that we give you thanks.

14TH SUNDAY IN ORDINARY TIME (B)

2 Samuel 5:1–5, 9–10; Psalm 48
2 Corinthians 12:2–10; Mark 6:1–13

Jesus' friends and neighbors are astonished at his teaching. They wonder about the source of his wisdom, and his authority to perform mighty works. He is only a carpenter's son. They can't accept him. Jesus replies to their rejection in words now familiar to all: "Prophets are not without honor, except in their hometown, and among their own kin, and in their own house." We too downgrade the gifts of those nearest us, and no marvels of grace can be performed in our midst.

Call to Worship   Psalm 48

Leader: Great is the Lord and greatly to be praised in the city of our God.

People: Your name, O God, like your praise reaches to the ends of the earth.

Leader: We ponder your steadfast love, O God, in the midst of your temple.

People: We will tell the next generation that this is our God who will be our guide forever.

Leader: Let us worship God!

Prayer of Praise and Adoration

Your faithfulness is as firm as the heavens, O God; righteousness and justice are the foundation of your throne. Your steadfast love goes before you as you set the planets in orbit and establish your covenant here on earth. You still the raging waters, and calm perturbed hearts. You are God above, beyond, and within all creation. We extol you, Our God, the Rock of our salvation.

Prayer of Confession

Unison: Forgive us, O God, for our self-important boasting. We take credit for our strength without thought of your gifts. When honors are bestowed, we treat them as our due. We claim as our victories the triumphs of your grace. You shower us with blessings, which we ignore. You bring new life; we take it for granted. Deliver us from our vain ways, and forgive our smug complacency. Turn our boasting to thanksgiving for Christ's power within us.

Assurance of Pardon

Leader: Paul declares that, "even when we were dead through our trespasses, God made us alive together with Christ. . . . For by grace you have been saved through faith, and this is not your own doing; it is the gift of God . . . so that no one may boast" (*Eph. 2:5, 8*). Let us then boast of God's grace within us, and claim with assurance the new life in Christ.

Prayer of Dedication

God of steadfast love and faithfulness, who made a covenant with the house of David, we bring our gifts so that your covenant with him may be extended throughout the world. We offer ourselves here as temples of your chosen one, David's royal son, Jesus Christ. Alive in the Spirit and empowered by service, we go forth in his name to proclaim your love as a sanctuary for those who are in need.

Prayer of Thanksgiving

O God, we give you thanks for Jesus, whose word enlightens our lives. He wrought mighty works and taught what it meant to have faith. He relied on a greater authority than that granted by earthly rulers, and freed us from bondage to principalities and powers. Though he was a stranger among his own, we proclaim him our Savior and serve him as members of his true family.

We give thanks for strangers and all those whose behavior challenges the accepted norm. In them we can learn what it means to be led by the Spirit. They can show us how to discern your will as they respond to your living Word. Their freedom can release us from standard morality and dead rules.

We give thanks for those whom others do not honor, angels of mercy who desire only to be useful to you. Their strength comes from the abiding sense of your indwelling Spirit. From them we learn how to love one another and to overcome selfishness.

Through strangers and angels you show us a better way. There is much we will never comprehend, but in Christ you have made known your love once and for all. For the gift of love and for loving ones, we give you thanks.

15TH SUNDAY IN ORDINARY TIME (B)

2 Samuel 6:1–5, 12b–19; Psalm 24
Ephesians 1:3–14; Mark 6:14–29

The grisly story of John's death is told in detail. When Herod's daughter Herodias dances, Herod is taken by her and offers her whatever she wishes. Herodias asks her mother what she should ask for. Her mother replies, "The head of John the baptizer." Even though John had told him it was not lawful to marry his brother's wife, Herod respected him enough not to cause him any harm. Now that would no longer be necessary, since John's head was brought in on a platter.

Call to Worship
Psalm 24

Leader: The earth is the Lord's and all that is in it, the world, and those who live in it.

People: Who shall ascend the hill of the Lord? And who shall stand in God's holy place?

Leader: Those who have clean hands and pure hearts, who do not lift up their souls to what is false.

People: Such is the company of those who seek the Lord, who seek the face of the God of Jacob.

Leader: Let us worship God!

Prayer of Praise and Adoration

O God, we worship and praise you for your gift of redemption. In Christ you chose us before the world was created. You sent him to cleanse us of all our unrighteousness. He sacrificed himself for us that we should be blameless. Your grace surrounds us, and your peace dwells within us. Through Christ, who calls us and names us as your chosen people, we gather to praise you for your glorious grace.

Prayer of Confession

Unison: God of redeeming grace, have mercy upon us as we confess our sin. Charged to travel light, we overburden ourselves. Commissioned to preach repentance, we ourselves do not change. Cautioned to avoid violence, we are quick to confront others. Called to be reconcilers, we create divisions. As Christ sends us forth and equips us to serve him, cleanse us of abusing his trust and his name.

Assurance of Pardon

Leader: Remember that we have redemption through Christ's sacrifice on our behalf. We have forgiveness of sins, according to the riches of God's grace. For God has made known to us in all wisdom and insight the mystery of God's will, "to unite all things in him, things in heaven and things on earth." Therein lies our assurance of pardon.

Prayer of Dedication

O God, as David brought up the Ark of the Covenant with much dancing and singing, we also rejoice as we offer our gifts. As the Ark held the commandments, may our gifts receive your approval. As the Ark was a sign of your covenant, let our gifts bear witness to your love. As the Ark brought hope to the people, use our gifts to bring relief to the needy. Accept these offerings in response to your graciousness, and may all who receive them find joy in new life.

Prayer of Thanksgiving

God of David and the house of Israel, who confirmed your love for all people in the gift of a Savior, who are we that we should be so blessed by your grace? Yet in him we have been set apart as a chosen race, a royal priesthood, God's own people, called and sent into the world. We who are nothing apart from your saving mercy may yet stand holy and blameless before you, because of your grace shown in Jesus Christ.

We thank you for the household of Christ, called the church. In your infinite wisdom you have brought together a multitude of people and cultures and made them one family through baptism. Together we proclaim one Savior, Jesus Christ, and one faith. We give thanks for this universal witness to Christ's resurrection, and pray for the day when all Christians may join as one around the Table.

Thanks be to you, O God, for one Holy Spirit, who empowers each of us with gifts according to our individual strengths and abilities. We give thanks for those with voice and those with vision, for those called to teach and those who manage. We praise you that your Spirit enables each to labor and affirms us all as workers together in Christ.

We are grateful for the world into which Christ sends us. Its beauty and grandeur inspire us; its hunger and poverty challenge us to service and sacrifice. Make us sensitive to the cries of the needy, and resourceful in ways to serve them, for the sake of him who has redeemed us by his blood.

16TH SUNDAY IN ORDINARY TIME (B)

2 Samuel 7:1–14a; Psalm 89:20–37
Ephesians 2:11–22; Mark 6:30–34, 53–56

Upon their return from serving and teaching, the disciples withdraw with Jesus to a lonely place. They need leisure and time for renewal, but this time is denied them. The throngs watch where they go and get there before them. Amid the demands of the gospel, draw apart each day to commune with Christ and reflect on his teaching. Only in this way can you be renewed and equipped for ministry.

Call to Worship   Ephesians 2

Leader: You are no longer strangers and aliens, but members of the household of God.

People: We are built upon the foundation, with Christ Jesus himself as the cornerstone.

Leader: In him the whole structure is joined together and grows into a holy temple.

People: In the Lord we are built together spiritually into a dwelling place for God.

Leader: Let us worship God!

Prayer of Praise and Adoration

O God of promise, who in Christ assembled the alienated and the excluded into the folds of your compassion, we give you praise for your redeeming grace. You break down dividing walls of hostility, and fill us with your Spirit of reconciling love. You set our feet firmly on the foundation of your goodness, and impart to us wisdom that enlightens our days. You are God, who indeed promises new life to all.

Prayer of Confession

Unison: O God, sustained by your mercy we make bold to confess our sin. We expel strangers and deny hospitality. We judge others all too freely. Our hasty words cause conflict and tension. We are disturbers of your peace. As you sent Christ to reconcile your people, forgive the failings of our unredeemed humanity and show us once again the image of your Son, who loved his enemies and taught us to do the same.

Assurance of Pardon

Leader: "Now in Christ Jesus you who once were far off have been brought near by the blood of Christ. For he is our peace . . . and has broken down the dividing wall, that is, the hostility between us." As we dwell in Christ, so let us also receive his forgiveness of our sins.

Prayer of Dedication

Merciful Deliverer, you do not cast away your disobedient people but receive them blameless through Christ's all-encompassing sacrifice. We come before you made clean by your righteousness. As you redeem us, you also empower us through the gift of your Holy Spirit. We rejoice at how you restore the fortunes of your people, and bring you gifts in response to your love.

Prayer of Thanksgiving

Where would we be without your compassion, O God? Who could stand before your judgment? Yet you promised that you would never forsake us. You sent Christ as a sign of your faithfulness and a seal of salvation. He is a haven of hope and a source of rest for souls weary from strife and wrongdoing. We give thanks that he dwells by your side, there to intercede for us as we offer our prayers.

We give thanks that he taught his disciples to draw apart for prayer and quiet. As he walked the earth and sought time away from the demands of the crowd, we too need to learn how to "be still, and know that you are God." In trying to please others, we do not replenish our resources. Encourage us to take time for contemplation. Instill in us the discipline to reflect on your will.

We give thanks for the strength others give us as their spirits support us and make us glad. When we are exhausted, it is they who uplift us; when we are bent low, they help us stand tall. Keep us from taking their concern for granted and from burdening them with our problems beyond what they can bear.

Our righteousness Christ won through his sacrifice for us. Your patience sustains us as your Spirit consoles and guides us. Your commandments nourish us as we glimpse your will for our lives. We are surrounded by hosts of those who support us. For your eternal revelation and these continuing reminders of your boundless compassion, we give you thanks, O God.

17TH SUNDAY IN ORDINARY TIME (B)

2 Samuel 11:1–15; Psalm 14
Ephesians 3:14–21; John 6:1–21

Feeding the multitude is a miracle. Who would have guessed that so little can satisfy so many? Five loaves and two fish show the ways of God's economy, that what is needed will be provided. Indeed, there is more than enough, and what is left is gathered. Another day will come, and there will be more people to feed. Jesus knows the reality of God's encompassing care; there will be sufficient for today and enough for tomorrow.

Call to Worship   Ephesians 3

Leader: May Christ dwell in your hearts through faith, as you are being rooted and grounded in love.

People: May you have the power to know the love of Christ that surpasses knowledge.

Leader: Now to the One who is able to accomplish far more than all we can ask or imagine,

People: To God be glory in the church and in Christ Jesus to all generations, forever and ever.

Leader: Let us worship God!

Prayer of Praise and Adoration

O God of deliverance, our knees bow down before you; with our voices we sing you praises. Our hands are uplifted to give you honor; our eyes are opened to behold your blessing. You are merciful in providing us a haven; you are caring and know all our needs; your presence is our assurance that you accept our worship. To you be the glory in the church and in Christ Jesus to all generations, forever and ever.

Prayer of Confession

Unison: Blessed Redeemer, have mercy upon us as we confess our sin. You endow us with goodness while we squander your blessings. We yearn for the possessions that our neighbors enjoy. Envy, greed, and selfishness consume us. Satisfaction eludes us as our cravings increase. Quiet our longing for material riches, and help us trust in Jesus, who provides for our needs.

Assurance of Pardon

Leader: And now may "Christ dwell in your hearts through faith, as you are being rooted and grounded in love, that you may have the power to comprehend, with all the saints, what is the breadth and length and height and depth. May you know the love of Christ that surpasses knowledge, so that you may be filled with all the fullness of God." With that fullness will come the assurance that God forgives all our sin.

Prayer of Dedication

To you, O God, be all power and glory, blessing and honor, now and forevermore. Your mercy at work within us enables us to do and be more than we could ever ask. Your Spirit surrounds us as we dwell in the shadow of your gracious deliverance. It is Christ who guides us as we go forth to serve. May all that we do reveal your benevolence, and may what we offer reflect your goodness.

Prayer of Thanksgiving and Supplication

O God of tenderness, you cradle creation in your bosom. We give you thanks for how you care for its needs. You refresh it with the same waters that are poured on us at baptism, a reminder of your covenant, which brings new life. You cleanse it through the purging presence of your Holy Spirit, as fresh breezes replace stale air. Not a day goes by without countless reminders of how you brood over what you gave birth to; nor can we go anywhere and hope to escape the touch of your judgment. You fill us with awareness of your pervasive compassion. We give thanks for your care, which surrounds us.

We pray for the young, who begin new life in utter dependence, for the unborn and newborn, who drew their first nourishment from another body. We are reminded of how needful we are. Give us hearts that reach out to children. Give us wisdom to impart direction to them. Give us patience to bear their frustrations with them. Give us humility to listen to what they have to say without judging them. Give us imagination, so that we can enter into their hopes.

We pray for your children from whom we are alienated. If it is because of hostility or anger, give to us a spirit of reconciliation sufficient to approach them and seek forgiveness. If it is because their skin color is different or their race is not ours, give us a sense of the length of Christ's Table, around which all will dine and rejoice. If it is because they taunt us or otherwise cause us discomfort, give us grace enough to show them the tenderness you give to us. Make us your agents of compassion, understanding, and reconciliation. In Christ's name we pray.

18TH SUNDAY IN ORDINARY TIME (B)

2 Samuel 11:26–12:13a; Psalm 51:1–12
Ephesians 4:1–16; John 6:24–35

Every culture has its own bread. It may be leavened or unleavened, round or rectangular, flat or airy, sourdough or sweet dough. Jesus understands the significance of bread and uses it as a metaphor to describe God's comprehensive care for all people. Jesus himself is the Bread of Life, who satisfies all who hunger for righteousness.

Call to Worship   Ephesians 4

Leader: I beg you to lead a life worthy of the calling to which you have been called.

People: There is one Lord, one faith, one baptism, one God who is above all and through all and in all.

Leader: Each of us was given grace according to the measure of Christ's gift.

People: Speaking the truth in love, we must grow up in every way into him who is the head.

Leader: Let us worship God!

Prayer of Praise and Adoration

O God of grace and infinite goodness, you nourish us with the bread of life and sustain us with the peace that sets our longing hearts at rest. You fill our cup with kindness; it overflows with the bounty of your all-encompassing care. You chose to dwell among us and in us through our Savior, Jesus Christ. We praise you and adore you, O God of us all.

Prayer of Confession

Unison: God of mercy, be above us to judge us, and be within us to convict us of our sin. Teach us who worship false gods to fear you, the one true God. Teach us who commit evil deeds to obey you and you alone. Teach us who oppress our neighbors the ways of righteousness and truth. Teach us who do not pursue peace the futility of war and the blessing of *shalom.*

Assurance of Pardon

Leader: God was in Christ reconciling the world, satisfying our hunger and thirst after righteousness. Jesus is the Bread of Life. All who come to him and humbly confess their sin will be filled with God's mercy and sustained by God's grace. So taste and see how God cares for you. Know and believe the good news of God's love.

Prayer of Dedication

O God, in Christ you call us to lead a life worthy of our calling. We come before you and implore you to accept our gifts. We offer our diversity, that it may be made one by your reconciling Spirit. We return to you the talents conferred by your creative goodness. We present to you our acts of obedience in response to your trust. May who we are and what we do be acceptable in your sight, through Christ our redeemer.

Prayer of Thanksgiving

O God, who chose to dwell among us in Jesus Christ, we give thanks that we can behold your glory and learn of your will. As Jesus taught of old in the synagogue, so your truth is made known today in pulpit and classroom. We give thanks for this ageless wisdom set in the context of history, a history which belonged to those who went before us, which is ours today, and which will be for those who come after us. As you judged David, so also you judge us today. As David repented and worshiped you, so also have we confessed and been cleansed.

We give thanks that you have chosen us as your covenant people. You have taken these earthen vessels and transformed them, molding and fitting us to conform to your purpose. You have fired us with your Spirit, and given each unique talents. Though diverse, we are one through Christ. We give you thanks that your Spirit continues to inspire us to use your gifts. It is the Holy Spirit who takes what seems impossible and makes it become reality.

We give thanks that in you we can truly be servants. In Christ you have shown us how to serve neighbors, to carry with us the towel and basin of hospitality, to empty ourselves of superficial vanity, which impedes our reaching to those who are hurt, and to be filled with conviction to see justice realized. Aware of the responsibility of being chosen, we go forth with thanksgiving for our one baptism, for the Spirit who guides us, and for your kingdom, which reigns over all.

19TH SUNDAY IN ORDINARY TIME (B)

2 Samuel 18:5–9, 15, 31–33; Psalm 130
Ephesians 4:25–5:2; John 6:35, 41–51

Jesus is aware that whatever authority he possesses God has bestowed on him. It is God working in him that enables him to call disciples to follow. Those who respond will learn God's will, obey God's commandments, receive the Bread of Eternal Life, and be guided throughout their days by the Holy Spirit. Answer God's call, become followers of Christ, and you will receive whatever is needed for the journey of faith!

Call to Worship

Ephesians 4

Leader: So then, putting away falsehood let all of us speak the truth to our neighbors.

People: Let no evil talk come out of our mouths, but only what is useful for building up.

Leader: Do not grieve the Holy Spirit of God, with which you were marked with a seal.

People: Let us be kind to one another, tenderhearted, and forgive one another.

Leader: Let us worship God!

Prayer of Praise and Adoration

Your mercy is fresh every morning, O God. Your ways are just and true. You cause the day to dawn with the promise of life everlasting; in Christ we learn of your will. Your Spirit surrounds us with wisdom and guidance; you do not forsake us when we seek your counsel. Be pleased as we praise you and make haste to hear us, for we assemble to honor you, God of new life.

Litany of Confession and Assurance of Pardon

Leader: Therefore, since we are members of one another, put away falsehood and speak the truth.

People: Forgive us, O God, for we deceive one another.

Leader: Be angry, but do not sin; do not let the sun go down on your anger.

People: Forgive us, O God, since we are prone to hold grudges.

Leader: Do not steal, but work honestly; make yourselves able to give to those in need.

People: Forgive us, O God, for we squander your mercies and take no delight in sharing our means.

217

Leader:	Let no evil talk come out of your mouths, only talk that builds up your neighbor.
People:	Forgive us, O God, for we slander one another without being conscious of the destruction we cause.
Leader:	Know that Christ loved us and gave himself for us, a fragrant offering and sacrifice to God.
People:	If we are sorry and truly repent of our sin, in Jesus Christ we are forgiven.

Prayer of Dedication

Eternal God, who gave us Jesus Christ, the Bread of Life, we respond to your goodness by offering ourselves as dough to be made alive by the leaven of the gospel. Knead us and mold us to fit your will for us. Flavor us with the richness of Christ's teaching. Shape us by his sacrificial love on our behalf. Infuse us with your Spirit, and send us forth to be bread for the world.

Prayer of Thanksgiving and Supplication

O God, we give you thanks for the household of faith. Your authority establishes it; your promise gives it assurance of your abiding presence; your Messenger, Jesus Christ, calls us to live as its members; your Spirit pervades and enlivens it. We give thanks for those who have lived before us as heirs of your goodness. They have passed on their vision to us. From them we receive examples of faithfulness as they responded to Christ's teachings. Through them we are aware of your comfort during times of trial and temptation. Because of them we may face boldly the times that await us, led by their insight and upheld by their courage. As Christ calls us and names us, we seek to follow their example of loyalty and devotion. Look with favor upon us as we offer our prayer.

Make us more conscious of those who yearn to hear your word, who seek direction for otherwise aimless lives. Let us be for them the clear call to commitment, a source of hope and meaning in the midst of change and dislocation. Lead us together to new respect for the mysteries of faith that defy easy comprehension and marginal discipline. Guide us in our probing to be confronted with that sense of your grandeur and our own limited and temporal existence. Help us to follow in the footsteps of saints who dwell eternally at your throne of grace. May the course they charted direct our pilgrimage, and the lessons they learned remain a heritage that we can pass on to those who come after us.

20TH SUNDAY IN ORDINARY TIME (B)

1 Kings 2:10–12; 3:3–14; Psalm 111
Ephesians 5:15–20; John 6:51–58

"When we break the bread, is it not a sharing in the body of Christ? When we give thanks over the cup, is it not a sharing in the blood of Christ?" These are words spoken as a minister takes the loaf, breaks it in full view of the congregation, and then pours the fruit of the vine into the cup. The bread and the cup are gifts of God for the people of God.

Call to Worship   Psalm 111

Leader: I will give thanks to the Lord with my whole heart, in company with the congregation.

People: Your work is full of honor and majesty, O God, and your righteousness endures forever.

Leader: The works of your hands are faithful and just; all your precepts are trustworthy.

People: The fear of the Lord is the beginning of wisdom; all those who practice it have a good understanding.

Leader: Let us worship God!

Prayer of Praise and Adoration

Eternal God, your mercy is everlasting, your goodness eternal. Your name endures to all generations. As we gaze at the stars, they dance to your music; the moon shines, reflecting your glory. We greet the sunrise and rejoice in creation. Tasting the rain, we affirm how you care for us. Touching the sand, we are in awe of your power. You enliven our senses to the scope of your grandeur. We give you all honor as we worship your name.

Prayer of Confession

Unison: O God, deliver us from the burden of sin as we make our confession. Remove the scales from our eyes, for we overlook neighbors in need. Cleanse us of selfishness, which keeps us from serving them. Purge us of vanity, since we expect them to be grateful. Help us not to brood over the seeming ingratitude of some we serve. Restore us by Christ's redeeming sacrifice, and purify our intentions. Make us fit for your service. In Christ's name we pray.

Assurance of Pardon

Leader: Jesus has said, "I am the light of the world; those who follow me will not walk in darkness, but will have the light of life." "Therefore, it is said, 'Awake, O sleeper, and arise from the dead, and Christ shall give you light.'" Arise; walk in the light, since in Christ you are forgiven.

Prayer of Dedication

Eternal God, you redeem us in Jesus; we can boldly approach you. Sustained by his word to us, we are enabled to serve. Impelled by your Spirit, we respond to your commands. Direct us and guide us as we seek to accomplish your will. We bring our offerings; use them for your purpose. We dedicate our time; fill it with your presence. We give ourselves; satisfy your intentions. All that we have, we present to you.

Prayer of Thanksgiving and Petition

O God of tender mercies, we give thanks for the example of David as he ends his ministry and Solomon who rules in his stead; for the psalmist who takes delight in your honor and majesty; for Jesus, who is touched by all who were afflicted; and for Paul, whose suffering never keeps him from proclaiming the good news. Give us tender hearts and courage in the face of sorrow and personal pain.

We pray for those who grieve the loss of a loved one. Surround them with your embracing compassion; care for them in their solitude, and comfort them during the lonely hours. May the Spirit of the living Christ abide with them to encourage them, and may Christ's resurrection from death give them hope for life that lasts eternally.

We pray for those who lament their condition. Hear them as they plead for some sign of relief. Help us to sit with them and soothe their anxiety, to understand them in a way that will bring consolation. Keep us from denying them amid their affliction, from shaming them or compounding their burden. May we be for them the balm that anoints them with courage.

We pray for those afflicted with sundry ailments. Send Christ's healing power, which can restore them to wholeness. Use us as instruments of your mercy, so that we sit with the lonely, feed the hungry, show hospitality to the stranger, and clothe the naked. Grant those who are healers the patience to allow your miraculous powers to work, O God, and those who are sick the resources to cope with pain and discomfort. Give to all your people the hope, confidence, and dignity that come from being children of God.

21ST SUNDAY IN ORDINARY TIME (B)

1 Kings 8:(1, 6, 10–11) 22–30, 41–43; Psalm 84
Ephesians 6:10–20; John 6:56–69

Jesus speaks the words of eternal life. He offers himself as spiritual food. Christ provides us with all that is necessary; we are able to proceed on the journey of faith. The words will guide us toward the right path to take. They will keep us from becoming wayward or getting lost along the way. The food will sustain us and satisfy our hunger. Christ is our guide and provider!

Call to Worship   Psalm 84

Leader: How lovely is your dwelling place, O Lord of hosts!
People: Happy are those who live in your house, ever singing your praise.
Leader: For a day in your courts is better than a thousand elsewhere.
People: O Lord of Hosts, happy is everyone who trusts in you.
Leader: Let us worship God!

Prayer of Praise and Adoration

All blessing, glory, and honor be unto you, O God, for your way guides our behavior and your saving power redeems us when we stray. You are beneath us as a sure foundation. You are above us as a canopy of light. You go before us as a revealer and guide. You stand behind us as the source of righteousness and peace. God of all that was, is, and shall be, we praise and adore you.

Prayer of Confession

Unison: O God, redeem us, for we stand in need of forgiveness. We squander your mercy when we abuse your creation. We slander our neighbors and seek not your peace. Nations rise up against nations, and threats of terrorism fill the air. Those without work find no hope of relief. The homeless wander without protection from harm. Christ had compassion on all those who suffered. Cleanse us of the sin that closes our hearts to our brothers and sisters.

Assurance of Pardon

Leader: Know that God hears our prayer and will have mercy on all who humbly repent of their sin. Did not God send Christ our Savior to cleanse us of unrighteousness? Does not Christ intercede on behalf of those who confess? Lay aside your burden then, and take courage from the gospel. God forgives us through Christ.

Prayer of Dedication

God of goodness and mercy, we bring you our offerings. We laud you with thanksgiving for the blessings you bestow. You fill us with hope; we give you our commitment. You instill in us confidence; we offer our trust. You teach us how to sacrifice; we seek to be faithful. You call us to obey you; we pledge our allegiance. All that we have we place before you. Use us and mold us to conform to your will.

Prayer of Thanksgiving

Merciful God, who in Jesus Christ established the household of faith, we praise you for those in whose midst we are privileged to dwell. We give thanks for relatives who surround us with love. You created us dependent upon others for our nurture and growth. You gave us parents and guardians to care for us, siblings and age peers as companions along the way. We give thanks for our homes and the names we bear.

We are heartily thankful as well for partners and lovers, who share our sorrows and our joys, and for the young and the old, who season our lives with wisdom and verve. As Jesus chose a few in whom to confide, so we are grateful for those we can trust.

We give thanks for friends who cheer us on. In them we see your Spirit of counsel and might. They stand beside us to encourage us when we are doubtful. They go before us to mark a trail we can follow. They stand behind us to push when we are indecisive, and they hold us up when we are weighed down with trouble. For all those named and unnamed who surround us with compassion and patience, we give you thanks. Reflecting the splendor of your grace, the richness of your benevolence, and the scope of your love, we join together with those in Christ's household committed to serving you as the family of faith.

22ND SUNDAY IN ORDINARY TIME (B)

Song of Solomon 2:8–13; Psalm 45:1–2, 6–9
James 1:17–27; Mark 7:1–8, 14–15, 21–23

What pollutes? Is it what we take into our systems or what we ourselves generate? Jesus declares it is the latter and warns his critics to act consistently with what God commands. Ceremonial washing is meaningless if we foul the environment with evil words and deeds. It is meaningless to honor God with our lips if we do not love our neighbors as ourselves.

Call to Worship
James 1

Leader: Let everyone be quick to listen, slow to speak, and slow to anger.

People: Let us welcome with meekness the implanted word that has the power to save our souls.

Leader: Be doers of the word, and not merely hearers, so you may be blessed in all you do.

People: Pure religion is to care for orphans and widows and not to be stained by the world.

Leader: Let us worship God!

Prayer of Praise and Adoration

God of steadfast love, you have written your testimonies upon the hearts of your people; your commandments have guided them throughout the ages. We praise you for Jesus, who makes your will known to us. We sense your Spirit at work in our lives. Throughout all creation, you maintain your presence and give us cause for rejoicing. We acknowledge your marvelous deeds and give you all praise.

Prayer of Confession

Unison: God of strength and might, we confess our neglect of salvation's armor. We have not girded our loins with truth. The breastplate of righteousness is tarnished by our lax behavior. Our feet are caked with mud from battles fought unshod by the gospel of peace. We have laid aside the shield of faith, and weakened our defense in a hostile world. Help us once again to don the helmet of salvation and to raise the sword of the word against the powers that oppose you, so that in all our struggles we may rely solely on your strength.

Assurance of Pardon

Leader: Hear for your comfort the words of Paul: "For I am convinced that neither death, nor life, nor angels, nor rulers, nor things present, nor things to come, nor powers, nor height, nor depth, nor anything else in all creation, will be able to separate us from the love of God in Christ Jesus our Lord" (*Romans 8:38–39*). Accept your forgiveness and rejoice in a love stronger than our sin.

Prayer of Dedication

O God, who alone can keep us from falling, we come bearing gifts in response to your grace. Thanksgiving we offer for the mercies you give us. Glad praises we sing for the salvation Christ has won for us. Our acts we commit to your righteous judgment. We acknowledge the guidance your Holy Spirit bestows. All that we have is a gift of salvation; we commit ourselves to you in response to Christ's call.

Prayer of Thanksgiving and Supplication

Almighty God, whose testimony is sure and whose ordinances provide a stable foundation, we come with thanksgiving for the guidance your commandments impart. They are a bulwark that defends us against temptation. They are your gift to us to keep us attuned to your will for our lives. We thank you that we may walk faithfully before you, full of the wisdom you have revealed.

We give you thanks for Jesus, who taught his followers the full meaning of the law. He would not allow it to constrain him from serving those in need. Help us to be bold in following his example. Give us also the freedom to move beyond the law in order to fulfill it. Keep us from interpreting your commandments in ways that inhibit our ability to respond to what you intend us to do. May we see in your precepts our charge to become disciples, and hear in them your pervasive desire for our allegiance.

We give thanks for the Holy Spirit, who interprets your law in specific occasions. We are protected thereby from our own whims and desires. When we would stray from the tasks to which you call us, help us sense your Spirit frustrating our attempts. When our own insights fail us, or we are misled by the counsel of others, give us the patience to wait for your direction, and the strength to heed it.

Gird us, O God, once again with the truth of Christ's gospel. Make our feet ready to do whatever is necessary to bring peace. Armed with the breastplate of your reconciling forgiveness, we go forth as ambassadors, your kingdom to proclaim.

23RD SUNDAY IN ORDINARY TIME (B)

Proverbs 22:1–2, 8–9, 22–23; Psalm 125
James 2:1–10 (11–13) 14–17; Mark 7:24–37

Jesus made "the deaf to hear and the mute to speak." There are many blocks to our hearing and speaking. Attentive listening is necessary before we can clearly proclaim the good news of salvation. Amid society's clamor, listen for what God intends and then, without stammering, boldly announce the hope of the gospel.

Call to Worship   Proverbs 2

Leader: Incline your ear and hear my words, and apply your mind to my teaching.
People: It will be pleasant if you keep them within you, if all of them are ready on your lips.
Leader: So that your trust may be in the Lord, I have made them known to you today.
People: The rich and poor have this in common: the Lord is the maker of them all.
Leader: Let us worship God!

Prayer of Praise and Adoration

Make your face to shine upon us, O God, and be pleased to dwell in our presence. We gather before you to give you our praise. Our ears have been opened to the sounds of angels singing hosannas; our tongues have been loosed to shout "Alleluia! Amen!" We listen attentively for your word, which brings wisdom. We wait expectantly to confess anew our allegiance in faith. Make your face to shine upon us, O God, and be pleased with our worship.

Prayer of Confession

Unison: O God, Giver of mercy, in Christ's name hear us as we confess our sin. We speak when we should listen; we hesitate when we should act. Anger prevents us from working your righteousness; selfishness inhibits our responding in faith. We are called to proclaim boldly the dawn of your kingdom, but our shouts turn out to be mere whispers. Cleanse us of wickedness, and fill us with meekness. Redeem us in Christ, in whose name we pray.

Assurance of Pardon

Leader: Remember that "As many of you as were baptized into Christ have clothed yourselves with Christ. There is no longer Jew or Greek, there is no longer slave or free, there is no longer male and female; for all of you are one in Christ Jesus" (*Gal. 3:27–28*). So live as free people, abounding in the hope of the gospel, for in Jesus Christ you are forgiven.

Prayer of Dedication

Gracious God, accept the tributes we bring, and bless our endeavors in your name. With our voices we will sing your praises; with our hands we will care for the suffering. With our feet we will seek to walk faithfully; with our hearts we will love you completely. All that we have we return to you, who endow us with bountiful gifts.

Prayer of Thanksgiving

O God, you drape our shoulders with the mantle of your protection; we give you thanks for the countless ways you care for creation. Through our Savior, the Christ, you have cast away doubt and fear, even of death itself, and loosened the chains of our ultimate bondage. We give thanks for his Spirit, who dwells within us and around us and surrounds us with truth as we pursue the way of your glorious kingdom.

We are thankful for Christ, who has opened the portals of heaven and enables us daily to catch a glimpse of your glory. Through his sacrifice once and for all, he delivered us from striving after our own righteousness. We give thanks that by his grace he invites us to partake of the fruits of your mercy. As baptism is a sign of our cleansing, help us to walk daily in newness of life. As the bread is broken and offered as sustenance, keep us ever mindful of those who still hunger. As the cup of blessing is passed, deepen our commitment to serve those who thirst after righteousness.

We are thankful for our companions in this pilgrimage of faith: *thinkers*, who ponder your mysteries and point to new boundaries of truth and understanding; *doers* of the word, who press on with ceaseless energy to fulfill the kingdom's goals; *healers*, who translate the compassion of Christ into acts of human renewal and restoration. All these prepare the way for us as we journey to your new day.

24TH SUNDAY IN ORDINARY TIME (B)

Proverbs 1:20–33; Psalm 19 or Wisdom of Solomon 7:26–8:1
James 3:1–12; Mark 8:27–38

Jesus asks his disciples, "Who do people say that I am?" They answer, "John the Baptist, Elijah, one of the prophets." Jesus then reveals to them the cost of discipleship. To follow him will involve self-denial, sacrifice, and obedience. Such is the way of the cross!

Call to Worship

Psalm 19

Leader: The law of the Lord is perfect, reviving the soul.
People: The decrees of the Lord are sure, making wise the simple.
Leader: The precepts of the Lord are right, rejoicing the heart.
People: The commandment of the Lord is clear, enlightening the eyes.
Leader: the fear of the Lord is pure, enduring forever.
People: The ordinances of the Lord are true and righteous altogether.
Unison: Let the words of my mouth and the meditation of my heart be acceptable to you, O Lord, our rock and our redeemer.

Prayer of Praise and Adoration

O God of glory, you bless the poor in spirit with the richness of your eternal favor. You choose the meek to inherit the earth. You comfort those who mourn, the hungry and thirsty you satisfy. The pure in heart catch sight of your splendor, and those who make peace you call your own. We join with the merciful, who throughout the ages have lived by your graciousness and worshiped your name.

Prayer of Confession

Unison: God of justice and righteousness, have mercy upon us as we confess our sin. We say we love our neighbors, but we still make distinctions. We favor the rich and discount the poor. We say we have faith, but our works do not show it; we preach Jesus Christ while we send the hungry away. While our lips praise you, our hands cast off strangers. We are not worthy to ask your forgiveness except for the name of Christ, who pardoned the thief on the cross and forgave those who put him to death.

Assurance of Pardon

Leader: Remember the words of Scripture, where it says, "Since we have confidence to enter the sanctuary by the blood of Jesus . . . and since we have a great priest over the house of God, let us approach with a true heart in full assurance of faith, with our hearts sprinkled clean from an evil conscience and our bodies washed with pure water" (*Heb. 10:19, 21–22*). In Jesus Christ we are forgiven!

Prayer of Dedication

O God, in Jesus you call us to follow; we come confessing that he is the Christ. We offer ourselves to be filled with his commandments. We dedicate our actions to match his desires. We commit our intentions to be led by his Spirit. With all that we have we seek to be faithful. Accept our endeavors and bless our ambitions. Honor our commitment, in Christ's name we pray.

Prayer of Thanksgiving and Supplication

Merciful God, in Christ Jesus you call believers to the new and living way of the gospel; we give thanks that we are numbered among those so chosen. We are thankful for Peter, who testified boldly that Jesus was the Messiah, even though he was confused about what discipleship meant. From him we learn how we too need to make our confession, although we may not be clear about what you intend us to do.

Give us confidence to step up to the brink of uncertainty and face the abyss of our own doubt. We give thanks for Jesus, who could cry out for you to save him, since we too are afraid of what the future might bring. Help us to feel his comforting Spirit surrounding us, giving us assurance that we are not alone. Help us hear anew the testimony of those who have gone before us, that you do not forsake those who put their trust in you. Turn our heads from gazing on what has been the security of the past, and help us accept the vision and promise of your glorious reign.

Give us courage, then, to take those leaps of faith which will transport us from the known to the unknown, from idolatry to obedience, from selfishness to service. We give thanks for Christ, who himself spanned the chasm from death to new life. From him we learn of your will as he makes known your commandments. Through him we can obey you, since he intercedes on our behalf. Because of him we shall henceforth serve you, for he calls us to repent and follow him. Forgetting what lies behind, we can press on to approach the portals of your kingdom and give you thanks for Jesus, who shows us forevermore the new and living way.

25TH SUNDAY IN ORDINARY TIME (B)

Proverbs 31:10–31; Psalm 1
James 3:13–4:3, 7–8a; Mark 9:30–37

The kingdom of heaven turns traditional values upside down. The least become greatest, masters become servants, the first shall be last, and children set examples. Whoever receives Jesus really welcomes not him, but God who sent him. Whatever we do in Christ's name is done not by us but by the Spirit within us. To live in God's reign is to welcome surprises. Be open to change, as you believe in the gospel.

Call to Worship   Psalm 1

> *Leader:*   Happy are those who take delight in the law of the Lord.
> *People:*   They are like trees planted by streams of water. In all that they do they prosper.
> *Leader:*   For the Lord watches over the way of the righteous.
> *People:*   May God number us with the righteous as we worship the Lord.
> *Leader:*   Let us worship God!

Prayer of Praise and Adoration

We seek to dwell in your presence, O God, and behold evermore the warmth of your love. For you shelter your people during their time of adversity; you cradle them in your arms when they are afraid and lonely. You beckon us to embrace you and put an end to our fearfulness. Entering your sanctuary, we give you praise for your mercy. Be pleased with our worship as we honor your name.

Prayer of Confession

Unison: All wise and understanding God, hear our prayer as we confess our sin. Have mercy upon us, for we are deceitful and foolish. Ambition controls our relations with others; cheating and lying help us gain more control. We are surrounded by values that bring disorder. We are victims of selfishness that distorts your truth. Save us from boasting and serving unworthy ends; save us for Christ, in whom alone abides peace.

Assurance of Pardon

Leader: Hear the good news: In Jesus Christ we are forgiven. "For in him all the fullness of God was pleased to dwell, and through him God was pleased to reconcile all things, whether on earth or in heaven, by making peace through the blood of the cross" (*Col. 1:19–20*). In the peace that Christ won abides our assurance of pardon.

Prayer of Dedication

Mighty Redeemer, whose judgment is righteous and whose mercy has no bounds, we bring you our offerings in response to your grace. You sent Christ, who calls us; we give you commitment. You gave the Spirit to nurture us; we enthusiastically follow. You provide the commandments as guidance; we seek to obey you. Take us and use us to fulfill your will.

Prayer of Thanksgiving

God of all wisdom, you put the stars in the heavens and assign the planets their orbits; we give you thanks for the care you bestow on the earth. As the rains fall, the soil is nurtured; as the sun shines, the plants reach upward. You also set the seasons of life to fit your purposes; you grant us years of productivity because of your grace. Our ultimate goal is to glorify you; our richest gain is to enjoy you forever.

We are thankful for Jesus, who made known your wisdom once and for all. By his healing touch, he overcame the power of disease and injury. We give you thanks that disabilities and illness can never render us incapable of knowing your love. We can face unafraid whatever befalls us, and rejoice with assurance that we shall dwell forever made whole by your touch.

We are thankful that through his sacrifice, Christ challenged the finality of death. We can henceforth trust in your eternal care of those closest to us, and look for the day when we shall be reunited with those departed, as in that day we gather around the table of Christ's heavenly banquet.

We are thankful for the Holy Spirit, who guides us through the valleys of the shadow of doubt. When we question your judgment, it is your Spirit who reveals your will to us. When we seek wisdom and understanding, it is your Spirit who sustains and nurtures us. Gently you care for us; with peace you comfort us. For all of your mercies, which are signs of your wisdom, we give you glory and thanks, O God.

26TH SUNDAY IN ORDINARY TIME (B)

Esther 7:1–6, 9–10; 9:20–22; Psalm 124
James 5:13–20; Mark 9:38–50

A cup of water, a millstone, and salt are three distinct images of discipleship. A cup of water is what one offers; it portrays refreshment, cleansing, and the promise of abiding life. A millstone is what one avoids; it stands for burden, bondage, and the threat of death. Salt is how one behaves; it depicts adding zest to life, unique abilities, and distinct service. Common images characterize an exceptional ministry.

Call to Worship
James 5

Leader: Are any among you suffering? They should pray. Are any cheerful? They should sing songs of praise.

People: The prayer of faith will save the sick and whoever has committed sins will be forgiven.

Leader: Therefore confess your sins to one another, and pray for one another, so that you may be healed.

People: The prayer of the righteous is powerful and effective.

Leader: Let us worship God!

Prayer of Praise and Adoration

You do not tarry, O God of all goodness, to show us your favor. You hasten to hear us whenever we call. Bathed in the brightness of your radiant love for us, we can see clearly your care for creation. Through Christ, now open our eyes to the splendor of your redeeming judgment; by the Spirit continue to lead us to behold your dazzling grace. We worship you—God, Christ, and Holy Spirit, blessed Trinity forevermore.

Prayer of Confession

Unison: O God of mercy, you know our lives are but an illusion when we do not dwell in your favor. Our acts are but vapor when we do not obey your will. We boast of our good deeds, and flaunt righteous behavior, but they are conceived in arrogance and born of conceit. Forgive our deception and the damage it causes. By your mercy forgive us, and through Christ make us free.

Assurance of Pardon

Leader: Hear again the words of assurance. Christ is "the mediator of a new covenant, so that those who are called may receive the promised

eternal inheritance, because a death has occurred that redeems them from
. . . transgressions. . . . For Christ . . . entered into heaven itself, now to
appear in the presence of God on our behalf" (*Heb. 9:18, 24*).

Prayer of Dedication

Born anew with the hope of your redeeming grace, O God, we come
before you, bearing our gifts. Use them to spread abroad the good news
that in Christ resides the promise of release from captivity, hope that peace
can prevail among all your people, and assurance that you usher in the
dawn of a new day.

Prayer of Thanksgiving

Mystery of mysteries, whose wisdom surpasses the farthest reaches of
our imagination, whose compassion comforts us when shadows lengthen
and our busy lives are hushed, whose mercy restores us when we stray, we
give you thanks.

You are never far from us. If we take time to acknowledge your presence among us, we can sense that you are near. You can do all things;
nothing can surpass your care for all creation. What your commandments
have taught us, the prophets declared and your poets sung of your goodness and providence, we see all about us. We praise you for your work in
our midst, and will honor your name among the nations. We are thankful
for your comforting presence during times that try our faith. You have
shown how you accompany your people during their wilderness wanderings. They have sung of your guidance through the valley of the shadow
of death. Your own Son felt your presence when he was tempted by Satan.
You can be trusted; we need only rely on your guidance.

Have patience with us when we are wayward, and lead us back into
your way for us. When we are fearful of what tomorrow may bring, reassure us through Christ's example. You, who gave us our baptism as a sign
of our cleansing through Christ, invite us to be nourished at the table of
new life. You who spoke through the prophets of promised deliverance,
now send your Spirit to accompany us as we seek the paths of righteousness. Give us a measure of your wisdom to sustain us through our pilgrimage, and lead us at the last to your Promised Land.

27TH SUNDAY IN ORDINARY TIME (B)

Job 1:1; 2:1–10; Psalm 26
Hebrews 1:1–4; 2:5–12; Mark 10:2–16

A child's faith is a lesson in trust. Jesus uses such trust as an attitude befitting God's kingdom. Children depend on others to feed them, clothe them, care for them, and instruct them. Does not God know of our needs before we express them, and has not Christ proven faithful throughout the ages? Like a child, have faith that God cares for you, and trust in Christ who intercedes on our behalf.

Call to Worship

Psalm 26

Leader: I will sing a song of thanksgiving, O Lord, and tell of all your wondrous deeds.

People: O Lord, I love the house in which you dwell, and the place where your glory abides.

Leader: But as for me, I walk in my integrity; redeem me, and be gracious to me.

People: My foot stands on level ground; in the great congregation I will bless the Lord.

Leader: Let us worship God!

Prayer of Praise and Adoration

God of the ages, whose care for your children spans generations, we praise and adore you. We hear how you led Israel through their wanderings and brought them safely to the Promised Land. We are taught that Christ calls us to enter your covenant, that you open your kingdom to all who believe him. We take part in your graciousness and live by your mercy. Hear our worship of you as we confess our faith anew.

Prayer of Confession

Unison: O God of creation, you entrust us as stewards; we confess our abuse of what you place in our care. We foul the water by deliberate disposal; the air is polluted with emissions we create. We burn the forests through carelessness; the oceans are poisoned with toxins. Forgive our neglect of nature's delicate balance, and have mercy upon us as we renew our commitment to the created order.

Assurance of Pardon

Leader: As we confess our sin we see Jesus, "who for a little while was made lower than the angels, now crowned with glory and honor because of the suffering of death, so that by the grace of God he might taste death for everyone." Now be assured that Christ who sanctifies and those who are sanctified all have one origin. In Jesus Christ we are forgiven.

Prayer of Dedication

God who creates us, Christ who redeems us, Holy Spirit who fills us with wondrous gifts, we come, blessed Trinity, with our tithes and our offerings. Accept them and use them to further your kingdom. Grant that they may enlighten a corner of darkness and bring the truth of your love to those seeking freedom from bondage.

Prayer of Thanksgiving and Supplication

God of wonders, in many and various ways you speak to your people. We give thanks that you speak to us through Jesus Christ, the eternal Word made flesh. He who was with you at creation now upholds it by your providence, offering redemption for our sin, cleansing us of unworthy behavior, reconciling all things unto you, and promising peace. We give you thanks that he pioneered our salvation through suffering on behalf of all your people, and that he now sits at your right hand to intercede on our behalf when we pray.

Hear us then, as in his name we make our common supplications unto you. Teach us to trust that in your providence you will care for our needs. Quiet fears within us, when events do not occur according to our will. Help us to be less self-centered in our lives and freer to respond to your will for us. Then as we hear Christ's call to obedience, enable us to be converted by the destiny to which you call us, shaped to conform to your commandments, and sent forth to follow as his faithful disciples.

Help us to regain a child's sense of wonder and awe for your created order. Teach us to marvel at its intricate balance, rather than interfere. Lead us to work within it, since we are subject to it for our own health and well-being. Renew within us the commitment to stewardship, whereby all that we do becomes a response to the sacred trust inherited in Christ's name. To the end that your name is praised and you gain the glory, we offer our prayer and give you our lives.

28TH SUNDAY IN ORDINARY TIME (B)

Job 23:1–9, 16–17; Psalm 22:1–15
Hebrews 4:12–16; Mark 10:17–31

Discipleship involves sacrifice as well as obedience. One without the other is never complete. Sacrifice without obedience is an empty gesture, however costly. Obedience without sacrifice is to behave in such a way that personal comfort is not disturbed. Jesus was obedient even unto death on the cross, so that those who believe in him might receive the gift of eternal life.

Call to Worship

Hebrews 4

Leader: Before the Lord no creature is hidden, the one to whom we must render an account.

People: Since, then, we have a great high priest, let us hold fast to our confession.

Leader: For we have one who in every respect has been tested as we are, yet without sin.

People: Let us approach the throne of grace, that we may find grace to help in every time of need.

Leader: Let us worship God!

Prayer of Praise and Adoration

Eternal God, you have been our resting place through the ages. Generations come and pass away, but you abide forever. We praise you for your presence among us. You bring us comfort amid our trials, clarity where confusion persists, peace in the midst of conflict, and hope of eternal life. Hear us now as we pay you our tribute, in glad adoration that you are God of our lives.

Prayer of Confession

Unison: God who creates us, Christ who redeems us, Spirit who renews us, hear our confession. We hide from you when we should heed you; your voice we neglect. Disobedience hinders our being more faithful. We claim that others mislead us when we stray from your will, but it is our doing. Have mercy upon us and grant us forgiveness, so that we may rest in your peace.

Assurance of Pardon

Leader: Scripture reminds us that "in the days of his flesh, Jesus offered up prayers and supplications with loud cries and tears . . . and was heard because of his reverent submission. Although he was a Son, he learned obedience through what he suffered; and having been made perfect, he became the source of eternal salvation for all who obey him" (*Heb. 5:7–9*). In Jesus Christ, we are forgiven.

Prayer of Dedication

God of grace and mercy, we sing you our praises, we recite our confessions, and we offer our commitment in response to your love. You did not spare your only Son, but gave him up so that we may be saved. We pledge our trust in Christ to deliver us worthy of your call to discipleship. Accept what we give you as signs of obedience, and bless our efforts as we seek to be faithful.

Prayer of Thanksgiving and Supplication

God of all ages and of every generation, whose wisdom extends beyond the horizon and whose care reaches the farthest depths of the sea, we give thanks that we abide in the shelter of your encompassing love. We hear how nothing, not even death itself, can separate us from resting eternally in your presence. We give thanks for Christ's sacrifice on our behalf, how he arose victorious from the fetters of that ultimate bondage and now prepares a place for us by your side.

We pray, O God, that you will remove from us any encumbrances that keep us from realizing our destiny. Remove the scales from our eyes so that we can see clearly what you would have us do. Help us to put our trust in Christ, who alone can keep us from falling by the wayside of self-deception, avarice, false pride, or boredom. Let our faltering steps be strengthened by his willingness to suffer defeat on our behalf, so that we can henceforth walk boldly in his name.

Cleanse us of whatever foolishness causes us daily to betray him. When we expect him to work wonders on our behalf, remind us through the testimony of Scripture how he cared for all people. When we would serve him only at our convenience, startle us with his call to sacrifice all that we have and follow him. When we would betray him before others by our unwillingness publicly to proclaim him our Savior, send your Spirit among us to renew our commitment. O God, you have been "our dwelling place in all generations. . . . So teach us to number our days that we may get a heart of wisdom."

29TH SUNDAY IN ORDINARY TIME (B)

Job 38:1–7 (34–41); Psalm 104:1–9, 24, 35c
Hebrews 5:1–10; Mark 10:35–45

To serve other people is a high calling. It requires sensitivity, sympathy, and self-sacrifice. Sensitivity is the ability to feel and to hear another's needs. Sympathy describes willingness to share the burden. Self-sacrifice is the extent to which one will go to alleviate the need. All three are important and require discipline. That is why Jesus makes such a point of calling the disciples to serve others.

Call to Worship   Psalm 104

Leader: O Lord my God, how great you are! You are clothed with honor and majesty.

People: O Lord, how manifold are your works! In wisdom you have made them all.

Leader: You make the clouds your chariot, you ride on the wings of the wind.

People: You make the winds your messengers, fire and flame your ministers.

Leader: Bless the Lord, O my soul. Let us worship God!

Prayer of Praise and Adoration

Your praise is ever on our lips, O God. Songs of joy swell within us. We gaze at creation and behold goodness; we hear of your covenant and discover righteousness. Your love is boundless, your care without limits. We enter your sanctuary to give you honor; we bow down before you with glad adoration. Receive our worship and accept our thanksgiving. You are God whom we serve evermore.

Prayer of Confession

Unison: O God, who sent Christ to make intercession, have mercy on us as we confess our sin. He was oppressed; we afflict others. He was judged; we declare others unworthy. He was stricken; we cause others pain. He was put to death; we likewise destroy the innocent. Numbered with sinners, he bore our transgressions. Through Christ make us righteous, so that in him we can obey you.

Assurance of Pardon

Leader: Since we have a great high priest, Jesus Christ, who has passed through the heavens, let us hold fast our confession. For we have not a high priest who is unable to sympathize with our weaknesses, but one who in every respect has been tempted as we are, yet without sin. Let us then with confidence draw near to the throne of grace, with assurance that in Christ we are forgiven.

Prayer of Dedication

We draw near your throne of grace, O God, renewed by your mercy and enlivened by your power. You have given us the gift of a Savior so that in you "we live and move and have our being." Your Spirit resides with us as a source of encouragement and strength. Accept what we bring now as signs of our faithfulness and bless what we do hereafter as we express our commitment.

Prayer of Thanksgiving and Intercession

O God of righteousness, who spared not your own Son but sent him to save us, we give you thanks for Jesus, who is Christ evermore. He loved us enough to suffer on our behalf; he was afflicted, yet remained faithful. We are thankful that he can sense our weaknesses, uphold us during trials, plead for us when you judge us unworthy, and reconcile us to you as he sits by your side.

We pray for those who cause us suffering, whatever the reasons. Restrain in us the temptation to strike back at them. Keep us from grudges that block reconciliation. Help us to make of wrongdoing an occasion for understanding and compassion for the offender.

We pray for our enemies. Give us strength to withstand their blows. When gossip turns to slander, and envy to malice, keep us from becoming self-righteous. By your reconciling Spirit, replace pride with sympathy, anger with empathy, and resentment with conviction to work for justice and truth.

We pray for those who feel of no account in the world. Help them recover their dignity and use us in the process. As those who share Christ's ministry to the oppressed, equip us with the insight and skills to fulfill that task. Where systems oppress people, empower us to change them. Where persons abuse persons, give us the wisdom to redirect the lives affected. Make us useful servants of your righteousness and mirrors of your goodness, for the sake of him who gave his all for us.

30TH SUNDAY IN ORDINARY TIME (B)

Job 42:1–6, 10–17; Psalm 34:1–8 (19–22)
Hebrews 7:23–28; Mark 10:46–52

A blind man cries out to Jesus for mercy. Jesus asks what he wants him to do. "To see," the man says. "Your faith has made you well," replies the Master, and sends him on his way. Sight restored, he follows Jesus. What seems like a miracle to the reader is recounted as an everyday occurrence. To have faith in Jesus is to accept the fact that being restored to wholeness will become commonplace.

Call to Worship
Psalm 34

Leader: My soul makes its boast in the Lord; let the humble hear and be glad.

People: O magnify the Lord with me, and let us exalt God's name together.

Leader: When I sought you, O God, you answered me. You delivered me from all my fears.

People: O taste and see that the Lord is good; happy are those who take refuge in the Lord, our God.

Leader: Let us worship God!

Prayer of Praise and Adoration

Merciful God, whose benevolence extends to all corners of the planet, we give you praise. You seek the lame that they may walk in your glory. You call the blind to behold your grandeur. You fill the hungry with good things, and offer release to those imprisoned. Your kindness follows us wherever we go. Your grateful people gather before you with glad adoration.

Prayer of Confession

Unison: O God, who appointed Christ our high priest, may he intercede for us as we confess our sin. We are lame when we do not walk by faith. We are blind when we do not seek your truth. We crave self-fulfillment, rather than your righteousness. We are in bondage to ourselves. Through Christ, release us from our captivity, and in him forgive us.

Assurance of Pardon

Leader: Remember that Christ did not exalt himself to be made a high priest but was appointed by God, who said to him, "You are a priest for ever." As we confess our sins, we have assurance that Christ intercedes on our behalf. God hears our prayer. Through Jesus Christ we are forgiven.

Prayer of Dedication

God of goodness, you lavish your gifts on us. You have given us health; we dedicate our vigor to following Christ. You have given us strength; we offer our energy to serve neighbors in need. You have given us the commandments; we commit a portion of our wealth as signs of our faithfulness. Accept the tributes we bring. Use them to accomplish your will.

Prayer of Thanksgiving

Great are your words, O God; you make our hearts glad. Wherever we look we see your goodness. Throughout history you have restored the fortunes of your chosen people. In barren lands you led them to living waters. When they were hungry, you sent manna to sustain them. Those who went forth weeping returned home with shouts of joy, recounting the benefits of your wondrous love.

We give thanks for Christ, in whose name we inherit your mercy, and confess anew our faith in him as our high priest. He bore our weaknesses in his body, and thereby made us strong. We give thanks that he lives among us today to encourage the fainthearted, empower the weak, comfort the lonely, and bring release to the captives. Through him we are able to serve above and beyond our collective capacities, and for that legacy we give you thanks.

We give thanks for your Holy Spirit, who renews our flagging spirits and sends us forth with praise on our lips. In the midst of doubt, your Spirit brings clarity; when we are weary, your Spirit revives us. We can rely on your Spirit during lonely adventures; throughout our wanderings, we are never without your presence.

Our hearts beat with joy, thanks to your graciousness. Our eyes see more clearly, thanks to the vision of Christ our Savior. Our whole selves move more freely, thanks to your indwelling Spirit. We shout glad alleluias, so great are your works!

31ST SUNDAY IN ORDINARY TIME (B)

Ruth 1:1–18; Psalm 146
Hebrews 9:11–14; Mark 12:28–34

The truth of the gospel is that what God requires, God also provides. God requires ultimate love and obedience. God provides Christ, who on our behalf has been made perfect forever. God requires that we love our neighbor as ourselves. God provides Christ, who as high priest always lives to make intercession on our behalf. In God we truly live, move, and have our being, thanks to Christ's perfect sacrifice for us.

Call to Worship   Psalm 146

Leader: I will praise the Lord as long as I live; I will sing praises to my God all my life long.

People: Happy are those whose help is the God of Jacob, whose hope is in the Lord their God.

Leader: The Lord lifts up those who are bowed down; the Lord loves the righteous.

People: The Lord will reign forever, your God, O Zion, for all generations. Praise the Lord!

Leader: Let us worship God!

Prayer of Praise and Adoration

Your ways are just and true, O God, and your commandments trustworthy. Your steadfast love is never far from us in the person of Jesus Christ, our Savior. In him we know your righteous judgment, your reconciling redemption, and your encompassing care for the whole of creation. Through him we shall walk humbly, live justly, and worship you joyously, God of our lives!

Responsive Prayer of Confession

Leader: O God, give me understanding, that I may keep your law and observe it with my whole heart.

People: God, have mercy upon us, for we do not obey you.

Leader: Lead me in the path of your commandments, for I delight in it.

People: Christ, have mercy upon us, since we take no delight in serving our neighbor.

Leader: Turn my eyes from looking at vanities, and give me life in your ways.

People: God, have mercy upon us, because we are selfish and prone to evil.

Leader:	Behold, I long for your precepts; in your righteousness give me life!
People:	Christ, have mercy upon us, forgive us our sin, and by your grace may we walk in new life.

Assurance of Pardon

Leader: The testimony of Scripture affirms our pardon when we hear the words "How much more will the blood of Christ, who through the eternal Spirit offered himself without blemish to God, purify our conscience from dead works to worship the living God!" (*Heb. 9:14*). In Jesus Christ, we are forgiven.

Prayer of Dedication

Redeeming God, cleansed by your mercy, sustained by your grace, and led by your righteousness, we come before you bearing our gifts. Purify them to serve your purpose, and nurture us to act according to your will, so that all we have and do may bring justice on earth.

Prayer of Thanksgiving

Merciful Creator, hear our prayer, as we give you the honor and praise due your glorious name. We thank you for Jesus, who himself offered up prayers and supplications to you. He partook of humanity so that through death he might destroy the power of evil once and for all. He suffered on our behalf, yet without sinning. In his anguish he cried unto you that the burden of the cross be taken from his shoulders, yet he remained faithful. We give thanks that in his being made perfect he intercedes for us.

We praise your name for his passage through heaven, that he has prepared a way for us into your glorious sanctuary. We give thanks that by his death and resurrection he tore asunder the veil that kept us from beholding your glory. He taught the commandments, and he assured their fulfillment.

We give you thanks that in him we can faithfully walk the path of discipleship. He teaches us what it means to obey you. Because of his faithfulness, we can hold fast our confession of hope without wavering. Through his commandments we hear how to stir up one another to love and good works. By his example, we gather as his disciples to sing you psalms of adoration and feast on the sacrament that he ordained. The bread of the covenant will sustain us and nourish us through the trials that wait us. The cup of new life assures us that you will never forsake us. For all that, O God, we give you the honor and praise.

32ND SUNDAY IN ORDINARY TIME (B)

Ruth 3:1–5; 4:13–17; Psalm 127
Hebrews 9:24–28; Mark 12:38–44

The widow's mite has become a symbol of stewardship. She gave not out of abundance but out of poverty. Jesus says that she gave everything she had. Stewardship is a sacred trust bestowed by God, an opportunity to care responsibly for all of God's creation. Stewardship grows out of faith that God will sufficiently care for all of our needs. The widow knew what it meant to enter God's sacred trust.

Call to Worship

Psalm 127

Leader: Unless the Lord builds the house, those who build it labor in vain.

People: Unless the Lord guards the city, the guard keeps watch in vain.

Leader: It is in vain that you rise up early and go late to rest.

People: We shall put our trust in the Lord who gives rest to God's beloved.

Leader: Let us worship God!

Prayer of Praise and Adoration

We praise you, God of all being! You give food to the hungry, set prisoners free, open the eyes of the blind, and lift the spirits of those bowed down. Because you are righteous, you sent Christ to redeem the lost and the wayward. We come into your presence enlivened by your Holy Spirit and full of new hope to give you the honor due your glorious name.

Prayer of Confession

Unison: Merciful God of compassion and justice, take pity on us as we confess our sin. We are not the stewards Christ calls us to be. Riches possess us while others go hungry. We mismanage creation with our pollution and strife. Your goodness is betrayed by our lust for power. We abuse your provision for us by our selfish desires. Help us hear once again Christ's call to be faithful, and through him forgive us as we repent of our sin and turn from it.

Assurance of Pardon

Leader: Remember the words of Scripture where it says, "For Christ has entered . . . into heaven itself, now to appear in the presence of God on our behalf . . . to remove sin by the sacrifice of himself." All who repent and eagerly await him have the assurance that their sins are forgiven.

Prayer of Dedication

God of grace and glory, all that we have is a gift of your mercy. You shower blessings upon us out of your goodness. You redeem us from the evil one, and rescue us from the pit of our own selfishness. We come before you, seeking to be faithful to Christ's call to stewardship. Accept what we offer as signs of our yearning to be better caretakers of your creation.

Prayer of Thanksgiving and Supplication

Author of all creation, Sovereign over all creatures, we praise you for your goodness and give thanks for your mercy. We give thanks that in Christ Jesus you have called us to be disciples, and that you delight to fill us with your Holy Spirit, who prods us to greater faithfulness.

We give thanks for Jesus, who calls us to be caretakers of the treasures nature provides. Help us through him to relinquish our lust to control all that we see. Make us responsive to what is around us, so that we sanctify the world rather than subdue it, rely on the created order and not always have to remake it, and support the natural course of events rather than always subjecting them to our own purposes.

Sanctified by Christ's sacrifice on our behalf, we give thanks for your Spirit, who reconciles us anew with your will. Through the Spirit, transform our surroundings from the mundane to the sacred, so that in all that we do we can respond to your divine trust. Help us use our time wisely and to your advantage. Give us discipline to nurture the talents you give, and zeal to use them to your honor and glory.

Subject to Christ who calls us, attuned to your Spirit who empowers us, and commissioned to proclaim you Author and Finisher of all creation, we go forth to the respective scenes of our labors. Bless our intentions and sanctify our efforts. May their effect be acceptable in your sight, O Lord, our Rock and Redeemer.

33RD SUNDAY IN ORDINARY TIME (B)

1 Samuel 1:4–20; 1 Samuel 2:1–10
Hebrews 10:11–14 (15–18) 19–25; Mark 13:1–8

The Word of God is eternal, surpassing all earthly knowledge. God sent the Word into the world, so that those who dwell on earth may have life, and that abundantly. Earthly life shall pass away, yet those who believe in Christ shall live eternally, for such is God's promise. Amid the trials and the burdens of mundane existence, hope in the Word, who brings order out of chaos and life beyond death.

Call to Worship   1 Samuel 2

Leader: My heart exults in the Lord; my strength is exalted in my God.
People: There is no Holy One like the Lord, no one besides you; there is no Rock like our God.
Leader: For the pillars of the earth are the Lord's, and on them God has set the world.
People: The Lord will guard the feet of the faithful ones and judge the ends of the earth.
Leader: Let us worship God!

Prayer of Praise and Adoration

God of dominion, power, glory, and honor, God of tenderness, compassion, patience, and comfort, we come extolling your virtues and praising your name. You are too wonderful for comprehension; we live because of your embracing mercy. We bless you for Christ, through whom we may know you, bow down before you, worship and adore you, God of all ages. Alleluia! Amen.

Litany of Assurance

Leader: When Christ had offered for all time a single sacrifice for sins, he sat down at the right hand of God.
People: In Jesus Christ, we are forgiven.
Leader: For by a single offering he has perfected for all time those who are sanctified.
People: In Jesus Christ, we are forgiven.
Leader: And the Holy Spirit adds, "I will remember their sins and their lawless deeds no more."
People: In Jesus Christ, we are forgiven.

| *Leader:* | Where there is forgiveness of these, there is no longer any offering for sin. |
| *People:* | In Jesus Christ, we are forgiven. |

Prayer of Dedication

"Ancient of Days, who sit enthroned in glory, to you all knees are bent, all voices pray; Your love has blest the wide world's wondrous story with light and life since Eden's dawning day" (*The Worshipbook,* no. 297). We come before you, O God, beholding your glory, and offer you gifts in praise of your name. May your light so shine that all creation discerns your dominion, and may whatever we do bring you honor and praise.

Prayer of Thanksgiving

O Triune God, whose dominion is eternal, we praise you for unwarranted blessings bestowed on your people throughout the ages. You led them through the barren places, providing food by day and protection by night. You made them wise through the voice of the prophets, and called them to account for their deeds. You gave them the Ark that contained the commandments, as a seal of your promise that they were your chosen people. We give thanks that we inherit this legacy of promise and fulfillment, and partake with our ancestors in faith of your wondrous love.

We praise you for Jesus, who calls us as heirs of your favor. It is through him that we dare to come into your presence. Once and for all he rent the veil in the heavenly sanctuary, and invites all who believe in him to come, enter in. We give thanks for the peace we receive when we follow, for the assurance that comes with your redeeming pardon. He remains with us as we seek to obey you. We give thanks for the teachings he bequeathed to his disciples, words of wisdom that continually guide us as we hear your living word proclaimed anew.

We praise you for the Spirit, who renews confidence and grants endurance for the paths of discipleship that lie ahead. We will not shy away from threatening encounters with your Spirit to guide how we act. Our knees will not tremble, nor will our hands remain idle, as long as the Spirit enables response. You have seen to it, O God, that we are empowered for service. May all our works praise you, and all your saints bless you.

34TH SUNDAY IN ORDINARY TIME
(REIGN OF CHRIST OR CHRIST THE KING) (B)

2 Samuel 23:1–7; Psalm 132:1–12 (13–18)
Revelation 1:4b–8; John 18:33–37

Again Jesus is questioned about his authority. Whence came the right to do what he did? What special insight enabled him to utter profound teachings? What source did he tap to perform healing deeds? Today it may be easier to answer such questions, but it is still as difficult to believe in his authority. Otherwise, why do some doubt him, deny him, and distrust him? Is he, or is he not, the Savior?

Call to Worship   Psalm 132

Leader: The Lord has said, "Zion is my resting place forever; for I have desired it.

People: "I will abundantly bless its provisions; I will satisfy its poor with bread.

Leader: "Its priests I will clothe with salvation, and its faithful will shout for joy.

People: " There I will cause a horn to sprout up for David, a lamp for my anointed one."

Leader: Let us worship God!

Prayer of Praise and Adoration

O God of enduring compassion and mercy, your dominion is unending, your judgment forthright. We live by your grace, assured of your love. We praise you for Jesus, who taught how to honor you; we are awed by your Spirit, who guides and sustains us. We come into your presence to learn your will for us, to worship and adore you as we abide in your realm.

Prayer of Confession

Unison: O God of mercy, woe be upon us, for we do not obey you. We confess one baptism, yet we foster divisions in Christ's body. We observe the Lord's Supper but work not for Christ's peace. We confess our reluctance to extend your favor to those we don't like. Forgive and restore us for the sake of your Son, Jesus Christ. You are a God of dominion; we live by your grace alone.

Assurance of Pardon

Leader: We are told in Scripture that the days are coming when God will raise up a righteous Branch, who shall reign and deal wisely, who

247

shall execute justice and righteousness in the land. We believe that Christ has come and performed all that was foretold by the prophets. I can assure you that in Jesus Christ we are forgiven.

Prayer of Dedication

Source of deliverance and hope, you invite us to live evermore in your favor. We offer ourselves to you in response to Christ's call. Out of the abundance of your love we offer gifts to you. From the storehouse of your mercy we bring you treasures. Accept the gleanings of our labor as we lay them before you. To you belong the glory and the dominion forever and ever.

Prayer of Thanksgiving and Intercession

Benevolent Ruler of nations and Protector of peoples, we come with thanksgiving for your mighty care. You do not draw apart from your people, but through Christ choose to dwell in our midst. We give thanks that he became the servant of humanity and stooped to the needs of the lowly and humble. In him we have assurance that you hear us when we pray, grieve with us when we are afflicted, mourn as we do the loss of loved ones, and care enough to judge and redeem us when we stray from your way.

We pray for those who govern us in society. Give to them a sense of your compassion and care. Keep them from setting themselves apart from the needs of those whom they serve, and endow them with patience and wisdom to work for the well-being of all. As we elect them to office, lead us to entrust them with sufficient authority to perform their duties. Keep us from ignoring their judgments, and help us to serve with them toward the common good of all people.

We pray for leaders of foreign lands, those aligned with us and those antagonistic toward us. Help us to work with our allies for common strength, shared benefits, and greater commitment to justice and peace. With those who are antagonistic, grant us understanding, compassion, and the humility to see their point of view. Keep us through Christ from rebuilding the walls of enmity and hostility he came to abolish. And may we through your Spirit be granted significant wisdom and courage to work peaceably with all peoples. We yearn for the time when your vision is realized, and the lion shall lie with the calf, and war shall be no more.

ALL SAINTS' DAY (B)

Wisdom of Solomon 3:1–9 or Isaiah 25:6–9; Psalm 24
Revelation 21:1–6a; John 11:32–44

Jesus goes to the aid of Mary and Martha as they grieve over the death of their brother Lazarus. We see the compassionate side of Jesus as he weeps with those who weep. We see his absolute obedience to God as he thanks God for having heard his unspoken prayer. We see the faith of Jesus as he cried with a loud voice for Lazarus to come out of the tomb. When Lazarus comes out of the tomb bound in the bonds of death, Jesus tells those about him, "Unbind him, and let him go." As we believe, Jesus can likewise unbind us and give us new life.

Call to Worship
Psalm 24

Leader: The earth is the Lord's and all that is in it, the world, and those who live in it.

People: Who shall ascend the hill of the Lord? And who shall stand in God's holy place?

Leader: Those with clean hands and pure hearts, who do not lift up their souls to what is false.

People: Such is the company of those who seek the Lord, who seek the face of the God of Jacob.

Leader: Let us worship God!

Prayer of Praise and Adoration

God of compassion and mercy, you wipe the tears from our eyes that we may behold the new heaven and new earth. We come into your presence with praise and thanksgiving. In Christ you promise that you will never forsake us. Because of your Spirit your abiding presence is forever with us. In you is our firm conviction that death will be no more, and mourning and crying will cease, for the first things have passed away and we dwell in the assurance of your eternal life.

Litany of Assurance

Leader: On this mountain the Lord of hosts will make for all peoples a feast of rich foods.

People: Lo, this is our God for whom we have waited and who will save us.

Leader: The Lord will destroy on this mountain the shroud that is cast over all peoples.

People: Lo, this is our God for whom we have waited and who will save us.

Leader:	The Lord will swallow up death forever.
People:	Lo, this is our God for whom we have waited and who will save us.
Leader:	Then the Lord God will wipe away the tears from all faces.
People:	Lo, this is our God for whom we have waited and who will save us.
Leader:	And God will take away their disgrace from all the earth.
People:	Lo, this is our God for whom we have waited and who will save us.

Prayer of Dedication

Gracious God, you set us upright and cause our feet to stand firm on the foundation of Jesus Christ, the cornerstone of our faith. We bring you ourselves in response to your grace and mercy. You test us in Christ and find us worthy of your benevolent care and compassion. Through the visitation of your Spirit you allow us to shine forth to your glory and honor and cause your light to shine forth on the nations. We bring you our gifts in response to your graciousness and ask that you will watch over us as we go forth to serve you in thought, word, and deed.

Prayer of Thanksgiving and Supplication

Author and Finisher of our faith, you have set our feet firmly on freedom's foundation; we praise you and give you thanks. Witnesses of old have taught us of the deliverance of God's people from peril. Scripture recounts their covenant promise: You will be our God and we your people. You, O Christ, have sealed a new covenant in your blood and won for us the victory of life everlasting.

Draw us into a right relationship with you and our neighbor. Help us to stand fast by your Spirit and not abuse your trust. Make our inheritance as your sons and daughters a lasting legacy, one that we are eager to pass on to our heirs. Help us by our example to teach them what it means to love you completely and our neighbor as ourselves.

We pray for neighbors both near and far. Give an extraordinary sense of your delivering power to those who live in peril for your sake. Allow them to walk free from care. Lift from their shoulders the weight of anxiety, and yoke us to them during their time of trial.

There are those for whom freedom is costly: martyrs, prisoners, and the oppressed. Let them not be denied the birthright of your blessing. Give to prisoners the hope that their confinement does not separate them from your mercy. Lift the oppressed and let them glimpse your glory. Set us on the path of freedom's journey and we shall recount what great deeds you have done.

Year C

1ST SUNDAY OF ADVENT (C)

Jeremiah 33:14–16; Psalm 25:1–10
1 Thessalonians 3:9–13; Luke 21:25–36

A day of great glory is forecast. The people are told to watch for it at all times. Signs will precede its coming, as trees in leaf declare that summer is near. Advent is a time of such expectancy; its sign is a babe full of promise and hope. Therefore, "look up and raise your heads, because your redemption is drawing near."

Call to Worship
Psalm 25

Leader: To you, O Lord, I lift up my soul. In you I put my trust.
People: Make me to know your ways, O Lord; teach me your paths.
Leader: Lead me in your truth, and teach me, for you are the God of my salvation.
People: According to your steadfast love remember me, for your goodness' sake, O Lord!
Leader: Let us worship God!

Prayer of Praise and Adoration

God of redeeming grace, you lead us in paths of righteousness and make your ways known through the birth of a child. We praise your goodness and rely on your wisdom. Accept the sounds of rejoicing we raise to you, and guide our hearing as we seek your instruction. Grant that we may not only worship you joyfully but also follow you faithfully all the days of our lives.

Prayer of Confession

Unison: Great Deliverer, we entrust to you our confession of sin. We are easily discouraged when our good deeds do not make things better. We fear harm to ourselves if we take too firm a stand. Portents of danger arise about us, and we doubt the future you have promised. We close our eyes to the signs and live for the moment. God, in Christ, forgive our cowardice and blindness, for the sake of him who endured the cross for us.

Assurance of Pardon

Leader: The words of the psalmist remind us that the Lord is upright and good. God instructs sinners in the way of righteousness and leads the humble along paths of steadfast love. So wait upon God all the day long, abide in the covenant, and rely on the truth: God is our salvation and worthy of trust.

253

Prayer of Dedication

God of promise, you cause the branch of hope to bud and flower; we offer you the fruit of our labor. May what we do bring reassurance to those seeking evidence of your goodness. Use our gifts as signs of what deliverance can mean. We join with the Christ in the struggle for justice; we commit ourselves to the quest for peace.

Prayer of Supplication

Guardian of our lives, it is you who remain faithful when all else falls away. Amid the darkening skies of world events, your vision of righteousness provides a ray of hope. When prophets see empires crumbling, your promise of deliverance sustains us. We trust not in riches, but in your goodness alone to meet our daily needs. You have sheltered your people in the past. We watch for signs of your presence among us still as we endure the trials that continue to confront us.

Grant us a vision of your will to lead us through the unknown morrow. When choices abound, and voices clamor for attention, show us a clear path. We rely on your mercy and would be led by your truth; we yearn to be faithful to the love you have shown.

When we are tempted to waver, help us to step out with confidence. Advent marks a new beginning; we hear anew of the redemption the Messiah brings. Help us embark on faith's journey in spite of the risks. When we are alone, comfort us by your Spirit's presence. When we hurt, ease our pain with the healing touch of the Great Physician. When we are confused because the way is uncertain, speak once more those words of reassurance: "Behold, the days are coming when you shall cause a Branch to spring forth who shall execute justice and righteousness in all the land." For we pray in the name of the one who reveals that righteousness, even Jesus the Christ.

2ND SUNDAY OF ADVENT (C)

Malachi 3:1–4; Luke 1:68–79
Philippians 1:3–11; Luke 3:1–6

The news is out! The messenger is coming! He will bring with him the covenant in which we delight. The valley shall be filled, mountains and hills made low; the crooked shall be made straight, the rough places smooth. Ah, but who can endure the day of his coming? For he will sit in judgment to purify the people until that which they offer is pleasing to God.

Call to Worship

Luke 1

Leader: Blessed be the Lord God of Israel, for you have looked favorably upon your people.

People: You have raised up a mighty savior for us in the house of his servant David.

Leader: By the tender mercy of our God, the dawn from on high will break upon us.

People: To give light to those who sit in darkness and guide our feet into the way of peace.

Leader: Let us worship God!

Prayer of Praise and Adoration

O God, you are a refining fire and a purifying agent. We praise you that in Christ you make us whole again. We gather to hear his coming announced, and anxiously wait the dawn of your redeeming grace. Fill our mouths with laughter at the prospect of our liberation, and our tongues with shouts of joy at the news of our redemption. You continue to do great things for us, O God. Therefore we come into your presence with singing.

Prayer of Confession

Unison: God of abounding grace, have mercy upon us. Our valleys are deep when we are encompassed with care. Our mountains are high when our burdens are heavy. We grope in the maze of our tangled alliances and reap the pain of bad choices and ignorant gambles. You promised that all flesh shall see your salvation. Show us the straight path and the smooth way that lead to your righteousness, through Jesus Christ, who is the way.

Assurance of Pardon

Leader: Paul prays "that your love may overflow more and more with knowledge and full insight to help you to determine what is best, so that in the day of Christ you may be pure and blameless, having produced the harvest of righteousness that comes through Jesus Christ for the glory and praise of God." Friends, in Christ live in the assurance of righteousness to the glory of God.

Prayer of Dedication

Searcher of hearts, you know our thoughts before they are spoken. You refine our impure acts so they conform to your will. May what we say reflect your purpose for creation, and what we do be consistent with your intent. Shape what we give you to suit your pleasure, and fashion us to fit your design.

Prayer of Thanksgiving and Intercession

O God, you cleanse our tarnished souls and purify our thoughts by the refining fire of your judgment. We wait for the day of your Messenger's coming, and give thanks for his righteousness by which we are saved from your wrath. He walks with us in the valley. He levels the barriers we raise to evade his will. His paths are straight; we need only follow. We can endure the day of his coming, thanks to your mercy; our prayer can be pleasing to you because of his sacrifice for us.

We intercede for those who are despairing. For them the valley seems endless, with no hope of escape. The walls of their own sense of inability close in upon them; they feel along in their ordeal. Help us to speak to them a word of comfort and assurance, to offer the embrace of companionship and concern. Together may we smooth the rough places and fill the valley, so that your will for them may have free course.

We pray on behalf of those encumbered with burdens too heavy to bear. Some of the weight is of their own choosing, some is not. May Christ, who bore our sin upon the cross, ease the burden of all who strain beneath the load. Yoke us with him and with all who are heavy laden, so that together we may complete the task you have assigned to us.

3RD SUNDAY OF ADVENT (C)

Zephaniah 3:14–20; Isaiah 12:2–6
Philippians 4:4–7; Luke 3:7–18

The prophet proclaims a festival when all God's people will celebrate that God dwells in their midst. It will be a day for rejoicing, for singing songs of salvation, for exclaiming about all the deeds God has done among the nations. People in all lands will be united. Peace will be the priority, with judgments erased, enemies cast out, and evil feared no longer, since God will gather all people together.

Call to Worship
Isaiah 12

Leader: Surely God is my salvation; I will trust, and will not be afraid.

People: For the Lord God is my strength and my might, and has become my salvation.

Leader: With joy you will give thanks to the Lord and call on God's name.

People: We will sing you our praises, O God, for you have done glorious things.

Leader: Let us worship God!

Prayer of Praise and Adoration

You put a glad song on our lips, O God of salvation, for in you we can trust and not be afraid. In Christ is announced our source of deliverance; through him the lame walk and the outcast are praised. Soon you will gather your people for a festival of salvation; we assemble now in Christ's name to rejoice and boast of your goodness.

Prayer of Confession

Unison: Source of salvation, what shall we do? Our lives are unworthy of the goodness you offer. We complain of our condition when our wants go unnoticed. Contentment eludes us, since when we have plenty we still yearn for more. Millions face hunger, while we fret over abundance. Through Christ forgive us, yet grant us no peace until we share our bread with the hungry and our homes with those who lack shelter.

Assurance of Pardon

Leader: "Rejoice in the Lord always; again I will say, Rejoice. . . . The Lord is near. Do not worry about anything, but in everything by prayer and supplication with thanksgiving let your requests be made known to God. And the peace of God, which surpasses all understanding, will guard your hearts and your minds in Christ Jesus." In Christ we are forgiven.

Prayer of Dedication

Gracious God, whatever is true we owe to your mercy. The honorable and just reflect your goodness. When we are pure, it is because you forgive us. Whatever is lovely is a gift of your grace. All of our excellence is due to your kindness. Receive now what we offer as signs of thanksgiving.

Prayer of Thanksgiving and Supplication

Glorious God, we approach you this day with a song in our hearts and praise on our lips. You have chosen to dwell in our midst and bring us salvation. You are the wellspring of all goodness from whom we draw life-giving sustenance. Your glory is manifest throughout creation. We will proclaim to the nations how your name is exalted.

As a warrior in battle, you attack the forces of oppression. Make us as determined to see that justice prevails. Where there is hunger, help us do more than allay it. Give us the insight and conviction to attack its causes. Helps us to provide shelter for those who are homeless. Forbid that our warmth should lull us into neglecting their misery. Make us advocates for the voiceless, and a tower of strength for the powerless. Let others see in us a force for justice and peace as we combat whatever keeps your people in chains.

Separate the chaff from the wheat in our lives, and help us to focus on the good we can do and be to your glory. When in response to our baptism we ask, "What shall we do?" make us receptive to the guidance your Spirit provides. The storehouse of our faith is cluttered with well-meaning intentions; many of the past year's resolutions lie forgotten. Remove the gap between our words and our actions as we seek consistency in faith and living. We have offered our prayer; now we commit to you our time and our efforts.

4TH SUNDAY OF ADVENT (C)

Micah 5:2–5a; Luke 1:47–55 or Psalm 80:1–7
Hebrews 10:5–10; Luke 1:39–45 (46–55)

Two women meet; greetings are exchanged. They are about to be mothers, and have much in common. Elizabeth, full of the Holy Spirit, exclaims that Mary is blessed. Mary, her spirit rejoicing, recites how God has been merciful. Expectation abounds for what is about to occur; those of low degree shall be exalted, and the hungry shall be filled with good things.

Call to Worship   Psalm 80

Leader: Give ear, O Shepherd of Israel. Stir up your might, and come to save us!
People: Restore us, O God; let your face shine that we may be saved.
Leader: Let us worship God!

Prayer of Praise and Adoration

O Shepherd of Israel, from whom comes forth one who shall feed your flock, we gather as those who dwell in the folds of your embrace and care. Your love envelops us like swaddling cloths wrapped around a babe in a manger. Your countenance shines like a star that led the wise men one night. We behold your radiance as we enter your sanctuary and praise your name for the Christ who brings us salvation.

Prayer of Confession

Unison: Most holy God, in Christ you pour out your mercy to forgive our transgression. Hear us now as we confess our sin. We err in our judgment of what you want from us. We seek to appease you with offerings, earn your favor by doing good deeds, or garner a blessing through making some sacrifice. Forgive us our nature that is prone to buy favor, and in Christ restore us to a right relationship with you.

Assurance of Pardon

Leader: Micah foresees the Coming One, who shall stand and feed the flock. The people shall dwell secure in the majesty of God's name. Christ is our peace, and we can dwell secure in the knowledge that through him we are forgiven.

Prayer of Dedication

"Ancient of Days, who sit enthroned in glory, to you all knees are bent, all voices pray." All that we bring you have bestowed upon us. Whatever good we do is a sign of your grace. Accept these glad offerings we lay before you as praise for "the goodness that does crown our days" (*The Worshipbook, no. 297*).

Prayer of Thanksgiving and Supplication

Source of salvation, your name is holy. From you comes forth One who shall govern your people. As a shepherd calls the sheep, so will your servant call humanity to come and enter into sanctuary, where they may dwell secure. There they shall be nourished by the word of your covenant, and surrounded with hope that you abide in their midst. Their days shall be spent following the Shepherd's command; their nights will pass quickly as they rest secure in your love. We give thanks that we may be numbered among those whom through Christ you have chosen; we seek to be faithful to the call we receive.

We pray for courage to respond to Christ's will in spite of the risk. Make us persistent in our ministry as a shepherd in search of lost sheep. Where persons are lost or bewildered, help us to stand as shining rays of hope. To those who wander aimlessly or unsure of themselves, let us bring fresh esteem, clarity of mind, and renewed purpose. To those beguiled by false hopes and vain promises, our prayer is that your Spirit will impart wise counsel and true hope. For those who are pursued and attacked by ruthless forces, we pray for determination and strength to come to their aid.

Make us worthy in all that we do to bear the stamp of your approval and election. Secure in your love, may we be bold in facing the forces of evil. Nourished by your Word, may we extend to all Christ's gift of new life. Fill our days with moments that please you, and our nights with the peace of the reconciled.

CHRISTMAS EVE/DAY (B) — *See Year A*

1ST SUNDAY AFTER CHRISTMAS (B)

1 Samuel 2:18–20, 26; Psalm 148
Colossians 3:12–17; Luke 2:41–52

Jesus causes his parents some anxious moments. He wasn't where they thought he was, so they search for him. Three days later they find him in the Temple at Jerusalem, amazing those gathered with his understanding and insight. His reason for being there is straightforward and simple: "Did you not know that I must be in my Father's house?" His mother has things to ponder as they go down to Nazareth.

Call to Worship   Psalm 148

Leader: Praise the Lord! Praise the Lord from the heavens; praise God in the heights!

People: All the shining stars praise you, O God, for you commanded and they were created.

Leader: Praise the Lord from the earth, young men and women alike, old and young together!

People: Let everyone praise the name of the Lord, for your glory is above earth and heaven.

Leader: Let us worship God!

Prayer of Praise and Adoration

We will indeed praise you, O God, and cause your works to be known. Your mercy and grace shall endure forever. As we obey your commandments and abide by your wisdom, we shall proclaim to the nations how you can be trusted. Upheld by the covenant you established, our feet firmly placed on an unshakable foundation, we enter your presence to give you all glory.

Litany of Exhortation

Leader: Put on then, as God's chosen ones, holy and beloved, compassion, kindness, lowliness, meekness, and patience.

People: Above all we will put on love which binds everything together in perfect harmony.

Leader: Forbear one another and, if one has a complaint against another, forgive each other.

People: Above all we will put on love which binds everything together in perfect harmony.

Leader:	Let the word of Christ dwell in you richly; sing psalms and hymns and spiritual songs with thankfulness to God.
People:	Above all we will put on love which binds everything together in perfect harmony.
Leader:	And whatever you do, in word or deed, do in Christ's name, giving thanks to God.
People:	Above all we will put on love which binds everything together in perfect harmony.

Prayer of Dedication

Giver of every good and perfect gift, tribute and glad praises we bring to you. Let the words of our mouths proclaim the dawn of redemption Christ inaugurates. Use our talents to spread abroad the good news of his reconciling love. Accept the gifts we offer to further his teachings, so that all people may find in him the abundant life he so richly promised.

Prayer of Thanksgiving and Intercession

Fountainhead of all wisdom, we have come into your courtyard to sing your praises; within the sanctuary your Word is proclaimed. Surrounded by your Spirit, we hear anew the promise of the covenant, that Christ came to earth so that all could be saved. We are amazed at how Jesus taught with authority and marvel at the poignancy and relevance of his words for today.

We pray for teachers who commit their lives to instructing others how to grow in wisdom, stature, and favor with you and their neighbors. We remember with gratitude those who have influenced us in our growing; we give thanks for their patience, insight, and supportive compassion. They knew how to prod us when we were lax, support us when we feared to venture forth, and applaud us when the task was completed. Grant those who teach an insatiable thirst for continuing enlightenment, and the needed strength to pursue their arduous tasks.

We pray for students who must discipline themselves to the never-ending quest for truth. Teach them that truth must serve goodness, and that the fear of God is the beginning of wisdom. Give them a sufficient measure of insight to satisfy their hunger for the moment, while implanting a craving for further revelation.

Teach us alike to hunger for righteousness and seek to be fed the bread of life. We give you thanks for Christ's household of which we are members, for his table around which we gather with brothers and sisters, and for the sustaining nourishment which brings us wisdom, growth, and your continued favor.

2ND SUNDAY AFTER CHRISTMAS (C) — *See Year A*

EPIPHANY OF THE LORD (C) — *See Year A*

BAPTISM OF THE LORD

Isaiah 43:1–7; Psalm 29
Acts 8:14–17; Luke 3:15–17, 21–22

There are great expectations! One is coming who will baptize with the Holy Spirit and with fire. The threshing floor will be cleared; the chaff will burn with unquenchable fire; good tidings will come to the afflicted. This one will bind up the brokenhearted and set captives free. Those who mourn will find comfort. The heavens shall open and all will hear, "You are my Son, the Beloved; with you I am well pleased."

Call to Worship
Psalm 29

Leader: Ascribe to the Lord, O heavenly being, ascribe to the Lord glory and strength.

People: Ascribe to the Lord the glory of God's name; worship the Lord in holy splendor.

Leader: The voice of the Lord is powerful; the voice of the Lord is full of majesty.

People: May the Lord give strength to God's people! May the Lord bless God's people with peace!

Leader: Let us worship God!

Prayer of Praise and Adoration

God of good tidings, you gladden our hearts with your favor. Our ears are attuned to your words of mercy. Wherever we look, we see the signs of your presence: Christ has truly come to set the captives free. Washed clean by your grace and renewed by your Spirit, we put on the mantles of praise and raise our voices in glad adoration. All glory be to you, O God of splendor and majesty, for in Christ we receive the gift of new life.

Prayer of Confession

Unison: You, who in Christ have assured redemption, hear our confession and forgive our sin. Christ proclaims your goodwill toward all people, yet we pursue vengeance. Those who mourn go uncomforted, as warfare continues in the earth. Captives without number await deliverance while we take freedom for granted. The afflicted await some sign of good news. Amid the ruin of cities and the clamor of protesting voices, we confess our disobedience. Save your people, O God, and cleanse us of our sin, for the sake of your Anointed One, Jesus Christ.

Assurance of Pardon

Leader: Recall John's words, "I baptize you with water; but he who is mightier than I is coming . . . (who) will baptize you with the Holy Spirit and with fire." As we repent our wickedness, Christ, who knows the intents of our hearts, cleanses us of all sin. The threshing floor is stirred and sifted so the wheat can be gathered. May the unquenchable fire of the Spirit purge our beings and prepare us for the reign of God.

Prayer of Dedication

Source of all we have and are, you have sent Christ to save us. We commit our lives to serve him. Your Spirit abides with us as counselor and guide. We offer our actions to be led by her wisdom. The waters of baptism are a sign of your forgiveness. We dedicate our talents as symbols of faithfulness. May what we bring prove worthy of your benevolence to us.

Prayer of Thanksgiving

O God, who spoke as the heavens opened to declare your pleasure in Jesus Christ, we praise you that we are called in his name and find favor in your sight. As your obedient servant, he was baptized by John and received the Holy Spirit. We praise you for our baptism, and that in Christ you seal our adoption as your sons and daughters. We thank you for the Spirit, who abides with us as a legacy of that inheritance, and for mothers and fathers in ages past who were faithful in transmitting your promises to our generation. From them we have received our confessions of faith. With Christ as the cornerstone you form us into a building of God. With Christ as our closest kin, you blend us into one household of faith.

We rejoice in the remembrance of our initiation into that fellowship. You set us apart and named us; the confession of faith was made and we received your divine blessing. As hands were laid upon us and we joined with brothers and sisters in ministry, so now we commit ourselves again to go into all the world, to proclaim good news and make disciples. Through the grace of our Savior and empowered by your Holy Spirit we will teach them all that you have commanded us—even to the close of the age.

2ND SUNDAY IN ORDINARY TIME (C)

Isaiah 62:1–5; Psalm 36:5–10
1 Corinthians 12:1–11; John 2:1–11

A wedding is no time for the wine to give out, but that's what happens. Jesus and his mother are wedding guests, so Mary has a word with her son. As a result, when the steward tastes what he thinks is water from a jar, he finds instead that it is good wine. Usually hosts serve the good wine first, and the poor wine last. With Jesus, guests continue to dine on the abundance of God's richest blessings.

Call to Worship   Psalm 36

Leader: Your love, O God, extends to the heavens; your righteousness is like the ever-rolling mountains.
People: We shall feast on the abundance of your goodness, O God, and drink our fill of your mercy, O Fountain of life.
Leader: Let us worship God!

Prayer of Praise and Adoration

Source of delight and rejoicing, you call us to assemble and partake of your banquet. The tables are spread with the abundance of your everlasting grace. Our cups overflow with the drink of new life. With Christ, our host, we join brothers and sisters to sing glad praises for all the wonders you have done.

Prayer of Confession

Unison: We blend our voices in common confession, O God; you are our hope of salvation. The Apostle teaches that there are varieties of gifts, yet we judge others because they do not fit our mold. There is one Savior, yet we mistrust those who do not believe as we do, and doubt that they are led by the same Spirit. Forgive us for the many ways we sever the parts of Christ's body. Through him reconcile us and pardon our estrangement.

Assurance of Pardon

Leader: Remember that Christ "is our peace, who has made us both one, and has broken down the dividing wall of hostility." It is Christ who reconciles us "both to God in one body through the cross" (*Eph. 2:14, 16*). Through Christ, live in assurance that you are forgiven, and be joined together as fellow citizens of God's household.

Prayer of Dedication

God of steadfast love, you give to each a measure of your bounteous mercy; accept what we offer in return as a gift of love from your family here. If it is service, make it pleasing in your sight. If it is wisdom, let it lead others to worship you alone. If it is dollars, multiply their effectiveness. Do this for the sake of Christ, whose gift of himself has made us one.

Prayer of Supplication

God of inspiration and truth, you call us to serve and through your Holy Spirit empower us with varieties of gifts. We praise you for your grace and mercy. Your grace is living water that cleanses us of all impurity; your mercy is fine wine that enlivens our spirit. Renewed by your grace and mercy and made whole by the truth that sets us free, we offer all that we are in obedience to Christ's call.

We give you our knowledge. It was your gift to us in creation, for you implanted within us the taste for inquiry. May what we have learned be used to sustain and ennoble the life of all. Help us to interpret to others the mysteries we have probed. Make our speech intelligible; so that others may hear and respond, and help us translate knowledge into action. Endow us with the daring to set challenging goals, and the energy and discipline to attain them.

We give you our ability to heal. May the Spirit of the living Christ continue to infuse us with compassion. May we always be responsive to those in need and sensitive to their unspoken cries for understanding and support. Give hope a name and a face as we move out toward the wounded in our world.

We give you our faith. Through Christ you taught us how to believe. By your Spirit's power we shall never forsake the quest for greater maturity in the Christian life. Make us eager to learn more of what it means to be Christ's faithful disciples. In all things guide us by your Holy Spirit, and make us instruments of your love and truth.

3RD SUNDAY IN ORDINARY TIME (C)

Nehemiah 8:1–3, 5–6, 8–10; Psalm 19
1 Corinthians 12:12–31a; Luke 4:14–21

Jesus confesses at Nazareth that God's Spirit is upon him. He has been anointed to preach good news to the poor, release to the captives, sight to the blind, and liberty to the oppressed. Isaiah's prophecy is fulfilled in the presence of those who hear him. Be led today by the same Spirit as Christ addresses you, that you may hear afresh the news of liberation.

Call to Worship   Psalm 19

Leader: The law of the Lord is perfect, reviving the soul; the decrees of the Lord are sure, making wise the simple.

People: The precepts of the Lord are right, rejoicing the heart; the commandment of the Lord is clear, enlightening the eyes.

Leader: The fear of the Lord is sure, enduring forever; the ordinances of the Lord are true and righteous altogether.

People: Let the words of my mouth and meditation of my heart be acceptable to you, O Lord, my rock and my redeemer.

Leader: Let us worship God!

Prayer of Praise and Adoration

Your law is perfect, O God; your ways are just. We praise you for Christ, who makes known your Word. Gold's value is nothing compared to the salvation you offer. The sweetness of honey is a foretaste of the feast you prepare. Made alive by your mercy and renewed in your Spirit, we come adoring your goodness, O Lord, our Rock and Redeemer.

Prayer of Confession

Unison: O God, have mercy upon us, and through Christ forgive our sin. He called the church to be one body with parts to make it function. We sever that one body through suspicion and hostility; we cannot dine around one common table. We divide into separate bodies and pretend to be the church. We take from one another what belongs to us all. By your grace make us one in Christ.

Assurance of Pardon

Leader: Paul declares that "as the body is one and has many members, and all the members of the body, though many, are one body, so it is with Christ. For in the one Spirit we were all baptized into one body . . . and we were all made to drink of one Spirit." Friends, affirm your baptism and be made one in Christ, since in Christ we are forgiven.

Prayer of Dedication

Great God, we lift up our hands to bring offerings to you. We bow our heads in prayer to give you honor. We worship your name with praise and thanksgiving. In Christ you bless us and call us your own. Full of joy in belonging to Christ's holy family, we join with brothers and sisters everywhere in presenting our gifts.

Prayer of Thanksgiving and Supplication

O God of the prophets and the apostles, and of all women and men who speak the truth and do it, we thank you for Jesus, who brought good news to the oppressed and sealed his message with his blood. Now we need no longer mourn, for he is the life. Now we need no longer grope in darkness, for he is the light. Now we need no longer groan in chains, for he is the liberating Word.

O God in Christ, you call us to be prophets; give us a clear vision and the courage to make it known. You call us to be apostles; make us eager to be sent, and steady in our mission. You call us to be teachers; give us needed skills of communication. Keep us faithful in the study of your word in Scripture. Make us partners with you in the quest for truth.

You call us to administer the parts of the body; give us the sense of how the whole ought to function. Teach us patience with the weaker members of the body, and above all deliver us from the pride of position and arrogance of power. Make us ministers of peace and encouragement, so that the body may remain whole.

We give you thanks for all who help and heal, and perform miracles of ministry. Grant zeal for your church to each of us and love for its unity, so that in your time sisters and brothers everywhere may gather at one table and confess one God of all.

4TH SUNDAY IN ORDINARY TIME (C)

Jeremiah 1:4–10; Psalm 71:1–6
1 Corinthians 13:1–13; Luke 4:21–30

It is nice when people speak well of us and marvel at the wisdom we seem to possess. But how quickly initial acceptance turns to suspicion when they hear utterances with which they do not agree. At first, those who heard Jesus thought he was marvelous, but when they understood the implications of his message, they became angry and sought to destroy him. Indeed, "no prophet is accepted in his own country."

Call to Worship
Psalm 71

Leader: In you, O Lord, I take refuge; let me never be put to shame.

People: In your righteousness deliver me and rescue me; incline your ear to me and save me.

Leader: Be to me a strong fortress, to save me, for you are my rock and my refuge.

People: For you, O Lord, are my hope, my trust. My praise is continually of you.

Leader: Let us worship God!

Prayer of Praise and Adoration

Source of all life, you give birth to the nations; we are conceived by your love. You sustain us in the womb of your mercy; we are nourished and grow in the folds of your grace. You have sent Jesus our Savior to deliver us, and have surrounded our days with your Spirit. Through Christ you conceive us as children of the covenant; we gather in his household to give you our praise.

Prayer of Confession

Unison: If love is patient, why are we irritable? If love is kind, why are we hostile? If love is not jealous or boastful, why do we flaunt our achievements in the presence of others? O God, in Jesus you have shown love which forgives imperfection; only in him can we forsake childish ways. Forgive our lack of love, and have mercy upon us.

Assurance of Pardon

Leader: Remember that God has done what the law, weakened by the flesh, could not do. God sent Christ in order to fulfill the law. Now we walk according to the Spirit, who bears witness with our spirit that we are God's children. Friends, claim your legacy; we are forgiven.

Prayer of Dedication

O God of faith, we put our trust in you. Source of hope, we are confident you shall never forsake us. Giver of love in ways too countless to be numbered, we return but a portion of what we have received from you. Use our gifts so that others may be assured of new life and enriched by the gift of your Holy Spirit.

Prayer of Thanksgiving and Supplication

Conceiver, Comforter, and Deliverer of all that lives, moves, and has being, we will continually praise you. You conceived a people who call you beloved. You brought them forth from bondage and gave them a name. You comforted them with the seal of your promised covenant; you nurtured them to have hope and to trust in your will. You sent Christ to deliver your people, and by your Spirit gave birth to the body we call the church. We feel the breath of your Spirit upon us and within us, strengthening, encouraging, and impelling us to faithfulness. O God, we thank you for our lives, and the inheritance of your love. Lead us to maturity in Christ.

Build our faith, O God, on the rock of Christ's own obedience. We give thanks that he has gone before us to show the way. Save us from hesitation when the path looks forbidding and from shrinking back when suffering and hardship block our way. Help us to stand firm in the assurance that you will not forsake us. Hope born of faith will sustain us when the journey becomes perilous. Though doubt may cause us to stumble, we will not despair. Give us your Spirit of power when our knees are shaking, reassure us by your comforting presence. May the love of Christ we seek to imitate be reflected in our every act. As the imperfect passes away and we draw nigh to your heavenly splendor, let us do so with rejoicing, for in Christ you set us free.

5TH SUNDAY IN ORDINARY TIME (C)

Isaiah 6:1–8 (9–13); Psalm 138
1 Corinthians 15:1–11; Luke 5:1–11

What does Jesus know about fishing? After all, Peter and his partners toiled all night and caught nothing, and Peter made his living as a fisher. "Let down your nets," Jesus insists, and soon the nets are breaking with the catch that is taken. The story is told to make a point: henceforth they will follow Jesus, and their catch will be men and women.

Call to Worship   Psalm 138

Leader: I bow down and give thanks to your name for your steadfast love and faithfulness.

People: On the day I called, you answered me, you increased my strength of soul.

Leader: Though I walk in the midst of trouble, you stretch out your hand and deliver me.

People: Your steadfast love, O Lord, endures forever. Do not forsake the work of your hands.

Leader: Let us worship God!

Prayer of Praise and Adoration

You are high and lifted up, O God of hosts; the seraphim sing of your glory. Holy, holy, holy, you are the one we adore. The whole earth is full of your splendor; we see all about us signs of your grace. We come into your temple chanting your praises. You are God of steadfast love and faithfulness; hear us as with our hearts we give you our thanks.

Litany of Affirmation

Leader: I delivered to you as of first importance what I also received, Christ died for our sins in accordance with the scriptures.

People: By God's grace I am what I am.

Leader: Christ was buried and on the third day was raised in accordance with the scriptures.

People: By God's grace I am what I am.

Leader: Christ appeared to Cephas, then to the twelve, then to more than five hundred, and to all called as apostles.

People: By God's grace I am what I am.

271

| Leader: | God's grace was not in vain; so we preach and so you believe. |
| People: | By God's grace I am what I am. |

Prayer of Dedication

Holiest of all, you call us to witness your divine splendor; you touch our lips, and with our voices we praise you. You are uplifted, yet you stoop to hear us, cleansing our guilt and forgiving our sin. We are here in response to your calling; we offer our gifts of time, talents, and tithe. Send us forth as your witnesses; so that hosts may know you and give you glory.

Prayer of Thanksgiving and Supplication

You, before whose throne the nations shall one day bow down in sacred joy, accept the praise we offer now with our whole hearts. You are high and lifted up; we are humbled by your presence. Yet you have crowned us with the jewel of your sovereign love and given Christ to open for us the way into the holiest of all. Your Spirit surrounds us as we wait; our every sense is filled with the wonder of your presence. You are holy and worthy of our praise; accept our sacrifice as in Christ's name we approach your divine majesty.

Let the coal of your sacred word touch our lips and take away our guilt. Loose our tongues to declare your grandeur, and open our mouths to proclaim your goodness to all people. With Isaiah, make us contrite in confessing our unworthiness to speak for you, yet send us forth by your Spirit to bear witness to your judgment and mercy revealed in Jesus Christ.

Make us strong so that we may bear the good news of your love to the ends of the earth. Kindle our zeal with burning brands from the altar of your love. Grant that our enthusiasm may ignite the lives of others, so that together we may minister to people whose eyes and ears are yet closed to the Word of Truth. Through our faithfulness may the coal from the altar touch their lips and make them clean. For the sake of Christ, your faithful one.

6TH SUNDAY IN ORDINARY TIME (C)

Jeremiah 17:5–10; Psalm 1
1 Corinthians 15:12–20; Luke 6:17–26

A touch can have healing power; a blessing can work wonders. Jesus used both throughout his ministry. "All in the crowd were trying to touch him, for power came out from him and healed all of them." When he blessed the poor, they received God's realm; when he blessed the hungry, they were satisfied. So, in Christ's name reach out and touch someone! It may work wonders.

Call to Worship   Psalm 1

Leader: Happy are those who take delight in the law of the Lord.

People: They are like trees planted by streams of water. In all that they do they prosper.

Leader: For the Lord watches over the way of the righteous.

People: May God number us with the righteous as we worship the Lord.

Leader: Let us worship God!

Prayer of Praise and Adoration

O God, you are like an ever-flowing stream, watering the earth and refreshing creation. We draw from your Holy Spirit life-giving sustenance. We are cleansed of all sin through Christ our Savior. We receive from your Word wisdom to guide us; we sing praises to you for your life-giving care.

Prayer of Confession

Unison: Forgive our vain repetitions, O God of mercy, for our deeds do not match our words of belief. We mouth pious slogans but fail to correct injustice. We claim to be righteous, while practicing bigotry and rejecting others. We glory in your gifts that bring success and comfort, yet we deny neighbors their right to prosper. Help us to confess Christ risen for all people, and forgive our failure to translate faith into action.

Assurance of Pardon

Leader: Paul writes, "If Christ has not been raised, your faith is futile and you are still in your sins. . . . But in fact Christ has been raised from the dead . . . so all will be made alive in Christ." For I assure you, in Jesus

Christ we are forgiven. So live in Christ that all may see your good works and glorify God who is in heaven.

Prayer of Dedication

God of deliverance, who in Christ brings soundness of mind, clarity to vision, wholeness of bodies, and wisdom to all we say and do, receive now the fruits of Christ's work in us. May what we give be used to make known Christ's healing presence, so that all may live with assurance of the new life you offer.

Prayer of Praise and Intercession

Merciful Healer, you cause the dawn to break and turn the night into morning. We give you thanks for promised new life. In you is hope, which has endured throughout the ages; with you abides the assurance that we are not alone. When perils confront us and cause anxious moments, you ease our unrest with your comforting presence.

There are some for which daybreak brings foreboding; they are the lonely, the forgotten, and the terminally ill. For them the flush of the morning is tinged with the grim reality that confronts them. Help us bring consolation to those known to us, and return to our memory those whom we have forgotten. May we reach out to touch them and remind them we care. When the time comes for some to cross over, may we be their companions until they abide eternally with you.

For others who embark on the day full of promise, we rejoice in their anticipation and give you the glory. Let their laughter be a chorus of alleluias to your mercy, their confidence a tribute to your Spirit within them. May their enthusiasm be contagious, so that we all may become infused with ardor for tasks the day brings. We shall join them and dance through the hours that await us, uplifting others to the new life in Christ.

7TH SUNDAY IN ORDINARY TIME (C)

Genesis 45:3–11, 15; Psalm 37:1–11, 39–40
1 Corinthians 15:35–38, 42–50; Luke 6:27–38

Jesus has a way of expecting the unpredictable. Who would assume we are to love our enemies? To offer the other cheek would just compound the offense. If we gave to all who begged for handouts, would there be anything left to put away for our future? Ah, but Jesus also teaches that God is merciful and will restore abundantly. "For the measure you give will be the measure you get back." Accept the unpredictable, for God can be trusted!

Call to Worship   Psalm 37

Leader: Trust in God, and do good; so you will dwell in the land, and enjoy security.
People: We shall be still before God, and wait patiently, refraining from anger and forsaking wrath.
Leader: Let us worship God!

Prayer of Praise and Adoration

God of Jacob, Leah, and Rachel, you caused a people to journey; they became a great nation. You named your servant Israel, for you would dwell in their midst. You are God Almighty and worthy of worship; we follow our ancestors and assemble to praise you. Be among us to guide us as we honor and adore you, and sanctify our gathering, O God Most High.

Prayer of Confession

Unison: O God Most High, our bodies are perishable, but you have sent Christ, the promise of our resurrection. Aging limits us, disease burdens us, and disabilities undermine our capacity to function. We are frail creatures at best. Yet we glorify these bodies; they are temples we worship. When some threat afflicts them, we are distraught or destroyed. We confess our idolatry. Teach us to number our days to Christ's glory, and forgive our vain worship of ourselves.

Assurance of Pardon

Leader: Remember that in all things we are more than conquerors because of God's love. "For I am convinced that neither death, nor life, nor angels, nor rulers, nor things present, nor things to come, nor powers, nor height, nor depth, nor anything else in all creation, will be able to separate us from the love of God in Christ Jesus our Lord" (*Rom. 8:38–39*). In Christ we are forgiven.

Prayer of Dedication

O God, who in Christ taught us how to be faithful, we respond to his instruction, seeking your favor. Be pleased with the offerings we give you; may our actions contribute to the well-being of others. Surprise the offender with our peaceful solutions and startle the beggar by our willing response. For then we shall love neighbors as Christ bade us to do.

Prayer of Thanksgiving and Supplication

Guardian of our lives, you have carried a people in your womb and given birth to a nation. You have fed them and sustained them, watched over their comings and goings, and welcomed them home from their wayward journeys. We thank you that we are heirs of your covenant with that nation and that your beloved Christ has called us to be part of the household of faith.

Take to your bosom those whose journeys are perilous, who venture for a time through uncertain terrain. Embrace them and lead them with your comforting presence; make them aware of your Spirit, who accompanies them in their plight. As Christ, who walked the bitter path to Calvary, guides them, may their travail give birth to new life, nurtured by hope.

When risk is certain, we pray for those who fear taking steps of faith. Grant them courage to embark on new paths of discipleship, and sufficient training and discipline to follow your will. Place their feet on the firm foundation of your eternal faithfulness, and help them trust your promises.

To those engaged in responding to Christ's sermon, loving enemies and feeding strangers, give support and continuing challenges. Help us to learn from them what bold commitment can mean. As you called Jacob Israel and set apart a people, we join with our ancestors in response to your grace.

8TH SUNDAY IN ORDINARY TIME (C)

Sirach 27:4–7 or Isaiah 55:10–13; Psalm 92:1–4, 12–15
1 Corinthians 15:51–58; Luke 6:39–49

A new day was dawning while Jesus walked this earth. Instead of fasting, there was eating and drinking. Indeed, those invited were not usually found on acceptable guest lists. Some folks had questions about what was happening. How would the new ways blend with the traditional? Would the old be forsaken as the new was embraced? Jesus was splitting the seams of past custom, and change would be the order of the day.

Call to Worship   Psalm 92

Leader: It is good to give thanks to the Lord, to sing praises to your name, O Most High.
People: I will declare your steadfast love in the morning, and your faithfulness throughout the night.
Leader: For you, O Lord, have made me glad by your work.
People: At the works of your hands I will sing for joy.
Leader: Let us worship God!

Prayer of Praise and Adoration

It is good to give you thanks, O God, and to sing praises to you, O Most High. The dawn is a gift of your abiding mercy; the night passes safely, thanks to your grace. We arise to grant you all glory and honor; we bow down before you and worship your name. We can herald the coming of a new day of faithfulness because of Christ Jesus, in whose name we pray.

Prayer of Confession

Unison: Let the trumpet sound, O God, and waken us from slumber. The day passes quickly and our time is soon spent. We are caught sleeping when we should be wakeful; there are tasks to be done, fulfilling your will. Forgive our failure to obey your commandments and our drowsiness when hearing Christ's word.

Assurance of Pardon

Leader: "Listen, I will tell you a mystery! We will not all die, but we will all be changed, in a moment, in the twinkling of an eye. . . . Thanks be to God, who gives us the victory through our Lord Jesus Christ." Receive the victory over sin that Christ has won, and arise to a newness of life.

Prayer of Dedication

Author of a new day, you have written in our hearts the promise of your unending covenant; we bring now our gifts in response to your Word. Translate our faith into acts that please you. Renew our subscription to our baptismal vows. May what we confess lead others to worship you, and our responses accomplish your purpose on earth.

Prayer of Thanksgiving and Supplication

God of all times and places, as rain and snow come down from heaven and water the earth, giving seed to the sower and bread to the eater, so shall your Word accomplish its purpose. O Christ, Savior of nations and Redeemer of peoples, as your Word goes forth and returns not empty to you, we give thanks for all who hear your words and do them. O Holy Spirit, Giver of life and Source of all joy, we break into singing, with mountains and hills, and join with trees in clapping our hands. O blessed Trinity, the cypress shall sprout as a memorial to your mercy and the myrtle shall stand as a sign of your undying love.

As we dine at Christ's table and there receive gifts of bread and wine, we acknowledge your provision for us from day to day, and pray that whatever we have we shall always share.

You word continues to guide and correct us. We give thanks that we live surrounded by abiding and abundant testimony to your everlasting promise. Keep us from muting your pledge with halfhearted witness or muffling your purpose by disobedient denial.

As your Holy Spirit continues to achieve harmony amid diversity, bring peace and concord to all our acts, that your kingdom may come, your will be done.

TRANSFIGURATION OF THE LORD
(SUNDAY PRECEDING LENT) (C)

Exodus 34:29–35; Psalm 99
2 Corinthians 3:12–4:2; Luke 9:28–36 (37–43)

As Jesus was praying, he was transfigured. God acted upon him in a way that changed his appearance; a voice spoke from a cloud declaring that Jesus was God's chosen. Prayer did not end when Jesus and the three disciples descended the mountain; its effects would be felt throughout Jesus' ministry. Prayer is an involving process, capable of radically changing our lives.

Call to Worship   Psalm 99

Leader: God reigns; let the peoples tremble! God is enthroned upon the cherubim; let the earth shake!

People: We will extol you, O God, and worship at your holy mountain; for you our God are holy!

Leader: Let us worship God!

Prayer of Praise and Adoration

Great are your works, O Holy One, and greatly to be praised. Not a day passes without our sensing your presence. You appeared in Jesus, removing the veil from your countenance. You spoke through Christ, that we might know your will. Henceforth we shall behold your glory as your Spirit leads us. Blessed Trinity, we praise your name.

Prayer of Confession

Unison: Mystery of mysteries, hide not your face from us. Hear our confession and forgive us of sin. We go to the mountains to escape our involvement. We hear your commandments, then hide from their truth. We disguise our faces to conceal our identities. Christ unmasks our pretense and strips us of pride. Help us not to be afraid to encounter your presence, and through Christ to stand before you cleansed of our sin.

Assurance of Pardon

Leader: The truth is this: As the heavens opened God spoke and proclaimed that Christ was the chosen one; listen to him. Our Savior proclaims that all who truly believe are cleansed of their sin. Friends, believe the good news of the gospel. In Jesus Christ we are forgiven.

Prayer of Dedication

God of Moses and Elijah, of Christ and the disciples, we too could build you booths, but you would not be pleased. We could bring you burnt offerings, but you do not desire them. You ask us to do justice, to love mercy, and to walk humbly with you. We come now before you, placing our lives in your service. Take us, women and men, young and old, to use us, as you deem fit.

Prayer of Thanksgiving

God of Moses and Zipporah, Aaron and Miriam and all, who have appeared before you and spoken on your behalf, we give you thanks. Through them you made known the awesome mystery of your transcendent glory. We give thanks for Christ Jesus, who tore in pieces the curtain that separated us from you. In his name we can approach you and call you by name.

We praise you for the hope we can have in Jesus, who walked among earthly folk, transforming all manner of ills into newness of life. When grief besets us we can turn to him to lift our spirit. When burdened with cares, we are assured that Jesus shares the yoke with us. When our own death confronts us we can see on the cross that he too passed victoriously through his time of trial.

We give thanks for the freedom we gain through life in the Spirit. We can arise and shame our captors through our confession of faith; we can lead those who oppress others to change of heart and life. We proclaim aloud the day of liberty for all of your children, with thanksgiving to Christ, who arose victor over all oppressions.

We are transfigured by your mercy and radically changed by your grace. We set our sights now on the ministry that awaits us, whereby the veil of mystery shall be lifted from your face, and all shall know that you are "God with us," at our side always, in Jesus Christ.

ASH WEDNESDAY (C) — *See Year A*

1ST SUNDAY IN LENT (C)

Deuteronomy 26:1–11; Psalm 91:1–2, 9–16
Romans 10:8b–13; Luke 4:1–13

Jesus was tempted for forty days in the wilderness. It was a test between apparent weakness and presumed power. Satan presumed that Jesus would respond powerfully to what Satan offered, but Satan mistook the meaning of God's power, and of Satan's own power as well. During those forty days, the devil began to comprehend the true power of Jesus' "weakness."

Call to Worship   Psalm 91

Leader: You who live in the shelter of the Most High, who abide in the shadow of the Almighty,
People: We will say to the Lord, "My refuge and my fortress; my God, in whom I trust."
Leader: Because you have made the Lord your dwelling place, no evil shall befall you.
People: God will protect those who call on the name of the Lord and show them salvation.
Leader: Let us worship God!

Prayer of Praise and Adoration

We call upon you, O God; hear our prayer. We raise our voices in glad adoration. You have brought your people out of bondage. You ministered to Jesus when he was tempted by Satan. You know when your people are afflicted, and understand their estrangement when they are alone and dismayed. We pause along our journey of faithfulness to bow down before you and worship your name.

Prayer of Confession

Unison: O Judge and Redeemer, we come before you, shorn of all pretenses and without cause for pride. We care more about bread than our confession of Christ our Savior. We worship many gods and do not serve you alone. We offer bribes to garner your favor; we do not rely on your promised goodwill. Forgive our deceit and grant us forgiveness. Through Christ we repent of our sinful ways.

Assurance of Pardon

Leader: Paul writes, "if you confess with your lips that Jesus is Lord and believe in your heart that God raised him from the dead, you will be saved." John writes, "If we confess our sins, he who is faithful and just will forgive us our sins and cleanse us from all unrighteousness" (*1 John 1:9*). Friends, in Jesus Christ we are forgiven.

Prayer of Dedication

Fostered by your tender care and secure in the haven of your redeeming love, we are emboldened to approach you, O God, with our gifts and offerings. May they be used to bring refuge to the aimless, deliverance to the captives, and protection to all who call on your name. For we bring them in Christ's name, our source of salvation.

Prayer of Thanksgiving and Supplication

Great God of the covenant, we bring you our offerings of praise and thanksgiving; your love is a legacy of Christ's death on the cross. You have given us a good land in which to dwell; you surround us with the evidence of your bounteous mercy; our cup overflows with the grace you bestow. You are a God for all seasons; through Christ you have poured out manifold signs of your abiding love.

As Christ was tested by Satan, we too at times face alluring temptation. Help us to recognize the wiles of the devil and withstand the challenges of evil. If bread is the issue, remind us that you provide sufficient for each day. If authority and glory seduce us, help us to recall that the meek shall inherit your promised splendor. If we are led to tempt God by some plunge into a fruitless and perilous venture, restrain us with your outstretched are.

We confess our abiding faith in Christ Jesus. Help us to enact with our bodies what we proclaim with our lips. Make our hearts receptive to those who seek understanding; with open arms may we embrace the lonely. Make our feet ready to step out on behalf of the lame and the crippled. May what we say and do enable all your people to pursue their pilgrimage of faith with dignity, poise, and conviction. We raise our hands to praise you, O God, as with our voices we herald you, Great God of the covenant.

2ND SUNDAY IN LENT (C)

Genesis 15:1–12, 17–18; Psalm 27
Philippians 3:17–4:1; Luke 13:31–35 or Luke 9:28–36

There is both anger and pathos in Jesus' gospel. Neither is unusual when dealing with matters of faith. Jesus was angry when Herod threatened his mission. He did not want anything to stand in the way of fulfilling God's will. Jesus lamented when his followers and others of faith were persecuted. To believe to the point of conviction was cause for support, nurture, and protection. Jesus sought to provide them all.

Call to Worship   Psalm 27

Leader: The Lord is my light and my salvation; whom shall I fear?
People: The Lord is the stronghold of my life; of whom shall I be afraid?
Leader: One thing I asked of the Lord, to live in the house of the Lord all the days of my life.
People: "Come," my heart says, "seek the face of the Lord." Your face, Lord, do I seek.
Leader: Let us worship God!

Prayer of Praise and Adoration

God of the heavenly commonwealth, we praise you for Jesus who came as your servant; he opened the gates for us to enter your kingdom. We laud you for the prophets who proclaimed your vision; through them we see clearly what your covenant involves. We give you all honor for what the disciples delivered to us; they taught us to worship you, and to that end we now lift our voices.

Prayer of Confession

Unison: Beloved God, whose mercy is everlasting and whose grace endures forever, look with favor upon us as we confess our sin. Lift our minds from earthly things to the vision of your heavenly commonwealth. We revel in self-glory; we delight in vain pursuits; we worship the idols of our base desires. Forgive our shortsighted behavior and reconcile us through Jesus to your eternal will.

Assurance of Pardon

Leader: Brothers and sisters, be assured that our commonwealth is in heaven. From it we await a Savior, who is Christ Jesus, who shall change our bodies into glory, and we shall dwell eternally in God's realm. Trust in Christ, for therein lies our forgiveness.

Prayer of Dedication

Great Shield and Defender, you visited Abram and made him a great nation. You sent to earth Jesus, who called out the church. We join with the hosts who have gone before us, pilgrims on a journey toward your promised land. We pause on the way to give you our offerings, and dedicate ourselves anew to the faithful quest.

Prayer of Thanksgiving and Supplication

O God of Abraham, Hagar, and Sarah, who fashioned a covenant out of promise and hope, we give you thanks that we are numbered among your sons and daughters. Through Christ you have called us and named us. You have made our bodies your temple, and by your Spirit you empower us for ministry.

As you have shown favor to countless before us, make us now fitting citizens of your commonwealth. Discipleship requires discipline; give us determination to set aside time for prayer and study. Amid the pressures of daily life, help us to be quiet so that we can hear you speaking.

Forbid that we should grow complacent about Christ's call to ministry. Shape our endeavors to coincide with your desires, and refine our efforts with the fires of your judgment. When we are lax, invade our consciences, so that we cannot rest until we abide at your side. If we shy away from confronting evil, inspire us to greater efforts to bring you our offerings of justice and peace.

Lead us as you led the Israelites unto the promised land. If you do not build the house, we shall toil in vain. If you do not guard the city, our watch will be worthless. Having called us in Christ, send forth your Spirit to watch over the course of our journey. May what we do be cause for rejoicing, and who we are reflect the radiance and glory of your promise and hope.

3RD SUNDAY IN LENT (C)

Isaiah 55:1–9; Psalm 63:1–8
1 Corinthians 10:1–13; Luke 13:1–9

The themes are repentance and bearing fruit. One leads to the other. To repent is to do an about-face. To bear fruit is to use bestowed gifts for the well-being of others. Both repentance and bearing fruit imply that someone other than we ourselves will influence our behavior. To repent is to obey God. To bear fruit is to serve our neighbor. Therein lies the great commandment.

Call to Worship   Psalm 63

Leader: O God, you are my God, I seek you, my soul thirsts for you.
People: So I have looked upon you in the sanctuary, beholding your power and glory.
Leader: Because your steadfast love is better than life, my lips will praise you.
People: So I will bless you as long as I live; I will lift up my hands and call on your name.
Leader: Let us worship God!

Prayer of Praise and Adoration

Merciful God, you have set the heavens above us as a sign of your splendor; you water the earth and cause it to bloom. With Christ as the vine and we the branches, our lives can reflect the radiance of your love and glory. Wherever we look we see your benevolence; with the dawn comes new life because of your grace. We gather to worship, praise, and adore you, God of all mercy and joy sublime.

Prayer of Confession

Unison: We have tasted your goodness, O God, in Christ our Savior. In that name we come asking forgiveness. We confess that we are greedy, while others go hungry. The daily bread you give is not enough; we must indulge our appetites. Our egos need feeding as well; we crave recognition and ignore our neighbors. Show us once more that Christ is our cup and our portion; may we find in him our heart's delight.

Assurance of Pardon

Leader: Know that whoever is in Christ is a new creation. The "old has passed away; see, everything has become new. All this is from God, who reconciled us . . . and has given us the ministry of reconciliation." Friends, put on the new being and become ambassadors for Christ, for we are forgiven.

Prayer of Dedication

God of all creation, who caused the manna to rain from heaven, the land to bear fruit, and parched grain to sustain your people, we come bearing gifts in response to your goodness. You are with us in lean times; when the bounty is great we shall not forget you. As in Christ we feed daily on the bread of new life, so through Christ we dedicate ourselves to your abiding covenant.

Prayer of Thanksgiving

God of Abraham and Sarah, Isaac and Rebekah, Jacob and Leah and Rachel, Moses and Zipporah, and countless men and women of the promise, you are remembered throughout generations as the God who will be what you will be. We give you thanks that through Christ we can know you. By your Spirit we sense your presence among us, yet we are not consumed. Speak and we shall listen. Send us forth and we shall serve you. Gather us and we shall worship your holy name. All blessing laud, and honor, great God who was, is, and evermore shall be.

Yet, who are we that you should speak to us? Christ calls us to follow, and we hesitate to do his bidding. Our ears pound with anxieties that afflict us, drowning out the cries of our neighbors. Clear the channels of communication of whatever keeps us from hearing your voice, and make us effective spokespersons of Christ's summons to ministry.

We shall go where you send us and shall strive to do whatever you command. Armed with the mercy that you bestow on us, how can we fail if we but remain faithful? Yet we admit our unworthiness of so great a distinction. Any gifts we have are the result of your grace.

We yearn to please you, O God, as a response to the favor you have shown us. We want our faith to amount to more than casual observance of days and ceremonies. We are sorry for our past, which has been less than well pleasing, and look to a future of absorbing commitment. Through Christ receive us anew as your faithful people.

4TH SUNDAY IN LENT (C)

Joshua 5:9–12; Psalm 32
2 Corinthians 5:16–21; Luke 15:1–3, 11b–32

A son takes his share of the inheritance and travels to a far county. There he squanders the wealth until it is depleted. Cast into squalor, he envisions the situation back home; he repents of his wrongdoing and returns to accept his fate. However, instead of rejection he finds a forgiving father who rejoices that his son is alive. The parable describes the ways of God's kingdom on earth. Whoever is in Christ is indeed a new creation.

Call to Worship
                                                                    Psalm 32

Leader: Happy are those whose sin is forgiven, and in whose spirit
            there is no deceit.
People: Therefore let all who are faithful offer prayer to the God of
            deliverance.
Leader: I will instruct you and teach you the way you should go, as
            you trust in the Lord.
People: Be glad in the Lord and rejoice, O righteous; shout for joy,
            all you upright in heart.
Leader: Let us worship God!

Prayer of Praise and Adoration

You are the source of our deliverance, O God, and rightly to be blessed. Your name shall ever be upon our lips. You have heard the poor and saved them from trouble. You have enlightened believers; their faces reflect your radiance. Aglow with the splendor of your promised redemption, we rise up to worship you, ruler of nations.

Prayer of Confession

Unison: O God, our Rock and Redeemer, hear our confession. We worship idols of our own making; when temptation overtakes us we submit to its charm. We find it easier to grumble at hardships than to praise you for mercies we receive day by day. We test you in every way. Yet you promise that you will not test us beyond our endurance. Forgive us when we take advantage of your loving nature, and restore us to communion with you.

Assurance of Pardon

Leader: Brothers and sisters, remember that "God is faithful, and . . . will not let you be tested beyond your strength, but with the testing . . .

will provide the way out so that you may be able to endure it." Christ is the foundation of our salvation; therein lies assurance that we are forgiven of sin.

Prayer of Dedication

Refuge of those who put their trust in you, you do not seek vain sacrifice, nor will you hear empty praises. You take delight in contrite hearts that are ready to do your will. Accept our offerings of praise and thanksgiving, mingled with these tangible gifts that we willingly surrender. They are symbols of our response to your call to repentance and our earnest desire to become more faithful stewards.

Prayer of Thanksgiving and Supplication

Reconciling God, through Christ you have granted your creatures the hope for new life; we praise your name and give you thanks. The old has passed away; behold the new has come. We no longer fear the wilderness, nor aimless wandering, tempted by forces beyond our control. You have sent us a Savior, who has passed through the wastelands, and has borne our sins for us, since we could not escape them ourselves. We herald our adoption as reconciled sons and daughters and approach the dawn of your everlasting covenant with joy in our hearts.

You have opened the doors of your heavenly home and warmly embraced your returning children. Our feet are made light by your Spirit within us; we can run and not grow weary within your gates. We give thanks for your discipline as a wise parent. You have not allowed us to stray too far from your will.

Assured that you await our return from our ventures, we shall be bold while we journey in faith here on earth. We shall strive to be ambassadors of your promised redemption. Armed with the righteousness Christ has won for us, we shall act for justice and reach out in compassion to neighbors. Through Christ hear us as we go forth rejoicing.

5TH SUNDAY IN LENT (C)

Isaiah 43:16–21; Psalm 126
Philippians 3:4b–14; John 12:1–8

The house was filled with the fragrance of ointment as Mary wiped Jesus' feet with her hair. Judas objected to this display of affection, since he could have gotten money for the nard she used. He made some objection about how the poor were forsaken, but Jesus quickly saw through his pretense. Legitimate concern for the poor would continue to be a sign of discipleship; the anointing of Jesus was simply the showing of proper respect.

Call to Worship   Psalm 126

Leader: You fill our mouths with laughter, O God; with our tongues we shout for joy.

People: You have done great things for us, O God; we come before you with praise on our lips.

Leader: Let us worship God!

Prayer of Praise and Adoration

Great Guide and Deliverer, you make a way in the wilderness and cause rivers to flow in the desert; we come repeating your name in glad adoration. You have led your people through wastelands where wild beasts and jackals even honor your name. We number ourselves as among those you have chosen. Hear us as in Christ we come before you, declaring you worthy of all worship and praise.

Prayer of Confession

Unison: God of mercy, hear us as we confess our sin. Power beguiles us and we deem ourselves worthy. Our good works convince us that we can assure our salvation. We heap treasures about us as signs of merit and status, then build elaborate defenses to keep our prizes secure. Forgive the illusion of our own greatness, and in Christ humble us to receive your reward.

Assurance of Pardon

Leader: Paul reminds us that he counted everything as loss because of the surpassing worth of knowing Christ Jesus his Savior. Through Christ came the righteousness from God based on faith, not personal attainment. From faith came the promise of resurrection from the dead. Friends, forgetting what lies behind, let us "press on toward the goal for the prize of the heavenly call of God in Christ Jesus." Therein lies assurance that we are forgiven.

Prayer of Dedication

Giver of every good and perfect gift, if you would be pleased with costly ointments, we would bring them to you. If adornments brought you pleasure, we could make images of you and bedeck them with fine jewelry. But you are not found in images, nor do you wish useless offerings. Accept our gifts of money as tokens of our abiding allegiance and use them in ways that will enhance your dominion; we pray in Christ, the giver of new life.

Prayer of Thanksgiving and Intercession

God of Mary, Martha, and Lazarus, you are full of compassion and abound in mercy. We give you thanks that we dwell in the realm of your grace. You have passed over our sins in sending us Jesus; we have a glimpse of new life through his days here on earth. When he was tempted, you ministered to him. You gave him authority to cast out the demons. When he cried out for guidance you heard him. He placed his life in your hands; he now dwells by your side. We live evermore with assurance that you will never abandon your people; for that comfort we thank you and praise your name.

Hear us as we pray on behalf of those who for some reason cannot trust your benevolence. They struggle in darkness and stumble through life, for they have not accepted the light. Help us to befriend them. Give us the sense to detect what causes their hearts to turn from you, and help us to deal sensitively with the sources of their resistance to your gospel.

We pray on behalf of those whom our culture despises; they must endure hardships that others inflict on them. Through your Spirit give them counsel. Enable us through Christ to bring them comfort. May we like Mary stoop to their need and anoint them with the balm of compassion and care. Empower us with the truth of Christ's resurrection, so that in sharing their sufferings, we may lead them from despair to the hope of new life.

PASSION/PALM SUNDAY (C)

Palm: Luke 19:28–40; Psalm 118:1–2, 19–29
Passion: Isaiah 50:4–9a; Psalm 31:9–16; Philippians 2:5–11;
Luke 22:14–23:56 or Luke 23:1–49

The curtain of the Passion play is about to go up. People will cheer and pay Jesus homage, rejoicing and shouting, "Peace in heaven and glory in the highest!" Jesus has been billed as the one who will liberate God's people from oppressive forces. Will he play the role as a warrior, miracle worker, or charismatic leader? No, when the curtain falls, Jesus will have been tried and sentenced.

Call to Worship   Psalm 118

> *Leader:* We give thanks to you, O God, for you are good; your steadfast love endures forever!
>
> *People:* Open to me the gates of righteousness that I may enter through them and give God thanks.
>
> *Leader:* Let us worship God!

Prayer of Praise and Adoration

We give you thanks, O God, for opening to us the gates of your righteousness. The stone, which the builders rejected, has become the head of the corner. We dwell as family within Christ's household; because of your grace we have been saved. Morning by morning we shall arise to praise you; day by day we shall be led by your word. Hear our rejoicing and receive our thanksgiving; blessed be Christ our Redeemer!

Prayer of Confession

Unison: O God of love, who sent Jesus among us, hear our confession and forgive our sin. When we invoke Christ's name for selfish reasons, have mercy upon us. When our faith is convenient and does not lead to commitment, surround us with grace, that we may repent. We are prone to call on you to satisfy our needs; we practice obedience without cost to our comfort. Forgive our leisurely approach to your sacrifice for us as Christ intercedes on our behalf.

Assurance of Pardon

Leader: Hear Paul's words when he reminds us to "let the same mind be in you that was in Christ Jesus, who . . . being found in human likeness . . . humbled himself and became obedient to the point of death—even death on a cross." As we confess Jesus Christ as Savior, God is just and forgives our sin. Therein lies our assurance.

Prayer of Dedication

Glory be to you, O God, for the gift of creation and its bounteous mercies. Praise be to you, O Christ, for redeeming love and the promise of new life. Thanks be to you, O Holy Spirit, for guidance, counsel, and abiding revelation. O blessed Trinity, we honor and worship you in presenting our offerings. Take our lives and let them be consecrated, O God, to thee.

Prayer of Thanksgiving and Supplication

Merciful God, who bestowed on Christ Jesus the name above every name, we bow down before you and give you the glory. Each morning we awaken to the new life you promise; Christ's teachings instruct us throughout the day's course of events. We hear the voice of your Spirit giving counsel and guidance.

Grant us serenity as we pursue routine tasks. Amid the clamor of demands, help us to bow to your desires. We hear the voices of those around us; their opinions affect our judgment about how we should live. When the crowd shouts approval, we are uplifted. When their response is rejection, we feel forsaken and lost. Help us to discern amid the fanfare and fatigue the persistent prodding of your divine will.

When the way is strewn with the garlands of victory, may we give you the praise and thanksgiving due your glorious name. Keep us from hungering for human adulation. Rather, let us seek your favor. You alone enable us to fulfill our ministry.

At times, O God, the cross will loom on the horizon. We shall be asked to take on burdens too great to bear. Support us at such times by the strength of your compassion. May the living presence of Christ continue to inspire us as he intercedes for us in spite of our fears. Sustained by the servanthood he assumed on our behalf, we shall face freely and boldly whatever awaits. O God of Easter, glorious is your name in all the earth!

MAUNDY THURSDAY (C) — *See Year A*

GOOD FRIDAY (C) — *See Year A*

RESURRECTION OF THE LORD/ EASTER (C)

Acts 10:34–43 or Isaiah 65:17–25; Psalm 118:1–2, 14–24
1 Corinthians 15:19–26 or Acts 10:34–43; John 20:1–18 or Luke 24:1–12

The time has come for the wolf and the lamb to feed together and the lion to eat straw like the ox. Former things shall not be remembered, for behold, God has created new heavens and a new earth. In place of weeping shall be rejoicing, and gladness shall reign among God's chosen people. Christ has risen and opened the gates of God's righteousness. Let the people enter and embrace their salvation.

Call to Worship   Psalm 118

Leader: Open to me the gates of righteousness, that I may enter through them and give thanks to God.

People: This is the day that God has made; let us rejoice and be glad in it.

Leader: Christ is risen!

People: Christ is risen indeed!

Prayer of Praise and Adoration

God of salvation, you have rolled the stone away and the tomb is empty. Nothing can defeat your love for humankind. The night is passed and with dawn comes new creation. Christ is risen to bring us new life. We herald with gladness your anointing of Jesus and rejoice in your promised redemption from sin. Hear our shouts of glad adoration as we enter the courtyard of your redeeming grace.

Litany of Assurance

Leader: God anointed Jesus of Nazareth with the Holy Spirit and with power. He went about doing good and healing all that were oppressed.

People: Everyone who believes in Jesus Christ receives forgiveness of sins through this name.

Leader: They put Jesus to death by hanging him on a tree; but God raised Jesus on the third day and made him manifest.

293

People:	Everyone who believes in Jesus Christ receives forgiveness of sins through this name.
Leader:	And Jesus commanded us to preach to the people, and to testify that he is the one ordained by God.
People:	Everyone who believes in Jesus Christ receives forgiveness of sins through this name.

Prayer of Dedication

God of eternal salvation, we come abounding with joy, transformed by your love. Through Christ you have broken the bonds of oppression, removing all barriers to your unending love. You have made us free to give you praise and thanksgiving. You have our undying devotion for the grace we receive. All our lives long we shall call your name blessed and give you the glory for this gift of new life.

Prayer of Thanksgiving

O God, you lift the veil of darkness; we awaken to the dawn of your glorious splendor. The gates are open and we can enter your dominion; the stone is rolled away and there is life everlasting! Christ is risen and intercedes for us; nothing can separate us from your love.

Trumpets announce your powerful victory; bells ring out announcing your triumph. There is joy in the land! Our weeping is ended. The causes of distress have been overcome by your love. "No more shall there be . . . an infant that lives but a few days, or an old person who does not live out a lifetime," for all shall live as adopted children, inheriting your favor through Christ our Savior.

We bless you for Mary Magdalene, Joanna, and Mary, the mother of James. They were the heralds of good news that first Easter morning. They ministered to Jesus in his time of trial and would not desert him when he was forsaken and lonely. They remind us this day that we should not doubt your benevolence. You will answer before your people call you; while they are yet speaking, you will hear their cries.

Hear our prayers of rejoicing as we enter your realm of redemption. You have fashioned a land flowing with milk and honey, and granted us days in which mercy has no end. Time has been redeemed by your undying presence and all space is sanctified by your inexhaustible grace. We are your Easter people made alive by Christ's rising. Alleluia and hosanna, thanks be unto you!

2ND SUNDAY OF EASTER (C)

Acts 5:27–32; Psalm 118:14–29 or Psalm 150
Revelation 1:4–8; John 20:19–31

Jesus came bringing peace. He demonstrated peace by the way he lived. He gave peace by the gift of the Holy Spirit. The peace of Christ would dispel all doubt from Thomas. Truly Jesus Christ was God with us! Generations have passed and countless persons have confessed their faith. In Jesus Christ resides the hope that all people may one day dwell together in peace.

Call to Worship   Psalm 150

Leader: Praise the Lord! Let everything that breathes praise the Lord!
People: We will praise you for your mighty deeds, O God, according to your surpassing greatness!
Leader: Praise the Lord with the sounds of the trumpet, with tambourine and the dance!
People: We will praise you with strings and pipe and loud clashing cymbals.
Leader: Let everything that breathes praise the Lord!

Prayer of Praise and Adoration

You are Alpha and Omega, O God, the beginning and the end of creation. You caused the formless void to burst into splendor, filling space and revealing your goodness. Your only begotten, Jesus Christ, came to bring peace and reconcile those who are estranged. We who have been made one gather to praise your goodness, and raise our voices in glad adoration.

Litany of Affirmation

Leader: We must obey God rather than human authority.
People: To God be glory and dominion forever and ever.
Leader: The God of our fathers and mothers raised Jesus, who was killed by hanging on a tree.
People: To God be glory and dominion forever and ever.
Leader: God exalted him at God's right hand as Leader and Savior.
People: To God be glory and dominion forever and ever.
Leader: Christ brings repentance and forgiveness of sins.
People: To God be glory and dominion forever and ever.

Leader: And we are witnesses to these things, and so is the Holy
           Spirit whom God has given to those who obey.
People: To God be glory and dominion forever and ever.

Prayer of Dedication

O God, who sent Jesus, making the nations his heritage, the ends of the earth his possession, all that we have is a gift of your love. Our wealth is measured by the mercy you have shown us; even life itself is due to your grace. Entrusted by Jesus as stewards of your dominion, we come before you with the fruits of our labor. Accept them as signs of our gratefulness and use them to further your rule over all creation.

Prayer of Thanksgiving and Supplication

Bringer of peace to the nations, we herald the good news: Christ is risen and we are risen with him. We are delivered from thinking of ourselves more highly than we ought, for we were dead in our sins and Christ rescued us. Since Christ broke down walls of hostility that separated us from our brothers and sisters, we are saved to think of others with new appreciation for their gifts and talents. We are saved as part of your eternal plan for all of creation, and united with your people everywhere in one holy communion.

Blend this diverse gathering of believers into one family, who confess one faith and one baptism. Make the peace Christ gave be the sinew that binds us together, the muscle that makes us strong to serve you, the bone that provides the structure for mission in the world. Keep us from petty rivalries, hasty judgments, and all factious elements of life that sap the body's strength.

United in Christ, may we become your agents of reconciliation in the church. Where class and race cause hurtful distinctions, help us to proclaim the rainbow of your covenant promise. Where peoples contend with one another over conflicting ideologies, make us the mediators of their differences. In all that we do, breathe the Holy Spirit upon us, so that we may stand united as brothers and sisters to the glory and praise of your holy name.

3RD SUNDAY OF EASTER (C)

Acts 9:1–6 (7–20); Psalm 30
Revelation 5:11–14; John 21:1–19

It was a long night for Jesus' followers, a fishing expedition with no fish. At dawn Jesus appeared on the beach, but they didn't know it was he. He showed them where to catch fish and then he cooked some, and took bread and fish and gave it to them—and then they knew. After breakfast Peter received a lesson on obedience: to love Jesus will mean caring for the sheep and tending the flock. The test of love is faithful service.

Call to Worship   Psalm 30

Leader: Sing praises to the Lord, O you faithful ones, and give thanks to God's holy name.
People: God has turned mourning into dancing; we are girded with gladness and will thank God forever.
Leader: Let us worship God!

Prayer of Praise and Adoration

Girded with gladness, we come rejoicing. You are God of salvation; we give you praise. When we cried for help you heard us; from out of the pit you rescued us. You have turned our mourning into dancing, loosed our sackcloth, and adorned us with favor. We raise our voices in faithful thanksgiving and give glory and honor to your wondrous name.

Litany of Affirmation

Leader: Worthy is the Lamb who was slain, to receive power and wealth and wisdom.
People: To the Lamb be blessing and honor and glory and might forever and ever!
Leader: Christ will send you into the city and tell you what you are to do.
People: To the Lamb be blessing and honor and glory and might forever and ever!
Leader: You are Christ's chosen instrument, called to suffer for the sake of Christ's name.
People: To the Lamb be blessing and honor and glory and might forever and ever!
Leader: Christ will restore your sight and fill you with the Holy Spirit.

People: To the Lamb be blessing and honor and glory and might forever and ever!

Prayer of Dedication

O Lamb of God, you take away the sins of the world. We come as your chosen instruments, called to serve. By your might we are empowered to do what you ask of us. With your blessing we can rejoice in the gift of new life. To your glory we have been granted the Spirit's counsel. Receive our gifts of thanksgiving as we give you all honor and praise forever and ever.

Prayer of Thanksgiving and Supplication

Keeper of the heavenly scroll, who sent forth the Lamb who shelters us with his presence, we give thanks that through Christ we may serve you both day and night. It was Christ who was slain on our behalf, whom you ransomed that we may have life unbound by the fetters of sin. Through Christ you gathered a people unto yourself, establishing a household we call the church. To you who sit upon the throne, and to the Lamb, we give all blessing and honor and glory and might.

We give thanks for time spent daily in common toil, for work to be done and the strength to accomplish those tasks set before us. Transform the common into the holy, and sanctify the scene of our labors through the presence of your Holy Spirit. May all that we do serve as a blessing, and the results of our efforts build up your dominion on earth.

As the risen Christ dined at dawn with the disciples, we give thanks that you grace our tables with your living presence. May we not take for granted the abundance of food, but use the strength we gain from adequate nourishment to work on behalf of the hungry. Let us not rest until there are guarantees that your children in all nations are sufficiently nurtured. Only then will the sheep be tended and the Lamb be given blessing and honor and glory and might.

4TH SUNDAY OF EASTER (C)

Acts 9:36–43; Psalm 23
Revelation 7:9–17; John 10:22–30

Jesus speaks of himself as the shepherd. Those who follow him belong to the flock. They hear his voice and obey him. He guides them to pastures where they are nourished; they find protection from whatever could harm them. Nothing can separate those who believe in Jesus from the love of God in whose name he tends the flock of faith.

Call to Worship   Psalm 23

Leader: The Lord is my shepherd; I shall not be in want.
People: You prepare a table before me in the presence of my enemies.
Leader: You anoint my head with oil, my cup overflows.
People: Surely goodness and mercy shall follow me all the days of my life.
Unison: And I shall dwell in the house of the Lord my whole life long.

Prayer of Praise and Adoration

Shepherd God, around whose table we gather, we give you praise. You lead us beside still waters, restoring our souls with your comforting presence. You lead us in paths of righteousness for the sake of Christ Jesus, who died for our salvation. Even though we walk through valleys that threaten us, we fear no evil. We shall dwell in your house all the days of our lives. For that assurance in Christ we give you glory and honor.

Litany of Assurance

Leader: Brothers and sisters, to us has been sent the message of salvation.
People: Salvation belongs to our God who sits upon the throne, and to the Lamb!
Leader: God raised Jesus from the dead; and for many days Jesus appeared to those who are now witnesses to the resurrection.
People: Salvation belongs to our God who sits upon the throne, and to the Lamb!
Leader: We bring you the good news that what God promised to our fathers and mothers has been fulfilled: Jesus is risen!
People: Salvation belongs to our God who sits upon the throne, and to the Lamb!

Prayer of Dedication

God of all nations, tribes, peoples, and tongues, you have redeemed us by the blood of the Lamb; we go into all nations announcing your victory. We confess with our tongues that Christ is risen, pledge our obedience to follow him faithfully, and proclaim your majesty to the ends of the earth. Hear our prayer and accept our commitment, for they are offered in the name of Christ our Savior.

Prayer of Thanksgiving

God our Shepherd, who set the Lamb in our midst to guide us, and to wipe away every tear from our eyes, we give you thanksgiving, honor, and praise. Our hearts shall not be troubled, for by your rod you guide us; neither shall we be afraid, for with your staff you comfort us. Goodness and mercy shall follow us all the days of our lives, and by your grace we shall dwell in your house forever.

We shall dwell with thanksgiving for Jesus, who keeps us from perishing; he is the door into the fold of your love. When we hunger, he sustains us with the bread of the covenant; he assuages our thirst with the waters of new life. He is the light of the world that chases away darkness. With him we can walk with assurance through the valley of death.

We shall dwell with honor, since you have come to shepherd us; we can no longer stray far from your path. We rest in green pastures and are refreshed by still waters; you set a table before us, reconciling our enemies; you anoint our heads with oil and mark us as your flock.

We shall dwell and continue to praise and worship you faithfully; we shall bow down before you to give you the glory. Led by your Spirit, we shall grow in wisdom and understanding of what it means to be Christ's disciples. We are encouraged by your mercy, enlivened by your grace, and directed by your guiding presence. We are the sheep of your pasture; all honor be to your name.

5TH SUNDAY OF EASTER (C)

Acts 11:1–18; Psalm 148
Revelation 21:1–6; John 13:31–35

Love is the way to give God glory. Jesus described how that love could occur. Soon Jesus would no longer be with the disciples. His inheritance to them would be the love they received. They were to show that same love to others, thereby continuing to obey Jesus after his departure. The commandment to love one another has been passed down through the ages, setting apart those who follow the Christ. So, love one another and give God glory, even as Jesus first loved you.

Call to Worship   Psalm 148

Leader: Let everything that has being praise the name of the Lord!
People: Mountains and hills, fruit trees and all cedars, shall praise the name of the Lord.
Leader: Young men and women alike, old and young together shall praise the name of the Lord.
People: We shall praise your name, O God, for your glory is above earth and heaven.
Leader: Let us worship God!

Prayer of Praise and Adoration

O God, you fulfill the desire of all who call upon you. We gather to worship and praise your name. You uphold those who are falling and raise up those who are bowed down. You are faithful in words, gracious in deeds, just in all ways, and kind in all that you do. Your dominion shall endure forever. With our mouths we will give you blessing and honor.

Litany of Affirmation

Leader: I saw a new heaven and a new earth; for the first heaven and the first earth had passed away, and the sea was no more.
People: God is the Alpha and the Omega, the beginning and the end.
Leader: I saw the new Jerusalem coming down out of heaven from God, prepared as a bride adorned for her husband.
People: God is the Alpha and the Omega, the beginning and the end.
Leader: Behold, God's dwelling is with all people. God will dwell with them, and they shall be God's people.
People: God is the Alpha and the Omega, the beginning and the end.

Leader: Behold, God makes all things new.
People: God is the Alpha and the Omega, the beginning and the end.

Prayer of Dedication

Living God, who made heaven, earth, the sea, and all that is in them, we praise you for rains and fruitful seasons. You satisfy our hearts with food and gladness. Through Christ you call us to walk in your ways. We offer our gifts as leaven, to spread the good news of Christ, the bread of life. We renew our commitment to serve you gladly and to love one another as you first loved us.

Prayer of Thanksgiving and Intercession

Fountain of life, who alone can satisfy all who thirst after righteousness, we give you all honor, blessing, and praise. Through your Holy Spirit you promise new beginnings; former things pass away as the new day dawns brightly. We shall live in the light of your trustworthy counsel and be guided by your wisdom as in truth we call upon your name.

We pray for those who have recently come to the fountain, confessing Jesus as the source of salvation. Open to them the vision of your dominion so that they can see clearly how they ought to respond. Give them clarity of mind as they seek to choose and decide in ambiguous situations.

We pray for those burdened with sorrow and pain; hear their cry and hasten to help them. Astonish them with the eternal presence of Christ their savior who can wipe away tears and restore wholeness of health. May they find comfort in those of us who reach out to embrace them. Give them patience to trust in the promise that you forsake not your own.

We pray for those who seek new beginnings, for whom Christ's resurrection is assurance that their past is forgiven. Some thirst after righteousness. Guide them beside living waters, where they may drink and be refreshed. Others hunger for justice. Lead them to the table of reconciliation, and nourish them on the bread of peace. You are the source of all wisdom, compassion, and reconciliation. Through Christ we bless you for hearing our prayer.

6TH SUNDAY OF EASTER (C)

Acts 16:9–15; Psalm 67
Revelation 21:10, 22–22:5; John 14:23–29 or John 5:1–9

Jesus foretells the coming of the Holy Spirit. The Spirit will teach and cause those who believe to remember what Jesus said. Jesus' promise is joined with the assurance of peace. In the midst of believing, the peace we receive will not be of this world. It will be the counsel of the Holy Spirit, who will make the word of Jesus penetratingly clear.

Call to Worship
Psalm 67

Leader: God be gracious to us and bless us and make your face to shine upon us.

People: Let the peoples praise you, O God; let all the peoples praise you.

Leader: The earth has yielded its increase; may God continue to bless us.

People: Let the peoples praise you, O God; let all the peoples praise you.

Leader: Let us worship God!

Prayer of Praise and Adoration

All nations on earth shall bless you, O God, for you have redeemed your people and brought them new life. Through Christ you have caused your Word to shine on the just and the unjust. By your Spirit all those who believe know of your saving power. We come confessing that Christ is our Savior; we give you all glory for your gift of redeeming grace.

Litany of Assurance

Leader: In the Spirit I saw the holy city Jerusalem coming down out of heaven from God.

People: Let not your hearts be troubled, neither let them be afraid.

Leader: I saw no temple in the city, for its temple is God the Almighty and the Lamb.

People: Let not your hearts be troubled, neither let them be afraid.

Leader: By its light shall the nations walk; and its gates shall never be shut by day—and there shall be no night there.

People: Let not your hearts be troubled, neither let them be afraid.

Leader: And the rulers of the earth shall bring into it the glory and the honor of the nations.

People: Let not your hearts be troubled, neither let them be afraid.

Prayer of Dedication

God of eternity, enthroned in glory, we come before you bringing our gifts. We humbly submit to your sovereign will. You are the source of all righteousness; we offer ourselves as ambassadors for peace. You are the source of justice; we give of our substance to alleviate hunger and want. You are the means by which all the earth shall prosper; we shall go into all nations and bless your name.

Prayer of Thanksgiving and Supplication

Gracious God, who sent Jesus into the world to proclaim peace to the nations and release for the captives, we stand at the portals of your everlasting dominion and behold your glory. We pledge our allegiance to foster your Word among peoples on earth.

Led by the Lamb, we carry your lamp into the cities to illumine the dark places. Let the lamp shine on all who struggle in the darkness: the addicted, the homeless, the unemployed, and the exploited. Help us to remove whatever stands in the way of their walking with dignity.

Full of that peace that Jesus gives, we bring the Spirit's counsel to those who are troubled. Open to them the gates of your guidance. We pray for those attacked by real or imagined demons; keep us from compounding their disease with unwarranted judgment, and guide them to discern the cause of their affliction. We pray for those with learning disabilities; surround them by people skilled in stimulating appropriate patterns for growth. We pray for those who are in hospitals and care centers; bless the doctors, nurses, and technicians who minister to them. We pray for those whom society has forgotten or would rather not remember; burn their plight upon our consciences. Continue to goad us out of complacency through your indwelling Spirit, so that we do not rest until the lost sheep are brought safely into the fold of the Lamb.

7TH SUNDAY OF EASTER (C)

Acts 16:16–34; Psalm 97
Revelation 22:12–14, 16–17, 20–21; John 17:20–26

Jesus prays for unity, a unity that portrays God's glory. Such a unity depends upon Christ's indwelling Spirit, which breaks down the barriers that keep people apart. Unity also depends upon faithfully hearing God's Word, as believers seek to discern God's will for their lives. Unity expresses itself in loving one's neighbors, reflecting the same concern for others that Christ had for all those in need.

Call to Worship   Psalm 97

Leader: The heavens proclaim your righteousness, O God.
People: And all the peoples behold your glory.
Leader: Rejoice in the Lord, O you righteous!
People: And we shall give thanks to God's holy name!
Leader: Let us worship God!

Prayer of Praise and Adoration

Strong Deliverer, righteousness and justice are the foundation of your throne. Your lightning enlightens the world; the earth sees it and trembles. Mountains melt like wax before you; Zion hears and is glad because of your judgments. We shall put aside our worship of vain images and cease our boasting of worthless idols. You are God who in Christ came to redeem us; we rejoice and give thanks to your holy name.

Litany of Assurance

Leader: Christ is the Alpha and the Omega, the first and the last, the beginning and the end.
People: The grace of Christ be with all the saints.
Leader: Blessed are those who wash their robes, that they may have the right to the tree of life and enter the city by the gates.
People: The grace of Christ be with all the saints.
Leader: Jesus is the root and the offspring of David, the bright morning star.
People: The grace of Christ be with all the saints.
Leader: Let whoever hears say, "Come"; let whoever is thirsty come, let whoever desires take the water of life without price.
People: The grace of Christ be with all the saints.

Leader:	Jesus testifies to all these things and says, "Surely I am coming soon." Amen. Come, Lord Jesus!
People:	The grace of Christ be with all the saints.

Prayer of Dedication

O righteous God, we have heard your Word, how we ought to obey you. We have confessed our faith in Christ our Savior. Full of your Spirit, we come now bringing our offerings. They symbolize our thanksgiving and reflect our commitment. Accept them and use them to spread the good news of salvation over all the earth.

Prayer of Thanksgiving

Holy God, you have redeemed us by Christ and reconciled us to yourself through him. We are bold to approach you and bless your name. You have not let the follies of humankind hinder your covenant from being enacted. Even a cross could not defeat your reconciling purpose. Throughout history you have revealed your gracious benevolence, and led the pilgrims through their perils toward your Promised Land. Now we stand on the eve of your Holy Spirit's appearance, and the day shall dawn brightly full of counsel and might. So, come, Creator Spirit, and enliven your children; make known your presence as you hear our prayer.

Washed clean by the blood of the Lamb, we shall don the robes of our baptism and enter the gates of your eternal dominion. We shall walk upright in the truth of your unrelenting assurance that our sins are forgiven. We shall reach the branches of the tree of life and eat of its fruit, no more to die. For in Christ you have banished the flaming sword from Eden; we can claim our inheritance as heirs of your grace.

Jesus, the bright morning star, shall enlighten our pilgrimage. Christ is the key who opens the prison cell and breaks the fetters of suspicion and hate. We shall listen to him and not grow weary in our endeavors. We shall make known your love to the ends of the earth. And may the grace of Christ, which passes all understanding, be with all your saints, even unto the end of the age.

THE DAY OF PENTECOST (C)

Acts 2:1–21 or Genesis 11:1–9; Psalm 104:24–34, 35b
Romans 8:14–17 or Acts 2:1–21; John 14:8–17 (25–27)

The nature of God is revealed in the face of Christ. "Whoever has seen me has seen the Father," Jesus says to Philip. To believe in Jesus is to do the works that Jesus does. Whatever the disciples ask in his name will be granted, to give God the glory. The Spirit will guide Jesus' disciples into all truth. A peace that the world cannot give shall be their legacy.

Call to Worship   Psalm 104

Leader: O God, how manifold are our works! You have made them all in wisdom; the earth is full of your creatures.

People: I will sing to the Lord as long as I live; I will sing praise to my God while I have being.

Leader: Let us worship God!

Prayer of Praise and Adoration

All the earth is full of your glory, O God; the heavens resound in praise of your name. Brooks ramble along the course you designed for them; leaves whisper of your manifold ways. Fields murmur as you pass through them; in the skies the thunder sounds its applause. With countless tongues and voices creation welcomes your presence. We join that throng and lift up our chorus, "Praise God, from whom all mercies flow!"

Prayer of Confession

Unison: God of wisdom and understanding, have mercy upon us as we confess our sin. Your children are scattered; language keeps them apart. Forgive us for the cultural pride that refuses to learn the language of another. Forgive us for the barriers of insensitivity that repel those whom you seek to call through us. By your Spirit's power undo the plight of Babel by the miracle of Pentecost, to the end that all may hear the gospel and praise the risen Christ with one voice.

Assurance of Pardon

Leader: As God confused the language of all the earth to keep the people from idolatry, so God sent Christ with the universal message of salvation: "Whoever calls on Christ's name shall be saved." Brothers and sisters, trust that name and be assured: In Jesus Christ we are forgiven!

Prayer of Dedication

O God, to you be the glory! We live to praise you; we trust your judgment; in all that we do we seek to obey you. Receive our offerings; they are the gifts of your Spirit. You have wrought the wonders that accompany new life. We shall not shrink from giving you glory, for we are called by Christ to be stewards of what you create.

Prayer of Thanksgiving and Supplication

Living God, with wondrous works and mighty deeds you continue to astound us with your grace and power. Like the rush of a mighty wind you make known your presence, interrupting our complacency, disturbing our lethargy. In hearing the first cry of a newborn, we sense your grace. You dry the tears of those who mourn; you calm the fears of those who face uncertain futures. You amaze us with wonders beyond comprehension. We stand in awe of your majesty and give thanks for your mercy.

Fill us with your Spirit and enlarge our vision. Open our eyes to the future that awaits beyond the scope of our finite perception. Attune our ears to your words of judgment so that we may discern our errors and forsake them. When we pursue courses of action that destroy your creation, correct our mismanagement and harness our greed. When we thoughtlessly make decisions that cause others to suffer, convict us of our cruelty and help us to right the wrongs.

Fill us with Christ and make us more daring. Implant your commandments within us so that we cannot mistake your truth. When we grasp after straws and are tempted to waver, balance our uncertainty with Christ's words of wisdom. When we stumble and fall in our pursuit of justice, strengthen our weak knees and set us on our path again. Alive in your Spirit and armed with your righteousness, we shall run the course you design for us.

TRINITY SUNDAY (C)

Proverbs 8:1–4, 22–31; Psalm 8
Romans 5:1–5; John 16:12–15

The Holy Spirit's role in the life of the disciples is defined. The Spirit leads believers in the way of God's truth, repeating what the Spirit has heard. The Spirit declares what is to come, guiding believers to behold God's glory and might. The Spirit takes what Jesus proclaimed and translates that message into relevant guidance. Through the Spirit, God's love in Christ is eternally known.

Call to Worship

Psalm 8

Leader: O God, your name is majestic in all the earth; your glory is chanted above the heavens.

People: You have crowned your people with glory and honor; we give you all praise in response to your grace.

Leader: Let us worship God!

Prayer of Praise and Adoration

Creator God, the earth is yours and all who dwell therein; the moon and stars reflect your radiance. You are the potter who fashions works of beauty from the mud, the painter who hangs the rainbow in the sky as the sign of your covenant. We join with those through the ages who have lauded your works of creation and redemption, evermore praising you and saying, "How majestic is your name in all the earth!"

Prayer of Confession

Unison: God of justice and love, you take away the sins of the world; have mercy upon us as we confess our sin. We call you God of creation, yet we serve idols of our own making. We confess Christ as our Savior, yet we rely on elaborate security systems for our protection. We claim the indwelling Spirit, yet we abide by our own counsel. Forgive our double-mindedness, and through Christ make us whole.

Assurance of Pardon

Leader: Through Jesus Christ we have obtained access to the grace in which we stand, and we can rejoice in the hope of sharing the glory of God. "God's love has been poured into our hearts through the Holy Spirit that has been given to us." Our assurance rests in the triune God, who grants us new life.

Prayer of Dedication

Set apart by your covenant, redeemed through Christ's sacrifice, and renewed by the refreshing winds of your living Spirit, we come bearing our gifts, O merciful God. They are but a portion of earth's treasure you abundantly give us; with them we commit our time and energy to be Christ's faithful servants. Use all that we bring, and all that we are, to bless your holy name.

Prayer of Thanksgiving

Great Designer of the universe, you fashioned creation to give you unending glory. We laud and honor the work of your hands. You gave depth to the waters and set the springs on their course. You shaped the mountains and brought forth the hills. You established the fields and determined the heavens, made firm the skies and fixed the planets in orbit. You commanded the seas to keep their limits and marked the continents where your people would dwell.

We praise you for Christ, your only begotten, the firstborn of creation to your eternal delight. Christ pioneered salvation through suffering on our behalf; Christ sanctified what you fashioned, purging it with hyssop and making it whiter than snow. Through Christ we can know you and enter the gates of your covenant, hear your words of wisdom and be led by your will.

We thank you for the Holy Spirit, by whom you pour your love into us. Our hearts take delight in your abounding grace. We find hope through the Spirit who grants us endurance, and know that you also suffer when we cry out in pain. Embraced by your compassion, counseled through your judgment, guided by your truth, and mercifully frustrated in our attempts at disobedience, we reaffirm our baptism in the name of the blessed Trinity. Bound by the Spirit as your covenant children, we rejoice in your creation's goodness and graceful redemption.

9TH SUNDAY IN ORDINARY TIME (C)

1 Kings 18:20–21 (22–29) 30–39; Psalm 96
Galatians 1:1–12; Luke 7:1–10

The centurion was a person of authority. When he issued commands to those under him, they were obeyed. His authority had its limits, however. He could not heal his slave, and thus he sought Jesus, whose authority was unequaled. "But only speak the word," he said, "and let my servant be healed." Jesus marveled at the centurion's faith.

Call to Worship   Psalm 96

Leader: O sing to the Lord a new song; sing to the Lord, all the earth.
People: We will sing to you and bless your name, O God. We will tell of your salvation from day to day.
Leader: Ascribe to the Lord, O families of the peoples, ascribe to the Lord glory and strength.
People: We come unto your gates with thanksgiving, O God, and into your courts with praise.
Leader: Let us worship God!

Prayer of Praise and Adoration

We lift our voices to bless you, O God; we bow down before you in humble adoration. You are honored among the hosts of heaven; your word spreads throughout the earth. We proclaim you God of all creation who sent Christ to redeem the nations. Filled with your Spirit, we sing in jubilation; we are your people and your love endures.

Prayer of Confession

Unison: God of all peoples and nations, hear our confession and forgive our sin. We make enemies of strangers when we distrust them. Fear and suspicion keep your people apart. Jesus came to reconcile our differences, yet your people do not dine at one common table. Heal our divisions and overcome our hostility. Unite us in the bond of your encompassing love.

Assurance of Pardon

Leader: Paul writes: "Grace to you and peace from God . . . and the Lord Jesus Christ, who gave himself for our sins to set us free from the present evil age, according to the will of our God . . . to whom be the glory forever and ever." In that grace and peace abides our assurance of pardon.

Prayer of Dedication

God of gladness, whose steadfast love endures forever and whose faithfulness is to all generations, we are your people and the sheep of your pasture. We rely on you for guidance along faith's journey; you protect us from harm. We shall dwell in the fold of your embracing mercy and give you the honor you are due. Accept our gifts, for all we receive are gifts of your grace.

Prayer of Praise and Supplication

You who keep covenant with all who walk faithfully before you, we give you thanks for Jesus, your Son, in whose name we journey. He came to set the nations aright, and was himself faithful even unto death. He called disciples to follow him. Their pilgrimage is ours today as we take up our crosses. He taught the meaning of sacrifice for others, and yoked us with him in service to you. We carry the name Christian wherever we wander. We give you thanks, O God, for that indelible sign of your unending covenant; we enter your gates with praise and bless your holy name.

Open the doors of your sovereign realm and give us a fresh vision of discipleship's course. Make us eager to embark on whatever path you choose. If the way is strewn with obstacles, level the rough places and keep us from stumbling. If there is more than one road, help us choose aright. When we meet strangers, may we not pass them by, but invite them to accompany us on the trek of faith. Clear the mists ahead so that we can see clearly. May we not abuse the authority that Jesus grants us.

Whatever strengths we have are gifts of your grace. Grant us humility in our relationships with neighbors; help us to see in them a reflection of your unmeasurable goodness. Chasten our judgment of those under us, and quicken our response to those who are above us. Make us as willing to give others the same benefit we would expect to receive. You prepare the table before us, O God, and give Christ the place of honor; you invite all of us to partake as faith's reconciling family. To you be the honor and glory forever and ever.

10TH SUNDAY IN ORDINARY TIME (C)

1 Kings 17:8–16 (17–24); Psalm 146
Galatians 1:11–24; Luke 7:11–17

A widow's only son had died and the funeral procession was leaving the city of Nain. Jesus saw the procession and had compassion on the widow, touched the bier and told the young man to arise. When the man spoke, the crowd was amazed, glorified God, and declared Jesus a prophet. Compassion, a touch, and newness of life were the trademarks of Jesus' ministry.

Call to Worship   Psalm 146

Leader: I will praise the Lord as long as I live; I will sing praises to my God all my life long.

People: Happy are those whose help is the God of Jacob, whose hope is in the Lord their God,

Leader: Who made heaven and earth, the sea, and all that is in them; who keeps faith forever.

People: The Lord will reign forever, your God, O Zion, for all generations. Praise the Lord!

Leader: Let us worship God!

Prayer of Praise and Adoration

Who is likened unto you, O God; with whom can you be compared? You are seated on high and look far down upon the heavens and the earth. You raise the poor from the earth, and the needy you lift from the heap of ashes. You visit calamity's child with the gift of new life, promised in Jesus our Christ and Savior. For all the mercy you shower upon us, we give you glory and sing you our praises.

Prayer of Confession

Unison: Merciful God, forgive us when we discredit the gospel through our actions. When we are frustrated, we blame you for our misfortune. We envy the well-to-do and forget to seek God's realm. Christ taught the meaning of faith, yet we are full of mistrust and are suspicious of your grace. We confess our faith even as we confess our failure. Forgive us our inconsistent behavior, and heal our divided natures.

Assurance of Pardon

Leader: As Jesus healed the afflicted and restored those who had died, so also through him our sins are forgiven and we are given new life.

313

Awaken to the assurance of your pardon, and arise to the promise of Christ's redeeming grace.

Prayer of Dedication

Like a potter, you fashioned the clay into designs of everlasting beauty. You set the heavens ablaze to your eternal glory. You create the fields and bring forth the harvest; its yield is ours because of your grace. Hear us, O God, as we give you heartfelt praise, and receive our offerings as signs of our love and gratitude.

Prayer of Thanksgiving and Intercession

O God, you visit the widow in her sorrow and comfort the suffering in their distress. We praise you for your mercy and compassion. Each day brings the knowledge of your reassuring presence; each night your Spirit watches over us. We awaken to the dawn of your promised salvation; we rest with the conviction that you will not leave us alone. The manifold signs of your graciousness surround us daily, O God, and for that we praise your wonderful name.

Be with all who mourn the passing of loved ones. Help them to find consolation in the outpouring of sympathy on their behalf. Fill the void left by their loss with abiding memories of those who have departed. Assure your servants of Christ's victory over death, that indeed as Jesus rose again, so those who sleep in him will themselves be raised to life eternal.

We pray for those afflicted with illness and pain. Ease their plight through the presence of your Holy Spirit. May they find comfort from arms that embrace them, guidance from hands that reach out to them, kindness in the eyes watching over them, and hope in the actions of all who care for them.

We who enjoy good health and freedom from ills give you the honor and thanks. Our days pass quickly by and we take so much for granted. Teach us to count the hours as a sacred trust from you, and our time on earth as the gift of your benevolence. Make of our bodies vessels for the extension of Christ's healing ministry and of our souls the receptacles of your divine love.

11TH SUNDAY IN ORDINARY TIME (C)

1 Kings 21:1–10 (11–14) 15–21a; Psalm 5:1–8
Galatians 2:15–21; Luke 7:36–8:3

The woman known as a sinner knew the meaning of forgiveness; Jesus' host, who was a Pharisee, did not. Luke contrasts how both treated Jesus. The woman kissed Jesus' feet and, weeping, anointed them with ointment, while the host did not give Jesus water for his feet, nor greet him with a kiss. She who was forgiven much loved much; he who was forgiven little showed little love. And yet, was not his need for forgiveness as great?

Call to Worship   Psalm 5

Leader: Give ear to my words, O Lord; give heed to my sighing, for to you I pray.

People: For you are not a God who delights in wickedness or sojourns with evil.

Leader: But I, through the abundance of your steadfast love will enter your house.

People: Lead me, O Lord, in your righteousness and make your way straight before me.

Leader: Let us worship God!

Prayer of Praise and Adoration

Giver of hope and gladness, who can turn our sorrow into exaltation, we praise you for Jesus, through whom we live anew. Christ quenches our thirst with living water; when we hunger for righteousness, our lives are filled with good things. We abide in the shelter of your love, O God, and raise our voices to worship and adore you.

Litany of Confession and Assurance

Leader: We know that a man or a woman is not justified by works of the law.

People: We have believed in Christ Jesus, in order to be justified by faith in Christ.

Leader: But if I build up again those things which I tore down, then I prove myself a transgressor.

People: We have believed in Christ Jesus, in order to be justified by faith in Christ.

Leader: I have been crucified with Christ; it is no longer I who live, but Christ who lives in me.

People:	We have believed in Christ Jesus, in order to be justified by faith in Christ.
Leader:	The life I now live in the flesh I live by faith in the Son of God, who loved me and gave himself for me.
People:	We have believed in Christ Jesus, in order to be justified by faith in Christ.

Prayer of Dedication

Messenger from on high, we come having heard your word of assurance; you will minister to us during our sojourn of faith. We shall not want, since you continue to watch over us; you will sustain us daily in response to our needs. Accept now our gifts, for they acknowledge your abundance. Whatever we offer is due to your grace. Take them and use them to your glory and honor as in Christ's name we pray.

Prayer of Thanksgiving and Supplication

God of the heavenly host, whose ministering angels visit the afflicted, we join the throng who sings your praises. We stand before your judgment seat redeemed through faith in Christ our Savior. We gather as sisters and brothers of your covenant family, called by Christ to obey your will. As we journey in faith, we bear the burdens of our neighbors and so lessen their strain as you have eased ours.

Speak to us as your angel addressed Elijah. When we are afraid, let us know that you are near. There are some who make light of our efforts to be faithful. Help us to hear your guiding words amid the distraction of other voices.

Nourish us for the journey. Help us to trust you for all of our needs. Feed us with the bread of heaven broken by Jesus; refresh us with the cup of new life. Anoint us with the oil of gladness and make us loving hosts. Show us afresh the joy of forgiveness. Help us to open the doors of your house to passing strangers, that they can enter therein and find rest. Make us unafraid to offer them the water of baptism, whereby they can be cleansed and find life anew.

Through grace you have sought us; in Christ you redeem us. By faith it is no longer we who live, but Christ who lives in us. God of the heavenly host, praise be unto you.

12TH SUNDAY IN ORDINARY TIME (C)

1 Kings 19:1–4 (5–7) 8–15a; Psalms 42 and 43
Galatians 3:23–29; Luke 8:26–39

Jesus arrives in the country of the Gerasenes and is met by a man possessed with demons. His affliction is so great that often he was bound in chains from which he would escape and be driven into the wilds. Jesus commands the demons to come out of the man, which they do, only to enter a large herd of swine, which ultimately drowns. Jesus is forces to leave the country while the healed man goes and tells all what Jesus has done for him. Many possessed with demons will find their lives right-wised, as they believe in the Christ.

Call to Worship   Psalms 42, 43

Leader: As a deer longs for flowing streams, so my soul longs for you, O God.
People: O send out your light and your truth; let them lead me to the throne of your grace.
Leader: Hope in God; for I shall again praise the Lord, my help and my God.
People: Then I will go to the altar of God and praise you with the harp, O Lord, my God.
Leader: Let us worship God!

Prayer of Praise and Adoration

O God of light and truth, lead us by your Word to your holy hill and to your dwelling. Then we shall come to your altar with exceeding joy and praise you with the lyre, for you are God. The wind cannot contain you, nor the fires consume you; the earthquake fails to encompass your power, for you are God. Speak as you have spoken with your still small voice, and we shall hear and be your people.

Prayer of Confession

Unison: Infinite Word of truth, breathe upon us the refreshing breath of your Holy Spirit and forgive our transgressions. Cleanse our hearts of false doctrine by the winds of righteousness and truth. Purge us by the fires of your eternal judgment and we shall be pure. Shake the foundations of our jealousy and selfishness and cast us anew in the image of Christ Jesus.

Assurance of Pardon

Leader: Before faith came, we were confined under the law, kept under restraint until faith should be revealed. Now that faith has come, we are no longer under a custodian; for in Christ Jesus we are God's children, through faith. So, inherit the promise of God's pardon through Christ, and live in the assurance that your sins are forgiven.

Prayer of Dedication

Guardian of our destiny, we come in response to Christ's call to discipleship. We offer our sacrifice of praise and thanksgiving with the prayer that you will deem it worthy of your grace. We offer our deeds of goodness; transform them into acts of benevolence befitting your mercy. We offer our treasure; turn it into the means of new life for all.

Prayer of Thanksgiving and Supplication

God of Elijah, Elisha, Miriam, and Naomi, we give thanks that throughout the ages you have revealed your Word. You temper us through the fire of your judgment and speak to us in a still, small voice. We praise you that you hide not your face from us, and we rejoice in the wisdom of your infinite Word.

Startle us with your pervasive Spirit. Disturb our way of living until it accords with your will. Keep us from becoming lulled by the comforts of the consumer society; make us willing to forsake false treasure in order to follow the Christ. When we are tempted to leave the path you choose for us, frustrate our efforts to go our own way.

Continue to guide us through Christ, who calls us. Let the freshness of your wisdom be as poignant as on the day of baptism, when we confessed our faith with ardor and zest. Keep our commitment attuned to the abiding revelation of Christ's teaching, and make us eager to pursue new ventures of ministry.

Continue to comfort us with your embracing tenderness. Surround those who long for your assuring presence. Be with those weakened by disabling diseases, and strengthen those burdened with cares and concerns. We pray for those who through death have lost loved ones. May we communicate to all those near to us your word of compassion, which is never far from us.

13TH SUNDAY IN ORDINARY TIME (C)

2 Kings 2:1–2, 6–14; Psalm 77:1–2, 11–20
Galatians 5:l, 13–25; Luke 9:51–62

To follow Jesus implies certain things. It may mean forsaking security in order to go where Jesus calls; decisions may need to be made now rather than after personal affairs are transacted. Once you make the choice, there is no looking back. Discipleship means today what it meant when Jesus walked: Choose this day whom you will serve.

Call to Worship   Psalm 77

Leader: I will call to mind the deeds of the Lord; I will remember your wonders of old.
People: I will meditate on all your work, and muse on your mighty deeds.
Leader: Your way, O God, is holy. What god is so great as our God?
People: You are the God who works wonders; you have displayed your might among the peoples.
Leader: Let us worship God!

Prayer of Praise and Adoration

We will boast of your presence among us, O God, and magnify your holy name. You still the avenger; you bring low the mighty; you exalt the humble and forget not your own. We are privileged to be numbered among those you have chosen, and through Christ seek to honor you in all that we do. Hear our praises, which we raise before you, as in glad adoration our tributes we bring.

Prayer of Confession

Unison: God of freedom, set at liberty we who are captive, and grant us absolution as we confess our sin. Prisoners of self-interest, we disregard neighbors. We bolster our own egos at others' expense. When slander is rampant, we seldom stop it. When rumors are rife, we seek not the source. Help us to check our destructive ways, lest we consume one another, and cause us to use our freedom in more loving ways.

Assurance of Pardon

Leader: "The fruit of the Spirit is love, joy, peace, patience, kindness, generosity, faithfulness, gentleness, and self-control. There is no law against such things." We who "belong to Christ Jesus have crucified the flesh with its passions and desires." Therefore, let us live in love and bear one another's burdens, in the assurance that we are forgiven and made alive in the Spirit.

Prayer of Dedication

Leader: O God, you cast your mantle upon us and mark us for ministry in Christ's name. We come before you with our tithes and offerings. We shall put on your cloak of righteousness as a sign to the nations of how you redeem all people. We shall carry the cross of salvation to the far corners of the globe. Accept these gifts as tokens of our commitment, and bless our endeavors as we serve you in Christ's name.

Prayer of Thanksgiving and Supplication

Author and Finisher of our faith, you have set our feet firmly on freedom's foundation; we praise you and give you thanks. Witnesses of old have taught us of the deliverance of God's people from peril. Scripture recounts their covenant promise. You will be our God and we your people. You, O Christ, have sealed a new covenant in your blood and won for us the victory of life everlasting.

Draw us into a right relationship with you and our neighbor. Help us to stand fast by your Spirit and not abuse your trust. Make our inheritance as your sons and daughters a lasting legacy, one that we are eager to pass on to our heirs. Help us by our example to teach them what it means to love you completely and our neighbor as ourselves.

We pray for neighbors both near and far. Give an extraordinary sense of your delivering power to those who live in peril for your sake. Allow them to walk, free from care. Lift from their shoulders the weight of anxiety, and yoke us to them during their time of trial.

There are those for whom freedom is costly: martyrs, prisoners, and the oppressed. Let them not be denied the birthright of your blessing. Give to prisoners the hope that their confinement does not separate them from your mercy. Lift the oppressed and let them glimpse your glory. Set us on the path of freedom's journey and we shall recount what great deeds you have done.

14TH SUNDAY IN ORDINARY TIME (C)

2 Kings 5:1–14; Psalm 30
Galatians 6:(1–6), 7–16; Luke 10:1–11, 16–20

Jesus commissioned those sent out to preach. They were to go in peace and remain only where they were welcome. Their charge was to heal the sick and to proclaim that God's reign was near. Where they were not received, they were not to fret, but shake the dust from their feet and move on. Throughout the ages the task has not changed: Go where Christ sends you and minister to all who are in need.

Call to Worship   Psalm 30

Leader: Sing praises to the Lord, O you his faithful ones, and give thanks to God's holy name.

People: Hear, O Lord, and be gracious to me! O Lord, be my helper!

Leader: You have turned mourning into dancing, and clothed us with joy,

People: So that my soul may praise you and not be silent. O Lord my God, I will give thanks to you forever.

Leader: Let us worship God!

Prayer of Praise and Adoration

God of the dawn, we arise to the hope of your redeeming grace. God of the dusk, we rest secure in the assurance that you neither slumber nor sleep. God of the noonday sun, we dwell in the midst of your unfailing mercy. You are above us, beneath us, and throughout all creation. Through the abundance of your encompassing love we worship and praise your glorious name.

Prayer of Confession

Unison: God of creation, you make all things new; look with mercy upon us as we confess our sin. The seeds of destruction find fertile soil in us; we nurture them to fruition. We pluck the yield and find it delightful; we rejoice in the evil harvest we have sown. Save us from our love of sinning, O God. Teach us to sow to your Holy Spirit, and reap eternal life.

Assurance of Pardon

Leader: Just as Paul bore on his body the marks of Jesus, so also may we glory in the cross of Christ Jesus. By it the world has been crucified to us and we to the world. So walk by this rule and dwell in God's mercy, for through the grace of our Savior we are forgiven.

Prayer of Dedication

O God of the heavenly vineyard, in Christ you have sown the seed of our eternal salvation. Through the Holy Spirit you have planted your Word of wisdom and might. We are surrounded by countless acts of your graciousness and are empowered in every way by your sustaining love. Receive the fruits of our labors, which we lay before you, and bless them to your glory.

Prayer of Thanksgiving and Supplication

Great God of love, in whose name we labor, we give thanks for the harvest of your redeeming grace. You have given us Jesus to guide us in our quest for faithfulness. You have sent your Spirit to enlighten our path. You watch over us as we endeavor to be his disciples, giving us faith, courage, and patience to pursue the course. We confess anew our commitment to obey more completely, trust more fully, honor more faithfully, and praise you more joyously all our days. You are God of our encircling years; we live, thanks to your love.

Bless us, loving God, as we go forth to labor, so that we may proclaim your peace that passes understanding. Amid the strife of nation with nation, help us to be your agents of righteousness, sounding the trumpet of judgment and boldly declaring your sovereignty over all the earth. Amid the turmoil that afflicts our cities, give us courage to confront the causes of hatred and fear, and point to a more excellent way. Within homes torn asunder by suspicion and selfishness, give us skills that can reconcile parents and children, sisters and brothers, and husbands and wives. Wherever we walk, may we plant seeds of your goodness and the vineyards of your unremitting grace.

Garnish our efforts with the flavor of humility that will bring the honor you are due. Keep us from usurping authority in order to build up ourselves, and from pride in self that makes a mockery of your mercy. May we be content that our names are inscribed as servants of your heavenly dominion. Lead us to boast only in your power, to flourish through faithfulness to Christ's high calling, and to triumph in the truth that makes us free.

15TH SUNDAY IN ORDINARY TIME (C)

Amos 7:7–17; Psalm 82
Colossians 1:1–14; Luke 10:25–37

A lawyer asked, "What shall I do to inherit eternal life?" He knew what was written but he wanted an example. Jesus replied by telling the story of the Good Samaritan. The Samaritan, a foreigner, knew what it meant to show mercy to someone in need. The religious authorities may also have known but did nothing about it. The lawyer learned that quoting the law is not enough; God calls us to acts of mercy.

Call to Worship   Colossians 1

Leader: We have heard of your faith in Christ Jesus and of the love that you have for all the saints.
People: We have heard of this hope before in the word of the truth, the gospel that has come to us.
Leader: We have not ceased praying for you and asking that you may be filled with the knowledge of God's will,
People: So that we may lead lives worthy of the Lord as we bear fruit in every good work.
Leader: Let us worship God!

Prayer of Praise and Adoration

Most Holy God, you know our every thought and deed; our lives are not hid from you. You dwell in the heights, yet you stoop to hear us. You inhabit the depths, yet you rise to support our efforts to serve you. You encompass the whole of creation, and are yet concerned for our needs. All praise to you, eternal God; we honor and glorify your holy name.

Prayer of Confession

Unison: God of compassion, we confess before you that we have sinned. We have passed by your neighbors, and ignored opportunities to show them mercy. We have mocked their misery by making excuses to avoid their plight. We who have been taught the law of love practice instead the law of self-interest. Forgive us, we pray, for the sake of the Christ who came to bind up the wounds of the one by the side of the road.

Assurance of Pardon

Leader: Hear Paul's words when he writes of God, who has transferred us from the dominion of darkness and to the care of Christ our Savior. So, walk in Christ's love with assurance of your redemption and the forgiveness of sins.

Prayer of Dedication

God of grace and truth, you fill us with the knowledge of your will, that we may gain spiritual wisdom and understanding. We seek to lead a life worthy of your calling in Christ. We bring you the fruit, born of your graciousness, with the prayer that it may be fitting of your blessing and glory.

Prayer of Thanksgiving and Supplication

All-knowing God, you discern our thoughts and are acquainted with all our ways. Before a word is on our lips you know it altogether. You lay your hand upon us as Christ calls us to ministry. You fill us with your Holy Spirit, who leads us by your wisdom and counsel. You guide us throughout our journey's length, forgiving our waywardness, equipping us to serve you, and fulfilling our needs. Nothing we can do escapes your eye. There is nowhere we can hid from you. You are within and without, before us and beyond us. O God of our being, we give you praise and thanksgiving.

Hasten the day when our love for you matches your mercy toward us. Enlarge our hearts to the dimensions of your mercy, and help us to return to you a measure of the love you give to us. Purify our souls with your continuing assurance of pardon, and save us from our love of idols and vain display. Strengthen us whereby we may serve you more effectively and glorify your name through obedience to Christ.

Give us the mind of Christ as we look upon our neighbor. Keep us from passing by those whom society overlooks. Plant indelibly on our hearts the plight of the homeless, the forsaken, and the poor. Lend us a portion of your grace as we seek to lift them from despair. Cause their fainting spirits to feel the gentle embrace of Jesus our Savior, who came that all may have life and have it abundantly.

16TH SUNDAY IN ORDINARY TIME (C)

Amos 8:1–12; Psalm 52
Colossians 1:15–28; Luke 10:38–42

Mary and Martha were sisters, each of whom had a special gift. Martha was intent on serving Jesus; Mary was content to listen to his teachings. When Martha objected to Mary's seeming disregard of household chores, Jesus gently rebuked her choice of values. At that point in his ministry, Martha's distraction with much serving was not what Jesus needed.

Call to Worship Psalm 52

Leader: I am like a green olive tree in the house of God. I trust in the steadfast love of God forever and ever.

People: I will thank you forever, O God, because of what you have done. I will proclaim your name, for it is good.

Leader: Let us worship God!

Prayer of Praise and Adoration

Great are you, O God, and greatly to be praised. Before we were born, you knew our inward parts and did knit them together in our mother's wombs. Our thoughts of you could exceed the sand and they would not suffice to exhaust your wonder. We marvel at the extent of your wisdom and graciousness as we bow down to worship your glorious name.

Prayer of Confession

Unison: God of hope and glory, through Christ hear our prayer and renew a right spirit within us. Hostility rages and battles continue; warfare is not ended and lives are lost. We yield to suspicion; our envy creates enemies. We confess that Christ came to create a new order, yet we continue complacently to dwell amid strife. O God, have mercy upon us.

Assurance of Pardon

Leader: Remember that you are chosen by Christ, who reconciles you to God. Christ presents you holy, blameless, and irreproachable before God. Continue in the faith, remain stable and steadfast, and do not shift from the hope of the gospel, which you heard. For in Christ you are forgiven.

Prayer of Dedication

We lean on the everlasting arms of your mercy, O God, and dwell in the hope of your grace fulfilled. Whatever good we do we owe to your power within us. The work of our hands is a gift of your love. Nourish our endeavors with your sustaining Spirit and accept our efforts, as in Christ we seek to fulfill your all-encompassing will.

Prayer of Thanksgiving and Supplication

Giver of life, who conceived creation's dawning and implanted the seeds of your eternal dominion, wonderful are your works. You are compassionate and lovingly embrace your creatures. You conceived their well-being and bore the Christ for them. You labored with their sinfulness and sent forth the Spirit. You did not forsake them when death's darkness enshrouded the earth. We live today, thanks to your love.

Hope of the world, we rely on your mercy. Continue to grant us hospice where we can live secure from harm. Help us to find in Christ the anchor of our faith, the haven of calm waters amid unsettling times. Root us and ground us in his teachings, so that when the wind blows, we remain steadfast; when stormy seas threaten, we do not desert you. When we are tossed to and fro, we may remain upright in the conviction that Christ died to free us from ultimate destruction.

Custodian of the future, we depend on your grace. Blend our thoughts with your thoughts. Leaven this lump of creation we call our existence, so that our days on earth reflect your splendor. Renew us with your Holy Spirit and align all that we do with your will for us. When we are depressed, be with us to uplift us; when we stray from your desire, frustrate our errant behavior. When our feet are light, dance with us; when we shout with joy, hear our praise. You have formed our days before we knew they existed. How precious to us are your thoughts, O God. How vast is the sum of them.

17TH SUNDAY IN ORDINARY TIME (C)

Hosea 1:2–10; Psalm 85
Colossians 2:6–15 (16–19); Luke 11:1–13

Jesus taught his disciples how to pray. First, hallow God's name and let God reign. Thereafter, pray daily for what you need to sustain you and seek forgiveness for the wrongs you have done. Keep away from temptations, since they lead to disobedience. Remember, above all, that God is faithful; God sends the Holy Spirit to fulfill every need.

Call to Worship   Psalm 85

Leader: Steadfast love and faithfulness will meet; righteousness and peace will kiss each other.

People: Faithfulness will spring up from the ground, and righteousness will look down from the sky.

Leader: The Lord will give what is good, and our land will yield its increase.

People: Righteousness will go before the Lord and make a path for God's steps.

Leader: Let us worship God!

Prayer of Praise and Adoration

You make us glad with the joy of your presence, O God, and fill our days with your steadfast love. Day by day you meet us with goodly blessings; night after night your steadfast love upholds us. Your glory is great; your help is unfailing. We bow before your splendor and majesty, and praise your name.

Litany of Assurance

Leader: In Christ the whole fullness of deity dwells bodily, and you have come to fullness of life in Christ.

People: As therefore you received Christ Jesus, abound in thanksgiving.

Leader: You were buried with Christ in baptism and were raised with Christ through faith in the working of God.

People: As therefore you received Christ Jesus, abound in thanksgiving.

Leader: You, who were dead in trespasses, God made alive together with Christ, having forgiven us all our trespasses.

People: As therefore you received Christ Jesus, abound in thanksgiving.

Leader:	God disarmed the principalities and powers and made a public example of them, triumphing over them in Christ.
People:	As therefore you received Christ Jesus, abound in thanksgiving.

Prayer of Dedication

Abounding in hope, we come before you, O God; you are deliverance and life divine. You build a storehouse of goodly blessings and set us within it to sample your love. Whatever our needs, you meet them completely. You surround us with your compassion and care. Receive the offerings that we lay before you. We dedicate all our possessions to your continuing glory.

Prayer of Praise and Supplication

Giver of countless blessings, your reign is divine. Your dominion exceeds the widest expanse of the oceans; your love extends beyond the heavens. Hallowed be your name into the eternal ages, for you have decreed that you alone are God. Hasten the day when all people shall know you, and let us be agents in proclaiming your will. Make of us stewards who tend your creation; help us teach others how to live at peace with the earth.

Give to us daily what we need to sustain us. Save us from greed and wanton desire. Deliver us from love of goods, the material things we tend to venerate and adore. Help us to be satisfied with the fortunes you heap on us: the grace, mercy, and peace only you can bestow.

We sin in spite of Christ's atoning sacrifice. Bathe us with assurance of Christ's redeeming love. When we judge others unfit for forgiveness, make us mindful of our own need for pardon. Give us a reconciling spirit toward those whom society scorns and rebukes.

Keep us from submitting to temptation. Perfect our faith and help us withstand Satan's lure. When we come asking, continue to receive us; when we seek guidance, help us to find your Spirit. As we knock at the door of your eternal dominion, help us to hear Jesus responding: Come, enter in!

18TH SUNDAY IN ORDINARY TIME (C)

Hosea 11:1–11; Psalm 107:1–9, 43
Colossians 3:1–11; Luke 12:13–21

The ledger showed a healthy profit. So, the landowner thought that it would be well to build larger storerooms. More grain could be stored and time could be taken to eat, drink, and be merry. Ah, but what if the landowner died during this life of ease, whose then would the riches be? Jesus taught the multitude to seek their treasure through obeying God rather than coveting earthly possessions.

Call to Worship   Psalm 107

Leader: Give thanks to the Lord, for God is good, whose steadfast love endures forever.
People: Those gathered from east and west and north and south are the redeemed of the Lord.
Leader: Those who cried to the Lord in times of trouble God delivered from their distress.
People: Let them thank the Lord for steadfast love and wonderful works to humankind.
Leader: Let us worship God!

Prayer of Praise and Adoration

Great Shepherd of Israel, you hear the voices of our supplications; you defend your people as their strength and shield. Through Christ you have established our eternal birthright; by your Spirit you make us to know your godly decree. As we dwell evermore in the fold of your heavenly heritage, we blend our voices with the multitudes and sing to you our songs of praise.

Litany of Confession

Leader: If then you have been raised with Christ, set your mind on things that are above.
People: For you have died, and your life is hidden with Christ in God.
Leader: Put to death therefore what is earthly in you: fornication, impurity, passion, evil desire, and greed, which is idolatry.
People: For you have died, and your life is hidden with Christ in God.
Leader: But now you must get rid of all such things—anger, wrath, malice, slander, and abusive language from your mouth.

People:	For you have died, and your life is hidden with Christ in God.
Leader:	Do not lie to one another, seeing that you have stripped off the old self with its practices and have clothed yourselves with the new self.
People:	For you have died, and your life is hidden with Christ in God.

Prayer of Dedication

Our Shield and Defender, you have taught us how to trust your goodness and lay up treasure in heaven; we offer you gifts in response to your Word. We bring you a portion of what our labor has gained in thankful praise for the abundance we have. We give you our souls in humble obedience, for in Christ we inherit eternal life. Be pleased with our offerings; they are signs of your mercy.

Prayer of Thanksgiving and Supplication

O God, our Rock and Redeemer, and solace for all who call on your name; we behold the vision of your holy splendor and bow down before you in humble submission. You are God; there is no other. All else fades and withers, while you endure throughout the ages. With angels, archangels, prophets, apostles, and martyrs who have gone before, we join in giving you praise and thanksgiving.

Your grace abounds. We receive of its abundance. You exceed our expectations and needs. There is never a day that we cannot list the manifold gifts of your abounding love. From morning until nightfall, we are upheld by your encompassing care.

Having been raised by Christ, we will set our minds on your heavenly splendor. We will trust your Holy Spirit to guide us when earthly desires distract us. We confess that we are prone to temptation, but by your grace we can put on the new nature Christ bestows.

Claiming our inheritance as your sons and daughters, we shall go forth to all people as witnesses to your love. Let us not covet what our neighbors enjoy. Prevent our worship of false gods, and stop our tongues when we would slander a brother or sister. When we eat, make us mindful that you are the source of all nourishment; when we drink, may it be the cup of new life. Help us to be merry in the joy of the Spirit, as we give you the glory and honor due your name.

19TH SUNDAY IN ORDINARY TIME (C)

Isaiah 1:1, 10–20; Psalm 50:1–8, 22–23
Hebrews 11:1–3, 8–16; Luke 12:32–40

Discipleship is costly, but it is not to be fraught with anxiety. God is to be trusted for all one's needs. With their treasure in heaven, disciples will not be afraid to give alms, for thieves cannot threaten their true possessions. Disciples free themselves of earthly care so they can wait and watch, for they do not know when the call will come.

Call to Worship   Psalm 50

Leader: God the Lord speaks and summons the earth from the rising of the sun to its setting.

People: God says, "Gather to me my faithful ones, who made a covenant with me."

Leader: Those who bring thanksgiving as their sacrifice honor the Lord.

People: To those who go the right way I will show the salvation of God.

Leader: Let us worship God!

Prayer of Praise and Adoration

O God in heaven, like a potter you framed the universe, and with your hands you made us. You fashioned creation to fulfill your purpose. Through Christ you restore that which is broken; by your Holy Spirit you enflame us with zeal to obey. Look down from heaven to see if there are any who act wisely; you will see us and hear us praising your name.

Prayer of Confession

Unison: By faith you called Abraham to sojourn, O God; by faith Sarah conceived even when she was past the age. We read of their witness and marvel at their obedience; our faith is meager by comparison. We rarely venture out without knowing the destination; we want to know what's in it for us before we commit ourselves to your call. Forgive our lack of daring and commitment and help us to trust you completely.

Assurance of Pardon

Leader: Remember that "faith is the assurance of things hoped for, the conviction of things not seen. . . . By faith we understand that the worlds were prepared by the word of God, so that what is seen was made from things that are not visible." We can therefore look "forward to the city that has foundations, whose architect and builder is God." For by the faith of Jesus, the Cornerstone, we are forgiven.

Prayer of Dedication

Righteous God, you cast out fear and open the doors to your dominion. We come bearing alms, as Christ would have us do. All that we own you have given to us. We set it apart to your glory and honor. Who we are is due to your graciousness; we commit our efforts to your service. Possess us and guide us through your Holy Spirit and we shall live out our days praising your name.

Prayer of Thanksgiving and Supplication

God of wisdom, righteousness, and grace, we are overcome by the benefits you have bestowed upon us. We need not fear, since in Christ you endow us with eternal life. You craft our talents and implant them within us; we live by your grace. Dying to sin and rising in the victory of Christ's atoning sacrifice, we can walk upright, thanks to your love.

Keep the lamp of your goodness burning brightly within us, as a sign of our welcome when Christ comes and knocks. If the candle of faith has grown dim and no longer leads us to obedience, trim our wicks and ignite us anew. As doubt and depression make our worship halfhearted, startle us with your grace so that we regain the sense of wonder. When our confession becomes casual and we have little intention of changing our ways, call us to account by your righteousness and purify our motives.

As Abraham stepped out with assurance, not knowing where he was to go, may we likewise venture forth by the light of your promise. Deliver us from the excessive need to control our own destinies, and restore our trust in your infinite goodness. By your power Sarah conceived, even when she was past the age. Help us to bear within us the hope that in Christ all things are possible. With faith rekindled, we set forth on our journey in the certain knowledge that we are ever at home with you.

20TH SUNDAY IN ORDINARY TIME (C)

Isaiah 5:1–7; Psalm 80:1–2, 8–19
Hebrews 11:29–12:2; Luke 12:49–56

The fire of judgment and the water of baptism were symbols of Jesus' compelling call to ministry; they still are. What one enflames, the other can quench. Jesus forecasts a time of division when households will be divided. Within the household of faith, baptism is the sacrament that binds us together; whatever our differences, we are still one. As the body of Christ, obey what Christ teaches and be reconciled one to another.

Call to Worship
Psalm 80

Leader: Give ear, O Shepherd of Israel, stir up your might and come to save us!

People: Restore us, O God of hosts; let your face shine, that we may be saved.

Leader: Then we will never turn back from you; give us life, and we will call on your name.

People: Restore us, O Lord of hosts; let your face shine, that we may be saved.

Leader: Let us worship God!

Prayer of Praise and Adoration

You lift our drooping hands, O God, and strengthen our weak knees. You make straight the ways of the faithful and keep those who trust you from falling. We shall make known your holiness among the nations and proclaim your peace unto the ends of the earth. In the name of Jesus, who sits at your right hand, we gather to praise you, God of all grace.

Prayer of Confession

Unison: Have mercy upon us, O God, for sin clings so closely and its burden is great. Because of sin our hands are at our sides when they should reach out to others. Our knees are shaky when we should be standing firm. We are victims of our own misdeeds; we cannot escape sin's weight on our lives. Through Christ's intercession lift the burden from us, and help us walk in freedom and in strength.

Assurance of Pardon

Leader: Know that God is gracious and just, and forgives all who repent and turn from their sin. So run with perseverance the race that is set, looking to Jesus, the pioneer and perfecter of your faith. Because Christ sits at God's right hand and intercedes for us, we have assurance that we are forgiven.

Prayer of Dedication

All praise and honor be unto you, O God, for your faithfulness throughout the ages. We could offer you nothing were it not for Christ our Redeemer. We could not walk obediently without your Holy Spirit to guide us. We could not bring you our offerings except for your grace. We are yours, blessed God. Use us now!

Prayer of Thanksgiving and Intercession

God of all knowledge, before whom nations rise and pass away, we bow down in awe of your infinite wisdom. You discern our inmost thoughts, sensing our needs. You are the quickening fire of judgment that renders us liable for our deeds and misdeeds. Yours is the reconciling Spirit of atonement, which can lift us from the depths of sin and failure. You set us aright, so that we may walk henceforth in your mercy. For all this and more we give you thanks.

God of compassion, we pray for those whose spirits are crushed by the weight of their afflictions. They cry in their anguish that there can be no God. Draw near to them during their time of trial, and deliver them from the abyss of despair. Help us be for them a source of encouragement and support, so that they may once more trust your promises. Let us hear in their cries our own call to be by their side.

God of justice, we pray for the doers of evil whose arms smite the weak and the powerful alike. They make no distinctions in their quest for power. They acknowledge no God who can requite their sin. When they are called to account before your throne, may Christ intercede on their behalf. Keep us from casting them aside as worthy only of punishment. Teach us our dependence with them on your mercy. Help us, O God, to pray for both the oppressed and the oppressors, to the end that all may one day be included in your gift of redemption.

21ST SUNDAY IN ORDINARY TIME (C)

Jeremiah 1:4–10; Psalm 71:1–6
Hebrews 12:18–29; Luke 13:10–17

Jesus laid his hands on a woman and enabled her to stand upright. When some took offense at his having healed on the Sabbath we hear the familiar argument about how there are six days to work; one should honor the Sabbath. However, when there are chores that need to be done seven days a week the argument no longer pertains. Jesus came to earth that people should be set aright. That knows no time limit or legal boundaries. God will not stop until the creation is restored to God's rightful intention.

Call to Worship   Psalm 71

Leader: In you, O Lord, I take refuge; let me never be put to shame.
People: In your righteousness deliver me and rescue me; incline your ear to me and save me.
Leader: Be to me a strong fortress, to save me, for you are my rock and my fortress.
People: For you, O Lord, are my hope and my trust. My praise is continually of you.
Leader: Let us worship God!

Prayer of Praise and Adoration

Blessed are those whose strength is in you, O God of hosts, in whose hearts are highways to your eternal dominion. A day in your courts is better than a thousand elsewhere, and you withhold nothing from those who walk uprightly. We shall dwell as doorkeepers in your heavenly household, there to give you the honor and glory that is due your name.

Prayer of Confession

Unison: With Christ as our hope, O God, we stand at the gates of your sanctuary seeking your pardon. We confess that we have not worshiped you alone. Life makes its demands and we push you to the margins. You are for leisure moments, when our own work is done. Forgive us for our small minds and mistaken priorities. Restore in us the sense of your greatness and your ultimate claim upon our lives.

Assurance of Pardon

Leader: Hear with grateful hearts that Jesus, the mediator of the new covenant, ushers us into the gates of God's eternal dominion. By his own blood he healed the estrangement between God, and us and by his sacrifice offers reconciliation to all who believe. In this Christ we have assurance that we are forgiven, and truly citizens of the heavenly city.

Prayer of Dedication

With praise and adoration we enter your temple. Thanksgiving spills from our lips as we approach your majesty. You are God who creates in splendor; holy and blessed is your glorious name. With your Spirit to guide us we shall strive to enter the narrow door, following Christ's teachings and the call to obey. Receive now these offerings as signs of our commitment, of our unceasing gratitude for the gifts you bestow.

Prayer of Thanksgiving and Supplication

How lovely is your dwelling place, O Lord of hosts. How spacious are the courts of your realm. Birds can come and build their nests. People can gather and find room at your table. Through Christ you have opened the gates to your heavenly Jerusalem, where we may enter in and taste the joys of salvation.

We thank you for the company of angels who teach us how to sing your praises. Make our life's journey a pilgrimage of praise and thanksgiving for the beauty, order, and worth you bestow on all of its parts. Keep us from taking our trek for granted, and from the misguided notion that whatever we do now affects not the whole.

We praise you for the firstborn already enrolled in heavenly splendor, prophets, priests, poets, and parents of our faith. Their visions of peace call us to greater endeavor. Their prayers on our behalf sustain us when our own words are found wanting. Their example abides with us still.

We rejoice at these tokens of your mercy, and are continually grateful for the gift of your Spirit. The Spirit strengthens us when temptation comes, and helps us to discern your will as we respond to the needs of our neighbors. Make us open channels of your love and clear signs to those who seek their way to you, to the end that all flesh may one day sing for joy.

22ND SUNDAY IN ORDINARY TIME (C)

Jeremiah 2:4–13; Psalm 81:1, 10–16
Hebrews 13:1–8, 15–16; Luke 14:1, 7–14

House rules are the theme of today's readings—that is, how to govern ourselves in the household of faith. For example, sit at table in the lowest place; you may be invited to move up higher. When you give a party, invite those whom others might shun; you will be blessed. Two lessons worth remembering: Be humble, and forget not the needy. God will exalt you and remember your faithfulness.

Call to Worship   Hebrews 13

Leader: Let mutual love continue. Do not neglect to show hospitality to strangers.

People: The Lord is my helper; I will not be afraid. What can anyone do to me?

Leader: Remember your leaders, those who spoke the word of God to you. Imitate their faith.

People: Through Christ, let us continually offer a sacrifice of praise to God.

Leader: Let us worship God!

Prayer of Praise and Adoration

O God of truth and justice, in Christ you have taught what it means to obey you. We glorify your name. You are the immovable rock of salvation, the stone upon which we build our faith. When trials beset us, you offer safe haven; amid tribulation, you remain a bulwark of strength. We shall dwell all our days atop your holy mountain, and there offer glad praises for the salvation you bring.

Prayer of Confession

Unison: Eternal Judge, cleanse our hearts of any ill will we may hold against neighbors. When they do not think as we do, we often judge them unenlightened. If they behave differently, we pin labels on them. We choose as our guests those we deem worthy of places of honor within our households. Yet through Christ you opened heaven to all without regard to their status in society. Forgive our inability to do the same, and save us from all pride and prejudice in our dealings with your children.

Assurance of Pardon

Leader: Sisters and brothers, recall the words of Scripture. "Jesus Christ is the same yesterday and today and forever." It is Christ who said, "I will never fail you nor forsake you." So, come to Christ and there find the assurance that in confessing our sin, we are forgiven.

Prayer of Dedication

God our Host, you invite us to dine at your table. You anoint us through Christ with the oil of righteousness. Our cup overflows with the gift of the Holy Spirit. We come to your banquet of eternal redemption with gifts befitting our new life in Jesus. Receive them as signs of our commitment to be your faithful stewards.

Prayer of Thanksgiving

Heavenly Teacher, your Word is everlasting. By it we are instructed. It shines like a beacon, guiding our way. Throughout the ages your Word has led your people along paths of righteousness. By it the wicked have turned from their evil deeds, and those who suffer have found havens of comfort. The neglected have felt its soothing balm, and those seeking salvation have found their way to your promised deliverance.

We give you thanks for Jesus, the Word made flesh. He taught what it meant to obey you completely. He lives today in the pages of Scripture, and in our hearts. Through him we hear your proclamation of freedom from all that binds us. His Word is alive in the waters of our baptism, cleansing us and clothing us in the garments of new life. He is alive as host of the heavenly banquet where all may gather and partake of the bread of reconciliation and the cup of salvation.

We praise you for the Holy Spirit, who guides us safely through every trial and tribulation. When valleys are deep and we despair of finding sure exit, the Spirit protects us and grants us clear passage. When we are captive to our creaturely comforts, the Spirit goads us to take that first step of faith. We shall seek to walk blamelessly in such counsel and wisdom. We shall speak the truth implanted once and for all by Jesus the Christ.

23RD SUNDAY IN ORDINARY TIME (C)

Jeremiah 18:1–11; Psalm 139:1–6, 13–18
Philemon 1–21; Luke 14:25–33

The subject is, again, the cost of discipleship. At what expense does one follow the Christ? It is well to consider the consequences before embarking on any major venture. Some forsake family and friendships in order to be faithful disciples. Any who cannot carry the cross ought to rethink their decision. To follow Christ involves renouncing allegiance to whoever and whatever may get in the way. Are you ready?

Call to Worship   Psalm 139

Leader: O Lord, you have searched me and known me, and are acquainted with all my ways.

People: Even before a word is on my tongue, O Lord, you know it completely.

Leader: For it was you who formed my inward parts; you knit me together in my mother's womb.

People: How weighty to me are your thoughts, O God! I try to count them—they are like the sand.

Leader: Let us worship God!

Prayer of Praise and Adoration

O God, our Rock and Redeemer, you are the stronghold and the refuge of faith, the foundation of hope and the safeguard for all who praise your name. With you we can walk and not stumble, run and not fall, and lie down in safety. We shall fill our days with visions of your lofty splendor, and consider each moment as sacred because of your grace.

Prayer of Confession

Unison: God in Christ, who endured the cross in your own flesh for our sakes, hear us as we confess our sin. We would be your bold disciples, but we fear suffering. We would carry our cross, but it weighs too much. We count the cost of following you—as long as there are benefits; but to renounce all we have is a devastating prospect. Forgive the conditions we make when we try to obey, and free us by your grace to forsake all and follow you.

Assurance of Pardon

Leader: God is just and takes no pleasure in the death of the wicked. Through Christ there is hope of eternal forgiveness. Turn back from your past and embrace God's promised assurance: In Christ there is redemption and release from all sin.

Prayer of Dedication

God of grace and peace, we come as free agents of Christ's reconciling love. We give our lives as a thank offering for the bountiful mercies you bestow on us. You refresh our hearts by the gift of a savior. May what we bring enrich others who seek your deliverance. Take us and use us as stewards of your grace and peace.

Prayer of Thanksgiving and Supplication

O God of freedom and justice, who alone can break the fetters of bondage which enslave us, we give you thanks that in Jesus we can walk freely as your sons and daughters. While we were slaves to sin, he rescued us. To us who were caught in the trap of self-deception, he showed your mercy. Yea, he himself endured death so that we might live eternally. It is through him that we can approach you in prayer.

Hear us as we offer our petitions and seek your grace to embark once more on faith's journey. Through your Holy Spirit continue to endow us with the wisdom befitting our high calling. When we are tempted to forsake you and live to ourselves, keep us from yielding to such vain notions. Help us rather to honor the yearning within to please you and be worthy of your trust.

Guide us in our quest for Christ's liberating righteousness, the keys that unlock whatever keeps our neighbors imprisoned. If it is disease, help us to give what we can for further research. If it is poverty, give us boldness to attack the systems of oppression and greed. If it is bigotry, purify us from our prejudice and enable us to proclaim Christ's reconciling atonement.

We pray for those who have not yet tasted the sweet fruits of freedom. Make us ever conscious of their plight. As Christ suffered for our sakes, make us willing to bear the cross on their behalf. As Christ rose victoriously, help us to demonstrate the risen life through acts of liberation from bondage. As Christ welcomes all to dine at your table, prepare us for the day when, united, we can feast on your grace.

24TH SUNDAY IN ORDINARY TIME (C)

Jeremiah 4:11–12, 22–28; Psalm 14
1 Timothy 1:12–17; Luke 15:1–10

To find what was lost is cause for rejoicing, even though the quest seemed endless. What is lost preoccupies our thinking; we retrace our steps in search of some clues. God's quest is consuming in search of lost ones. There is rejoicing in heaven when someone repents.

Call to Worship

Psalm 14

Leader: Fools say in their hearts, "There is no God." They are corrupt and do abominable deeds.

People: The Lord looks down from heaven on humankind to see if there are any who are wise.

Leader: Let us worship God!

Prayer of Praise and Adoration

Great and wonderful are all your works, O God; majestic is your name. Unto the ends of the earth you display your dominion. Beyond the reaches of the heavens your glory shines. Hear the praises we offer as we gather to worship. Receive the confession we make through your mercy and grace. As we open your Word, we discern your goodness. Your way is holy, great God of all.

Prayer of Confession

Unison: Praise be unto you, God of mercy and might, and to your only begotten, our Savior Christ Jesus. In spite of our sin, Christ calls us to ministry. Christ is patient and loving, reflecting your nature. We dishonor your name and persecute our neighbors; we are not deserving of the trust you place in us. We confess our wrongdoing and plead your forgiveness. Through Christ accept us and cleanse us of all sin.

Assurance of Pardon

Leader: "The saying is sure and worthy of full acceptance, that Christ Jesus came into the world to save sinners." By Christ's mercy we have been born anew into a life of hope, becoming, for those who would follow, an example of God's patience and trust. To the God of ages, "immortal, invisible, the only God, be honor and glory forever and ever. Amen."

Prayer of Dedication

O God, you desire steadfast love and not sacrifice; we seek to know you, not to placate you. We offer what we have, and ourselves. Accept our gifts as signs of our commitment to love you more fully, and receive our response in obedience as a symbol of our dedication to serve.

Prayer of Thanksgiving and Supplication

Great and wonderful are your works, O God. They are awesome to behold and worthy to be praised. You are a shepherd who cannot rest until all the sheep are safely gathered. You are the keeper of fine treasure who searches for even one coin until it is found. You are the God who sent Jesus to redeem a lost and fallen humanity. He bore our sins and paid the cost of our guilt.

Give us, we pray, a measure of your patience as we seek the wandering. Keep us from hastily disregarding their plight. Some are lost because they have been misguided. Help us to show them the proper way. Others choose to march to the beat of their own drummer. Give us ears to hear their source of enlightenment, and the boldness to share with them our faith in Christ. Uphold by your Spirit those who truly seek to repent of their past and start anew. May they be borne on Christ's shoulders to a homecoming within the confines of your beloved community.

We give thanks for the treasures stored within each of us. Keep them from becoming tarnished by neglect or abuse. As in Christ you have made us worthy of your grace, may all that we do radiate your blessing and glory. If it is to proclaim the good news of Christ, make our words clear and convincing. If it is to heal, teach us to be as consoling to others as Christ is compassionate with us. If it is voluntary service, show us the mind of Christ, who gave without thought of return.

25TH SUNDAY IN ORDINARY TIME (C)

Jeremiah 8:18–9:1; Psalm 79:1–9
1 Timothy 2:1–7; Luke 16:1–13

The lesson is clear: no one can serve two masters. If we treasure riches, then we are tempted to pile up as much as possible. If we treasure God, then all that we have is committed to the service of God. We must decide whom we will serve. There is no halfway ground.

Call to Worship   Psalm 79

Leader: Let your compassion come speedily to meet us, for we are brought very low.

People: Help us, O God of our salvation; deliver us and forgive our sins, for your name's sake.

Leader: Let us worship God!

Prayer of Praise and Adoration

Giver of every good and perfect gift, your steadfast love endures forever. You redeem the nations from distress and trouble. You gather your people from the corners of the earth. We enter your courts singing thanksgiving for the bountiful mercies you lavish upon us. Hear our glad praises and be pleased with our worship, for you are worthy of all honor.

Prayer of Confession

Unison: Merciful God, you lead us by the cords of compassion. We seek your forgiveness through Christ's intercession. Fill us anew with your Holy Spirit, so that we may faithfully obey your will. When we are vengeful, purge our thoughts of resentment and anger. When we bear false witness, turn us from deceit to truthfulness. Cleanse us of selfish desires, and free us to respond to your holy Word. In righteousness remake us, and through Christ restore us.

Assurance of Pardon

Leader: God our Savior desires that all should be saved and come to the knowledge of the truth. There is one God, and one mediator, Christ Jesus, who came as a ransom for all. With assurance and conviction I say to you: God in Christ forgives us our sin.

Prayer of Dedication

Redeemed by Christ and gathered to praise you, we come with thanksgiving, O God our Savior. You relieve our hunger and quench our thirst.

You fill us with good things and satisfy our needs. How shall we respond to such goodness and mercy? By committing all that we have to your honor and glory. Accept our offerings and receive our tributes, for they belong to you.

Prayer of Petition and Supplication

God our Savior, to lift our prayers to you is good and acceptable. Hear us now as we come before you. Christ dwells by your side to intercede for us when our words fail. Angel songs blend with our voices, filling the air with hymns of praise. You are clothed with all honor and majesty. You alone are God and we adore you.

Hear us as we pray for those to whom we have entrusted the authority of government. We pray for their health, that they may be able to withstand the pressures of office. We pray for those who advise them, that they may be given the wisdom required for each circumstance. We pray for the families, loved ones, and friends of our leaders, that they may be supportive in the midst of the burdens of public life.

Hear us as we pray for ourselves as citizens. Help us to be responsible and to blend the diversity of opinions into unified concern for the well-being of all. Deliver us from suspicions of one another, and help us to focus rather on the good of all. Save us from becoming high and mighty, and lead us in the paths of service.

You have taught us through Christ that we can serve only one. We commit our allegiance to you alone. May all that we do be to your glory, so that one day we may hear your "Well done, good and faithful servant."

26TH SUNDAY IN ORDINARY TIME (C)

Jeremiah 32:1–3a, 6–15; Psalm 91:1–6, 14–16
1 Timothy 6:6–19; Luke 16:19–31

The lesson of Scripture is plain: Riches blind us to the will of God and lead to temptations that destroy. The call to justice lies at the mansion gate, but we fail to show mercy to the homeless. The consequences of such neglect are eternal. Christ calls us now to hear and to repent. Those in the grip of famine cannot wait.

Call to Worship   Psalm 91

Leader: You who live in the shelter of the Most High will say, "My God, in whom I trust."

People: No evil shall befall those who make the Lord their refuge, the Most High their dwelling place.

Leader: God will deliver those who love the Lord and call on God's name.

People: When they call, God will answer, be with them in trouble, and show them salvation.

Leader: Let us worship God!

Prayer of Praise and Adoration

Your goodness goes before us, O Holy Redeemer, and the upright rejoice in your radiant splendor. Your touch turns deserts into pools of living water. As you embrace the land, its yield abounds. With wisdom you implant, we shall proclaim your virtue. Through our Savior Christ Jesus we shall sing your praise without ceasing.

Prayer of Confession

Unison: God of grace, we stand in need of your forgiveness. Desiring to be rich, we fall into temptation. Love of money ensnares us. Enough does not satisfy. The more we acquire, the greater our greed becomes. We become prosperous in our own eyes, and poor in your sight. Through Christ the Giver of life, rescue us from self-destruction.

Assurance of Pardon

Leader: Brothers and sisters, fight the good fight of faith. Aim at righteousness, godliness, love, and gentleness. Take hold of the eternal life to which you were called when you made the good confession in the presence of many witnesses. And Christ, who alone can keep you from falling, will deliver you blameless before the throne of God. In Christ, we are forgiven.

Prayer of Dedication

Merciful Provider, all that we have is a gift of your goodness; whatever we acquire we gain by your grace. You cause the rains to yield abundant harvests; you send the sun to nourish rich growth. We bring you gifts wrought by your handiwork and dedicate our lives to tending your creation. Accept us as stewards within your dominion, and bless our efforts on your behalf.

Prayer of Thanksgiving and Supplication

God of heaven, where angels dwell, we give thanks for Christ, in whom we glimpse your eternal realm. Through Christ you have poured out your Spirit upon all of your children. Those who believe see visions of your splendor and dream dreams of your glory. We praise you that we are numbered among those who can climb Calvary's hill and behold the heavens opening to reveal your majesty.

We are grateful for Christ's mediation as we make our confession. He intercedes for us when our words are found wanting and our actions fall short of your will for us. We would aim at righteousness, but greed devours us. We yearn for riches with consuming desire. Teach us again how you clothe and feed creation, and help us to trust in your design for our lives.

We would be more loving, but hostility hinders us. We are suspicious of our neighbors and begrudge them their due. As Christ bore the cross in spite of our sinfulness, make us more sympathetic to our neighbor's burdens. As you raised Christ on the third day and robbed death of its victory, raise us to renewed acts of compassion, so that brothers and sisters can see what it means to be free.

Teach us, O God, what it costs to obey. Send forth your Spirit to counsel and guide us. As we embark on faith's journey, keep us free from reproach. We look to the day when Christ shall come, and pray that we may be found ready.

27TH SUNDAY IN ORDINARY TIME (C)

Lamentations 1:1–6; Lamentations 3:19–26 or Psalm 137
2 Timothy 1:1–14; Luke 17:5–10

Relationship with God implies obedience, duties to be fulfilled in grateful response to what God has done. To be a servant of Christ is a high calling. Christ called the disciples and empowered them. They were to serve in Christ's name and give God the glory. Think of your discipleship as a mandate to be faithful. It is a gift you have received, not an honor you have won.

Call to Worship   Lamentations 3

Leader: The steadfast love of the Lord never ceases, with mercies that are new every morning.

People: Great is your faithfulness, O God, and the source of all hope.

Leader: You are good to those who wait upon you, O God, and whose souls seek the Lord.

People: It is good that one should wait quietly for the salvation of the Lord.

Leader: Let us worship God!

Prayer of Praise and Adoration

We shall dwell in your house forever, O God, and seek to live upright and blameless lives in Christ Jesus, our guide. You show us your mercy. Christ teaches us justice. We live by your Spirit, who enlightens our way. Blessed Trinity, you do not forsake us. We can walk with integrity because of your love. Hear our glad praises as we enter your sanctuary. You are worthy of all the glory your children can bring.

Prayer of Confession

Unison: O God, who by your Spirit can rekindle the embers of faith, purge us of all sin and make of us obedient servants. We are guilty of pushing you to life's periphery. We serve you only when it seems convenient. We follow the Christ when it is to our benefit. We call on the Spirit when our own efforts fail. Remake us in your image of righteousness, and teach us the meaning of discipleship.

Assurance of Pardon

Leader: "Do not be ashamed, then, of the testimony about our Lord . . . who saved us and called us with a holy calling, not according to our works

347

but according to his own purpose and grace . . . given to us in Christ Jesus before the ages began." By that grace we are saved as through Christ we are forgiven.

Prayer of Dedication

We sing of your loyalty and justice, O God; we tell of your handiwork to all generations. You call us to faithfulness; therefore we shall seek to be blameless in all that we do. Accept our commitment to ministry as your Spirit guides us, and be pleased with the offerings we bring. Make us useful within the gates of your righteousness, so that justice shall reign throughout the land.

Prayer of Thanksgiving

God of grace, mercy, and peace, we thank you for the ministry to which you call us, the teaching which guides us, and the intercession of Christ when we stumble and fall. We are mindful of his suffering for our sakes, and grateful for his victory over evil. No longer can the powers of death claim absolute control over us, for we are Christ's and he is victor over death.

We thank you for the Spirit who nurtures us toward our first steps in faith. The Spirit keeps us from falling, and plants our feet on the rock which none can move. By the Spirit we can see beyond today and catch a glimpse of a new heaven and a new earth.

With your Spirit to guide and Christ to intercede for us, we venture forth with confidence on our pilgrimage. We give thanks for ancestors in faith whose example we may follow. We stand on their shoulders and view the heavenly city. Their stories are a rich legacy of insight. They faced the abyss and remained steadfast. Their testimony is etched forever on the hearts of your people, O God. Send us forth in their spirit and make us worthy of generations to come.

28TH SUNDAY IN ORDINARY TIME (C)

Jeremiah 29:1, 4–7; Psalm 66:1–12
2 Timothy 2:8–15; Luke 17:11–19

Ten lepers begged Jesus for mercy. Jesus sent them to the priests and as they went they were cleansed. But only one, an outsider at that, returned to praise God for the healing received. "Where are the nine?" asked Jesus. The lesson is this: Have faith that your prayer will be answered, and in faith thank God for the mercy you received.

Call to Worship   Psalm 66

Leader: Make a joyful noise to God, all the earth. Sing glory to God and praise the Lord!

People: Come and see what God has done: how awesome the deeds among mortals.

Leader: Bless the Lord, O peoples, let the sound of God's praise be heard.

People: Truly God has listened; he has given heed to the words of my prayer.

Leader: Let us worship God!

Prayer of Praise and Adoration

We come within the gates of your heavenly dominion and enter your courts to give you our praise. You are God whose splendor fills the temple; our eyes behold the signs of your steadfast love. With our hands cleansed through the forgiveness of Jesus we shall go about your altar singing songs of thanksgiving. Your works are wondrous and worthy of tribute; hear our rejoicing as we lift before you glad adoration.

Prayer of Confession

Unison: In the name of Christ Jesus, descended from David and risen in glory, we make our confession. Disputes arise within congregations; brothers and sisters quarrel. Hostility fractures the body; conflict leads to suspicion and pain. Forgive us, O God, when we continue to bear grudges; reconcile us to our neighbor as you redeem us of sin.

Assurance of Pardon

Leader: "The saying is sure: If we have died with him, we will also live with him; if we endure, we will also reign with him. . . . Do your best to

349

present yourself to God as one approved by him, . . . rightly explaining the word of truth." The truth is this: In Christ we are forgiven.

Prayer of Dedication

God of goodness, you bind up the wounds of the afflicted. We come with thanksgiving for your boundless acts of mercy. Receive now our offerings. Use them to heal the suffering, to shelter the homeless, to comfort the lonely, and to make whole once again those whose lives are broken. We give what we have in the name of Christ, who gave to all who believe the gift of hope.

Prayer of Thanksgiving and Supplication

O God, who name is worthy of unending praise, we bow before you in humble submission. Words fail to communicate our depth of love to you and our yearning to obey your will. Without your Spirit day follows day in aimless succession. Nothing can compare with the love you have shown us, not the tribute of leaders, the fame of achievement, nor the applause of friends and loved ones. We owe all to your mercy; we will praise you at all times and call upon your name.

Hear us as we pray for cleansing. Rid us of the vanity that clutters our thinking. Show us the Christ who taught self-denial. Help us to hear once again how the humble received mercy, the sick were healed, and those whom good people rejected were loved and forgiven.

Increase our faith and save us from the need to boast of our own goodness. As we are quick to call on you for guidance when we are threatened, let us be as eager to give you the glory for whatever we gain. Fill us anew with your Holy Spirit, so that our words may be your words, our work your work, and our glory your glory. You are the God of our salvation to whom belong all glory, praise, and honor, now and forevermore.

29TH SUNDAY IN ORDINARY TIME (C)

Jeremiah 31:27–34; Psalm 119:97–104
2 Timothy 3:14–4:5; Luke 18:1–8

The widow was wearing out the poor judge! By his own admission he cared little about God or people, but what was he to do with this persistent woman? The Gospel tells us that he finally vindicated her, just to get her "off his back." If a judge like this will vindicate a plaintiff, God will surely vindicate the elect who cry for justice.

Call to Worship   Psalm 119

Leader: Oh, how I love your law! It is my meditation all day long.
People: Your commandment makes me wiser than my enemies, for it is always with me.
Leader: I have more understanding than all my teachers, for your decrees are my meditation.
People: I understand more than the aged. How sweet are your words to my taste.
Leader: Let us worship God!

Prayer of Praise and Adoration

Righteous One of all generations, how glorious is your name. You speak and worlds are created; you establish the boundaries of the seas and the land. Your countenance illumines the heavens above us. Your righteousness is known throughout all the earth. We live by your mercy and depend on your blessings; we give you all praise.

Prayer of Confession

Unison: O God, our Judge and Redeemer, we confess that we have failed in our ministry to others. We listen for teachings to our own liking. We yearn for doctrines that boost our egos. We follow those who flatter us. We seek comfort and not challenge from our confessions of faith. Renew a right spirit within us, O God, and train us in righteousness as you forgive our sin.

Assurance of Pardon

Leader: Brothers and sisters, "continue in what you have learned and firmly believed, knowing from whom you learned it, and how from childhood you have known the sacred writings that are able to instruct you for salvation through faith in Christ Jesus." For the truth of the gospel abides. In Jesus Christ, we are forgiven.

Prayer of Dedication

Source of all goodness, power, and strength, we come with gifts in response to your love. You pour out your goodness; we bring you thanksgiving. You infuse us with power; we offer the fruits of our labor. You sustain us with strength; all that we do we dedicate to your glory. Honor us and bless those endeavors, which are a testimony to your abiding grace.

Prayer of Thanksgiving and Supplication

Righteous Judge, you temper judgment with mercy; we praise and thank you for your loving-kindness. Though we are not worthy even to eat the crumbs from your table, you have set a place for us and invite us to dine. With Christ, the Bread of Life, we are continually nourished. Through Christ, the living Word, you reveal your gracious will for our lives. In Christ, who lives and reigns to guide us, we pray without ceasing.

Open our eyes to new insight into what it means to be called your people. When destruction is all about us hear our cries for direction and make us quick to respond. When your children cry out for refuge and safety, give us compassion to embrace them with care. When your people suffer from injustice and bondage, empower us in Christ's name to set them free. Place us in a tower as watchers over your creation, and grant us the vision of how the righteous shall live.

Give patience to endure and strength to withstand the trials that await. When we cannot rise above the movement of the masses, set our feet on higher ground and give us boldness to proclaim your will for all. When the cross weighs heavily and we strain to confront those who oppose your way, grant us sure faith and steady nerves to confess that you alone are God. From the vantage you give us may we become beacons of faith, hope, and love, to the end that all may know your goodness.

30TH SUNDAY IN ORDINARY TIME (C)

Joel 2:23–32; Psalm 65
2 Timothy 4:6–8, 16–18; Luke 18:9–14

How we pray says a lot about our understanding of God. Jesus told a story of two people at prayer: one was a Pharisee, the other a tax collector. The Pharisee thanked God that he was not like others—unjust, extortioners. The tax collector could only beat his breast and beg God for mercy. Jesus declared that the tax collector went away justified. Those who exalt themselves will be humbled, and those who humble themselves before God will be exalted.

Call to Worship

Psalm 65

Leader: Praise is due to you, O God, for you answer our prayer.
People: We shall be satisfied with the goodness of your holy temple.
Leader: By awesome deeds you answer us with deliverance.
People: You are the hope of all the ends of the earth and of the farthest seas.
Leader: Let us worship God!

Prayer of Praise and Adoration

Shield and Defender, how worthy you are of the praises we bring. We sing of your mercy. We tell of your glory. We speak of your greatness to the assembled throng. We need only cry aloud and you hear us, O God. You send your Spirit as our comfort and strength. We shall dwell evermore within your enfolding protection through the faith of Christ Jesus, in whose name we pray.

Prayer of Confession

Unison: To fear you is the beginning of wisdom, O God, and to confess our sins can lead to repentance. We acknowledge the wrongs we commit against neighbors; the remarks that aim at tearing them down, the actions that exclude, the subtle and not so subtle distinctions that "put them in their place." Forgive us for our love of comfort in a world that is hungry and thirsty. Help us to amend our ways, through the merit and intercession of Jesus Christ.

Assurance of Pardon

Leader: Hear the good news: Christ delivers those who are truly sorry and repent of their sins. Christ intercedes on their behalf before the judgment seat of Almighty God. Christ cleanses them and makes them fit to dwell in God's heavenly dominion. In Jesus Christ we are forgiven!

Prayer of Dedication

Merciful God, teach us to trust you to supply all our needs. You are the source of manna in our wilderness wanderings, the giver of the bread of life along the pilgrimage of faith. We bring you our offering with praise and thanksgiving for your constant care and protection.

Prayer of Thanksgiving and Intercession

O God, who so loved the world that you came in human form to live among us, we give thanks that through Christ we can open our hearts to you. Your people praise you amid the canyons of city streets. You hear their cries from the valleys of death's shadow. You welcome the shouts of joy from the mountaintops. You stoop to listen to sighs from the squalor of peasant villages. Wherever your people dwell, you sense their needs and receive their praises.

As in the Jerusalem of the prophets, so today there are conditions in our world that cry for justice. Cities are racially segregated, poverty abounds. People languish without hope for employment; frustration moves toward violent protest. There are homeless, exposed to the elements, passing through life's seasons with worn bodies and bowed heads. Neighbors prey on each other, trampling on the dignity with which you endowed all your children. We feel helpless to alter their lot.

We pray for them, O God, and for ourselves, that we may become instruments of change in this world. Embolden us to hold public officials accountable for human welfare. Make us wise in the ways of justice, so that laws are fair and fairly administered. Make us the threads of hope, which, when woven together by common endeavor, become the tapestry of a just society, through Christ, the giver of hope.

31ST SUNDAY IN ORDINARY TIME (C)

Habakkuk 1:1–4; 2:1–4; Psalm 119:137–144
2 Thessalonians 1:1–4, 11–12; Luke 19:1–10

Zacchaeus climbed a sycamore tree to get a better view. Jesus spotted him and said, "Come down; for I must stay at your house today." There was murmuring at this. Now Zacchaeus was a tax collector, and rich. He was also a sinner in the eyes of many. Jesus came to save sinners. Respectable people are easily offended!

Call to Worship   Psalm 119

Leader: Your righteousness is an everlasting righteousness, O Lord, and your law is the truth.
People: Your decrees are righteous forever, O God; give me understand that I may live.
Leader: Let us worship God!

Prayer of Praise and Adoration

O God of our salvation, with dread deeds you answer us with deliverance. You are the hope of all the ends of the earth and of the farthest seas. By your strength you establish the mountains and still the waters. You calm the troubled breasts of all who put their trust in you. We shall not cease to give you praise and bless your holy name.

Prayer of Confession

Unison: Righteous God, you deem it just to repay with affliction those who mistreat your children. Forgive the sins we commit which harm our neighbors. Temper your vengeance when we claim not to know you. Ease your wrath when we fail to obey the gospel Christ taught. Let the glory of your might undergird our endeavors, as through Christ you deliver us from our weakness and shame. O God, have mercy upon us and fill us with your splendor.

Assurance of Pardon

Leader: To this end we always pray for you, asking that our God will make you worthy of God's call and will fulfill . . . every good resolve and work of faith, so that the name of our Lord Jesus may be glorified in you, and you in him, according to the grace of our God and the Lord Jesus Christ." In Christ's name we are forgiven.

Prayer of Dedication

Chosen to serve you, we bring you our tributes. You are the God who delivers us; glad praises we sing. All that we have are gifts of your graciousness. You plum our potential, our yield increases. We are stewards of your mercy, called to serve. Accept these offerings as signs of our faithfulness throughout each day.

Prayer of Thanksgiving and Supplication

O God our Host, by whose gracious will Christ invites the household to dine, we give thanks that we are numbered among those who have places at your table. By your mercy you have broken the walls that divide us, uniting rich and poor, people of all shades, the lame and the spry, the bright and the bland, the loyal and the disloyal. All are reconciled by the One who broke bread that night so that our separations could be healed. We give thanks for the love displayed in that hospitable act.

Help us to climb with Zacchaeus above the press of the crowd and catch sight of Jesus, who came to make each person whole. Erase within us the tendency to blot our diversity, as if only those like us had anything to offer. Help us to see in all the stroke of your brush, the blending of hues, highlighting of shadows, harmonizing of subtleties, the rainbow of beauty your covenant foretold.

Make of this house a hospice where all find shelter, whose doors are opened when others are shut. Let there be no strangers here where Jesus is the host. Send us forth with renewed commitment to seek out those whom society has abandoned. Make us quick to recognize their dignity, to affirm their right to self-determination, and to assist them in their quest for wholeness. Help us to welcome sinners as we have been welcomed by you, Christ Jesus.

32ND SUNDAY IN ORDINARY TIME (C)

Haggai 1:15b–2:9; Psalm 145:1–5, 17–21 or Psalm 98
2 Thessalonians 2:1–5, 13–17; Luke 20:27–38

Human relationships here on earth have certain dynamics. At the resurrection a wholly different reality obtains. The Sadducees sought to relate the two orders. Jesus must answer that it cannot be done. In this age people marry and are given in marriage; in the age to come they neither marry nor are given in marriage. Whether now or in the age to come, God is God of the living, not God of the dead.

Call to Worship   Psalm 145

Leader: Every day I will bless you, and praise your name forever and ever.

People: Great is the Lord, and greatly to be praised; your greatness, O God, is unsearchable.

Leader: You fulfill the desire of all who fear you; you hear their cries and save them.

People: My mouth will speak the praise of the Lord, and bless your holy name forever and ever.

Leader: Let us worship God!

Prayer of Praise and Adoration

You are worthy of all praise, O God; your judgment is sure. Like a refiner's fire, you purify your people and temper their desires. The heat is your love for them; the flame is the Spirit's power within. The light is the light, which illumines the world. Come, fire from above, and fill our being, as we worship and adore our maker.

Litany of Assurance

Leader: Brothers and sisters, we must always give thanks to God for you.

People: God is faithful and will strengthen you and guard you from evil.

Leader: God chose you as the firstfruits for salvation through sanctification by the Spirit and through belief in the truth.

People: God is faithful and will strengthen you and guard you from evil.

Leader: Brothers and sisters, stand firm, and hold fast to the traditions that you were taught by us, either by word of mouth or by our letter.

357

People:	God is faithful and will strengthen you and guard you from evil.
Leader:	Now may God, who loved us, and through grace gave us eternal comfort and good hope, comfort your hearts in every good work and word.
People:	May the Savior direct your hearts to the love of God and to the steadfastness of Christ.

Prayer of Dedication

Gracious Comforter, we have sought to render true judgment, show kindness, accompany the sojourner, and devise no evil with our own hearts. May the tribute we render be worthy of the trust you place in us. Accept our offerings of praise and thanksgiving, as in Christ's name we pray.

Prayer of Thanksgiving and Supplication

Eternal God, from whom all goodness flows, we give thanks for Jesus Christ, who opens for us the gates to eternity. By your Holy Spirit lift us high above the cares that weigh upon us. Let our spirits soar on the clouds of your merciful redemption, so that we may catch sight of your dominion and glory. Teach us your perfect will and guide us in the path of righteousness. Speak peace to our restless minds, so that your ways become our ways and Christ's call our fervent desire.

You are present everywhere, in countryside and city street, in family and in solitude. Be a sign for us as we seek to follow you. Help us to move beyond the convenient boundaries of our lives and touch the lives of others. Let us sing the glad song that Jesus has come to heal every human hurt.

Grant that we may live, move, and have our being in constant awareness of your grace and blessing. As we traverse the hours you give us daily, grace our footsteps, that they may follow those of Christ. When the sunlight fades and our bodies grow weary, let all we have been and done throughout the day serve as our prayer of thanks, through Christ our Savior.

33RD SUNDAY IN ORDINARY TIME (C)

Isaiah 65:17–25; Isaiah 12
2 Thessalonians 3:6–13; Luke 21:5–19

Jesus foresees a time of distress and travail for his followers. Nation will rise against nation. There will be earthquakes, famine, terror, and signs from heaven. God's people will face persecution and be delivered to the authorities. Yet they are to endure and bear witness to the truth, for God will be with them.

Call to Worship   Isaiah 12

Leader: Sing praises to God, for the Lord has done gloriously. Let it be known in all the earth.
People: Surely God is my salvation, for the Lord is my strength and has become my salvation.
Leader: Let us worship God!

Prayer of Praise and Adoration

God of righteousness, truth, and justice, you judged your people according to the statutes delivered to Moses. We praise you for the mercy of Christ's intercession. In Christ's name we gather and are assured of your presence. We bow in adoration, and sing of your glory. Your Word is proclaimed for our guidance and nurture. Look now with favor on our worship, as in Christ we seek to be faithful.

Prayer of Confession

Unison: God of consuming fire, treat us not as stubble through the folly of our misdeeds. We are misled by arrogance as we boast of our goodness. We look with disdain on those less fortunate, and ignore the poverty of our own souls. Claiming to be among the mighty, we favor those gifted with similar strengths. As individuals and as a nation, we test your patience. Yet in Christ you love us still. Forgive our pride and restore our sanity, so that we may yet serve you.

Assurance of Pardon

Leader: Brothers and sisters, it is God who gives justice to the weak and maintains the right of the afflicted and destitute. God rescues the needy and delivers them from the hand of the wicked. As you confess your sins, God is faithful and just and will through Christ deliver you blameless in the day of God's judgment. In Jesus Christ we are forgiven.

Prayer of Dedication

Redeemer of the nations, great and wonderful are your works. All that we bring you have provided. Only your grace renders our acts worthy of praise. Receive our tributes as praise and thanksgiving for your benevolent care, and multiply our efforts to your everlasting glory. For we offer our gifts in the name of Jesus Christ, the obedient one.

Prayer of Thanksgiving and Intercession

Judge of the universe, you know that we live in a great and awful time. You have opened our minds to the secrets of nature, placed in our hands the power of the atom, and allowed us to explore the heavens. Through human skill the earth yields an abundance of food. Through the marvels of medicine our earthly span is extended beyond threescore and ten. We bow in humble thanksgiving and acknowledge your grace by which alone we survive.

As generations before us pled for your mercy, so we today entreat your goodness. We pray for modesty, as we inhabit the earth's surface. Save us from destroying such a beautiful home. Endow our leaders with wisdom and a love of creation. Fill them with zeal for peace to match their obsession for defense. We pray for the success and safety of the modern explorers. Grant that their discoveries may increase for all people the gifts of our providential care. Help us to be more faithful stewards of the resources you provide. Replace greed with a gracious sharing of our abundance. We pray for the healers and those who preserve life. May longer lives bring a greater sense of your saving love.

As in Christ you came to show your love for the world, so through Christ we pray that the world you love may be saved for future generations.

34TH SUNDAY IN ORDINARY TIME
(REIGN OF CHRIST OR CHRIST THE KING) (C)

Jeremiah 23:1–6; Luke 1:68–79
Colossians 1:11–20; Luke 23:33–43

Suddenly, we are cast back to the time of the crucifixion as Jesus hangs on the cross, one on his right and one on his left. If he is truly the Messiah why does he not just remove himself? Or, why, a person of his lofty position, can he not save himself and those who are punished with him. One says to him, "Jesus, remember me when you come into your kingdom." Jesus replies, "Truly, I tell you, today, you will be with me in Paradise." As they cast lots for Jesus' clothing the lot of those who believe in him will be eternal life.

Call to Worship
Luke 1

Leader: Blessed be the Lord God of Israel, for you have looked favorably upon your people.

People: You have raised up a mighty savior for us in the house of your servant David.

Leader: By the tender mercy of our God, the dawn from on high will break upon us,

People: To give light to those who sit in darkness and guide our feet into the way of peace.

Leader: Let us worship God!

Prayer of Praise and Adoration

We come into your courts with praise, O God, and sing in glad adoration. You fill the temple with your majestic presence. We bow in awe at the sight of your holiness. Your goodness and mercy shall follow us all the days of our life, as in Christ we shall dwell in your house forever.

Litany of Assurance

Leader: Give thanks to God who has enabled us to share in the inheritance of the saints in the light.

People: For in Christ all the fullness of God was pleased to dwell.

Leader: God has rescued us from the power of darkness, and in Christ we have redemption, the forgiveness of sins.

People: For in Christ all the fullness of God was pleased to dwell.

Leader: In Christ all things in heaven and on earth were created, things visible and invisible.

People:	For in Christ all the fullness of God was pleased to dwell.
Leader:	Christ is the head of the body, the church; Christ is the beginning, the firstborn from the dead.
People:	For in Christ all the fullness of God was pleased to dwell.
Leader:	Through Christ God was pleased to reconcile all things, whether on earth or in heaven, by making peace through the blood of the cross.
People:	For in Christ all the fullness of God was pleased to dwell.

Prayer of Dedication

O Christ, in whom the fullness of the Godhead dwells, we offer ourselves to your service. Let time be blessed by your presence. Let skills enrich the life of humankind. Receive what we bring as offerings to you. Make use of them and of us, for the sake of your holy gospel.

Prayer of Thanksgiving

God of the circling years, whose faithfulness spans generations, your grace and mercy continually astound us! Through Christ you have entered our world, walked where we walk, shared our infirmities, and been touched by our joys and sorrows. You hear the prayers of all who bow down before you as Christ intercedes on their behalf. We can utter our halting phrases with assurance that Christ will translate the idiom, genre, and metaphors into symbols that communicate our love.

We are thankful that we need hide nothing from you. You know our longings and desires, our fears and temptations. We hear again of how Christ drew apart to spend time in prayer, his tears testifying to the frightening prospect of death. We sense the sorrow he endured, and witness his unyielding confession of trust in your will. Through him we too can endure.

We await the day when all hearts shall love you and Christ shall reign supreme. In the meantime, we shall continue to call on your guidance, for we know not what each day will bring. We shall arise with assurance that the dawn brings resurrection, and confront each moment as a time of grace. When the sun sets and our ministry is done, we pray that our efforts will be found worthy of your mercy and grace.

ALL SAINTS' DAY (C)

Daniel 7:1–3, 15–18; Psalm 149
Ephesians 1:11–23; Luke 6:20–31

Luke's version of the Beatitudes strikes a familiar theme; Those who are in need will be blessed, and those who abuse God's graciousness will find their satisfaction is shallow. Also, a lot depends on how people treat their neighbors. Love goes a long way in defusing situations that otherwise could get ugly. Instead of antagonizing another through aggression Jesus offers the well-known alternative, "Do to others as you would have them do to you."

Call to Worship   Psalm 149

Leader:	Praise the Lord! Sing to the Lord a song of praise in the assembly of the faithful.
People:	For the Lord takes pleasure when the people of God offer their praise and thanksgiving.
Leader:	Let us praise God's name with dancing, making melody with tambourine and lyre.
People:	Let the faithful exult in glory; we will sing for joy and let the high praises of God be in our throats.
Leader:	Let us worship God!

Prayer of Praise and Adoration

May the words of our mouths and the meditations of our hearts be acceptable to you, O Lord. Day by day you guide us. Every breath we take is a gift of your mercy. You strengthen our knees to serve you. You lift our hands to give you all praise. We come before you in the company of brothers and sisters to give you the worship due your wonderful name. May our words be worthy of the trust you place in us and our meditations mindful of your benevolent care.

Litany of Assurance

Leader:	When you heard the word of truth, and believed in Christ, you were marked with the seal of the Holy Spirit,
People:	So that we might live for the praise of his glory.
Leader:	I have heard of your faith in the Lord Jesus and do not cease to give thanks for you as I remember you in my prayers,
People:	So that we might live for the praise of his glory.
Leader:	I pray that the God of our Lord Jesus Christ may give you a spirit of wisdom and revelation,
People:	So that we might live for the praise of his glory.

Leader:	So that, with the eyes of your heart enlightened, you may know what is the hope to which Christ has called you,
People:	So that we might live for the praise of his glory.
Leader:	God put this power to work in Christ, who now sits at God's right hand and intercedes on our behalf,
People:	So that we might live for the praise of his glory.

Prayer of Dedication

We know whatever we bind on earth will be bound in heaven; whatever we loose on earth will be loosed in heaven. We seek to bind ourselves to you, O God, and bring your heavenly kingdom here amongst us. May what we offer be a sign of our commitment to offer our finest for the sake of your mission. Use our gifts as firstfruits of our entrance into your heavenly realm.

Prayer of Thanksgiving

O God, you hold the keys to that house not made with hands, eternal in the heavens. We give you praise and thanksgiving. You have furnished your household with whatever is necessary to secure our blessed reign with you through Christ who intercedes on our behalf. You led him through times of trial and tribulation that we might be cleansed of our sin. You raised him victoriously from the tomb so that death could never claim victory over us. You seated him at your Side and tore the curtain of the temple in two so that we could have access into your Holy of Holies. Christ now sits by your Side and takes our halting words and turns them into pleasing offerings before your throne of grace.

We thank you for those who have gone before us, pillars of the faith who have helped to build the foundations of our trust in you. They have taught us what it means to believe. They have walked the paths of their pilgrimage so that we need not stumble. They have taught us what it means to confess our faith in language fit for our times. They have left a legacy of determination for us to follow, in order that the poor will inherit your reign, the hungry will be fed, those who weep will eventually laugh, and those who are ridiculed will leap for joy, for surely their reward will be great in heaven.

We thank you for the saints who surround us now, mentors and teachers who continue to open to us new truths of the gospel. We thank you for disciples who help us to see new vistas of opportunity to witness to your abiding love and care for all people. Help us offer hospitality and create a community where all may freely enter and serve. For we know that in so doing we will extend that great heavenly banquet table, where the Risen Christ is the host, into our lives here and now and hasten the day when your will is done.

Index of Scripture Readings: Year A

Numbers
11:24–30   The Day of Pentecost

Deuteronomy
30:15–20   6th Sunday in Ordinary Time
34:1–12   30th Sunday in Ordinary Time

Joshua
3:7–17   31st Sunday in Ordinary Time
24:1–3a, 14–25   32nd Sunday in Ordinary Time

Judges
4:1–7   33rd Sunday in Ordinary Time

1 Samuel
16:1–13   4th Sunday in Lent

Psalms
2   Transfiguration of the Lord (Sunday preceding Lent)
8   Trinity Sunday
13   13th Sunday in Ordinary Time
15   4th Sunday in Ordinary Time
16   2nd Sunday of Easter
17:1–7, 15   18th Sunday in Ordinary Time
19   27th Sunday in Ordinary Time
22   Good Friday
23   4th Sunday in Lent
                                  4th Sunday in Easter
27:1, 4–9   3rd Sunday in Ordinary Time
29   Baptism of the Lord
31:1–5, 15–16   5th Sunday of Easter
31:9–16   Passion/Palm Sunday
32   1st Sunday in Lent
33:1–12   10th Sunday in Ordinary Time
34:1–10, 22   Thanksgiving Eve/Day
                                  All Saints' Day
40:1–11   2nd Sunday in Ordinary Time
45:10–17   14th Sunday in Ordinary Time
51:1–17   Ash Wednesday
66:8–20   6th Sunday of Easter
68:1–10, 32–35   7th Sunday of Easter
72:1–7, 10–14   Epiphany of the Lord
72:1–7, 18–19   2nd Sunday of Advent
78:1–4, 12–16   26th Sunday in Ordinary Time
78:1–7   32nd Sunday in Ordinary Time
80:1–7, 17–19   4th Sunday of Advent
86:1–10, 16–17   12th Sunday in Ordinary Time

90:1–6, 13–17	30th Sunday in Ordinary Time
95	3rd Sunday in Lent
96	Christmas Eve/Day, Proper I
97	Christmas Eve/Day, Proper II
98	Christmas Eve/Day, Proper III
99	Transfiguration of the Lord (Sunday preceding Lent)
	29th Sunday in Ordinary Time
100	34th Sunday in Ordinary Time
	(Reign of Christ or Christ the King)
104:24–34, 35b	The Day of Pentecost
105:1–6, 16–22, 45b	19th Sunday in Ordinary Time
105:1–6, 23–26, 45c	22nd Sunday in Ordinary Time
105:1–6, 37–45	25th Sunday in Ordinary Time
106:1–6, 19–23	28th Sunday in Ordinary Time
107:1–7, 33–37	31st Sunday in Ordinary Time
112:1–9 (10)	5th Sunday in Ordinary Time
114	24th Sunday in Ordinary Time
116:1–2, 12–19	Maundy Thursday
	11th Sunday in Ordinary Time
116:1–4, 12–19	3rd Sunday of Easter
118:1–2, 14–24	Resurrection of the Lord/Easter
118:1–2, 19–29	Passion/Palm Sunday
119:1–8	6th Sunday in Ordinary Time
119:33–40	7th Sunday in Ordinary Time
119:105–112	15th Sunday in Ordinary Time
121	2nd Sunday in Lent
122	1st Sunday of Advent
123	33rd Sunday in Ordinary Time
124	21st Sunday in Ordinary Time
128	17th Sunday in Ordinary Time
130	5th Sunday in Lent
131	8th Sunday in Ordinary Time
133	20th Sunday in Ordinary Time
139:1–12, 23–24	16th Sunday in Ordinary Time
146:5–10	3rd Sunday of Advent
147:12–20	2nd Sunday after Christmas
148	1st Sunday after Christmas
149	23rd Sunday in Ordinary Time

Song of Solomon

2:8–13	14th Sunday in Ordinary Time

Isaiah

2:1–5	1st Sunday of Advent
7:10–16	4th Sunday of Advent
9:1–4	3rd Sunday in Ordinary Time
9:2–7	Christmas Eve/Day, Proper I

11:1–10	2nd Sunday of Advent
35:1–10	3rd Sunday of Advent
42:1–9	Baptism of the Lord
49:1–7	2nd Sunday in Ordinary Time
49:8–16a	8th Sunday in Ordinary Time
50:4–9a	Passion/Palm Sunday
52:7–10	Christmas Eve/Day, Proper III
52:13–53:12	Good Friday
58:1–9a (9b–12)	5th Sunday in Ordinary Time
58:1–12	Ash Wednesday
60:1–6	Epiphany of the Lord
62:6–12	Christmas Eve/Day, Proper II
63:7–9	1st Sunday after Christmas

Jeremiah

| 31:1–6 | Resurrection of the Lord/Easter |
| 31:7–14 | 2nd Sunday after Christmas |

Ezekiel

| 34:11–16, 20–24 | 34th Sunday in Ordinary Time (Reign of Christ or Christ the King) |
| 37:1–4 | 5th Sunday in Lent |

Joel

| 2:1–2, 12–17 | Ash Wednesday |

Micah

| 6:1–8 | 4th Sunday in Ordinary Time |

Matthew

1:18–25	4th Sunday of Advent
2:1–12	Epiphany of the Lord
2:13–23	1st Sunday after Christmas
3:1–12	2nd Sunday of Advent
3:13–17	Baptism of the Lord
4:1–11	1st Sunday in Lent
4:12–23	3rd Sunday in Ordinary Time
5:1–12	4th Sunday in Ordinary Time All Saints' Day Thanksgiving Eve/Day
5:13–20	5th Sunday in Ordinary Time
5:21–37	6th Sunday after Epiphany
5:38–48	7th Sunday after Epiphany
6:1–6, 16–21	Ash Wednesday
6:24–34	8th Sunday after Epiphany
9:9–13, 18–26	10th Sunday in Ordinary Time
9:35–10:8 (9–23)	11th Sunday in Ordinary Time

10:24–39	12th Sunday in Ordinary Time
10:40–42	13th Sunday in Ordinary Time
11:2–11	3rd Sunday of Advent
11:16–19, 25–30	14th Sunday in Ordinary Time
13:1–9, 18–23	15th Sunday in Ordinary Time
13:24–30, 36–43	16th Sunday in Ordinary Time
13:31–33, 44–52	17th Sunday in Ordinary Time
14:13–21	18th Sunday in Ordinary Time
14:22–33	19th Sunday in Ordinary Time
15:(10–20) 21–28	20th Sunday in Ordinary Time
16:13–20	21st Sunday in Ordinary Time
16:21–28	22nd Sunday in Ordinary Time
17:1–9	Transfiguration of the Lord (Sunday preceding Lent)
18:15–20	23rd Sunday in Ordinary Time
18:21–35	24th Sunday in Ordinary Time
20:1–16	25th Sunday in Ordinary Time
21:1–11	Passion/Palm Sunday
21:23–32	26th Sunday in Ordinary Time
21:33–46	27th Sunday in Ordinary Time
22:1–14	28th Sunday in Ordinary Time
22:15–22	29th Sunday in Ordinary Time
22:34–46	30th Sunday in Ordinary Time
23:1–12	31st Sunday in Ordinary Time
24:36–44	1st Sunday of Advent
25:1–13	32nd Sunday in Ordinary Time
25:14–30	33rd Sunday in Ordinary Time
25:31–46	34th Sunday in Ordinary Time
	(Reign of Christ or Christ the King)
26:14–27:66	Passion/Palm Sunday
27:11–54	Passion/Palm Sunday
28:1–10	Resurrection of the Lord/Easter
28:16–20	Trinity Sunday

Luke

1:47–55	3rd Sunday of Advent
2:(1–7) 8–20	Christmas Eve/Day, Proper II
2:1–14 (15–20)	Christmas Eve/Day, Proper I
24:13–35	3rd Sunday of Easter

John

1:(1–9) 10–18	2nd Sunday after Christmas
1:1–14	Christmas Eve/Day, Proper III
1:29–42	2nd Sunday after Epiphany
3:1–17	2nd Sunday in Lent
4:5–42	3rd Sunday in Lent
7:37–39	The Day of Pentecost
9:1–41	4th Sunday in Lent

10:1–10	4th Sunday of Easter
11:1–45	5th Sunday in Lent
13:1–17, 31b–35	Maundy Thursday
14:1–14	5th Sunday of Easter
14:15–21	6th Sunday of Easter
17:1–11	7th Sunday of Easter
18:1–19:42	Good Friday
20:1–18	Resurrection of the Lord/Easter
20:19–23	The Day of Pentecost
20:19–31	2nd Sunday of Easter

Acts

1:6–14	7th Sunday of Easter
2:1–21	The Day of Pentecost
2:14a, 22–32	2nd Sunday of Easter
2:14a, 36–41	3rd Sunday of Easter
2:42–47	4th Sunday of Easter
7:55–60	5th Sunday of Easter
10:34–43	Baptism of the Lord
	Resurrection of the Lord/Easter
17:22–31	6th Sunday of Easter

Romans

1:1–7	4th Sunday of Advent
4:1–5, 13–17	2nd Sunday in Lent
4:13–25	10th Sunday in Ordinary Time
5:1–11	3rd Sunday in Lent
5:12–19	1st Sunday in Lent
5:1–8	11th Sunday in Ordinary Time
6:1b–11	12th Sunday in Ordinary Time
6:12–23	13th Sunday in Ordinary Time
7:15–25a	14th Sunday in Ordinary Time
8:1–11	15th Sunday in Ordinary Time
8:6–11	5th Sunday in Lent
8:12–25	16th Sunday in Ordinary Time
8:26–39	17th Sunday in Ordinary Time
9:1–5	18th Sunday in Ordinary Time
10:5–15	19th Sunday in Ordinary Time
11:1–2a, 29–32	20th Sunday in Ordinary Time
12:1–8	21st Sunday in Ordinary Time
12:9–21	22nd Sunday in Ordinary Time
13:8–14	23rd Sunday in Ordinary Time
13:11–14	1st Sunday of Advent
14:1–12	24th Sunday in Ordinary Time
15:4–13	2nd Sunday of Advent

1 Corinthians

1:1–9	2nd Sunday in Ordinary Time

1:10–18	3rd Sunday in Ordinary Time
1:18–31	4th Sunday in Ordinary Time
2:1–12 (13–16)	5th Sunday in Ordinary Time
3:1–9	6th Sunday in Ordinary Time
3:10–11, 16–23	7th Sunday in Ordinary Time
4:1–5	8th Sunday in Ordinary Time
11:23–26	Maundy Thursday
12:3b–13	The Day of Pentecost

2 Corinthians
| 5:20b–6:10 | Ash Wednesday |
| 13:11–13 | Trinity Sunday |

Ephesians
1:3–14	2nd Sunday after Christmas
1:15–23	34th Sunday in Ordinary Time (Reign of Christ or Christ the King)
3:1–12	Epiphany of the Lord
5:8–14	4th Sunday in Lent

Philippians
1:21–30	25th Sunday in Ordinary Time
2:1–13	26th Sunday in Ordinary Time
2:5–11	Passion/Palm Sunday
3:4b–14	27th Sunday in Ordinary Time
4:1–9	28th Sunday in Ordinary Time

Colossians
| 3:1–4 | Resurrection of the Lord/Easter |

1 Thessalonians
1:1–10	29th Sunday in Ordinary Time
2:1–8	30th Sunday in Ordinary Time
2:9–13	31st Sunday in Ordinary Time
4:13–18	32nd Sunday in Ordinary Time
5:1–11	33rd Sunday in Ordinary Time

Titus
| 2:11–14 | Christmas Eve/Day, Proper I |
| 3:4–7 | Christmas EveDay, Proper II |

Hebrews
1:1–4 (5–12)	Christmas Eve/Day, Proper III
2:10–18	1st Sunday after Christmas
4:14–16; 5:7–9	Good Friday
10:16–25	Good Friday

James
| 5:7–10 | 3rd Sunday of Advent |

1 Peter
1:3–9   2nd Sunday of Easter
1:17–23   3rd Sunday of Easter
2:2–10   5th Sunday of Easter
2:19–25   4th Sunday of Easter
3:13–22   6th Sunday of Easter
4:12–14; 5:6–11   7th Sunday of Easter

2 Peter
1:16–21   Transfiguration of the Lord (Sunday preceding Lent)

1 John
3:1–3   All Saints' Day

Revelation
7:9–17   All Saints' Day

Sirach
15:15–20   6th Sunday after Epiphany

Index of Scripture Readings: Year B

6:1–5, 12b–19	15th Sunday in Ordinary Time
7:1–11, 16	4th Sunday of Advent
7:1–14a	16th Sunday in Ordinary Time
11:1–15	17th Sunday in Ordinary Time
11:26–12:13a	18th Sunday in Ordinary Time
18:5–9, 15, 31–33	19th Sunday in Ordinary Time
23:1–7	34th Sunday in Ordinary Time (Reign of Christ or Christ the King)

1 Kings

2:10–12; 3:3–14	20th Sunday in Ordinary Time
8:(1, 6, 10–11) 22–30, 41–43	21st Sunday in Ordinary Time

2 Kings

2:1–12	Transfiguration of the Lord (Sunday preceding Lent)
5:1–14	6th Sunday in Ordinary Time

Esther

7:1–6, 9–10; 9:20–22	26th Sunday in Ordinary Time

Job

1:1; 2:1–10	27th Sunday in Ordinary Time
23:1–9, 16–17	28th Sunday in Ordinary Time
38:1–7 (34–41)	29th Sunday in Ordinary Time
42:1–6, 10–17	30th Sunday in Ordinary Time

Psalms

1	7th Sunday of Easter
	25th Sunday in Ordinary Time
4	3rd Sunday of Easter
9:9–20	12th Sunday in Ordinary Time
14	17th Sunday in Ordinary Time
19	3rd Sunday in Lent
	24th Sunday in Ordinary Time
20	11th Sunday in Ordinary Time
22:1–15	28th Sunday in Ordinary Time
22:23–31	2nd Sunday in Lent
22:25–31	5th Sunday of Easter
23	4th Sunday of Easter
24	15th Sunday in Ordinary Time
	All Saints' Day
25:1–10	1st Sunday in Lent
26	27th Sunday in Ordinary Time
29	Baptism of the Lord
30	6th Sunday in Ordinary Time
31:9–16	Passion/Palm Sunday
34:1–8 (19–22)	30th Sunday in Ordinary Time

41	7th Sunday in Ordinary Time
45:1–2, 6–9	22nd Sunday in Ordinary Time
48	14th Sunday in Ordinary Time
50:1–6	Transfiguration of the Lord (Sunday preceding Lent)
51:1–12	5th Sunday in Lent
	18th Sunday in Ordinary Time
62:5–12	3rd Sunday in Ordinary Time
80:1–7, 17–19	1st Sunday of Advent
84	21st Sunday in Ordinary Time
85:1–2, 8–13	2nd Sunday of Advent
89:1–4, 19–26	4th Sunday of Advent
89:20–37	16th Sunday in Ordinary Time
97	Christmas Eve/Day Proper II
98	6th Sunday of Easter
103:1–13, 22	8th Sunday in Ordinary Time
104:1–9, 24, 35c	29th Sunday in Ordinary Time
107:1–3, 17–22	4th Sunday in Lent
111	4th Sunday in Ordinary Time
	20th Sunday in Ordinary Time
118:1–2, 14–24	Resurrection of the Lord/Easter
118:1–2, 19–29	Passion/Palm Sunday
119:9–16	5th Sunday in Lent
124	26th Sunday in Ordinary Time
125	23rd Sunday in Ordinary Time
126	3rd Sunday of Advent
127	32nd Sunday in Ordinary Time
130	13th Sunday in Ordinary Time
	19th Sunday in Ordinary Time
132:1–12 (13–18)	34th Sunday in Ordinary Time
	(Reign of Christ or Christ the King)
133	2nd Sunday of Easter
	12th Sunday in Ordinary Time
138	10th Sunday in Ordinary Time
139:1–6, 13–18	2nd Sunday in Ordinary Time
	9th Sunday in Ordinary Time
146	31st Sunday in Ordinary Time
147:1–11, 20c	5th Sunday in Ordinary Time
147:12–20	2nd Sunday after Christmas
148	1st Sunday after Christmas

Proverbs

1:20–33	24th Sunday in Ordinary Time
22:1–2, 8–9, 22–23	23rd Sunday in Ordinary Time
31:10–31	25th Sunday in Ordinary Time

Song of Solomon

| 2:8–13 | 22nd Sunday in Ordinary Time |

Isaiah

25:6–9	Resurrection of the Lord/ Easter Day
	All Saints' Day
40:1–11	2nd Sunday of Advent
40:21–31	5th Sunday in Ordinary Time
43:18–25	7th Sunday in Ordinary Time
50:4–9a	Passion/Palm Sunday
61:1–4, 8–11	3rd Sunday of Advent
61:10–62:3	1st Sunday after Christmas
62:6–12	Christmas Eve/Day Proper II
64:1–9	1st Sunday of Advent

Jeremiah

31:7–14	2nd Sunday after Christmas
31:31–34	5th Sunday in Lent

Hosea

2:14–20	8th Sunday in Ordinary Time

Jonah

3:1–5, 10	3rd Sunday in Ordinary Time

Mark

1:1–8	2nd Sunday of Advent
1:4–11	Baptism of the Lord
1:9–15	1st Sunday in Lent
1:14–20	3rd Sunday in Ordinary Time
1:21–28	4th Sunday in Ordinary Time
1:29–39	5th Sunday in Ordinary Time
1:40–45	6th Sunday in Ordinary Time
2:1–12	7th Sunday after Epiphany
2:13–22	8th Sunday in Ordinary Time
2:23–3:6	9th Sunday in Ordinary Time
3:20–35	10th Sunday in Ordinary Time
4:26–34	11th Sunday in Ordinary Time
4:35–41	12th Sunday in Ordinary Time
5:21–43	13th Sunday in Ordinary Time
6:1–13	14th Sunday in Ordinary Time
6:14–29	15th Sunday in Ordinary Time
6:30–34, 53–56	16th Sunday in Ordinary Time
7:1–8, 14–15, 21–23	22nd Sunday in Ordinary Time
7:24–37	23rd Sunday in Ordinary Time
8:27–38	24th Sunday in Ordinary Time
8:31–38	2nd Sunday in Lent
9:2–9	Transfiguration of the Lord (Sunday preceding Lent)
9:30–37	25th Sunday in Ordinary Time
9:38–50	26th Sunday in Ordinary Time

10:2–16	27th Sunday in Ordinary Time
10:17–31	28th Sunday in Ordinary Time
10:35–45	29th Sunday in Ordinary Time
10:46–52	30th Sunday in Ordinary Time
11:1–11	Passion/Palm Sunday
12:28–34	31st Sunday in Ordinary Time
12:38–44	32nd Sunday in Ordinary Time
13:1–8	33rd Sunday in Ordinary Time
13:24–37	1st Sunday of Advent
14:1–15:47	Passion/Palm Sunday
15:1–39 (40–47)	Passion/Palm Sunday
16:1–8	Resurrection of the Lord/Easter Day

Luke

1:26–38	4th Sunday of Advent
1:47–55	3rd Sunday of Advent
	4th Sunday of Advent
2:(1–7) 8–20	Christmas Eve/Day Proper II
2:22–40	1st Sunday after Christmas
24:36b–48	3rd Sunday of Easter

John

1:(1–9) 10–18	2nd Sunday after Christmas
1:6–8, 19–28	3rd Sunday of Advent
1:43–51	2nd Sunday in Ordinary Time
2:13–22	3rd Sunday in Lent
3:14–21	4th Sunday in Lent
6:1–21	17th Sunday in Ordinary Time
6:24–35	18th Sunday in Ordinary Time
6:35, 41–51	19th Sunday in Ordinary Time
6:51–18	20th Sunday in Ordinary Time
6:56–69	21st Sunday in Ordinary Time
10:11–18	4th Sunday of Easter
11:32–44	All Saints' Day
12:12–16	Passion/Palm Sunday
12:20–33	5th Sunday in Lent
15:1–8	5th Sunday of Easter
15:9–17	6th Sunday of Easter
17:6–19	7th Sunday of Easter
18:33–37	34th Sunday in Ordinary Time (Reign of Christ or Christ the King)
20:1–18	Resurrection of the Lord/Easter Day
20:19–31	2nd Sunday of Easter

Acts

| 1:15–17, 21–26 | 7th Sunday of Easter |
| 3:12–19 | 3rd Sunday of Easter |

4:5–12   4th Sunday of Easter
4:32–35   2nd Sunday of Easter
8:26–40   5th Sunday of Easter
10:34–43   Resurrection of the Lord/ Easter Day
10:44–48   6th Sunday of Easter
19:1–7   Baptism of the Lord

Romans
4:13–25   2nd Sunday of Lent
16:25–27   4th Sunday of Advent

1 Corinthians
1:3–9   1st Sunday of Advent
1:18–25   3rd Sunday in Lent
6:12–20   2nd Sunday in Ordinary Time
7:29–31   3rd Sunday in Ordinary Time
8:1–13   4th Sunday in Ordinary Time
9:16–23   5th Sunday in Ordinary Time
9:24–27   6th Sunday in Ordinary Time
15:1–11   Resurrection of the Lord/ Easter Day

2 Corinthians
1:18–22   7th Sunday in Ordinary Time
3:1–6   8th Sunday in Ordinary Time
4:3–6   Transfiguration of the Lord (Sunday preceding Lent)
4:4–7   1st Sunday after Christmas
4:5–12   9th Sunday in Ordinary Time
4:13–5:1   10th Sunday in Ordinary Time
5:6–10 (11–13) 14–17   11th Sunday in Ordinary Time
6:1–13   12th Sunday in Ordinary Time
8:7–15   13th Sunday in Ordinary Time
12:2–10   14th Sunday in Ordinary Time

Ephesians
1:3–14   2nd Sunday after Christmas
                               15th Sunday in Ordinary Time
2:1–10   4th Sunday in Lent
2:11–22   16th Sunday in Ordinary Time
3:14–21   17th Sunday in Ordinary Time
4:1–16   18th Sunday in Ordinary Time
4:25–5:2   19th Sunday in Ordinary Time
5:15–20   20th Sunday in Ordinary Time
6:10–20   21st Sunday in Ordinary Time

Philippians
2:5–11   Passion/Palm Sunday

1 Thessalonians
5:16–24   3rd Sunday of Advent

Titus
3:4–7   Christmas Eve/Day, Proper II

Hebrews
1:1–4; 2:5–12   27th Sunday in Ordinary Time
4:12–16   28th Sunday in Ordinary Time
5:1–10   29th Sunday in Ordinary Time
5:5–10   5th Sunday in Lent
7:23–28   30th Sunday in Ordinary Time
9:11–14   31st Sunday in Ordinary Time
9:24–28   32nd Sunday in Ordinary Time
10:11–14 (15–18) 19–25   33rd Sunday in Ordinary Time

James
1:17–27   22nd Sunday in Ordinary Time
2:1–10 (11–13) 14–17   23rd Sunday in Ordinary Time
3:1–12   24th Sunday in Ordinary Time
3:13–4:3, 7–8a   25th Sunday in Ordinary Time
5:13–20   26th Sunday in Ordinary Time

1 Peter
3:18–22   1st Sunday in Lent

2 Peter
3:8–15a   2nd Sunday of Advent

1 John
1:1–2:2   2nd Sunday of Easter
3:1–7   3rd Sunday of Easter
3:16–24   4th Sunday of Easter
4:7–21   5th Sunday of Easter
5:1–6   6th Sunday of Easter
5:9–13   7th Sunday of Easter

Revelation
1:4b–8   34th Sunday in Ordinary Time
                                   (Reign of Christ or Christ the King)
21:1–6a   All Saints' Day

Wisdom of Solomon
3:1–9   All Saints' Day
7:26–8:1   24th Sunday in Ordinary Time

Index of Scripture Readings: Year C

126	5th Sunday in Lent
137	27th Sunday in Ordinary Time
138	5th Sunday after Epiphany
139:1–6, 13–18	23rd Sunday in Ordinary Time
145:1–5, 17–21	32nd Sunday in Ordinary Time
146	10th Sunday in Ordinary Time
147:12–20	2nd Sunday after Christmas
148	1st Sunday after Christmas
	5th Sunday of Easter
149	All Saints' Day
150	2nd Sunday of Easter

Proverbs

| 8:1–4, 22–31 | Trinity Sunday |

Isaiah

1:1, 10–20	19th Sunday in Ordinary Time
5:1–7	20th Sunday in Ordinary Time
6:1–8 (9–13)	5th Sunday in Ordinary Time
12	33rd Sunday in Ordinary Time
12:2–6	3rd Sunday of Advent
43:1–7	Baptism of the Lord
43:16–21	5th Sunday in Lent
50:4–9a	Passion/Palm Sunday
52:7–10	Christmas Eve/Day Proper III
55:1–9	3rd Sunday in Lent
55:10–13	8th Sunday in Ordinary Time
60:1–6	Epiphany of the Lord
62:1–5	2nd Sunday in Ordinary Time
65:17–25	Resurrection of the Lord/Easter
	33rd Sunday in Ordinary Time

Jeremiah

1:4–10	4th Sunday after Epiphany
	21st Sunday in Ordinary Time
2:4–13	22nd Sunday in Ordinary Time
4:11–12, 22–28	24th Sunday in Ordinary Time
8:18–9:1	25th Sunday in Ordinary Time
17:5–10	6th Sunday after Epiphany
18:1–11	23rd Sunday in Ordinary Time
23:1–6	34th Sunday in Ordinary Time
	(Reign of Christ or Christ the King)
29:1, 4–7	28th Sunday in Ordinary Time
31:7–14	2nd Sunday after Christmas
31:27–34	29th Sunday in Ordinary Time
32:1–3a, 6–15	26th Sunday in Ordinary Time
33:14–16	1st Sunday of Advent

Lamentations
1:1–6   27th Sunday in Ordinary Time
3:19–26   27th Sunday in Ordinary Time

Daniel
7:1–3, 15–18   All Saints' Day

Hosea
1:2–10   17th Sunday in Ordinary Time
11:1–11   18th Sunday in Ordinary Time

Joel
2:23–32   30th Sunday in Ordinary Time

Amos
7:7–17   15th Sunday in Ordinary Time
8:1–12   16th Sunday in Ordinary Time

Micah
5:2–5a   4th Sunday of Advent

Habakkuk
1:1–4; 2:1–4   31st Sunday in Ordinary Time

Zephaniah
3:14–20   3rd Sunday of Advent

Haggai
1:15b–2:9   32nd Sunday in Ordinary Time

Malachi
3:1–4   2nd Sunday of Advent

Matthew
2:1–12   Epiphany of the Lord

Luke
1:39–45 (46–55)   4th Sunday of Advent
1:47–55   4th Sunday of Advent
1:68–79   34th Sunday in Ordinary Time
                               (Reign of Christ or Christ the King)
                               2nd Sunday of Advent
3:7–18   3rd Sunday of Advent
3:15–17, 21–22   Baptism of the Lord
4:1–13   1st Sunday in Lent
4:14–21   3rd Sunday in Ordinary Time
4:21–30   4th Sunday in Ordinary Time

5:1–11	5th Sunday in Ordinary Time
6:17–26	6th Sunday in Ordinary Time
6:20–31	All Saints' Day
6:27–38	7th Sunday in Ordinary Time
6:39–49	8th Sunday in Ordinary Time
7:1–10	9th Sunday in Ordinary Time
7:11–17	10th Sunday in Ordinary Time
7:36–8:3	11th Sunday in Ordinary Time
8:26–39	12th Sunday in Ordinary Time
9:28–36	2nd Sunday in Lent
9:28–36 (37–43)	Transfiguration of the Lord (Sunday preceding Lent)
9:51–62	13th Sunday in Ordinary Time
10:1–11, 16–20	14th Sunday in Ordinary Time
10:25–37	15th Sunday in Ordinary Time
10:38–42	16th Sunday in Ordinary Time
11:1–13	17th Sunday in Ordinary Time
12:13–21	18th Sunday in Ordinary Time
12:32–40	19th Sunday in Ordinary Time
12:49–56	20th Sunday in Ordinary Time
13:1–9	3rd Sunday in Lent
13:10–17	21st Sunday in Ordinary Time
13:31–35	2nd Sunday in Lent
14:1, 7–14	22nd Sunday in Ordinary Time
14:25–33	23rd Sunday in Ordinary Time
15:1–3, 11b–32	4th Sunday in Lent
15:1–10	24th Sunday in Ordinary Time
16:1–13	25th Sunday in Ordinary Time
16:19–31	26th Sunday in Ordinary Time
17:5–10	27th Sunday in Ordinary Time
17:11–19	28th Sunday in Ordinary Time
18:1–8	29th Sunday in Ordinary Time
18:9–14	30th Sunday in Ordinary Time
19:1–10	31st Sunday in Ordinary Time
19:28–40	Passion/Palm Sunday
20:27–38	32nd Sunday in Ordinary Time
21:5–19	33rd Sunday in Ordinary Time
21:25–36	1st Sunday of Advent
22:14–23:56	Passion/Palm Sunday
23:1–49	Passion/Palm Sunday
23:33–43	34th Sunday in Ordinary Time
	(Reign of Christ or Christ the King)
24:1–12	Resurrection of the Lord/Easter Day

John

1:1–14	Christmas Eve/Day Proper III
1:(1–9) 10–18	2nd Sunday after Christmas
2:1–11	2nd Sunday after Epiphany

5:1–9	6th Sunday of Easter
10:22–30	4th Sunday of Easter
12:1–8	5th Sunday in Lent
13:31–35	5th Sunday of Easter
14:8–17 (25–27)	The Day of Pentecost
14:23–29	6th Sunday of Easter
16:12–15	Trinity Sunday
17:20–26	7th Sunday of Easter
20:1–18	Resurrection of the Lord/Easter Day
20:19–31	2nd Sunday of Easter
21:1–19	3rd Sunday of Easter

Acts

2:1–21	The Day of Pentecost
5:27–32	2nd Sunday of Easter
8:14–17	Baptism of the Lord
9:1–6 (7–20)	3rd Sunday of Easter
9:36–43	4th Sunday of Easter
10:34–43	Resurrection of the Lord/Easter Day
11:1–18	5th Sunday of Easter
16:9–15	6th Sunday of Easter
16:16–34	7th Sunday of Easter

Romans

5:1–5	Trinity Sunday
8:14–17	The Day of Pentecost
10:8b–13	1st Sunday of Lent

1 Corinthians

10:1–13	3rd Sunday in Lent
12:1–11	2nd Sunday in Ordinary Time
12:12–31a	3rd Sunday in Ordinary Time
13:1–13	4th Sunday in Ordinary Time
15:1–11	5th Sunday in Ordinary Time
15:12–20	6th Sunday in Ordinary Time
15:19–26	Resurrection of the Lord/Easter Day
15:35–38, 42–50	7th Sunday in Ordinary Time
15:51–58	8th Sunday in Ordinary Time

2 Corinthians

| 3:12–4:2 | Transfiguration of the Lord (Sunday preceding Lent) |
| 5:16–21 | 4th Sunday in Lent |

Galatians

1:1–12	9th Sunday in Ordinary Time
1:11–24	10th Sunday in Ordinary Time
2:15–21	11th Sunday in Ordinary Time

3:23–29	12th Sunday in Ordinary Time
5:1, 13–25	13th Sunday in Ordinary Time
6:(1–6) 7–16	14th Sunday in Ordinary Time

Ephesians

1:3–14	2nd Sunday after Christmas
1:11–23	All Saints' Day
3:1–12	Epiphany of the Lord

Philippians

1:3–11	2nd Sunday of Advent
2:5–11	Passion/Palm Sunday
3:4b–14	5th Sunday in Lent
3:17–4:1	2nd Sunday of Lent
4:4–7	3rd Sunday of Advent

Colossians

1:1–14	15th Sunday in Ordinary Time
1:11–20	34th Sunday in Ordinary Time (Reign of Christ or Christ the King)
1:15–28	16th Sunday in Ordinary Time
2:6–15 (16–19)	17th Sunday in Ordinary Time
3:1–11	18th Sunday in Ordinary Time

1 Thessalonians

| 3:9–13 | 1st Sunday of Advent |

2 Thessalonians

1:1–4, 11–12	31st Sunday in Ordinary Time
2:1–5, 13–17	32nd Sunday in Ordinary Time
3:6–13	33rd Sunday in Ordinary Time

1 Timothy

1:12–17	24th Sunday in Ordinary Time
2:1–7	25th Sunday in Ordinary Time
6:6–19	26th Sunday in Ordinary Time

2 Timothy

1:1–14	27th Sunday in Ordinary Time
2:8–15	28th Sunday in Ordinary Time
3:14–4:5	29th Sunday in Ordinary Time
4:6–8, 16–18	30th Sunday in Ordinary Time

Philemon

| 1–21 | 23rd Sunday in Ordinary Time |

Hebrews

1:1–4 (5–12)	Christmas Eve/Day Proper III
10:5–10	4th Sunday of Advent
11:1–3, 8–16	19th Sunday of Ordinary Time
11:29–12:2	20th Sunday of Ordinary Time
12:18–29	21st Sunday of Ordinary Time
13:1–8, 15–16	22nd Sunday of Ordinary Time

Revelation

1:4–8	2nd Sunday of Easter
5:11–14	3rd Sunday of Easter
7:9–17	4th Sunday of Easter
21:1–6	5th Sunday of Easter
21:10, 22–22:5	6th Sunday of Easter
22:12–14, 16–17, 20–21	7th Sunday of Easter

Sirach

27:4–7	8th Sunday after Epiphany